Mary Queen of Scots' Downfall

Mary Queen of Scots' Downfall

The Life and Murder of Henry, Lord Darnley

Robert Stedall

PEN & SWORD HISTORY

First published in Great Britain in 2017 by
Pen & Sword History
an imprint of
Pen & Sword Books Ltd
47 Church Street
Barnsley
South Yorkshire
S70 2AS

ISBN 978 1 47389 331 3

A CIP catalogue record for this book is
available from the British Library.

Printed and bound in England
By TJ International, Padstow, Cornwall PL28 8RW

Pen & Sword Books Ltd incorporates the Imprints of Pen & Sword Books
Archaeology, Atlas, Aviation, Battleground, Discovery, Family History, History,
Maritime, Military, Naval, Politics, Railways, Select, Transport, True Crime,
Fiction, Frontline Books, Leo Cooper, Praetorian Press, Seaforth Publishing,
Wharncliffe and White Owl.

For a complete list of Pen & Sword titles please contact
PEN & SWORD BOOKS LIMITED
47 Church Street, Barnsley, South Yorkshire, S70 2AS, England
E-mail: enquiries@pen-and-sword.co.uk
Website: www.pen-and-sword.co.uk

We must not offhand condemn any man for the shape of his skull, but if ever there was a skull which the man in the street would describe as that of a moron or fool, it must certainly be Darnley's and his every action confirms such a judgment.

Pearson, *Biometrika*, Vol. XX pt 1 (July 1928),
p. 52; cited in Bingham, pp. 6–7

The elimination of Darnley was a first necessity of state, and this all the Scottish [nobles] recognized, if not for national reasons, at least for their own personal convenience and interests. ... These Scottish leaders were all unscrupulous, they were all unfaithful to their fellow conspirators ... There is no romance about the epoch, all is sordid, immoral, ruffianly. How does it differ from the state of affairs in England? Not in the least. ... There has been a false glamour cast over this period by the tragedy of Mary Stewart. It was an age of unshamed treachery.

Pearson, *Biometrica*, Vol. XX pt 1 (July 1928), pp. 26–7

Please also see the author's website on www.maryqueenofscots.net.

Acknowledgements

I am indebted to Claire Hopkins of Pen and Sword Books Ltd for her help and advice at every stage of the production of this book. She has been clear on what was wanted and supportive of new ideas. At a time when there is a focus on Darnley's appearance, it has been interesting to compare Darnley's portraits to the extraordinary drawings made by Karl Pearson in *Biometrica* in 1928, when he made minute measurements of Darnley's skull. His own narrative on Darnley's life shows a healthy disregard for the findings of acknowledged historians of his era. I have been able to take advantage of the views of more modern historians, to whom I am greatly indebted, but it is extraordinary how such a well-trodden subject is still able to unearth new theories on what happened. My efforts to establish the layout and location at Kirk o'Field, which I started in *The Challenge to the Crown*, have been corrected by Rob Maxtone-Graham, although his own more detailed assessment is keenly awaited. It is he who has established that the map made of the murder scene at Kirk o'Field by William Cecil's spy is extraordinarily accurate, despite its apparent shortcomings in perspective. I am grateful to David Atkinson for drawing all the maps and the view of Edinburgh. Without him, the presentation of its layout would make no sense at all. Needless to say, I turn to my son, Oliver, for all things technical, but particularly for his production of the website on www.maryqueenofscots.net, which contains much ancillary information, including family trees, surrounding this biography.

Robert Stedall

March 2017

Contents

List of Illustrations

Front cover

Henry Stuart, Lord Darnley, King of Scotland (oil on panel), English School (16th century), Hardwick Hall, (National Trust Photographic Library/ Bridgeman Images 15451567).

Maps

Picture section

Maps

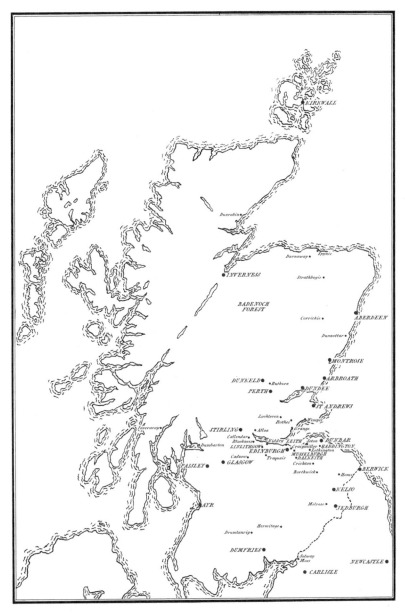

Map of Scotland, drawn by David Atkinson, Handmade Maps Limited.

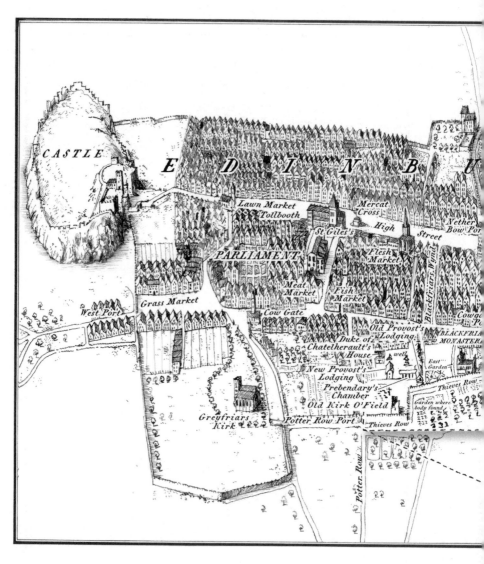

Edinburgh c. 1567 Drawn by David Atkinson, Handmade Maps Limited. Adapted f

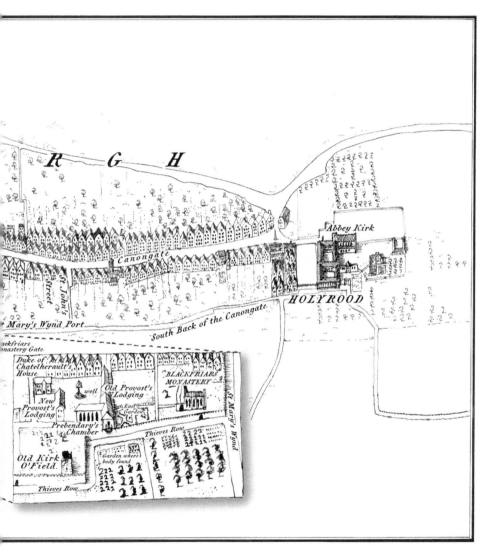

ap of Edinburgh by James Gordon, 1647 in the National Library of Scotland.

Preface

Henry, Lord Darnley, gained more notoriety in death than during his lifetime. His place in history arises from his marriage to Mary Queen of Scots and to his subsequent murder, in which Mary was implicated. To understand the significance of this, it is appropriate to outline the events of Mary's reign, both before their marriage and after his murder. Assessing the likely culprit has been a perennial puzzle for students the world over. This book reaches some surprisingly fresh conclusions, despite the ambiguity of the contemporary evidence, which was confused by hostile propaganda put about by the enemies of the Scottish Catholic Crown among both the Scottish nobility and the English government. Mary was not only the dynastic heir to the English throne, but, through her mother Marie of Guise, belonged to the fiercely imperialistic, and Catholic, Guise family. By marrying the Catholic Darnley, who was, after Mary, second in line to the English throne, their joint claim to be Elizabeth's heir was unassailable. This called for desperate action by those determined to maintain a Protestant government in England and one that was politically supportive in Scotland. It is a measure of their success that they undermined Mary's and Darnley's rule, giving each of them a place in history that their own political shortcomings should never have warranted.

To appreciate the difficulties facing Scotland, it is essential to understand the three great conflicts of Mary's reign. First, there were the competing efforts of France and England to maintain their influence over Scottish government. English belligerence had forced Scotland and France into a defensive alliance, in part to protect Scotland from English invasion but also to protect France by allowing diversionary attacks on England to take place from the north. Second, there was the religious hostility between Catholics and Calvinist Reformers, who were spreading their new doctrines through Scotland. The Reformers had been incited by Henry VIII as a means of protecting England, after its break with Rome, from a Catholic Counter-Reformation, which might be launched from across its Scottish border. Almost coincidentally, the Scottish Reformation provided a platform for discontented Scottish nobles to make a political stand, with English support, against a Scottish government dominated by French and Catholic interests. Third, there was the feudal conflict between central government and the powerful Scottish *mormaers* or Earls, who dominated their remote personal fiefdoms while maintaining their loose affiliation to the Scottish Crown. With the Crown being financially weakened by successive debilitating regencies and the cost of fending off English aggression, it no longer maintained a standing army and was reliant on the Earls and their clans for military support, and on the Catholic Church for funding.

There was a further difficulty, also faced by Elizabeth in England. The Tudor belief in an anointed monarch's dynastic right to govern unopposed was being questioned by Reformers in Scotland and by the Protestant government in England, both of whom believed that the monarchy should be accountable to the people. Strongly republican sentiments in Scotland questioned the authority of hereditary monarchy. These were conflicts that Darnley completely failed to comprehend. While James and Elizabeth developed the political acumen to survive attacks on their authority, Mary and Darnley's naïvety let them down. A particular example of this was Mary's appointment of David Riccio as her principal adviser. As a Piedmontese and a Catholic, he usurped a role generally reserved for a member of the Scottish hierarchy, and his Catholicism was unacceptable both to them and to Cecil, determined to maintain a politically supportive government across England's northern border.

There is a huge amount of literature on the murders of Riccio and Darnley. Recent scholarly studies by Lady Antonia Fraser, John Guy and Alison Weir, for example, have painted Mary as an innocent in the midst of intrigue, let down by those who might have helped her, and debased by politically motivated propaganda. They portray her as a Catholic martyr (as she wished her audience at Fotheringhay to believe), unfairly condemned both in her lifetime and by history. Their view is not shared by Dr Jenny Wormald, Roderick Graham or Susan Doran, who see the murder of her husband as a political necessity in which she was involved. None of their assessments is totally convincing. Yet to each of these eminent historians I owe a debt of gratitude for their scholarship. Of particular assistance has been Caroline Bingham in her largely unlauded *Darnley: a life of Henry Stuart, Consort of Mary Queen of Scots*. This demonstrates the exemplary research of an eminent historian of the period.

At certain points, I have provided comments on the text, which do not form part of the main narrative. I have included these as endnotes in the references section starting on page 289 and I have marked the relevant reference numbers with an asterix in the text.

Part 1

The Lennoxes' background and Scottish heritage

Chapter 1

The Marriage of the Earl of Lennox to Lady Margaret Douglas

On 6 July 1544, Henry VIII and Queen Catherine Parr attended the marriage at St James's Palace of Matthew Stuart, 4th Earl of Lennox to Henry's beautiful but headstrong niece, Margaret Douglas. This was an arranged marriage, which became a true love match. Lennox displayed all the courtly grace of having been brought up in France.

> He excelled in ability of body and dexterity of exercise. He was of strong body, well proportionate, of lusty and manly visage, straight in stature and pleasant in behaviour, wherefore at that time he was very pleasant in the sight of gentlewomen.[1]

'He was for manly courage and other virtues, as well of body as mind, inferior to none of his time.'[2] Margaret found him 'sufficiently gratifying to her ambition and followed by a mutual affection', despite her two earlier attachments, which had been thwarted by the English King.[3] She felt the marriage would 'banish my cares and my bliss augment. ... He was in my power, and I his true bride.'[4,5]

Most importantly, the marriage was of huge dynastic importance, linking as it did two close heirs to the Scottish and English thrones. Lennox became naturalised as an Englishman to assure English nationality for any children of the marriage and Henry announced that 'in case his own issue failed, he should be right glad if heirs of her [Margaret's] body succeeded to the crown'.[6] (Yet he later changed his mind.) Margaret never made any secret of her Catholicism and was a *confidante* of her cousin and contemporary, Princess Mary Tudor. Mary provided Margaret with a marriage gift of a selection of valuable gems including a gold brooch set with a large sapphire and other enamelled jewels depicting stories from the Bible. As a dowry, Henry provided the couple with the valuable Temple Newsam estate in Yorkshire with about 4,000 acres, and the Palace of Stepney in London. He strongly approved of Lennox. Not only had the Lennox Stuarts been traditional supporters of the Tudor dynasty, having provided troops to assist Henry VII in defeating Richard III at Bosworth Field, but Lennox was also quite prepared to adopt a Reformist stance to promote his marriage suit and to portray himself as a foil for Margaret's Catholic excesses. Yet, his Protestantism was no more than skin-deep and he continued to practise his Catholicism at home with his wife, who was soon dominating him with her astute intellect.

As a direct descendant of James II of Scotland, Lennox was next in line to Mary Queen of Scots on the Scottish throne after James Hamilton, 2nd Earl of Arran, and his legitimate progeny. (See table of The Scottish Succession pp. 278–9) Arran had been appointed regent of Scotland on behalf of Margaret's niece, the infant Mary Queen of Scots, a position generally reserved for the Crown's heir, but there was doubt about his legitimacy, which, if upheld, arguably left only the life of the infant Mary between Lennox and the Scottish crown.[7*]

Margaret Douglas was the daughter of Henry VIII's elder sister, Queen Margaret Tudor, the widow of James IV of Scotland. By James, Queen Margaret was the mother of James V and grandmother of Mary Queen of Scots. Following her husband's untimely death at Flodden in 1513, she struggled to maintain the regency for her infant son with assistance from Archibald Douglas, 6th Earl of Angus, the leading Scottish magnate of the English party. Whether from 'passion, policy or pressure', Margaret, now Queen Dowager, leaned heavily on Douglas clan support and in 1514, without Henry's prior approval, she remarried Angus, who recognised the advantage of cementing his English ties. Henry soon accepted Angus as his brother-in-law and close ally, providing him with an English pension. Dynastically, their daughter Margaret was in line to the English throne after Henry's legitimate children and her niece, Mary Queen of Scots. (See table of the English succession pp. 276–7)

Henry VIII saw a dynastic marriage between Lennox and Margaret Douglas as a means of establishing Scotland's loyalty. In 1532, he had set the English reformation in train by breaking with Rome to enable him to divorce Catherine of Aragon, who had been unable to provide him with a male heir. This made it of critical importance for him to secure his northern border to prevent Scotland, which remained adamantly Catholic, from becoming a bridgehead for an invasion by Continental Catholic powers. It was recognised that whoever effected a marriage into the Scottish Crown was likely to control Scotland. Although Henry promoted his daughter, Mary Tudor, as consort for her cousin, James V, the Scots turned to France to protect them from English domination.

Alliance with France encouraged the Scots to adopt aggressive tactics against England. James V died in anguish in December 1542 after the disastrous failure of his army at Solway Moss. His 10,000 men had been defeated by 4,000 Cumberland farmers armed with pitchforks strengthened by a nucleus of 300 trained English troops. Only twenty Scots were killed, but 1,200 were taken prisoner when they sank into the bog. Henry VIII had given instructions for members of the Scottish nobility to be captured, so that he could seek their future allegiance as the price of their freedom. He arranged for them to be released only against assurances of their future loyalty and required them to provide their children as hostages to reinforce this understanding.

With James's newborn daughter, Mary, becoming Queen of Scots, Henry had another opportunity to promote a consort to confirm Scotland's allegiance to England. He was determined that she should marry his 5-year-old son, Prince Edward. In March 1543, Sir Ralph Sadler, the English Ambassador, met with Arran to negotiate marriage terms in the expectation that Mary would be brought up in England. Arran's only interest was to see how he would benefit, but he offered to support Henry's break with Rome. Henry secretly proposed his daughter, Princess Elizabeth in marriage to Arran's eldest son to cement a Protestant union between England and Scotland. He even offered to raise Arran to the Scottish Crown in the area north of the Firth of Forth. Although Arran found this highly satisfactory, particularly when Henry offered him 5,000 men, he really wanted £5,000.

With his colleagues mistrusting all things English, Arran had little hope of gaining their support for his deal, and an English marriage was an anathema to Mary's French mother, Marie of Guise, now the Queen Dowager. To hold the marriage plan together, Arran tried to stop her from communicating with France. Yet she managed to send warning of her plight to her mother, Antoinette de Bourbon, who advised the French government. Henry now faced an uphill struggle, but marriage between Lennox and Margaret Douglas opened dynastic possibilities.

Chapter 2

Matthew Stuart, 4th Earl of Lennox

Born at Dumbarton on 21 September 1516, Lennox had faced a difficult upbringing. In 1526, his father, John Stewart, 3rd Earl of Lennox, with estates to the north of Glasgow, was killed while trying to assist the Dowager Queen Margaret to effect the escape of her son, the young James V, from the control of Angus, from whom she was now estranged (see p. 11). This forced the 10-year-old Matthew, now 4th Earl of Lennox, to travel to France with his brother, John, for their upbringing. Meanwhile, their mother, Anne Stewart, daughter of the Earl of Atholl, and her two other children, Robert and Helen, remained in Scotland, where Robert was trained for the Church and became Bishop of Caithness. France was an obvious destination for the two brothers, as the junior branch of the Lennox Stuart family, the Seigneurs d'Aubigny, made a living there as mercenaries.[1*] (See table of the Stewart (Stuart) of Lennox family pp. 280–1) They were brought up in Provence and served as soldiers with their great uncle, the childless Robert, 3rd Seigneur d'Aubigny, Marshal of France. Lennox became Captain of the *Garde Écossaise* and adopted the French spelling of the Stewart name, resulting in the Scottish Royal family becoming Stuart on his son Lord Darnley's marriage to Mary Queen of Scots, although, while in France, Mary also adopted the French spelling of her name.

In 1543, Lennox returned to Scotland to conduct a complex mission on behalf of the French government. He was given the task of escorting the young Mary Queen of Scots to France, while his brother John remained behind. At this time Cardinal David Bethune, Archbishop of St Andrews, was being held in ward at Blackness Castle, having been caught out for having forged James V's will in an attempt to prevent the anglophile Arran from becoming regent. This had left Arran in control of the infant Mary. The initial French plan had been to send the Duke of Guise to Scotland with a sufficient force to distract Henry from making a proposed invasion of the Continent. In the end, they sent Lennox, who was seen by Bethune as a useful ally to overthrow Arran. Having slipped the English fleet, he arrived north of the border, well supplied with French gold for distribution to offset the effect of English pensions.

For Mary to be spirited away, the Queen Dowager needed to remove her from Arran's direct control at Linlithgow. She planned to take her to Stirling, which was strongly fortified and had formed part of her dowry on her marriage to James. This would provide security while Mary awaited transfer to Dumbarton and a ship for France. In a brilliant game of double bluff, the Queen Dowager enlisted Sadler's help. Following his negotiation with Arran, he visited her at Linlithgow to see Mary, whom he dandled on his knee. He later confirmed to Henry that she was 'as goodly a child as I have seen of her age, and as like to live, with the Grace of God'.[2] The Queen Dowager charmed him with a story that, although she favoured Mary marrying Prince Edward, Arran had no intention of agreeing because he wanted Mary to marry his son. He was simply seeking an English bribe and, when Henry died, he intended to usurp the Scottish throne. Henry could prevent this by helping to move Mary to Stirling. Sadler was taken in and promised not to reveal his sources to protect her. He sanctioned the move without realising her true intent, but for the time being Mary remained where she was.

On Lennox's arrival in Scotland, he went straight to Linlithgow to see the Queen Dowager. If Arran were to be prevented from implementing the English marriage plan, Lennox and the Queen Dowager would need support from the Scottish Catholic Church. With Bethune being held under the control of George, 4th Lord Seton, the Queen Dowager's close ally, Lennox approached him to seek Bethune's return under ward to St Andrews. In mid-1543, Bethune was formally released from detention.

Once freed, Bethune 'began to rage as any lion loosed of his bond', galvanising anti-English public opinion.[3] He encouraged Arran's illegitimate half-brother, John Hamilton, Abbot of Paisley, to persuade Arran to drop the English alliance, threatening him that if he continued to abandon the Catholic cause, the question of his legitimacy would be reopened. Arran was offered French subsidies, which compared favourably with those from the English. Yet, while Bethune wanted a French alliance, he stopped short of supporting a French marriage for Mary, fearing that Scotland would be subsumed into France, thereby weakening the authority of the Scottish nobility and its Catholic Church. If Arran could be persuaded to drop the English alliance, Bethune would support his son's betrothal to Mary.

Bethune's deal with Arran placed him at odds with both Lennox and the Queen Dowager. He soon became aware that Lennox had a personal agenda. If Arran were shown to be illegitimate, Lennox would be next in line to the Scottish throne. He planned to marry the Queen Dowager and to claim the regency for himself, allowing Mary to make a French marriage. The first step was to remove her from Arran's control by taking her to Stirling, but this would need Bethune's support.

Henry VIII was quick to react to Bethune's release and was aware that Lennox was hoping to kidnap Mary to take her from Dumbarton to France. He *ordered* Arran to raise forces to bring her into the safety of Edinburgh Castle. With the English marriage plan lacking support, Arran used the excuse that Mary was suffering from the 'breeding of teeth', but had to admit to Sadler that Henry's terms for an English marriage were not acceptable.[4] Henry threatened war. He needed a quick resolution, as he was about to embark on his invasion of France. Arran compromised and, in the Treaty of Greenwich, signed on 1 July 1543, agreed to the marriage in terms which guaranteed Scottish independence and with Mary to be brought up and educated in Scotland. If she remained childless after marriage, she was to be returned home as an independent queen. These terms allowed the Queen Dowager to retain Mary under her control and, when Sadler reported French ships being sighted off the coast, she at last had military support.

Faced with the threat of Mary making an English marriage, Lennox received Bethune's backing to move her with her mother to Stirling, out of Arran's reach. On 24 July 1543, the Catholic hierarchy in Scotland arrived at Stirling with 7,000 men, before marching to Linlithgow to thwart Arran's attempt to move the infant queen to Edinburgh. On arrival two days later, Arran capitulated. On 27 July, Mary was escorted with her mother to Stirling by 2,500 cavalry and 1,000 infantry, followed by a baggage train, which extended for almost a mile. She would remain there for the next four years.

Henry continued to bludgeon Arran into honouring the English marriage plan. The English fleet captured Scottish merchant ships en route for France, and he tried to take control of castles south of the Forth. He failed to appreciate the adverse effect of his bullying tactics. His pro-English allies were turned against marriage to Prince Edward, and in Edinburgh, Sadler found himself being threatened. In November 1543, he was escorted across the border. Safely on English soil, he reported: 'Nor do I think never man had to do with so rude, so inconsistent, and beastly a nation as this.'[5]

With Arran no longer controlling Mary, Bethune persuaded the General Council to depose him as regent in favour of the Queen Dowager, and to appoint Angus (Margaret Douglas's father) as Lieutenant General. With Angus having traditionally supported the English, this shows the extent of his disillusionment with English policy. Arran realised that he had to compromise, but refused to surrender the regency. On 3 September, only a week after ratifying the Treaty of Greenwich, he held a secret meeting with Bethune at Falkirk. They embraced and rode on to Stirling, where Arran revealed the full extent of the secret marriage plans he had made with Henry. On 8 September, after threatening Arran with excommunication, Bethune persuaded him to repudiate the English alliance, but again proposed that his son, James, should marry Mary rather than Elizabeth, and he threatened to question his legitimacy if he did not revert to Catholicism. Arran seems to have blindly accepted the doubts over his legitimacy. On 8 September 1543, 'the unhappy man', as John Knox disparagingly referred to him, received the Catholic sacrament, thereby losing any trust that Henry VIII had placed in him.

Although Arran remained regent, Bethune stood at his side as Chancellor. Angus was confirmed as military commander, perhaps in an effort to assure his loyalty. Yet he remained in contact with Henry and was soon induced to rejoin the English camp. When Lennox tried to claim the regency on the grounds that he was heir to the throne ahead of Arran, he gained no support and his loyalty to the Scottish Crown was questioned. Arran and Bethune now appointed a council headed by the Queen Dowager drawn from members of both the French and English parties.

The Scottish nobles closed ranks behind Arran. On 9 September, Mary was taken in procession to the Chapel Royal in Stirling for her Coronation. Arran carried the crown, Lennox the sceptre, and Archibald Campbell, 4th Earl of Argyll, militarily the most powerful of the Scottish lords, the sword of state. While the 9-month-old child howled, Bethune, dressed in the full panoply of a cardinal, held the crown over her head and used chrism to anoint her as queen, a position that God alone could bestow and call to account. The bishops and nobles present swore allegiance, but the English party, including Angus, stayed away. The ceremony lacked the pomp associated with such events in England and France, and the English ambassador reported it as having 'such solemnities as they do use in this countrie, which is not very costlie'.[6] Mary would quickly learn that ceremony gained prestige for the Crown, despite its extravagance.

Despite Arran receiving the backing of both the Queen Dowager and Bethune, Lennox again attempted to undermine Arran's position by proposing marriage to her. She was attracted by Lennox's assurances of loyalty, particularly if Arran should again oppose her. With Mary's coronation being a time to celebrate, the Queen Dowager wanted amusement and held a party at Stirling for her twenty-eighth birthday. She was still one of the most beautiful ladies in Scotland and it was 'like Venus and Cupid in the time of fresh May, for there was such dancing, singing, playing and merriness ... that no man would have tired therein'.[7] She already had another admirer in Patrick Hepburn, 3rd Earl of Bothwell, and could not miss the opportunity to play Lennox off against him. He had even divorced his wife, Agnes Sinclair, on 16 June 1543 to make way for his intended marriage.[8*] Like Lennox, he had only recently returned to Scotland, having been exiled to the Continent for opposing James V's authority. As a soldier full of bravado, he was ready to participate in chivalrous pursuits such as duelling and jousting to promote his suit. In words resonant of comments on his son, Sadler described him as 'the most vain and insolent man in the world, full of pride and folly, and here nothing at all esteemed'.[9] Yet father and son had a charm which could captivate women.

Suddenly Bothwell had a sophisticated rival. Lennox was aged 27 and had lived at the French Court. He spoke fluent French, was very good-looking, was a capable dancer and an accomplished lute player. They both recognised that, by winning the Queen Dowager's hand, they would be strongly positioned to displace Arran as regent and, in Lennox's case, to usurp his position as heir to the throne. They postured like peacocks before her, running up enormous bills on clothing, while they danced, sang and recited poetry, or engaged in shooting and jousting matches. She loved all the attention, but offered 'nothing but fair words'.[10] Bothwell resorted to subterfuge by circulating a rumour, which Lennox believed, that he was already secretly betrothed to her. Within a month of Mary's coronation, Lennox had retired to Dumbarton to lick his wounds; he was determined on revenge. Although Bothwell continued to court the Queen Dowager, rumours of a liaison are probably unfounded and they did not marry.

Francis I supported Lennox in his efforts to restore traditional French links with Scotland by sending Jacques de la Brosse, his ambassador to Scotland, with six ships containing money and artillery to support the Queen Dowager. On arrival at Greenock on the Clyde in October, de la Brosse was met by Lennox. Assuming his continuing loyalty, de la Brosse handed over his precious cargo, which Lennox took to Dumbarton Castle. Yet he had no means to defend the castle and, as a French citizen, realised that his action was treasonable. Most of the prize was thus handed back to de la Brosse for delivery to the Queen Dowager, but he seems to have retained a proportion for himself. Nevertheless, she was able to distribute 59,000 crowns as pensions to her adherents. This did much to buy support for her; the Pope also sent Mary a subsidy. With Bethune taking control, on 15 December the

Scots signed a treaty with France reconfirming the *Auld Alliance* and they cancelled the understanding that Mary would marry Prince Edward.

Although Lennox was reconciled with the Queen Dowager, she had been stringing him along and made clear that she would not marry him. He needed another way to build his powerbase and, in fury, approached Angus with an offer to support Henry VIII, if permitted to marry Angus's daughter, the beautiful but headstrong Margaret Douglas. Lennox gave a letter to Sadler to be delivered to Margaret with Henry's approval. He needed to wait for Henry's assurance of support and some financial compensation, as he was likely to lose his Scottish and French estates if he joined the English. He did not completely relinquish his hopes of marrying the Queen Dowager until this was forthcoming. On 17 May 1544, he signed an agreement with the English Commissioners at Carlisle. In return for Margaret's hand in marriage, he promised to recognise Henry VIII as protector of Scotland, to arrange the marriage of Mary Queen of Scots to Prince Edward, to place the Queen of Scots in English custody, to transfer several Scottish strongholds, including Dumbarton, into English possession and to allow the Protestant scriptures to circulate in Scotland. On achieving all this, he would be appointed Governor (regent) of Scotland and heir to the throne ahead of Arran. There was also a proviso that, as he had never met Margaret, they both had the right when they did meet to confirm their agreement to the marriage. The person who suffered most from Lennox's abandonment of the Auld Alliance was his brother John, now Seigneur d'Aubigny, in France. Francis I had him thrown in the Bastille, where he languished for three years while Lennox made efforts to gain his release and to bring him to England.

Chapter 3

Lady Margaret Douglas

Margaret's background was no less fraught than that of her future husband. She had been born in 1515 after her mother, the Queen Dowager, had been forced out of Scotland, heavily pregnant, following the arrival from France of John Stewart, Duke of Albany, who had been invited by James Hamilton, 1st Earl of Arran, to replace her as regent. On reaching the Borders, she was received by Lord Dacre, the English military commander, who escorted her to Harbottle near Otterburn in Northumberland for Margaret's birth. The birth proved difficult, but, as soon as mother and daughter were able to travel, they were moved to more comfortable surroundings at Dacre's principal residence at Morpeth. Although Angus visited her, he returned to Scotland to make his peace with Albany and to resume his affair with his long-term mistress, Janet Stewart of Traquair, to whom he had been betrothed. From Morpeth, Margaret was taken by her mother to London to see Henry VIII, arriving in May 1516. In early 1517, when Albany returned to France, Henry sent them back to Scotland, still hoping that his sister would be able to eliminate French influence and would be reconciled with Angus. They arrived on 15 June 1517 to be met by Angus at Lamberton Kirk. Henry 'was persuaded that [Angus] would serve English interests more efficiently than [the Queen Dowager] and "better than five Earls of Arran"'.[1] Their reconciliation did not prove successful as Albany, from France, restored the Queen Dowager to care for James V. With Arran's assistance, she escaped with Margaret from Angus's control to Linlithgow and later to Stirling. Albany agreed to assist the Queen Dowager's efforts to obtain a Catholic divorce from Angus on the grounds of his continuing relationship with Janet Stewart of Traquair. The Queen Dowager, meanwhile, began a passionate affair with Henry Stewart, second son of Lord Avandale, ten years her junior. Henry VIII's sympathies remained with Angus, and he told her to be reconciled with her husband.

During this time, Margaret Douglas remained with her mother. Being in the Royal nurseries she was brought up speaking Scots, and always retained a strong Scottish accent. With growing antagonism between Angus and Arran, Albany had to return from France to settle matters. Angus was exiled to France 'to rid Scotland of [his] disruptive presence'.[2] He remained there from 1522 to 1524, but was given a pension by Henry VIII. With Angus out of the way, consideration was given to Margaret becoming betrothed to Arran's son James, but this was vetoed by Albany as such a powerful union threatened his position as regent. Another suitor was James Stewart, Earl of Moray, an illegitimate son of James IV, but this also came to nothing. Eventually, consideration was given to her marrying Matthew Stewart, son of the 3rd Earl of Lennox, who was supportive of the Queen Dowager against Angus. Yet following Lennox's death, this proposed suit seemed to have been put on one side.

On Albany's departure from Scotland in 1525, Angus returned and was admitted to the Council, which formed a rota to take responsibility for James V's safety. This included Arran, Lennox and Colin Campbell, 3rd Earl of Argyll. Angus took control from August 1525, but, in November, he refused to hand James over in accordance with the agreement. With English support, he now took control of Scottish government, continuing to hold James against his will. On 4 September 1526, Lennox made a rescue attempt at Linlithgow, but was captured and murdered by one of the Hamiltons, causing lasting antagonism between the two families. Although James remained under Angus's control, he was supportive of his mother, who, in 1526, shocked Henry VIII by at last obtaining a divorce from Angus, so that she could marry Henry Stewart. This was provided by Pope Clement VII on the grounds that Angus had not been free to marry her because he had already entered into a betrothal contract with Janet Stewart of Traquair. The Queen Dowager managed to protect her daughter's legitimacy, by arguing that she had been unaware of this precontact when she married Angus, and Margaret's legitimacy was confirmed by the Pope. Yet James V always referred to Margaret as his 'base-sister'.

In May 1528, James at last managed to escape from Angus's control and received widespread support from the Scottish nobility. Having turned to his mother for help, he appointed Henry Stewart as Lord Treasurer and created him Lord Methven. Methven and the Queen Dowager seized control of Scottish government with assistance from Archbishop James Bethune of St Andrews (uncle of the Cardinal), leaning it back towards the *Auld Alliance*. Angus retired to his impregnable fortress at Tantallon, having already taken Margaret there to supervise her upbringing. He was well aware of her potential value as both niece of Henry VIII and half-sister of the King of Scots, and he ensured that she was properly educated. Angus was now her mainstay and she never saw her mother again.

Although Angus attempted to restore his influence by storming Edinburgh, he was rebuffed, and was besieged at Tantallon. Eventually he escaped with his daughter and her governess across the English border. Cardinal Wolsey, who was Margaret's godfather, provided protection by arranging a home for her with Captain Thomas Strangeways at Berwick. Strangeways, who was the Comptroller of Wolsey's household, warned that she

> might be stolen and withdrawn into Scotland which caused me to take more labour for her sure-keeping; yet I know well she was never merrier nor more pleased and content than she is now, as she oft-times repeats.[3]

She had no interest in being returned to her mother, and was considered of sufficient lineal importance to be brought to London with her father, who received another English pension. Henry VIII sent gowns so that she would look the part, and she was educated as a royal princess. In the spring of 1530, she was brought to her aunt, Princess Mary, Duchess of Suffolk and then to Newhall in Essex to join her cousin and contemporary, Mary Tudor, with whom she developed a lasting friendship, united in their Catholicism.

Margaret was considered one of the most attractive women of her generation, with the fair complexion and red hair characteristic of the Tudors. This gained her Henry VIII's affection. She dressed with taste and elegance and, when Henry sought a divorce from Catherine of Aragon to marry Anne Boleyn, she showed remarkable tact by retaining Princess Mary's friendship, while cultivating Anne and her relations. During 1532 and 1533 she was retained as first lady in Princess Mary's household. On 7 September 1533, to Henry's great disappointment, Queen Anne gave birth to a daughter, Elizabeth, rather than a hoped for son. In October, Mary was reduced from the rank of princess to become the 'illegitimate' Lady Mary. She was obliged to enter the household of her new half-sister, where Margaret, now presiding as its first lady, held precedence over her. Margaret also became first lady-in-waiting to Anne Boleyn. Remarkably, this reversal of fortune did not disrupt the firm friendship between Mary and Margaret.

In the circle surrounding Anne Boleyn was her uncle, Lord Thomas Howard, although he was young enough to be her brother. Despite not being an appropriate match for a royal lady, he was encouraged to make suit for Margaret by Queen Anne and was genuinely in love with her; they wrote courtly verses to each other. Yet, with Queen Anne's star starting to wane, it is clear that Henry VIII disapproved of his niece forming a relationship with a member of the Howard family. Yet the attachment continued to develop in secret, and the couple were betrothed before witnesses. This was a reckless step for a king's niece to take without royal approval. Although the betrothal should have allowed their union to be consummated, Margaret always hotly denied that intercourse took place.

Anne fell rapidly out of favour and was beheaded on 19 May 1536; Elizabeth was deemed illegitimate like her half sister Mary. It was Margaret, who carried the train of the new queen, Jane Seymour, at the feast of Corpus Christi on 15 June the same year. With both of his daughters now made illegitimate, and Jane Seymour yet to produce an heir, Henry realised that the succession was between James V and Margaret Douglas, who might be preferred as she had been born in England. Shortly before 8 July, Henry learned of Margaret's precontract with Howard. (Suggestions that Henry had approved the betrothal beforehand appear unlikely.) By wooing her, Henry considered that Howard had been tilting at the throne. He was impeached and, on 18 July 1536, the couple were consigned to the Tower for treason, where they continued to write poems of love for each other. In an attempt to establish Margaret's illegitimacy, Henry sought out Janet Stewart of Traquair to confirm her betrothal to Angus, prior to his relationship with the Queen Dowager, which had been the grounds for the Queen Dowager divorcing him, as approved by the Pope. Yet, on her deathbed in 1541, the Queen Dowager made a declaration confirming that she had been unaware of the precontract at the time of their marriage. This made Angus her lawful husband, and removed any stigma of illegitimacy from her daughter. This did not stop Henry using the evidence of Angus's precontract to declare Margaret illegitimate.

Following the birth of Prince Edward on 12 October 1537, with the succession at last resolved, Thomas Cromwell offered to arrange Margaret's rehabilitation – if she would renounce Lord Thomas Howard. As she was still under sentence of death, she pragmatically agreed and, having confirmed her virginity, was at last released. Lord Thomas, who appears to have been suffering from typhoid, died in the Tower two days after Margaret's departure, leaving her distraught. Given doubts over Prince Edward's legitimacy within the Catholic Church, Henry again barred Margaret from the throne, this time on the grounds that her mother's marriage to Angus lacked royal approval in advance. He then returned her to favour and, on 12 November, she rode in the funeral procession for Queen Jane, being recorded as 'Lady Margaret Howard, the king's niece'.[4] She too had been suffering an intermittent fever in the Tower and it was on her mother's intercession that Henry agreed for her to be moved with her servants to the Abbey of Syon on the Thames near Isleworth. She was to remain there for five months, recuperating in the care of the abbess, still wracked with guilt over Howard's death. She was only 22.

In November 1539, Henry appointed Margaret as first lady-in-waiting to his new queen, Anne of Cleves, a marriage that he found abhorrent. In the following year, Margaret became first lady-in-waiting to the new queen, Catherine Howard. Yet again, she formed an impulsive attachment, this time to Sir Charles Howard, Queen Catherine's brother, although there is no evidence that this was encouraged by the young queen. Sir Charles fled to Flanders, only returning to England in 1544, which suggests that Margaret's virtue was not seriously compromised by the affair. She did, however, feel that he had let her down by leaving her to face Henry VIII's wrath on her own. He served under Hertford in Scotland, but died in France later in 1544, probably at the siege of Boulogne.

On 13 November 1541, Margaret was moved from Hampton Court to Kenninghall, the Duke of Norfolk's country residence, while Queen Catherine, who was by then in even worse trouble after conducting extra-marital affairs, was transferred to Syon. With Henry needing the support of the Douglases in Scotland, Angus was able, in mid-1543, to arrange Margaret's rehabilitation to Court. She became a bridesmaid to Catherine Parr, while Angus attempted to re-assert English influence in Scotland after the Scottish disaster at Solway Moss and the death of James V. Henry needed to find a husband for his 27-year-old headstrong niece, and marriage to Lennox would offer a new dynastic link between the Scottish and English crowns. Immediately after their marriage, with Lennox away on active service on Henry's behalf, Margaret retired to Temple Newsam, where, out of sight of the English Court, she established herself as a catalyst for Catholic intrigue. When Henry learned of this, he excluded her from the succession under his will. During the reign of Edward VI, she remained in Yorkshire, but, as soon as Mary Tudor became queen, she returned to London, bringing her young son, Henry, Lord Darnley, with her.

Chapter 4

Lennox's involvement in English efforts to subsume Scotland under its control

Henry still hoped to rekindle the marriage between Prince Edward and Mary Queen of Scots, but needed to weaken Bethune's stranglehold on the regency. He had two strings to his bow. The first was to bludgeon Scotland into submission with a series of punitive raids, which became known as the Rough Wooings, in retribution for Scottish broken promises. The second was to infiltrate Protestant preachers to promote a Scottish Reformation and to show up the shortcomings of the Scottish Catholic Church. This left him uncertain of the loyalty of the Catholic Angus. As a Protestant, even if out of convenience, Lennox seemed a more natural ally for Henry, despite Margaret's Catholicism. After returning to Scotland, Angus had remarried Margaret, daughter of Robert 5th Lord Maxwell; he was now reintegrated into Scottish society. Margaret resented him taking a much younger wife, not least because she provided him with a male heir, thereby putting her expected inheritance in question, but the child died in 1548.

Henry continued to provide Angus and his dwindling group of Scottish supporters with pensions, but knew that they lacked the military muscle to gain control of Mary. His bullying tactics pushed Angus and Arran into supporting Bethune and the Queen Dowager. With Henry continuing to provide Angus with financial inducements, he was still treated with suspicion by his fellow Scots. Having confirmed his loyalty to Bethune, Angus was sent to the Borders to make a raid into England, but nothing effectual took place. In January 1544, he showed his true colours; he captured Leith for the English, while his brother, Sir George Douglas of Pittendreich, took Musselburgh. With Lennox now betrothed to Angus's daughter, he returned to Glasgow to provide them with support.

The Queen Dowager retaliated with her modest contingent of French soldiers, who were garrisoned around Scotland, but she was in need of help from the Scottish nobles. Bothwell, who continued to have ambitions to marry her, drove Sir George out of Musselburgh. The Douglases

were outnumbered and were forced to submit, giving new sureties of loyalty to the regency. Yet they also wrote to Henry to confirm their continuing support for him. In April 1544, Arran used French troops to capture
Glasgow, which Lennox had fortified. Sir George Douglas and Maxwell,
Angus's new father-in-law, went to Lennox's assistance but were taken hostage. When Angus went to intercede, he too was arrested and warded first
at Hamilton Castle and later at Blackness. With Lennox now isolated, he
became extremely unpopular. When Arran threatened him and his remaining pro-English allies with forfeiture, they were forced into a secret bond
with the regency, but also wrote to Henry to confirm their loyalty, providing
him with a detailed invasion plan.

Henry now accused Bethune of inciting the Scots against the English.
On 5 March 1544, he appointed Prince Edward's uncle, Edward Seymour,
Earl of Hertford, as Lieutenant General of the North. With Henry about
to embark on his invasion of France, he wanted to forestall any diversionary interference from Scotland. With Lennox's efforts having petered
out in the west, Hertford led a lightning strike, known as the first of the
Rough Wooings. He was given three weeks, during which he was to besiege
Edinburgh and its castle, to destroy the port of Leith and ravish the lowland
region between Edinburgh and Stirling. Having accomplished this, he was
to devastate Fife, razing Bethune's castle at St Andrews.

At the end of April, Hertford landed 15,000 men at Granton just west
of Leith, where he overwhelmed 6,000 Scottish troops and secured Leith
to unload his provisions. When his cavalry arrived from Berwick, he
attacked Edinburgh, but ignored the castle, which was well fortified. He
wanted unconditional surrender and his men looted and burned houses and
churches in a fire that raged for three days. He went on to Fife, where his
troops ravaged and burned Kinghorn and the area round Kirkcaldy. With
insufficient time to reach St Andrews, he destroyed the area to within six
miles of Stirling, resulting in Mary being moved north to the relative safety
of Dunkeld. On his return, he razed Leith before departing south along
the east coast route, burning market towns and flattening fortified towers as
he went. He arrived in Berwick on 18 May, and, when his fleet reappeared
from Leith, his crack troops were shipped to Calais to join Henry in his
Continental campaign. Hertford personally went to London as Lieutenant
of the Kingdom. Yet, such was his military reputation that he was recalled
to France for the capture of Boulogne.

Having fostered the English alliance, Arran was blamed for this Scottish
disaster, but Bethune's confrontational policies also faced criticism.

The nobility started to believe that the Queen Dowager, with her prudent and cheerful disposition, should be involved in the regency. Although she sought control, parliament appointed her only as co-regent with Arran, leaving deadlock between them until Bethune again stepped forward to broker a compromise. Despite lacking control, she now sat regularly in the Privy Council, leaning them towards a French marriage for Mary as the only means of combating the English. Yet the climate of Scottish opinion, progressively more Reformist, was not ready for this, and Bethune continued to back her marriage to Arran's son.

On 17 May 1544, after visiting the English commissioners at Carlisle, Lennox signed a formal alliance with Henry VIII confirming the terms for his marriage to Margaret Douglas. With the anglophile Alexander Cunningham, 5th Earl of Glencairn, he agreed to kidnap Mary at Stirling and bring her to England. They were also instructed to gain control of the principal Scottish fortresses and to impose Protestantism. In return, they were granted English pensions and Lennox was promised the regency with Glencairn to be Protector. A week later, Lennox took 600 men on a naval expedition of eighteen ships up the west coast to seize Dumbarton Castle, while Glencairn went on foot with 500 spearmen, only to meet Arran with double that number. In a fierce conflict, Glencairn suffered severe losses including his second son, Andrew. He retired with a few remaining adherents to await Lennox at Dumbarton, while Arran took control of Glasgow. When Lennox arrived, he enticed a number of Scottish lairds into giving him support by providing them with pensions. Yet, after meeting Glencairn, he left to obtain further assistance from Henry, leaving the lairds with an opportunity to defect. It was on this visit that his marriage to Margaret took place.

When Lennox returned with reinforcements, he found Glencairn too demoralised to continue fighting. The new expedition was now abortive. Believing the English position to be untenable, Glencairn defected to the regency. With Arran still seeking a marriage between Mary and his son rather than the French Dauphin, he was soon at loggerheads with the Queen Dowager. She was furious with the untrustworthy Scots, who were still accepting any largesse that Henry VIII offered. She had always favoured a French marriage for Mary, not least because it would promote Guise family interests in France. Bethune still doubted its merits and, overlooking any concern about Arran's legitimacy, again promoted Mary's marriage to his son. She had little choice but to play along with this and was persuaded by Bethune to realign with Arran.

By 1546, the Queen Dowager had gained parliamentary agreement to repudiate the Treaty of Greenwich, thereby ending further thought of Mary marrying Prince Edward. Henry was furious. Yet, his continuing aggression had whittled away any remaining loyalty among the English party. The regency released Angus, Sir George Douglas and Maxwell from imprisonment, when they gave assurances of support against the English. Angus was shocked at the wholesale destruction caused by the Rough Wooings and, from now on, he supported Scottish interests, while continuing his conciliatory noises to Henry. He fought valiantly on Arran's behalf at the siege of Coldingham Priory on the Berwickshire coast, when Arran showed every sign of fleeing. Although Glencairn had rejoined the English, he felt isolated and again sought rehabilitation with the regency. In December, Angus and his allies were absolved from treason and restored to their estates. The French recognised his bravery at Coldingham by granting him the Order of St Michel, together with a gold collar and 4,000 crowns. When Henry heard this, he gave orders for Sir George's castles at Pinkie and Dalkeith to be destroyed. Yet when an English raiding party desecrated Melrose Abbey, the Douglases' traditional burial place, a smaller Scots force ambushed them and took many prisoners. This greatly improved Scottish morale.

In late 1544, Lennox had crossed over to Dublin, where he put together a new expedition to capture Dumbarton Castle, which was strongly garrisoned with French troops. With its almost impregnable fortifications, he failed to regain control. Only he among the Scottish nobility now remained loyal to the English. Angus tried to neutralise him by proposing a two-month truce, promising him that it would result in him becoming 'ruler of Scotland' after marrying Margaret Douglas, who Angus 'loved most in all the world'. This was only a ruse to try to stop his expedition in its tracks. Angus was also the key to Arran's victory over the English at Ancram Moor on 27 February 1545, although he may have been bribed by the Scottish government to assure his continued loyalty. Henry now posted Lennox back to Ireland. In his absence, in 1545, he was attainted for treason by the Scottish Parliament with his Scottish estates being forfeited and granted to Arran. This seriously undermined his claim to the Scottish succession, but he continued to use the Lennox title.

In May 1545, the French distributed another round of pensions to assure Scottish loyalty and sent 500 more troops. With both Douglas and French support, the regency moved onto the offensive. Angus and Sir George Douglas crossed the English border in July, but no great action resulted and Angus cynically sent messages of goodwill to Henry, assuring him of his continued support for Mary's marriage to Prince Edward. He was no doubt seeking a restoration of his pension, as he was by then actively opposing the marriage in the Privy Council and signed the Act of Parliament revoking the Treaty of Greenwich.

Henry made a second attempt to bludgeon the Scots into submission. By September 1545, Hertford had been able to leave Boulogne. Having mustered 12,000 troops at Newcastle, he crossed into Scotland at Berwick. Fearful of the strength of the new French reinforcements, he was more circumspect and limited his attack to the ransacking of the locality around Jedburgh and Kelso, before returning to Newcastle after three weeks. With France and England exhausted by war, he returned to France to broker a truce that was to include Scotland, but this was overtaken by events.

In March 1546, Bethune's persecution of Protestant preachers infiltrated by Henry and of those lairds who had been converted by them, culminated in one of their most effective spokesmen, George Wishart, being burned at the stake in Bethune's presence at the castle of St Andrews. In retaliation, a group of lairds from Fife managed to break into the castle with Henry's connivance to murder Bethune. Henry sent provisions by sea to support the 'Castilians', who were besieged by Arran's troops, enabling them to hold out with increasing English support for fourteen months.

After Bethune's assassination, the Queen Dowager again sought to wrest the regency from Arran and reverted to the French marriage plan as the only way to protect Scotland for her daughter. In 1544, Catherine de Medici had at last provided a son for the Valois dynasty in France and he became the prize on offer. With all their bullying, the English had driven the Scots into France's welcoming arms and more battle-hardened French troops arrived in Scotland. The Scottish nobility was now united behind Arran against the English.

In May 1546, Lennox made another attempt to gain control of Dumbarton, and the governor admitted him to the castle. Arran immediately laid siege to it, forcing Lennox to abandon his project and to return to England, where he rejoined Margaret, who retained her prominent status at Court.

Following Henry's death in January 1547, Edward VI succeeded to the English throne. Hertford now became his Protector as Duke of Somerset, and tried to reinstate the Scottish marriage plan by offering to concede Scottish autonomy and provide a free trade agreement. With the French party in Scotland now in the ascendancy, they had the promise of French support against further English aggression. In a final round of Rough Wooings, Somerset adopted a two-pronged attack, hoping to play on growing conflict between Catholics and Reformers. While Lennox was put in command of a force in the west, Somerset led the main English army of 15,000 men, which advanced along the Scottish east coast shadowed by the English fleet.

Arran hurriedly moved Mary north to the Erskine Priory at Inchmahone, on the Lake of Menteith. It was here that she was joined for the first time by the four Maries: Mary Fleming, Mary Livingston, Mary Seton and Mary Bethune, with whom she was later to travel to France. (Despite her mother being French, the young queen was brought up in Scotland speaking Scots. It was only after they travelled to France that she and her companions started to converse in French.) On 10 September 1547, Arran advanced from Edinburgh with 12,000 hastily gathered troops and a further large contingent of poorly-armed clergy dressed in black. Although they took up a well-entrenched position bristling with spears at Pinkie Cleugh near Musselburgh, they lacked discipline, and Arran was unsure whether his lieutenants were in receipt of English pay. When 4,000 Irish mercenaries on the Scottish left broke ranks to charge the English right, they were scattered by fire from the English fleet. Angus led the van on the Scottish right where his pikemen drove back the English horse, but when he attempted a flanking movement his men were broken by a hail of English arrows and by fire from Italian musketeers. Sadler, as Secretary of the English Army, showed great resource in rallying his cavalry; their greater discipline won the day. Instead of providing support to Angus, Arran's men retired from their strategic position only to be picked off by English cavalry and guns. Arran fled the field 'scant with honour', leaving 10,000 Scots dead and 1,500 more as prisoners; the English had lost 200 men. This was a disaster on the scale of Flodden. Although Edinburgh was at his mercy, Somerset failed to follow up on his victory despite burning Leith and, on 29 September, he left Scotland after planning to build a network of English forts. In April 1548, an English garrison of 2,500 men was stationed at Haddington.

During the hostilities, several members of the Douglas family were arrested by the English at Dalkeith, to be sent to London where they were lodged in the Tower. These included Sir George's wife, Elizabeth, and her sons, David (later 7th Earl of Angus), James (later 4th Earl of Morton), together with Angus's illegitimate son, George Douglas (later better known as the unsavoury Postulate of Arbroath, who was involved in Riccio's murder), and cousin, Sir Archibald Douglas of Glenbervie. (See table of the Douglas of Angus family pp. 282–3) Angus wrote to Margaret in June 1548, seeking assistance for them to be 'gently treated'. She was able to arrange for them to stay under the Lennoxes' 'sure-keeping' at Temple Newsam, although they were subsequently moved to the Tower.

Meanwhile, Lennox had moved to Carlisle for the planned diversionary assault on western Scotland. Having remained outwardly Protestant, Lennox had ingratiated himself with Somerset by employing an 'army of spies' at his own expense to infiltrate Scottish government. These provided valuable information for the English Council. He also provided maps of the rugged Scottish topography, which, hitherto, had confounded invading forces. His sole motive was to seek revenge on the Hamiltons for the murder of his father. Early in 1548, he advanced with Lord Wharton up the west coast after being promised 2,000 men by the Master of Maxwell, Angus's brother-in-law. To confirm his undertaking, Maxwell provided hostages to Wharton, but failed to deliver the agreed troops; this left Lennox without local reinforcements. Wharton's force was attacked by Angus at Dumfries and forced back to Carlisle, where Lennox called for the ten hostages to be tried, resulting in four of them being hanged. This gained for him undying enmity in Scotland and Angus particularly disapproved of his brutality. In 1549, Margaret, always a devoted daughter and his only surviving legitimate child, was disinherited from the Angus Earldom, which had been open to 'heirs general', including female heirs. Angus preferred David Douglas, the son of his brother Sir George, as a male successor. This always rankled with Margaret. She was furious at her father's disloyalty particularly after she had ensured the proper treatment of her Douglas kinsmen brought to England. She continued to try to reconcile him with Lennox, but without success. She refused to accept the change to the title's entail and, after her father's death in 1557, signed her correspondence 'Margaret Lennox and Angus'. Although she appealed in the Scottish Court of Chancery, she was deemed to be the wife of a forfeited traitor, and the case languished unsettled.

The Battle of Pinkie Cleugh caused a huge anti-English backlash. Angus, who had retired to Calder, joined those infuriated with all things English. Arran took the blame and was now regent in name only, while the Queen Dowager progressively took control and restored Mary to Stirling. Without the means to resist the English, she called for more French support, and Henry II offered to liberate Scotland, if Mary were betrothed to his son, the infant Dauphin. Arran was bought off with the French dukedom of Châtelherault in Poitou, and a further annual pension of 12,000 livres. In January 1548, the French marriage was approved by the Scottish Parliament. The terms needed little discussion, and even Angus confirmed his support. Scotland was to retain its autonomy and was promised new French garrisons at Dunbar and Blackness. Yet Mary was to travel to France for her upbringing.

Henry II was as good as his word. The Queen Dowager's Guise brothers provided the Scots with an expeditionary force of well-trained veterans of the Italian campaign with professional officers. The main force disembarked at Leith on 17 June 1548, confirming France's determination to protect Mary's Scottish Crown. Mary was moved to Dumbarton, out of English reach, in readiness for her departure. Henry II sent his personal galley with a party of senior diplomats to collect her. On 29 July 1548, Mary departed, while her mother remained behind to protect her throne on her behalf. Meanwhile Angus took command of the combined Scottish and French forces, which made several incursions into England. By 1551, the English had been ousted and Mary's throne was secure. This resulted in Somerset's dismissal as Protector for Edward VI. He was replaced by John Dudley, Duke of Northumberland.

With Lennox being associated with Somerset in the skirmishes into Scotland, he was also out of favour and retired to Yorkshire to manage his estates. Nevertheless, Margaret travelled to London in November 1551 to meet the Scottish Queen Dowager as she was returning from a visit to her daughter in France. She later received an invitation from Angus to visit him at Tantallon. Although Northumberland initially refused his consent for her to travel, he relented and Margaret stayed with her father at Tantallon for two months in mid-1553, but was not restored as heir to the Angus estates. While she was away Edward VI died of tuberculosis. Margaret played no part in Mary Tudor's effort to gain the Crown, following the attempted coup promoting Lady Jane Grey to secure a Protestant succession, but did return to London to attend her friend's coronation in October. She never saw her father again, and, when he died in January 1557, she was excluded from his will.

Chapter 5

Efforts to secure a Protestant succession for the English throne

Notwithstanding the dynastic rights of his Tudor connections, Henry VIII, and perhaps more importantly his Protestant advisers, were determined to secure a Protestant succession to prevent the English Reformation being reversed after his death. Any continuing pockets of Catholicism needed to be stamped on. In 1544, the English Parliament under the Third Act of Succession empowered Henry to nominate his heirs under his 'last will and testament signed with the king's own hand'.[1] When his will was prepared shortly before his death in 1547, he was too ill to sign it, and it was completed with a metal stamp of his signature inked in afterwards by a clerk, causing doubts as to whether he had been conscious during its preparation. This called its validity into question. It nominated his three children, Edward, Mary and Elizabeth, notwithstanding that Mary and Elizabeth had previously been declared illegitimate. Elizabeth was also illegitimate in Catholic eyes, as Catherine of Aragon was still rightfully Henry's wife at her birth.

If his own line were to fail, Henry decreed that the throne should pass to the descendants of his favoured Protestant younger sister Mary, who had married his great friend Charles Brandon, Duke of Suffolk. This overlooked those of his Catholic elder sister Margaret, despite her prior dynastic right. In order to bar Queen Margaret's heirs, Henry ordained that no one born outside England could inherit, although at the time of her marriage to James IV of Scotland no such impediment had been put in place. While this barred the Scottish-born Mary Queen of Scots, it did not debar Margaret Douglas, who had been born in the north of England and had been nominated as a potential heir at the time of her wedding. Yet her Catholicism had caused Henry to declare her illegitimate to protect the claims of his daughters, by arguing that her mother had not sought consent to marry Angus as required by the Royal Marriage Act of 1536. It has been suggested that Margaret was overlooked following a row with Henry, shortly before his death, but this does not appear to have been the case. She had always depended on Henry for her position at Court, and it is apparent that she mourned him deeply. Yet her Catholicism was not so much unacceptable to Henry, who had remained a Catholic at heart, as to the caucus of powerful nobles around the Crown, who would stop at nothing in their attempts to retain a Protestant monarchy.

The only straightforward part of the succession was that Henry was succeeded by his son, Edward VI, backed by his mother's family, the Seymours, Earls of Hertford and later Dukes of Somerset, the Dudleys, Earls of Warwick and later Dukes of Northumberland, and the Greys, Marquesses of Dorset and later Dukes of Suffolk. These were supported both by parliament and the up-and-coming Cambridge graduate, William Cecil, who, as Somerset's Secretary and Master of Requests, had become the architect of the English Reformation. Henry Grey, Marquess of Dorset, had married Henry VIII's niece, Frances Brandon, now first in line after Henry's own children under Henry's will. When Margaret brought the infant Darnley to court, she received a cool reception from the young king and prudently retired back to Yorkshire, where she remained for six years, apart from infrequent London visits.

When it became clear that Edward VI was dying of consumption, the Protestant caucus was determined to thwart his sister, the Catholic Mary Tudor, from succeeding him. They persuaded Edward to change his will to appoint as his successor the 15-year-old Jane Grey, Dorset's eldest daughter and granddaughter of Princess Mary. Despite rumblings of disquiet, Privy Councillors and leading judges were pressured into approval, cutting out not only Mary Tudor but also Elizabeth, in addition to Queen Margaret's descendants. A somewhat bemused Jane was hastily married to Lord Guildford Dudley, Northumberland's fourth son, and, on Edward's death, she was proclaimed queen, in what seemed a perfect coup with a semblance of legality to it, leaving Northumberland as the power behind the throne. Yet Mary Tudor also had herself proclaimed queen, rallying overwhelming support in Catholic East Anglia and from elsewhere in the shires. This forced Northumberland to lead an army out of London to challenge her as she came south. Freed from Northumberland's dominating influence, the Privy Council did a *volte-face* declaring their support for Mary, as the proper dynastic heir. Radical Protestantism as imposed by Edward VI's government had not sufficiently taken root. Not unnaturally, Elizabeth also backed her sister, thoroughly piqued that she too had been overlooked. They marched into London together and, to great acclaim, Mary was pronounced queen. Northumberland was arrested and executed for high treason, while Jane Grey and Guildford Dudley were thrown into the Tower.

Mary's accession meant that Margaret and Lennox could return to London, parading their Catholicism. Margaret now took precedence over Elizabeth, who remained illegitimate in Catholic eyes. They were showered with gifts. Margaret received two gowns of gold tissue, a gold girdle set with rubies and diamonds and a large pointed diamond repossessed from Anne, Duchess of Somerset. They were provided with luxurious apartments in the Palace of Westminster. These were

> furnished at the queen's expense with ten beds and twenty-one pieces of tapestry, enough to furnish a large suite of rooms for family and servants. The bed provided for Margaret herself was of purple velvet and cloth of gold "with St George figured on it in sundry places". Lennox was appointed Master of the Hawks and given the best horse from the stable of Edward VI.[2]

In late 1553, the 38-year-old Mary Tudor made herself unpopular by becoming betrothed to Philip, soon to become King of Spain and eleven years her junior. On 25 July 1554, Margaret carried the train at their wedding in Winchester Cathedral. England was now threatened with a Spanish invasion to restore Catholicism. This caused uproar, and Sir Thomas Wyatt led a rebellion from Kent to place Elizabeth on the throne. Mary showed great courage when the rebels reached London, and they were easily dispersed. They had been supported by Henry Grey, now Duke of Suffolk. His action resulted in his daughter, Lady Jane Grey, and her husband, Lord Guildford Dudley, being executed. Elizabeth was summoned to Court to answer for her involvement, but no evidence could be found to implicate her. She was now housed in a room immediately below the Lennoxes' apartments at the Palace of Westminster. Margaret deliberately turned the area above it into a kitchen, causing her continual disturbance from the 'casting down of logs, pots and vessels'.

With one attempt having already been made to set aside Henry VIII's will, it was rumoured that Mary would name Margaret Douglas or her son as her successor, and Margaret seized every opportunity to blacken Elizabeth by reporting every snippet of gossip that might implicate her in Wyatt's rebellion. Certainly in the first part of her reign Mary openly treated Margaret as her heir presumptive. The prospect of royal status greatly boosted Margaret's sense of financial security. With the Lennox estates in Scotland being attainted, and Margaret being cut out of her rightful inheritance of the Angus estates by her father, they had been extremely short of money. They now received generous treatment from Mary Tudor to supplement their income from their Yorkshire estates. This enabled them to finance their extravagant lifestyle and provide an appropriate education for their son. It was in this mood of optimism that the Lennoxes appear to have commissioned a handsome enameled locket now known as the Lennox Jewel to demonstrate their mutual love. (See illustrations).

The Lennox Jewel is a locket initially designed in celebration of the mutual love until 'death shall dissolve' of Matthew and Margaret Lennox. This is depicted within two hinged openings by two hearts above 'MSL' (for Matthew and Margaret Stuart Lennox) and a memento mori (a skull and crossbones). There are differing views on when it was made, but it seems most likely to have been during the reign of Mary Tudor, when Margaret had expectations of being nominated as Mary's heir. It was only then that she would have had the resources to commission such a valuable piece. In the centre is a large blue stone with the appearance of a cabochon sapphire (but in fact glass) surrounded by enamelled inscriptions in Scots appropriate for those waiting patiently to be nominated to the English crown. On the interior are symbols to denote Margaret's steadfast Catholicism, while a Roman soldier (Lennox) slays another carrying a red shield (Angus the Red Douglas).

When Elizabeth was named as Mary Tudor's heir, the Lennoxes focused their ambitions on the marriage of their son, Darnley, to Mary Queen of Scots. Margaret seems to have arranged for the locket to be adapted to make it appropriate as a gift to Mary in contemplation of her marriage to Darnley. On the front, there is now a jewelled crown containing a fleur-de-lys, symbolising Mary as the widowed Queen of France. On the reverse, which had previously been undecorated, there is now a crowned salamander (the crest of the French kings) and a phoenix (Mary being reborn by her marriage to Darnley). An inscription shows her to be of 'rare goodness', living in peace (a dove with a laurel branch) and piety (a pelican feeding its young). On marriage to Darnley, they will create a radiant new dynasty (a sunflower growing from his loins).

Margaret's hopes of gaining royal status appear to have been thwarted by Philip II, who saw the Lennox connection with France as threatening; he wanted the English crown to retain a Habsburg affiliation. He proposed that Princess Elizabeth should be married to Emmanuel Philibert, Duke of Savoy, and later, when it was clear that Mary Tudor did not have long to live, he considered marrying Elizabeth himself. While she successfully sidestepped these suits, it put paid to either Margaret or Darnley being named as Mary's heir. Shortly before her death, Mary nominated Elizabeth, notwithstanding that she was Protestant. Had Margaret or anyone else been named, it would have resulted in civil war. On Mary's death, Elizabeth was welcomed to the throne with a surge of enthusiasm. Although Margaret was the chief mourner at Mary's Catholic funeral at Westminster Abbey, the Lennoxes were forced back to Yorkshire, and Elizabeth appointed Cecil to act as their go between with the Court. This was a big come down for the second lady in the kingdom, but Elizabeth had every reason to hate her. Back at Temple Newsam, the Lennoxes continued as leading Catholics, while Elizabeth's advisers kept a close watch to gather evidence against them. Margaret was 'beyond measure hostile to the Protestant religion, more violent even than Mary herself'.[3] One reason for this seems to be that a Calvinist mob desecrated her mother's tomb during an attack on the Charterhouse at Perth in 1559. Her body was burned and her ashes scattered. She now planned to use her faith as a political weapon to bolster Darnley's claim to the English throne.

Mary's death from a malignant tumour had ended a reign fraught with disasters. Her burning of heretics had caused widespread revulsion. Her involvement with Philip in war with France had resulted in the loss of Calais, the last remaining part of England's Continental dominions.[4] Cecil had seen her as fulfilling his worst nightmare. English politicians learned a hard lesson. Her Catholicism had not stopped her being recognised as queen. You ignored the dynastic succession at your peril. Although he had continued to work undercover to support Protestantism, when his plotting was discovered, he too was forced to take Mass at his Wimbledon home. It was only too clear to him that Elizabeth's legitimacy needed to be upheld. If it were doubted, Mary Queen of Scots, as a Catholic and a Guise, followed by Margaret Douglas and Darnley, were the next in line.

On Elizabeth's accession, Cecil became her senior adviser, providing her with both political and liturgical advice to develop her policies. In April 1559, with her position on the throne now secure, he steered the Act of Religious Settlement through parliament to confirm England as Protestant; he was now formally appointed as her Secretary of State. Catholic heirs had no place in Cecil's plan. He knew the justice of their dynastic claims, but they were politically unacceptable, and Mary, with her Guise connections, was militarily threatening.

From now on every policy that Cecil adopted towards Mary Queen of Scots and Darnley was designed to weaken their claims to the English throne. Mary, as Queen-Dauphiness of France was quartering her arms with those of England. This was a huge insult to Elizabeth, as it implied that she was illegitimate. Cecil needed either to bring her down or to make her amenable to amity with England and the Protestant faith. He retained every scrap of evidence that could be used against her in the future and built a network of relationships with those in influence in Scotland, who would either encourage her to follow his objectives or, failing this, would destroy her. His two earliest recruits were Lord James Stewart, Mary's illegitimate half-brother, and William Maitland of Lethington, the queen regent's up and coming Secretary. They were well educated, astute, discreet and arguably the ablest men north of the border. They gained positions of influence with him that Angus and Lennox had enjoyed with Henry VIII. He could watch Darnley for himself, but Darnley being only 13 years old, does not appear to have been considered a serious political threat.

Chapter 6

The upbringing of Lord Darnley

S oon after her marriage, Margaret Douglas found that she was pregnant. The Lennoxes first son Henry, Lord Darnley, was born at their
London residence, the Palace of Stepney, in March 1545, but he died
eight months later.[1] Despite this great sadness, Margaret conceived again
and a second son, also Henry, was born at Temple Newsam on 7 December
1546 and was thus four years younger than his future wife Mary Queen of
Scots. He and his sickly brother Charles, nine years his junior, were the only
two of the Lennoxes' ten children to survive infancy, so it is understandable
that they were indulged by their doting parents. He was named Henry after
his godfather, Henry VIII, but was brought up as a Catholic. From an early
age, he was groomed by his mother as a royal prince with every expectation of becoming king with a dynastic status close to both the Scottish and
English thrones.

Darnley's tutors included John Elder, the Scottish scholar, and John
Lallart, who visited Scotland in 1562. Elder seems to have concentrated on
Darnley's study of Latin, while Lallart taught him French, so his parents
could ensure that he was equally conversant in English, Scots and French.
Elder was a cleric from Caithness and a canon of the Collegiate Church of
Dumbarton. He owed his appointment to Lennox's brother, Robert, then
Bishop of Caithness and provost of Dumbarton. He was 'a sycophant and
a hypocryte', well able to change his views in religious matters to suit the
occasion.[2] When Lennox transferred his allegiance to Henry VIII, Elder
addressed a beautifully written *Proposal* to the English king promoting the
marriage of Mary Queen of Scots to Prince Edward, vituperating 'against
the Scottish bishops as "the Dewil's convocation" and against "David Beton
ther cardinall, with Beelzebub's fles[h]mongers the abbots" ...'[3] Yet he
also drafted a fulsome letter from Temple Newsam in 1554 written out by
Darnley in immaculate italic script to Mary Tudor, describing her as a 'most
triumphaunte, moste victorious, and most gratious Princesse' after her success in putting down Wyatt's rebellion.[4] It was in this letter that he averred:
'I am enflamed and stirred, even now my tender aige not withstanding, to be
serving Your Grace, wishing every hair of my head to be worthy of a soldier.'[5]

The objective was to convince Mary that Darnley was 'precocious, devoted, and in every way suitable to be recognised as her heir'.[6] He studied *Factorum ac Dictorum Memorabilium Libri IX* (Nine books of Memorable Deeds and Sayings) of Valerius Maximus full of 'shallow, sententious and bombastic' rhetoric suitable for addressing people of importance. He even translated them into English. The intention was to provide him with a veneer of classical knowledge without having to study more serious classical authors in depth. 'The superficial polish and moral vacuity universally attributed to Darnley probably mirror[ed] the character of his tutor'.[7]

Yet Darnley excelled at sports and music. He was strong and athletic, becoming a magnificent horseman with a passion, 'almost to the point of obsession', for hunting and hawking.[8] He was trained in swordplay, shooting, running at the rings (a game for practising jousting, where the rider attempted to strike an object or ring with his lance), tennis, golf and pell-mell (croquet). As the son of handsome parents, he was always recorded as good-looking with a slim physique. Yet it was his stature at six foot two inches (which compared well with Mary, who was only about three inches shorter) and his elegant legs which were his principal attraction. Facially he was somewhat effeminate, and from the shape of his skull, which received minute inspection by Karl Pearson in 1928, it can be seen that he had a swept back forehead, providing him with a somewhat 'ape-like' appearance, and a broad bridge to his nose. It was Pearson's opinion, that the portrait on the front cover of this book was a good likeness of him, and other depictions were designed only to flatter. (See picture section.) Darnley and Mary towered above their contemporaries at a time when few men stood more than five foot six inches. By the time of Edward VI's death in 1553, Darnley was already known to be musical; he inherited Edward's lutes, and three suits of clothing. He was later acknowledged to be an expert lutenist, singer and an elegant dancer.

It was clear to Margaret that Darnley should become king, but her issue was to find a way for him to overcome the prior dynastic claims of Mary Queen of Scots, now Queen-Dauphine of France, who was likely to receive French military assistance to support her claim. Margaret had no means to compete, except that Mary was banned under Henry VIII's will for having been born in Scotland. Darnley was male, was seen as less threatening and had been born in England. Yet he was only 13, was also Catholic, and Elizabeth might yet marry and have children of her own. Perhaps Elizabeth would die of small pox or some other prevalent disease. Margaret's best hope was to keep her elegant son in Mary's eye, and should the sickly Dauphin die young, as seemed likely, he could be promoted as her husband. The Lennoxes focused all their attention on events as they unfolded in France.

Beneath his outward gloss, Darnley was growing into an objectionable and self–opinionated dolt. Despite his careful education, he lacked common sense. Unable to hold his tongue, he revealed everything he was told to his friends and servants, who themselves were not always discreet. He was arrogant, idle and, when thwarted, could be petulant and uncouth with a violent temper. He was tactless and failed to keep his word. He was also selfish, vain and extravagant, spending substantial sums on food and clothing. He was often drunk and was openly homosexual. Knox wrote that he 'passed his time hunting and hawking, and other such pleasures as were agreeable to his appetites, having in his company gentlemen willing to satisfy his will and affections'.[9] In his *Historie of James the Sext*, Melville recorded that he was 'much addicted to base and unmanly pleasures'.[10] In February 1566, when Mary was pregnant, Drury wrote to Cecil of a matter that had taken place at Inchleith 'too disgraceful' to be named in a letter. Such practices were very much the vogue among pleasure-loving males associated with the French Court. One of many adverse comments described him as 'mentally and morally weak, and his imbecility was conjoined with reckless courage … and fatal obstinacy'. His parents seemed blind to his shortcomings and failed to guide him to a more moderate stance. It is not difficult to understand why he alienated most of those with whom he came into contact. Sir James Melville summarised him as being 'haughty, proud, and so very weak in mind as to be a prey to all those that came about him'. He went on:

> He was inconstant, credulous and facile, unable to abide by any resolutions capable to be imposed upon by designing men, and could conceal no secret, let it be either to his own welfare or detriment.[11]

Chapter 7

The Scottish Reformation

Prior to Wishart's death at St Andrews, he had been a formative influence on John Knox, a young St Andrews University graduate and Catholic priest. This resulted in Knox being converted to Protestantism. While the Castilians were being besieged at St Andrews, Knox managed to enter the castle during an armistice over Easter 1547 and was persuaded to preach to them of 'the abominable idolatry of the Mass, blasphemous to the death of Christ and a profanation of the Lord's Supper', and he described the Catholic clergy as a 'greedy pack', developing the zeal for which he would become renowned.[1,2] Knox was ahead of his time, but he used his evangelism to convert many to Protestantism. Following the fall of the castle, most of the Castilians, including Knox, were forced to spend eighteen months on the French galleys, but, having served his time, he was brought back to England by Somerset in February 1549 and ultimately became a chaplain for Edward VI, where he befriended Cecil. On the accession of Mary Tudor, Knox escaped back to the Continent, where he eventually arrived in Geneva to train under John Calvin.

With Knox no longer in Scotland, there was no evangelical theologian of stature to provide leadership for a Scottish Reformation, but a group of Scottish nobles were becoming progressively warier of French ambitions to subsume Scotland under French rule. Their growing influence was triggered by Knox's return to Scotland for a short period in 1556, when he preached at Calder to Lord James Stewart and Argyll. They now joined a group of like-minded Reformers among the nobility, who formed the Lords of the Congregation. Although their faith was based on genuine personal conviction, their grouping conveniently offered a political platform, from which to face Marie of Guise, now queen regent. Knox brazenly wrote to her, demanding that she should become a Reformer or face 'dejection to torment and pain everlasting'.[3] She contemptuously treated his letter as a joke. Although he returned to Geneva, he was invited by Lord James, Argyll and Glencairn to return in the following year.

While waiting for a ship at Dieppe in 1557, during his return to Scotland, Knox wrote the document that gained him, for all time, a reputation as a political embarrassment. He produced his *First Blast of the Trumpet against the monstrous Regiment of Women*, a diatribe against the rule of both Mary Tudor and the queen regent published in early 1558. He saw it as 'a subversion of good order, of all equity and justice' for women to rule men.[4] His timing was unfortunate, as Mary Tudor died later in the year and Elizabeth also saw it as an affront. In an effort to make amends, he wrote to her in July conveying his unfeigned love and reverence, but told her that she ruled by the will of the people and not by dynastic right. Elizabeth now saw him as an anathema and would not have his name mentioned. He remained insensitive to criticism and showed no Christian sympathy for his opponents, relishing any bloodthirsty brutality that brought about their end. Elizabeth's opposition forced him to return to Scotland, rather than to gain a more glittering Protestant post in England. On arrival, he quickly went onto the attack against the Catholic Church. This was an unfortunate approach, as, since the time of James V, senior Scottish nobles, including Lord James Stewart had been granted the use of Catholic Church lands as lay 'Commendators'. The Lords of the Congregation needed to steer Knox into addressing the political concern of ending the queen regent's 'tyranny of strangers'.

The Lords of the Congregation started to gather support, in part, because the Reformist faith was less financially demanding on its adherents than the Catholic Church, but, in the main, because of their political concerns about French domination. It might have been thought that Huguenot influence in France now offered them a better prospect of support than Catholic England under Mary Tudor, so it was political rather than spiritual concerns that was their stronger influence.

Starting with Mary's marriage to the Dauphin in April 1558, a number of factors moved the Lords of the Congregation from a body concerned with reform of the Church to one determined to oust French influence from Scotland. The queen regent's additional military strength and the security provided by Mary's marriage made her feel less vulnerable. On 28 April, she approved the burning of a former priest-turned-Reformer, Walter Myln, at the stake at St Andrews. This caused an inevitable backlash. The Reformers erected a pile of stones to mark Myln's burial place and, although the Catholic clergy had them removed, they were always replaced. This *cause célèbre* provided the Lords with a motive to incite opposition, and the queen regent had a fight on her hands.

Another of those converted by Knox in 1556 was William Maitland of Lethington. It was he who first began to fear the increase in the queen regent's forces, not in terms of protecting the kingdom for her daughter, but in subjugating Scotland to French and Catholic domination. His concerns may have been coloured by his own position as Secretary being threatened at a time when she was appointing so many French advisers. He started to persuade other Reformist nobles to share his views and, in 1559, resigned, so that he could oppose her. Châtelherault had lost credibility, but, when persuaded by Arran, his son, to join the Lords of the Congregation, his move swung the balance in favour of those who sought to oust the French.

Reformist unrest began initially in Perth. When Knox arrived to preach at St John's on 11 May 1557, his sermon caused a riot, leading to the sacking and looting of the nearby Catholic monasteries, during which Queen Margaret's grave was desecrated. The provost, Patrick, 3rd Lord Ruthven, refused to assist the queen regent's French garrison in suppressing the insurgency. Even the Catholic George Gordon, 4th Earl of Huntly, supported an end to French domination and failed to come to her rescue. Glencairn and Andrew Stewart, 2nd Lord Ochiltree, raised 2,500 men to support Ruthven. Knox went to St Giles's in Edinburgh, from where he galvanised Reformers from the pulpit to back military action. Thomas Randolph, the English Ambassador claimed that he 'is able in one hour to put more life into us than 500 trumpets continually blustering in our ears'.[5] On 4 June 1557, Lord James and Argyll left Edinburgh with 300 men to link with other Reformist groups at St Andrews. Within a week, 13,000 troops from further afield were encamped above the town at Cupar Muir. The queen regent avoided confrontation, but agreed to remove her French troops from Fife. When they demanded the departure of the French garrison from Perth, it surrendered on 26 June. She was forced back to the safety of the French garrison at Dunbar, and, on 29 June, the Lords of the Congregation entered Edinburgh unopposed.

With her well-trained French forces securely based in fortified garrison towns, the queen regent was positioned to counterattack. With additional help from France, she made continuing attempts to stamp out heresy and provided a liberal distribution of French pensions to keep the Scottish nobility at bay. When these dried up, however, the Reformers gained increasing support to topple her. Following Mary Tudor's death, and with Elizabeth now on the English throne, Maitland pushed them into seeking an English alliance, while Cecil encouraged Lord James and Argyll to protect England's northern border by taking control. It was the Reformation that broke the Auld Alliance with France. The issue for the Lords was to demonstrate that they had the military strength to challenge the French. On 19 July 1558, they wrote an urgent letter to Cecil seeking English help. With Lord James emerging as their leader, he adopted a façade of religious objectives to cloak his personal plan to oust the queen regent. He must have assumed that he would gain English assistance. He wanted Mary kept safely out of the way in France and wrote carefully to Cecil hinting at her deposition to create a united Protestant Britain. Yet his colleagues pulled back from this radical step.

Elizabeth was in a quandary. She did not believe that the legitimate succession in Scotland should be overridden by religious preconditions. She also wanted to avoid a war with France. She needed time to recover from the financial turmoil and military disaster of the loss of Calais left by Mary Tudor. Despite supporting Protestant government in Scotland, she could not be seen to offer the Lords of the Congregation overt backing and preferred to limit it to financial assistance. She did not initially feel secure on her throne, and when she did, she was a party to the Peace of Cateau-Cambrésis between France and Spain signed in April 1559, and would not risk jeopardising her relationship with them. Yet the Peace had reduced the authority of the Guises in France, which limited the military assistance that they could now offer the queen regent.

Cecil did not agree with Elizabeth. When financial support alone proved insufficient to defeat the queen regent's French forces, he wrote lengthy reports to fellow members of the English Privy Council to justify military action, even if it meant supporting rebels to oust a legitimate government. He hoped that Elizabeth would recognise England's security as more important than protecting an anointed Tudor queen on her Scottish throne. The queen regent was militarily dangerous. Her French troops were garrisoned all over Scotland and she had a smattering of Scottish support. The powerful Catholics in Scotland feared that Lord James, the eldest son of James V, even though illegitimate, was tilting at the Crown.

Having grouped her forces at Dunbar, the queen regent denounced Lord James and Argyll as rebels and accused Lord James of seeking the Crown. He hotly denied it, promising her his support, if Reformers were tolerated. He told her that their only objective was 'to maintain and defend the true preachers of God's word'. To retain her supply lines, she fortified the port of Leith where a French garrison was stationed. This forced the Lords to withdraw from Edinburgh. Lord James now approached the waverers among the nobility. In September 1559, he was joined by Châtelherault and his son Arran for a conference of Reformist nobles at Stirling. On 21 October, Châtelherault signed documentation to suspend the queen regent, which she ignored. Yet, as heir to the throne, he had a right to replace her, and this gave the Lords a semblance of legality.

Lord James made a direct approach to Elizabeth, but she now feared that Spain would join with France to place Mary on the English throne. She preferred to blur her decisions in a manner that exasperated her advisers, but did much to protect her in the early part of her reign. She refused to invade Scotland to back a rebel cause, but provided more money, while hotly denying any involvement to the foreign ambassadors in London, 'at which she was expert to the point of genius'. Her powers of dissimulation were such that the ambassadors had to admit, 'She is the best hand at the game living.' Although 4,000 foot and 2,000 horse were quartered at Berwick, she would not send them across the border. Instead, she sent the young and able Admiral William Winter with English ships from Berwick to harry reinforcements and supplies arriving from France, but with instructions to say that he was seeking out pirates without her authority if caught.

On 31 October, Elizabeth used Cecil's agent, Thomas Randolph, to send £3,000 secretly to Lord James, but the queen regent was warned and sent James Hepburn, 4th Earl of Bothwell to ambush the courier. Bothwell took his prize to Crichton, hotly pursued by Lord James and Arran. On 9 November, after fleeing with his booty, he offered to fight Arran in a duel, but Arran refused. Bothwell was now Lord James's implacable enemy.

On 21 October, Lord James re-entered Edinburgh with 15,000 men. Yet the Castle Governor, John, 6th Lord Erskine, was protecting the queen regent, now suffering from dropsy, and would not desert her. Although Ruthven presided over a meeting of the nobility to appoint a Council of twenty-four to replace her as regent, she took no notice, despite her doctors unhelpfully advising rest and a warmer climate. She was moved to Leith, now well fortified and garrisoned with 3,000 French troops. Lord James's occupation of Edinburgh had achieved nothing in military terms, and negotiations with her proved fruitless.

Despite reinforcements sent from France being lost in a huge storm in the North Sea, the queen regent made good use of her garrison at Leith. On 6 November, Lord James and Arran sent a force out from Edinburgh to protect a convoy of provisions stuck in the marshes between Holyrood and Restalrig. The French sallied out, pushing them back into Edinburgh at the Canongate with the loss of more than 1,000 of Lord James's men.

The Lords of the Congregation agreed to withdraw from Edinburgh to Stirling with 15,000 men, on condition that the queen regent called parliament to meet on 10 January 1560. She still commanded their grudging respect; Randolph paid tribute to her 'craft and subtleties' during this negotiation, and Throckmorton admired her 'queenly mind'.[6,7] He wrote to

Cecil, for the love of God 'to provide that she were rid from hence, for she hath the heart of a man of war'.

At last, on 27 December 1559, Cecil persuaded the English Privy Council to intervene, after citing the unique opportunity to establish Scotland as a dependency. Two thousand more troops arrived at Berwick, and, on 23 January, Winter blockaded Leith; the queen regent demanded an explanation, refusing to believe that he was acting without authority. The Lords of the Congregation took half of their men to Fife, where Ruthven joined them to await the arrival of English troops. The remainder went to Glasgow to protect the west of Scotland.

Bothwell, like his father before him, was one of the few Scottish nobles to support the queen regent. He was given command of her troops and, on 24 November 1559, took Linlithgow and regained Edinburgh, which had been left undefended. He took 800 men to capture Stirling and advanced into Fife to attack Lord James and Arran at Cupar Muir. Buoyed up by a sermon on the field from Knox, the Lords of the Congregation, with an inferior force, kept Bothwell's men at bay for twenty-one days, giving Winter the opportunity to capture two French men–of–war and vessels carrying military supplies. In need of provisions, the French were forced back through Stirling to Leith. Although the queen regent applied to James Macdonald, the strongest of the western chiefs, to support her with his 700 men, Argyll persuaded him to assist the Lords in blockading her French garrison in Leith.

At last, Maitland made arrangements for Lord James to negotiate a military alliance at Berwick with the young Thomas Howard, 4th Duke of Norfolk, who was in command of the English troops. The English agreed to protect the Scots 'in their old freedoms and liberties' while Mary remained in France.[8] Mary angrily wrote to her mother promising undying love and more French troops, but the Guises were out of power, and none were available. Although she begged her mother to heed her health, the queen regent remained dangerously ill. She wrote to d'Oysel: 'I am lame and have a leg that assuageth not from swelling. If any lay a finger upon it, it goeth in as into butter.' On 2 April 1560, Norfolk's troops crossed into Scotland, to join Lord James and Glencairn with their Scottish forces at Prestonpans, from where they advanced on Edinburgh.

On 17 April, when the queen regent failed to call the promised parliament, forty-nine Scottish nobles of all persuasions signed a bond to expel the French. Yet the French were still a force to be reckoned with. Elizabeth's earlier prevarication had left Norfolk with inexperienced and underfunded men. Although Leith was attacked on 7 May, the English were soundly rebuffed. A group of Scottish whores, determined not to lose their regular French clientele, caused considerable injury by throwing burning coals on the attackers from the battlements. With Seton's help, Bothwell ambushed and captured the English commander. The French retained control of Leith and, although the Scottish Parliament met outside its walls three days later, the disappointed Commissioners could do no more than ratify the Treaty of Berwick, hoping that Elizabeth would send more men.

By holding the port of Leith, the queen regent could still receive reinforcements and she dispatched Bothwell to France for help. Given their urgent plight, he sailed to Denmark, hoping to transport 5,000 German mercenaries with Frederick II's fleet, while he went on over land to France. The queen regent, now aged 45 was terminally ill and died at Leith on 11 June, swollen and in great pain. Shortly beforehand, she had written to Argyll regretting the hostilities and blaming the Catholic lords, probably unjustifiably, for their advice. Such was the personal respect for her that Lord James, Argyll and Glencairn called a ceasefire to visit her on her deathbed. She asked them to believe that she wanted to protect Scotland as much as France. She proposed, as a compromise, the removal of both French and English troops.

The Reformers initially opposed the shipment of her body back to France in a lead-lined coffin. It was only in July 1561, more than a year after her death, that she was at last laid to rest in Reims. From the distance of France, Mary needed to assert her authority in Scotland, but with the Guises having lost power, they could not help, and the remaining French garrisons were forced to leave Scotland.

With the Lords of the Congregation now able to govern without interference, they sought closer ties with England. Châtelherault was appointed regent with Lord James as his deputy. The French government instructed their ambassador, Charles, Sieur de Randan, to broker a peace before their costs in Scotland brought 'the ruin and desolation of France'. The Guises swore revenge on Elizabeth for backing the Scottish rebels, but were in no position to put pressure on her. With Mary in fear of losing her throne, they asked Philip II to mediate to defend Catholicism in Scotland. He agreed, but it suited him to be pragmatic; his main interest was in retaining England as an ally. He managed to prevent Elizabeth from being excommunicated by the Pope for twelve years after her accession. He did not want Mary, the Queen of France, also as Queen of England, able to threaten his means of communication through the Channel. Without consulting Mary, Spanish and French representatives began to negotiate with Châtelherault and Lord James in Edinburgh, and Cecil arrived from London.

The Spanish saw the negotiations as a natural follow-on from the Treaty of Cateau-Cambrésis, while the Guises considered them to be a French sell-out. After a month's discussion, the Treaty of Edinburgh was signed on 6 July 1560. Elizabeth was recognised as the rightful English Queen, and Mary's claims were dropped. All French and English troops were to leave Scotland, except for sixty French soldiers at Inchleith and Dunbar, with their other forts and garrisons being razed to the ground. Châtelherault and Lord James were reconfirmed as Governor and Deputy, heading a Council of twenty-four Scottish nobles to govern so long as Mary remained abroad. Catholic services were banned. It was even confirmed that Elizabeth's role had been that of an impartial umpire to create the conditions for a negotiated treaty, and not that of ally to the Lords of the Congregation. Always with an eye to personal benefit, Châtelherault saw to it that he was restored to his French estates, which had been attainted in the meantime. Finally, if Francis and Mary failed to ratify the terms, England could intervene to uphold the Presbyterian faith. Mary still had her throne, but at a price. It is hard to imagine how the negotiators expected her to endorse it. Yet the agreement cemented lasting friendship between Lord James and Cecil. On 1 August 1560, it was ratified by the Scottish Parliament. Maitland spoke as 'harangue maker' to confirm the abolition of papacy, and Knox agreed to prepare a new Confession of Faith based on Calvinist doctrine. Christmas and Easter festivities were banned as being Papist, although the pagan festival of Hogmanay was allowed to survive!

On returning to London, Cecil fully expected a reward both for the Scottish negotiators and for himself, but Lord Robert Dudley, his political opponent, had the Queen's ear. He received nothing, despite having faced considerable personal expense, and his request for pensions for the key Scottish lords was turned down. Elizabeth claimed she had spent £247,000, more than a year's revenue, providing men and equipment to free the Scots from France and that was benefit enough. Cecil could only brood on her folly in favouring Dudley, whom he disliked intensely.

Lennox used the opportunity of the French demise in Scotland to approach the Spanish seeking their armed support for a coup for him to replace Mary on the Scottish throne, promising that he would restore Catholicism north of the border with the aid of their Scottish allies. This came to nothing as Philip II was determined to retain his strategic alliance with the English, who were supporting the Reformers. Cecil gained wind of these negotiations and threatened Lennox that his private dealings with foreign powers were in contravention of the terms of his marriage agreement.

The Scottish Parliament did not wait for royal approval of the Treaty of Edinburgh and met to dismantle the Scottish Catholic Church.[9*] Presbyterianism became the standard religion, with the General Assembly as its highest court, empowered to criticise Catholics and Reformers alike. Knox was instructed by parliament to arrange for a committee of Reformers to draw up a Book of Discipline 'learnit in the mysteries of the new testament'.[10] It provided a Scottish Confession as a clear statement of Calvinist faith braced against a Counter-Reformation. It opposed the Mass and considered ordination of clergy to be superstitious. Knox's most laudable objective was to establish a morally upright community with universal schooling for women as well as men, with secondary and university education for those who would benefit. This gained the backing of the burgesses of the towns and the people at large. All 'monuments of idolatry' were to be destroyed. This was carried out in the south-west, but was more difficult to achieve in the Catholic north. It was only good sense that prevented civil strife.

Bothwell had learned of the queen regent's demise while in Denmark and decided to lie low. He had been graciously received by the king and entered into a misalliance with Anna, daughter of a Norwegian nobleman, Christopher Throndssen, an admiral in the Danish navy. He seduced her with a promise of marriage, and she sold her jewellery to finance their travel to Flanders. Having burned his boats with the Reformers, Bothwell needed to seek help from Mary in France. Still short of funds, he set off alone for the French Court, arriving there in September. He was well received after his support for the queen regent, but was described by Throckmorton, the English Ambassador, whom he met in Orléans, as 'a [vain]glorious rash and hazardous young man'.[11] Francis made him a Gentleman of the Bedchamber and Mary gave him 600 crowns to restore his finances. He later admitted that she 'rewarded me much more liberally and graciously than I deserved, which angered my enemies to the greatest degree'.[12] She respected his vitality and, before his return to Flanders, she appointed him as a commissioner for her estates. Anna returned to Scotland with him on 17 November 1560, but he unceremoniously dumped her, despite her being pregnant.[13*] He now flitted between Scotland and France, never spending long enough in any one place for the Lords of the Congregation to catch up with him, but, as Hereditary Lord High Admiral, he arrived in Calais to transport Mary's baggage on her return to Scotland.

Part 2

Competing ambitions to be recognized as Elizabeth's heir

Chapter 8

Mary marries the Dauphin and becomes Queen Consort of France

The marriage of Mary to the French Dauphin in April 1558 must have been a blow to the hopes of Margaret Douglas. Suddenly she was competing to be recognised as the Catholic heir to the English throne with a rival who could expect French military support. The timing of the marriage had been triggered by the success, three months earlier, of Mary's uncle, Francis, Duke of Guise, in capturing Calais, England's last remaining outpost on the European continent. This had caused huge French celebration. Her marriage to the hapless and stunted Dauphin was full of spectacle. The 15-year-old Mary was 'arrayed in her regal trappings, so covered in jewels that the sun itself shone no more brightly, so beautiful, so charming withal as never woman was.'[1] She towered over her husband and, with the Guise family advising her, she dominated his every move. Although she was undoubtedly fond of him, he was almost certainly impotent.

There can be no doubt that Mary was considered outstandingly glamorous at this time. At five foot eleven inches, she was seven inches above the height at which women were generally described as tall, and was already close to her full height at her wedding. With flawless pale skin and a fine figure, she was always a sought-after subject for Court poets and artists, and this is borne out by pictures of her in childhood and adolescence. All the written evidence is unfailingly favourable. Even Knox described her as 'pleasing' and recorded that the people of Edinburgh called out, 'Heaven bless that sweet face.'[2] Sir James Melville saw her as 'very lovesome', and the poets around the Court saw her as 'a true goddess'.[3] The Venetian ambassador described her as a princess who was 'personally the most beautiful in Europe'.[4] Yet it was her voice, her complexion, height, her lissome figure with perfect breasts, her hands and her grace of movement that tended to receive praise. While Mary was always an attractive personality, when she reached maturity, she became less classically beautiful and her nose was to lengthen, but there are no remaining portraits of her made in the period immediately following her return to Scotland, so there are no visual means of judging her in her prime. When imprisoned in England, there were a number of portraits, which do not exude the glamour one might expect, but by then she was older and suffering from rheumatism and other ailments, and her nose seems to have become the dominating feature of her face, which shows signs of her having gained weight.

On 17 November 1558, Mary Tudor died childless in London without Darnley being nominated as her heir, as his mother had hoped. With deliberate provocation, Mary in France went into mourning for the loss of the English cousin she had never met. With Elizabeth illegitimate in Catholic eyes, the Queen-Dauphine was, by blood, the rightful successor. Yet the English government harboured no doubts over Elizabeth's legitimacy. She had been the focus of every Protestant plot to overthrow the Catholic Mary Tudor during her reign. She had been educated for her future role as queen. She was now 25, nine years older than Mary Queen of Scots, headstrong, academically capable and politically adept. She may have lacked the Queen-Dauphine's star quality, but her tutor Roger Ascham recorded: 'Her study of true religion and learning is most eager. Her mind has no womanly weakness, her perseverance is equal to that of a man ...'[5]

England's ready acceptance of Elizabeth as queen was a great blow for Henry II. When he sought to have her declared illegitimate, the widowed Philip II immediately opposed it. Despite her being Catholic, Philip did not want the Queen-Dauphine on the English throne with the prospect of France and England combining to control both sides of the Channel, his conduit between the two parts of his vast empire. He proposed marriage to Elizabeth, and she shrewdly strung him along. He pressurised the Pope not to confirm her as illegitimate, putting paid to Guise claims on Mary's behalf. On 21 April 1558, to Elizabeth's huge relief, Mary and Francis, as Queen and King of Scots, wrote to Elizabeth, endorsing her as queen, and vowing peace and friendship.

On 30 June 1559, Henry II was struck by a lance, which splintered while he took part in a jousting tournament in Paris; he died ten days later. The Dauphin was suddenly King Francis II and Mary was his Queen Consort. At this time, Darnley was with his parents in Yorkshire, although they were now spending much of their time at a second home, Settrington, in the Yorkshire wolds. The advantage of this was its proximity to Bridlington, a little port that traded with Dieppe. This enabled them to maintain close contact with affairs in France. With Mary now queen, Lennox's younger brother, John Stuart, 4th Seigneur d'Aubigny, was elevated to the French Court as the young queen's kinsman and became Captain of the *Garde Écossaise*.

After being captured at St Quentin during France's wars with Spain, he had received a substantial contribution from Lennox towards the ransom for his release. This placed Aubigny under an obligation to his brother.[6] He immediately sent word of the king's death. The Lennoxes secretly sent their 13-year-old son by sea with Elder to offer their condolences and to congratulate Mary and Francis II on their accession to both the French and the English thrones. After reaching the French Court at the palatial Château of Chambord, Aubigny acted as Darnley's mentor and arranged a secret audience with the young king and queen. Darnley delivered a letter from Lennox seeking the restoration of his Scottish estates and handed over pedigrees to show his close claims to both the Scottish and English thrones and his connection to the houses of Lennox and Douglas.[7] Although Mary turned down Lennox's request for restoration, she gave Darnley 1,000 crowns and invited him to attend Francis II's coronation. Elder was by then making a great show of Catholicism, and Nicholas Throckmorton, the English Ambassador in Paris, warned that he was 'as dangerous for the matters of England as any he knew'.[8] Yet Throckmorton does not appear to have recognised Darnley and reported only that 'a young gentleman, an Englishman or a Scottishman, who had no beard, was received with great distinction by the king and queen of France and Scotland'.[9] Darnley went on to stay with his uncle at Aubigny, where he was entertained by his aunt, Anne de la Queulle, and cousin, Esmé, who was later to play a key part in James VI's Government, ultimately becoming Duke of Lennox. He was taken hunting before returning home to Settrington, via Dieppe and Bridlington with his presence in France still unnoticed. Elder had become fascinated by the predictions of Nostradamus a French *savant* much respected by Catherine de Medici, who had foreseen Henri II's jousting accident. He was also predicting that his son would die before he was 18. Elder seems to have brought a copy of his predictions from France, and Lallart wrote a commentary on them for Margaret, who also had an interest in the occult.

By now Elizabeth was treating the Lennoxes with suspicion, and William Forbes, a spy in the pay of Lord Robert Dudley, was placed in their household. Forbes reported that Margaret retained 'a fool who was permitted "to rail uncorrected on the Queen's Majesty and upon Lord Robert"'.[10] Despite their reduced status in England, Lennox obsessively sought to be restored to his estates and to be cleared of treason in Scotland, which would be an impediment to Darnley being considered as a potential suitor for the Scottish queen. Towards the end of 1559, Lennox sent a 'confidential servant', Laurence Nisbet to Scotland to negotiate with Mary's mother.

He contemplated offering her support to combat the growing strength of the Reformers, in return for the restoration of his Scottish estates, but seems to have resisted this proposal. When Nisbet returned to London to meet the French ambassador, the Compte de Noailles, he was arrested and imprisoned. While both Lennox and Nisbet claimed that the only purpose of the Scottish visit was to seek restoration of the Lennox estates, Nisbet appears to have talked and the English believed the story of Lennox's treasonable intent to assist the queen regent, who was terminally ill and under great pressure against the Lords of the Congregation and the English. Margaret was called to London to explain, but continued to claim that the sole purpose of the visit was for Lennox to recover his estates and to try to limit the support for Châtelherault to become regent if Marie of Guise should die.

The news of the queen regent's death reached France on 18 June 1560, but it was withheld from Mary for ten days while negotiations over Scotland's future were hammered out. She then withdrew weeping to her rooms for a month, suffering a physical collapse. She adopted the *deuil blanc*, the mourning headdress that she would wear until she married Darnley five years later. Her mother's portrait remained a cherished possession and was among those found after her execution at Fotheringhay.

Mary was already greatly concerned over her husband's well being. His sexual shortcomings were common knowledge in the circle round the Crown, but he was becoming increasingly unwell caused by an abscess behind his ear. Mary knew that he was deteriorating, and realised that, if he died, she faced the prospect of returning to Scotland. In mid-November 1560, he complained of recurring dizziness and collapsed in church. When he died on 5 December, Mary was devastated. Her future 'dissolved like a mirage'.[11] She retired for forty days to mourn in a private chamber.

With the Guises diminished in authority, Mary needed allies. She was joined by her grandmother, Antoinette de Bourbon, and, despite her grief, had time to think. Although she contemplated returning to Scotland as a Catholic queen, this would cause conflict with the Reformers, who were likely to retain English support. Although large parts of Scotland remained Catholic, she would need significant additional military strength to promote a Counter-Reformation. This would require her remarriage to a powerful Catholic ally, but there were two problems. Firstly, there was a danger of Scotland becoming subsumed into her chosen spouse's homeland. Secondly, she was likely to live with him outside Scotland. Yet, if she returned unmarried, accepting the religious *status quo*, as Lord James was to suggest, she could promote her dynastic claim to the English throne. It was dynastic ambition that motivated her return. There is no evidence, at this time, that she remotely contemplated marriage to Darnley. He could not provide her with military support and, as a Catholic, would fall foul of both the Scottish government and Elizabeth, who would see the couple as a threat. Furthermore, he was only just 14.

Mary's Guise uncles hoped to restore their flagging influence by arranging her remarriage. The 9-year-old King Charles IX was suggested, but Catherine wanted to avoid a return to Guise supremacy. They approached Philip II to propose her marriage to Don Carlos, his son by the Infanta Mary of Portugal, who had died in childbirth. Don Carlos had physical and mental shortcomings that might have seemed even more deterring than those of Francis II had they been more generally known. He was a hunchback with twisted shoulders and never weighed more than six stone. He had become brain-damaged after fracturing his skull falling downstairs while chasing a servant girl, whom he enjoyed flagellating. Although his life had been saved by a trepanning operation, he was left epileptic and homicidal. Yet all of this appears to have remained hidden from the diplomatic community.

Neither Catherine nor Elizabeth approved of the Don Carlos suit. Faced with the prospect of open hostility from both France and England, Philip pulled back. He had no wish to upset the English so soon after brokering the Treaty of Edinburgh to destroy the *Auld Alliance* and he wanted Guise imperialistic ambitions to be curbed. Yet it was the prospect of the Don Carlos suit, which prevented Margaret Douglas from making any progress in promoting Darnley. With dynastic marriage negotiations coming to nothing, Mary could remain comfortably in France as Queen Dowager and Duchess of Touraine in her own right, where she might make a noble, if not a royal, marriage. Alternatively, she could seek to return as a widow to Scotland, from where the opportunity of the English throne might come her way. Her gambling streak plumped for the high-stake challenge of Scotland. Yet her choice of husband would be crucial. Candidates whom Cecil found acceptable included the kings of Denmark and Sweden and the dukes of Ferrara and Bavaria, but they offered little advantage to Guise family ambitions. He advocated deferring any decision until her return.

Although Throckmorton met Mary on several occasions, she refused to ratify the Treaty of Edinburgh, which she had played no part in negotiating. Approval would severely compromise her position on the Scottish throne. As a Catholic, she could not accept the banning of papacy and had no intention of forgoing her claim to the English throne. She reminded him of her Tudor lineage, and went on: 'I pray [Elizabeth] to judge me by herself, for I am sure she could ill bear the usage and disobedience of her subjects which she knows mine have shown to me.' She called for 'amity' with her 'sister Queen'.[12] This will have struck a chord with Elizabeth.

In Scotland, the stage was set for a power struggle between Lord James Stewart, backed by the Lords of the Congregation, and the Catholic Huntly. Huntly sent the Scottish Catholic priest John Leslie to propose that, if Mary would land at Aberdeen, she would be escorted by 20,000 troops on a wave of Catholic popularity to Edinburgh. Mary was too well aware of the military power of the Reformers to fall for this romantic notion. Yet she respected Leslie, and he remained in France to seek papal help for Scotland's Catholics on her behalf.

Lord James had visited Cecil in London on his way to France. They had concluded that Mary posed less of a risk in Scotland than if left under Guise control in France. Although Elizabeth was determined that she should ratify the Treaty of Edinburgh, thereby confirming Elizabeth as the rightful English Queen, Lord James's objective with Cecil was to establish a basis, acceptable to both the Scottish Parliament and the English, for Mary, as a Catholic, to return to her throne. So long as she aspired to the English Crown, alliance with France would be less appealing, and Cecil happily dangled this carrot before her. Once separated from her Guise relations, it was hoped that she might take a less dogmatic religious stance.

Cecil supported Maitland's view that Mary should make an appropriate Protestant marriage. This would reinforce the newfound Scottish alliance with England. He wanted Presbyterianism maintained in Scotland and expected Mary to suborn her personal religious beliefs to those of her future husband. Yet he wanted her claim to the English throne to be taken on trust, until she demonstrated her Protestant affiliation. He would never accept a committed Catholic as English Queen, unless cloaked in a politically Protestant exterior. He could not discuss such sensitivities with Elizabeth, still hoping that she would solve his problem by marrying and having children of her own. It is clear that Darnley did not come into consideration even though he had some support among English Catholics. He was just 14 and his mother Margaret was out of favour as a result of her Catholicism and earlier scheming against Elizabeth.

Lord James needed to persuade Mary, despite her Guise connections, that her return to Scotland as queen was dependent on her accepting the religious *status quo* with Lord James as head of her government. Although they did not admit it publicly, this was a relief to Philip II and Catherine de Medici, who had lost the appetite for war and wanted to dampen Guise aspirations. He spent five days building his rapport with her. If she accepted the religious *status quo*, he would arrange for her to receive the Catholic sacrament in private. This might be abhorrent to Knox, but his ranting was being seen as politically unhelpful.

Mary pragmatically accepted Lord James's proposal. His dour gravitas made him a natural choice as her adviser; she mistrusted Châtelherault and Arran, particularly after a proposal that Arran should marry Elizabeth to usurp the Scottish throne. Arran, who was already showing signs of mental instability, had appeared with his own proposal to marry Mary, but she turned this down not wanting Elizabeth's cast off. She envisaged Lord James as her *eminence grise* helping her to govern on her own. She was naïve in failing to realise his ambition for power. He returned to Paris to gain Throckmorton's backing for his plan, explaining the advantages for both Scotland and England. The fickle nature of the Scottish nobility made the success of the plan dependent on gaining English support. Throckmorton, who was trusted by Elizabeth, agreed to promote it, seeing him as 'one of the most virtuous noblemen'.[13] Elizabeth saw the advantage of allowing Mary to return, despite holding Catholic services in private, but would not recognise her as her heir. She knew only too well the danger of having an heir with a faith different from her own. She had been part of all the intrigue to oust her sister, and she was piqued that Mary had failed to ratify the Treaty of Edinburgh.

As hereditary Lord High Admiral, Bothwell arrived at Calais to command a dozen Dutch merchantmen chartered for Mary's baggage. Having provided sumptuous gifts for her Guise relations, she set sail for Scotland in a French galley on 14 August 1661. On leaving the French coast she broke down, saying: 'Adieu France, adieu France, adieu donc ma chère France.'[14]

Chapter 9

Margaret Douglas's initial efforts to promote Darnley as a husband for Mary

On hearing that Francis II had died, Margaret Douglas was determined to promote Darnley's suit to marry Mary. She immediately sent him to Orléans to pass on her condolences, and he was already on his way home before the official messenger arrived from Elizabeth. Margaret, who was in Yorkshire, plied Mary with the advantages of marriage to her long-legged son, which would combine their close claims to both the Scottish and English thrones. She even suggested that they should replace Elizabeth. Mary, however, was being guided by her Guise uncles, who had other ideas, and she knew that Elizabeth would see marriage to Darnley as hostile. She had no wish to be confrontational, and Margaret's hope of Mary falling for the leggy 14-year-old fell flat.

Margaret did not risk sending Darnley to greet Mary on her return to Scotland; his appearance would not have been welcome while she established herself as a tolerant queen in a Protestant country. Lallart was sent instead, ostensibly to deliver messages to Aubigny, although Aubigny did not accompany her from France; he did, however, send a 'Book of Emblems' for Darnley. This provided images of personal devices accompanied by Latin mottos. It was the vogue for these to be attached to clothing or to provide headings for correspondence.[1] Lallart's true purpose was to speak to the queen and he hoped to do this as she travelled around Scotland. Having followed her to Stirling, he managed a quick conversation as she mounted her horse en route for Perth, although this is unlikely to have been concerned with Darnley's suit. Following his visit, Lallart was investigated by the English Privy Council. He reported:

> I let her understand my Lord's mind regarding his estates, and also his request for his case to be heard before Parliament. The Queen replied that she was but newly returned into her realm, therefore she could not give such an answer as she would; but all she might do for my Lord and my Lady her aunt, she would do at proper time, desiring my Lady to be always her good aunt, as she knew her for to be; with remembrances to them both.[2]

Margaret considered this encouraging. Yet she was not aware that her recent intriguing at Settrington had been reported back to the English government, including the study of Nostradamus, the jibes against Elizabeth and Lord Robert Dudley, the reports of Darnley's second visit to France, and Lallart's trip to Scotland.

By this time, Châtelherault was professing to be a Reformer. Although Lennox remained in England, he dropped any pretence of being Protestant and joined the French party in Scotland to promote himself as Scotland's Catholic heir presumptive after Mary. This demonstrated a lack of good timing. Shortly before Christmas 1561, the Lennoxes were arrested at Settrington and were taken to London for confinement at their apartments in the Palace of Westminster. Although Margaret set out for London with all her family, Darnley seems to have gone to York, from where he travelled incognito back to France. How he achieved this is not clear, but he may have been able to join a ship at Bridlington. He did not go to the French Court – from where his extradition might be demanded, but probably travelled direct to Aubigny.[3] Lennox was confined to the Tower where he remained until 1564, while Margaret and their other children, including their son Charles, were placed in the custody of Anne Boleyn's cousins, Sir Richard and Lady Sackville, at Sheen, a former Carthusian monastery. Sir Richard was a respected lawyer and Chancellor of the Exchequer. Following the dissolution of the monasteries, Sheen had been granted to Henry Grey, Duke of Suffolk, who converted it into a mansion, but it had reverted to the Crown after his execution following Wyatt's rebellion in 1554. Mary I restored it to the Carthusians, but on Elizabeth's accession, Sir Richard was granted a lease.

Margaret was in serious trouble. Although she wrote to Cecil to demand an audience with Elizabeth, protesting 'fervent loyalty and devotion', Forbes's revelations made these unconvincing. There was a second mole in her household, Thomas Bishop, who had recently been dismissed by the Lennoxes for his disloyalty. For some time, he had been spreading a list of damaging half-truths about the Lennoxes' treasonable plottings in revenge for his poor treatment. He provided evidence that Margaret had been in secret communication with the ambassadors of France and Spain (even apparently attempting to garner support for the queen regent at the siege of Leith, which seems unlikely), with Mary Queen of Scots on several occasions over the dynastic advantages of her marrying Darnley (which was undoubtedly true), with the Lords in Scotland to sound out their support for Darnley to marry Mary (which again was true – but treasonable without

Elizabeth's consent), that she had celebrated mass in her private chapel, that she had referred to Elizabeth as a bastard (which was treasonable), that she intended to make a challenge for the English Crown, that she used sooth-sayers and witchcraft to promote her ambitions and 'to imagine the death of the monarch'. (When the spire of St Paul's cathedral collapsed after being struck by lightning, she was accused of having caused it by witchcraft.) In addition, there was independent evidence that she had been communicat-ing with Alvares de Quadra, Bishop of Aquileia, the Spanish Ambassador, to promote her Catholic claim to the English throne with Philip II. Cecil had bribed Quadra's Italian Secretary, Borghese Venturini, to confirm evi-dence of the correspondence of this scheming. Venturini reported Quadra's request that, if Philip were to support her,

> the Catholic religion would be restored, and that this could easily be done, the majority of the nobles being of that faith; and eight or ten of the nobility would rise in favour of Lady Margaret and her son. But until he move[d] they must keep quiet, and his long delay had much dismayed them.[4]

Yet Philip II wanted to retain his alliance with Elizabeth against France and was fearful of the Lennoxes' pro-French stance. Although the extent of Margaret's involvement in Quadra's scheme was not clear, while she was at Sheen, she unwisely claimed that she should rightfully be queen. There were unequivocal reports that she was now plotting against Elizabeth, and plans were made to arrest her as soon as the necessary evidence could be gathered.

Margaret was not made aware of the incriminating evidence being gathered against her. Despite being threatened with an investigation into her legitimacy by the Court of Star Chamber, this was dropped, probably because Elizabeth was nervous of its implications for her own status. It is clear that Elizabeth pulled back from treating her too harshly. She wanted to retain a Tudor alternative to Mary Queen of Scots with her Guise con-nections as heir to the English throne, and saw the 15-year-old Darnley as less threatening than Don Carlos or some other European Catholic prince as Mary's consort. Both Elizabeth and Catherine de Medici were determined to thwart the Don Carlos marriage proposition and it would appear that Catherine favoured her marrying Darnley. It was even hoped that Darnley might be persuaded to become Protestant. There is no doubt that Elizabeth preferred the Lennoxes to the rival claim of Catherine Grey, and it would seem that Dudley, who had become Margaret's ally, discouraged Elizabeth from punishing her too severely. Margaret was placed in the Tower and was again excluded from the succession based on unfounded doubts over her legitimacy.

After a year in the Tower, Margaret was returned under house arrest to Sheen. Realising that her own political ambitions were at an end, she now focused her considerable skills on promoting Darnley as heir to both the Scottish and English thrones, and on continuing to encourage his marriage to Mary. In early 1562, she approached the diplomat, Francis Yaxley, to seek information from Quadra, the Spanish Ambassador, presumably over the state of Mary's negotiations to marry Don Carlos, but also to canvas her marriage to Darnley among European Catholic powers to demonstrate their unassailable Catholic claim to the English throne. Yaxley was a Member of Parliament and had been an acolyte of William Cecil, even though he was known to be a 'good Catholic'. Yet he was notoriously unable to keep his mouth shut. On 14 February 1562, his scheming was caught out and he wrote to Dudley, after his support for Margaret, for assistance prior to being interviewed by the Privy Council. This was to no avail; he was arrested and imprisoned in the Tower until February 1565. Although Elizabeth gained wind of the renewal of Margaret's 'secret compassing of marriage betwixt the Scottish queen and her son', yet again, Margaret was not accused of treason.

Margaret was anxious about her husband's continuing incarceration after her own torrid experiences in the Tower. He was in solitary confinement and declining health. Although she wrote to Elizabeth to seek better treatment for him, she received no reply. Under interrogation, Lennox had affirmed that his messengers sent to Scotland were seeking only the restoration of his estates. Yet the Lieutenant of the Tower wrote to Cecil of his 'extreme passions' at his imprisonment.[5] When Margaret continued to plead for him, she had to use all her guile with flattering letters to redeem Elizabeth's mistrust. She denied any treasonable intent, claiming 'it was the greatest grief she ever had to perceive the little love the queen bears her'. When Elizabeth caught smallpox in October 1562, Margaret offered to nurse her in the hope of sympathy. This seemed to work and a month later, Lennox was released and was permitted to rejoin Margaret at Sheen. They were both freed in the following spring, when the queen declared 'that she had forgiven and forgotten their offence, yet she would not see them'.[6] It would seem that Dudley had brokered their release, seeing Margaret as the potential heir to the throne in preference to either Mary Queen of Scots or Catherine Grey, who had recently produced a second son in the Tower. Dudley's view was not shared by the Privy Council, who were still seeking confirmation that Margaret was a bastard. Yet the sticking point on this was the dispensation granted by the Pope, that confirmed Margaret's legitimacy because her mother had been unaware of Angus's precontract with Janet Stewart of Traquair. Margaret's release was made conditional on her making a solemn oath that she would not allow her son to marry without Elizabeth's consent. It is a measure of Elizabeth's tolerance that the Lennoxes were freed, given the compelling evidence that she held against them. They returned to Settrington, but were in extreme poverty as their Temple Newsam estates had not been properly managed and Lennox's Scottish property remained attainted. To meet the cost of their keep during imprisonment, Margaret had been forced to borrow money from the Sackvilles.

In February 1563, Darnley, who was now 17, returned from France to Yorkshire and money was found for Hans Eworth, the distinguished Flemish artist, to make a life size portrait of him with his brother Charles. This highlighted his remarkable stature and fine legs. It was painted in tempera on linen, suggesting that it was intended to be rolled for transportation, perhaps to Scotland. To keep tabs on them, Elizabeth brought Margaret and Darnley back to Court, where she 'made much' of his proficiency on the lute and kept him in daily attendance. He sang and performed in the evenings 'as indeed he plays very well'.[7] Yet Lennox was not immediately rehabilitated and remained in Yorkshire.[8]

Chapter 10

Events following Mary's arrival in Scotland

On arrival in Scotland on 19 August 1561, Mary relied on her charm to prevent religious conflict and, despite Catholic services being banned, she sought religious tolerance. Knox kept anti-Catholic propaganda to the fore and Lord James had to step in to prevent a build-up of opposition to his agreement for Mary to take mass in private. He was assisted by his half-brothers, the profligate Lord Robert and the amiable Lord John, who later married Bothwell's sister, Jean Hepburn. Although Mary's Catholic allies were determined that she should launch a crusade to restore papacy, she alienated them by reconfirming that she had agreed with Lord James only to seek Catholic services for herself in private. With Catholicism banned, she had access to Catholic Church funds to benefit loyal supporters and supplement Royal coffers.

Knox, who risked a reversal of the Scottish Reformation that he had worked so successfully to achieve, showed the 18-year-old Mary no sympathy. From the pulpit of St Giles's, he declaimed that 'one Mass was more fearful to him than ten thousand armed enemies being landed in any part of the realm'. When she called him to meet her to object to his incitement of armed revolt, he magnanimously agreed to tolerate her for the time being, claiming backhandedly 'to be as well content to live under your grace as Paul was to live under Nero'.[1] She was left in tears of frustration. Yet he respected her conviction in her own faith, writing to Cecil:

> Her whole proceedings do declare that [her Guise Uncles'] lessons are so deeply printed in her heart that the substance and the quality are likely to perish together ... If there be not in her a proud mind, a crafty wit and an indurate heart against God and his truth, my judgment faileth me.[2]

This was not what Cecil was hoping to hear, but Maitland was embarrassed at Knox's outbursts. He wrote to Cecil that she 'doth declare a wisdom far exceeding her age'. He went on:

The Queen my mistress behaves herself so gently in every behalf as reasonably we can require. If anything be amiss, the fault is rather with ourselves. You know the vehemency of Mr. Knox's spirit, which cannot be bridled, and yet doth sometimes utter such sentences as cannot easily be digested by a weak stomach. I would wish he would deal with her more gently, being a young princess unpersuaded.[3]

Yet Cecil was in correspondence with Knox and may well have encouraged him to test the strength of her faith.

In February 1562, she demonstrated her tolerance by bowing to Reformist pressure to provide one-third of Catholic Church income to support the Kirk's impoverished clergy. Although the Pope tried to persuade her to act against the heretics, this would have conflicted with her hope to be recognised as Elizabeth's heir. Although she might gain Elizabeth's favour by accommodating the Reformers, she still encouraged Catholics among the nobility to join her privately at Mass.

Mary's working relationship with Lord James started well, and she left him to manage the government on her behalf. As Cecil's close friend, he seemed to offer the best hope of gaining her recognition as Elizabeth's heir. He took control of the Privy Council; this was comprised of sixteen members, representative of all factions. This augured well for a period of settled government. He appointed Maitland and James Douglas, 4th Earl of Morton (Angus's nephew), as his two closest advisers. Maitland had already established a close bond with Cecil, staying with him when in London, where they could share their love of Classical literature. Although he had a rough manner, Morton was an outstanding administrator, despite a propensity for feathering his own nest.

Mary spent her time cocooned in her apartments with a close circle of courtiers. Her failure to become involved in government is in marked contrast to her mother and to her son James, when he came of age. Lord James treated her in a bluff, domineering manner, but Maitland was more obsequious. She showed all the surefootedness at Court that she lacked in politics, exuding charisma to captivate those around her. She was surrounded by her four Maries, Mary Fleming, Mary Seton, Mary Livingston and Mary Bethune, all members of families closely allied to the Crown. Mary Seton's brother, George 5th Lord Seton, was appointed Master of the Household. There were also a number of her mother's former French officials. George Buchanan reported, 'She was graced with surpassing loveliness of form, the vigour of maturing youth, and fine qualities of mind.'[4] Even Knox grudgingly admitted that she held 'some enchantment whereby men are bewitched'.[5] Yet, as she matured, her attraction lay in her elegance and charm rather than classic good looks. With the revenues of the Duchies of Touraine and Poitou as Queen Dowager of France, and her inheritance from her mother's French estates, she was able to indulge in an agreeably cultivated existence.

Mary was greeted with acclaim as she travelled to Stirling, Perth and Dundee, despite some Reformist heckling. Her palaces were refurbished with possessions she had shipped from France, so that she was soon every inch a queen, although she continued to wear the *deuil blanc* in memory of her mother and deceased husband. Despite this, she understood the importance of cutting a dash at state functions with glittering gowns of cloth of gold or silver, and her jewellery was valued at 491,000 crowns. She imported courtly entertainments from France, introducing equestrian masques, which included mock tournaments where participants, including Court ladies in costume or wearing masks, 'ran at the ring'. Teams competed on Leith sands and other places. The object was to see who could score the most points spearing a ring suspended above posts in an agreed number of turns. Her pastimes included music and dancing, which Knox considered 'offensive in the sight of god'.[6] When she asked him to discuss his concerns, he agreed to tolerate them, if she did not behave as a Philistine. Yet there was nothing unseemly, as he seemed to be implying.

At Christmas 1561, there was music, dancing and glittering hospitality. Overcoming his Calvinist scruples, Randolph reported, 'The ladies be merry, leaping and dancing, lusty and fair … My pen staggereth, my hand faileth farther to write … I never found myself so happy, nor never so well treated.'[7] He had taken a shine to Mary Bethune, which perhaps accounted for his euphoria. Knox found himself a lone voice in his criticisms and Mary was becoming much loved. Mary Fleming was involved in a two-year flirtatious courtship with Maitland, before agreeing to marry him, but there was no suggestion of an improper liaison beforehand. When Mary Livingston became engaged to the Catholic John Sempill, with whom she particularly enjoyed dancing, Knox implied that her marriage to 'The Dancer' was hastened by 'shame'.[8] Yet they married to universal approval at a long-planned ceremony, and their first child was not born until at least a year later. People began to ignore Knox's ranting. The Council formally confirmed Mary's right to hold Mass with her household in private, but drew the line at it being sung. Knox complained that they were seduced from extremism by the gentle and civilising influence of the Court.

Dancing at Court required music, with minstrels and musicians being retained as lute and viol players. Mary sang well and accompanied herself on the lute, seeing it as a means of showing off her elegant long fingers, but she was not so proficient as Darnley. During Mass at Easter in 1565, Randolph complained that 'she wanted now neither trumpets, drum, nor fife, bag-pipe or tabor'.[9] Her domestic staff sang part songs and played instruments. When short of a bass singer among her *valets de chambre*, they were joined by David Riccio, a young Piedmontese of good but impoverished family, who also played the lute. He was visiting Edinburgh in the suite of the Duke of Savoy's ambassador, Robertino Solaro, Count Moretta, and left his post to enter Mary's service.

Despite enjoying the trappings of royalty, Mary loved dressing up in disguise. She joined her Maries in donning men's clothing at a dinner for the French ambassador. In St Andrews they dressed as burgesses' wives, keeping house and doing their own shopping. In Stirling, they went through the streets in disguise begging for money, noting who was prepared to give and who refused. Mary tried this again with Darnley in Edinburgh, three weeks before their marriage. She enjoyed being outdoors and was never happy unless she had plenty of fresh air and exercise. As an expert horsewoman, she would ride out alone for up to three hours at a time and travelled on horseback to new destinations. She went hunting and hawking as she had in France; these were interests that she was to share with Darnley and Lennox. She went regularly to Falkland, rebuilt by her father in 1531 as a hunting lodge, and visited other lodges with their deer parks and forests. Hunting deer involved 'beating-in', as on a present-day pheasant shoot, to push the herd towards the participants, who laid chase with barking dogs, often Irish wolfhounds, accompanied by men with arrows, javelins and clubs. To ensure ample sport, deer were imported by litter beforehand, and wild boar had to be brought from France. Trained hawks were highly prized by royalty as presents and were among gifts sent to Elizabeth in 1562 in anticipation of their meeting. Mary, like Darnley, was proficient at archery, and indoors she played chess, backgammon, cards, dice and 'biles' (billiards). (Her library contained *The Rules of Chesse* translated by William Caxton from the French in 1474.)

When Bothwell returned to Edinburgh, he was singled out for his loyalty to Mary's mother with a gift of land, despite opposition from Lord James. He did not attend Privy Council meetings regularly and, after falling out with Arran, was barred from Court. Lord James's antipathy stemmed back to his capture of the English money sent to the Lords of the Congregation in October 1559. With Arran becoming increasingly mentally unstable, Bothwell took amusement in bating him. When his sister Jean became engaged to Mary's half-brother, Lord John Stewart, Bothwell hosted their wedding reception at Crichton. He also arranged a stag party. Late at night and dressed in masks, they escorted Lord John on a drunken sortie through Edinburgh in hope of catching Arran *in flagrante* with his mistress, Alison Craik, 'a good handsome wench'.[10] Although they gained access to the home of her stepfather, Arran was not there. On the following evening, they broke down the door and ransacked the house. Arran, who was now with his mistress, managed to escape by a back entrance, and lodged a complaint. Despite receiving a stern rebuke from Mary, this did not stop them trying once more. By the next evening, the Hamiltons had assembled 300 men to guard the Market Place armed with spears and jacks to oppose Bothwell, who arrived with 500 supporters. The common bell was sounded and it took the last-minute intervention of Lord James, Argyll and Huntly to calm matters down. Mary saw it as a joke that had gone badly out of hand. She reprimanded Bothwell and banished him to Crichton for a fortnight, hoping that all would soon be forgotten. When Lord James persuaded the General Assembly to demand a trial, Mary refused.

A month later, Bothwell hosted Lord John's marriage to Jean, with both Mary and Lord James attending. The couple were granted Dunbar Castle by Mary as a wedding gift. Knox was tasked with reconciling Arran with Bothwell, but it took him until February 1562 formally to arrange this. Arran, who was becoming increasingly eccentric, claimed that Bothwell had encouraged him to rekindle his suit for Mary. In all probability, Bothwell had been ridiculing him, and this caused more feuding. Mary was by now extremely wary of Arran, despite his close association with Lord James. He had become a man possessed, calling for a saw to cut off his legs and for a knife to slash his wrists. In March, he claimed to Knox that Bothwell had told him to murder Lord James and Maitland, and to carry the queen off to Dumbarton to marry her. At this stage, Dumbarton was being controlled by Arran's father, Châtelherault, who was in tears of distress over the whole incident, but Lord James insisted that the castle should be handed over to Mary as a precaution. Arran wrote to Mary and Lord James, who were at Falkland, claiming that Bothwell was trying to implicate him in a plan to share power. All this was treasonable and there had to be an investigation. It is hard to judge whether Arran's story was told out of spite to get even for the attack on his mistress, or whether Bothwell had put him up to it in jest, but he was undoubtedly insane. Châtelherault was distraught. He restrained

Arran at his house at Kinneil near Bo'ness, from where Arran smuggled out a second letter in code to Randolph, which told a similar story. This was shown to Mary, but his kinsman Gavin Hamilton told her to ignore it.

With Lord James looking for any excuse to bring Bothwell to book, Arran and Bothwell were arrested for conspiracy and, on 4 May, were brought to Edinburgh Castle. With nothing to hide, Bothwell came forward willingly. Arran was interviewed by Erskine and Morton, both of whom found him apparently mentally fit, but he relapsed and was handed back to his father's care. He promptly escaped from his window by climbing down knotted sheets in just his underwear. He went to the Stirling home of Sir William Kirkcaldy of Grange, where he continued to rave, and was confined at St Andrews to await a confrontation with Bothwell before Mary and the Privy Council. When this took place, Arran accused Bothwell of treason, while Bothwell challenged him to a duel, but Arran was in no state to participate.

Despite Arran's obvious lunacy, Lord James imprisoned him in Edinburgh Castle, although he was 'ill-bruited for the rigorous entertainment he faced there'.[11] He was later released to the care of his mother and lived on in confinement until 1609. Bothwell was exonerated without trial. Yet Lord James gained Mary's approval to retain him in Edinburgh Castle on the unlikely pretext that he was intriguing with the English. Lord James was anxious to stop him causing mischief, as he and Mary were contemplating a trip to the north to deal with Huntly. On 28 August 1562, Bothwell escaped after bribing a guard, hoping that Mary would see his three months of imprisonment as unjust. He went to his mother, Agnes Sinclair, at Haddington, where he asked Knox to intercede for him.

On 23 September, Bothwell submitted to Mary, but she was still in Lord James's thrall and was not amused at his escape. Randolph reported gleefully, 'Anything that he can do or say can little prevail ... her purpose is at the least to put him out of the country.' Mary was beginning to have some sympathy for his plight. In late December, he sailed for the Continent without consent, but his ship was wrecked in a storm off the Northumberland coast near Holy Island, where he was handed over to Thomas Percy, now restored as 7th Earl of Northumberland. Although he offered to repatriate Bothwell to Scotland, Lord James wanted him to face a London trial, knowing that the English hated him. On 24 January 1563, he was taken to the castle at Tynemouth, from where he was moved by Elizabeth to the Tower.

Despite Mary's friendship with Seton, now Master of the Household, he too had fallen out with Bothwell. More unfortunately, he had a row with Maitland, indispensable to Mary's marriage negotiations, and she forced him into exile. In March 1563, Seton went to France and was still there when Mary married Darnley. Yet such was his family's close association with the Crown that he provided Seton Palace for her honeymoon, despite remaining abroad. When he was recalled in August 1565, he remained her devoted supporter through all her tribulations.

Chapter 11

Rival efforts to be established as Elizabeth's heir

It was Mary Queen of Scots who was the initial focus among Catholics to be considered as Elizabeth's heir but this was an anathema to the English government. Darnley was only 14 in 1560 and the Lennoxes' treasonable activities were being watched. On 23 March 1560, while Mary was still Queen-Consort of France, Cecil had written to Elizabeth through the Privy Council:

> We do all certainly think that the Queen of Scots and for her sake her husband and the House of Guise be in their hearts mortal enemies to your majesty's person ... their malice is bent against her person and they will never cease as long as she and the Scottish Queen lives.[1]

Since then, Mary had refused to ratify the Treaty of Edinburgh, the terms of which obliged her to forgo her claim to the English Crown. Lord James and Maitland had hoped that, once back in Scotland and away from Guise influence, this unacceptable condition might be dropped. Although Cecil was determined on a Protestant succession, he was happy to string Mary along. She would hardly adopt a Catholic policy in Scotland with the prize of the English throne, as she assumed, within her grasp. In his eyes, her acceptability depended on her renouncing her Catholic faith, but this was not an option she would contemplate. Unlike Cecil, Elizabeth strongly espoused a dynastic rather than a political succession central to the Tudor philosophy of the divine right of kingship, while Cecil believed that the monarchy should be accountable to parliament. Neither Lord James nor Maitland realised the uncompromising attitude that Cecil was taking.

Mary's initial preoccupation on her return was to overcome the obstacles to her acceptability as Elizabeth's heir, wanting this to be resolved before considering marriage. Although she was the lineal heir, she was barred under Henry VIII's will, having been born outside England, and reinstatement required Elizabeth's approval. As early as 1559, Elizabeth had told parliament that she did not intend to marry, although this may have been a political manoeuvre to hold Philip II's suit at bay while negotiating the Treaty of Cateau-Cambrésis.

Even then, she was being dubbed the Virgin Queen. Yet in 1560, she contemplated marrying Dudley, with whom she enjoyed a fling lasting eighteen months, made all the more scandalous because he was already married to Amy Robsart.[2]* The Spanish ambassador reported: 'Lord Robert has come so much into favour that he does whatever he likes with affairs and it is even said that her Majesty visits him in his chamber day and night.'[3] Despite the innuendo, it seems unlikely that her virginity was compromised. When Amy died after falling downstairs, Elizabeth reluctantly decided not to marry him and tore up the grant to make him an earl. Cecil had threatened to resign if she did.

Having promoted Arran's marriage to Elizabeth to enable them to gain the Scottish throne, Maitland was extremely nervous before Mary's return. He wrote to her in France offering her 'faithful service'. On 29 June 1561, she replied, making clear that she knew exactly what he had been doing. She would forget the past and judge him only by his future loyalty, but, as the 'principal instrument' of the 'practices' attempted against her, she told him to curtail his 'intelligence' with Cecil.[4] She wrote:

> Nothing passes among my nobility without your knowledge and advice. I will not conceal from you that if any thing goes wrong after I trust you, you are the one that I shall blame first. I wish to live henceforth in amity with the Queen of England and am on the point of leaving for my realm. On arriving I shall need some money for my household and other expenses. There must be a good year's profit from my mint ...[5]

This was imperious stuff from an 18-year-old, and he was quickly reinvented as a faithful servant, despite him sending a copy of her letter to Cecil.

As Buchanan later pointed out, Maitland was 'chameleon'-like, and he now worked on regaining Mary's trust by renegotiating the unacceptable terms of the Treaty of Edinburgh. Even before her return, he and Lord James had agreed to approach the English with a 'middle way'. Lord James wrote to Elizabeth, and Maitland to Cecil, carefully constructed and coordinated letters. Lord James regretted Mary having claimed the English throne while in France, blaming the Guise family's bad advice. He proposed 'a perpetual quietness', with Mary renouncing her immediate dynastic claim in return for being 'allured' with recognition as Elizabeth's heir. If Elizabeth agreed, he would try to bring Mary 'to some conformity' in religion.[6] Maitland argued that, as soon as Mary set foot in Scotland, she would win hearts. Her Catholicism was unlikely to detract support from her, with the Reformation insufficiently established and many lords remaining Catholic. Even Reformist nobles were unlikely to oppose her and, being 'inconstant' and 'covetous', could be bought off. If Mary actively pursued a Catholic policy, it could be disastrous for the Scottish Reformation. He did not say so, but Lord James was implying that, if Elizabeth were to accept Mary as her heir, she could be persuaded to maintain the politically Protestant *status quo* in Scotland.

In September 1561, only thirteen days after the queen's return from France, Maitland, now aged 33, went to London to offer Mary's ratification of the Treaty of Edinburgh in return for acceptance as Elizabeth's heir. Mary also offered to keep the English Government informed of any efforts by the Lennoxes to promote Darnley in marriage to her. It is clear that at this time Mary considered that she had more important suitors to cultivate. Darnley was only 15, four years younger than herself, and she mistrusted the Lennoxes. On arrival, Maitland visited Elizabeth in company with Cecil and Dudley. He pointed out that Henry VII had not debarred Margaret Tudor's heirs from the English throne on marriage to James IV. He then made his offer, while admitting that it would require modification of the treaty's terms, under which Mary had to surrender her present and future claim. Elizabeth was sympathetic, but wanted her to take it on trust while she demonstrated her political affiliation with Protestantism. She explained her predicament frankly. While admitting that there was no claim she preferred to Mary's, she could not acknowledge her as her heir. (At this time, Darnley was in France and his parents were imprisoned.) 'Think you,' Elizabeth asked,

> that I could love my winding-sheet, when as examples show, princes cannot even love their children who are to succeed them? ... I know the inconstancy of the English people, how they ever mislike the present government and have their eyes fixed upon the person that is next to succeed ... They are more prone to worship the rising than the setting sun.

She admitted being the focus for plots against Mary Tudor, sometimes without knowledge of them, and, as the second person in the realm, was at their mercy. 'There were occasions in that time I stood in danger of my life ... so never shall my successor be.'[7] If Mary (or even Darnley) were acknowledged as her heir, there was no going back; it became a right. Yet she agreed to appoint commissioners to modify the treaty, so that Mary's claim was foregone only during her lifetime. She told Maitland to correspond with Cecil to confirm this, and he came away feeling that this had been a good opening.

By admitting that there was no claim that she preferred to Mary's, Elizabeth was not threatening to debar her under the terms of Henry VIII's will. She seemed to expect Mary to succeed her, if she gave certain assurances. She should confirm Elizabeth as the rightful queen, should give up any league with France, and remain friendly towards England. Maitland hoped to gain Cecil's blessing if he negotiated an acceptable Protestant marriage for her, but in this he was to be mistaken. Cecil wanted her to convert to Protestantism and would not countenance a Catholic heir. Maitland did not see her Catholicism as inviolable; he told Cecil: 'Surely I see in her a good towardness, and think that the queen, your sovereign, shall be able to do much with her in religion if they once enter in a good familiarity.'[8]

Despite Elizabeth's undertaking to renegotiate the terms of the Treaty of Edinburgh, this did not happen. Six weeks after Maitland's return to Scotland, she changed her mind, demanding ratification in its original form. Mary had nothing to gain and everything to lose by agreeing. Cecil no doubt saw that renegotiation would focus attention on Elizabeth's doubtful legitimacy. Elizabeth was playing on Philip II's continued goodwill, but, with Mary's stock rising, there were fears that he might support her.

Maitland tried to engineer a meeting between the two monarchs. Mary approached Randolph to propose it. By talking to her, Mary believed that she would so inspire her that any differences would melt away. As she had told Bedford while still in France: 'We are both in one isle, both of one language, both the nearest kinswoman that each other hath, and both Queens.'[9] By reaffirming their kinship, Elizabeth would be persuaded to recognise her dynastic claim. The English Privy Council was divided. Although Mary's religious tolerance had been well received, Cecil continued to follow Henry VIII's will by promoting Catherine Grey, despite her being out of favour. The will had also precluded Darnley, so it was their Catholicism as much as a fear of Guise influence that were the stumbling blocks. Elizabeth favoured Mary. She was a respectable widow who had not put a foot wrong and she was suspicious of Margaret's scheming.

Despite Scottish Catholic opposition, Mary persuaded her Council to give approval for her to visit England. Maitland went to London in May 1562 to advance plans for a meeting at York in August or September, despite Cecil's efforts to prevent it. Then bad news came from France. On 1 March 1562, Guise's men had attacked a group of Huguenots holding an unauthorised service in a barn at Vassy in Champagne. This was seen as the start of a Guise-inspired religious crusade, which could spread to England. England was poised for war against Mary's Guise relations. Mary called in Randolph to dissociate herself from her uncles' 'unadvised enterprise'. Although Elizabeth still wanted the meeting to go ahead, Cecil called for a postponement, citing wet weather and a shortage of 'wine and fowls' at York.[10] Without telling Elizabeth, he sent Sir Henry Sidney to Scotland to call it off. By 25 June, hostilities in France seemed to have come to nothing. Maitland was continuing to lobby Elizabeth and, to his relief, she overruled Cecil, confirming that she would visit York, despite the universal opposition of her Council. Maitland returned home in triumph.

News of the meeting received a muted reception among the Scottish nobility, but Mary was ecstatic. When she quizzed Randolph on Elizabeth's looks, he diplomatically confirmed that she could soon judge for herself and she 'would find much more perfection than could be set forth with the art of man'.[11] Yet, on 12 July, the day of Maitland's return, Elizabeth in London prevaricated. Fighting had again broken out in France, and she feared that England would have to intervene. She knew that the meeting would greatly strengthen Guise standing in France. When Mary was told of the postponement, she 'fell into such a passion as she did keep her bed all that day'.[12] Yet Elizabeth recognised Maitland's worth, providing him with a pension to assure his loyalty.

The Huguenots, under Louis, the Prince of Condé, enjoyed a number of initial successes. They captured Orléans, Angers, Tours and Blois. When Lyons fell, Catherine had to recall the Guises to recover lost ground. While she turned for help to the papacy and other Catholic powers, the Huguenots approached the English, promising to restore Calais. Yet Elizabeth prevaricated over whether to send an invasion force under Dudley.

With Mary being caught in the middle, she kept her head down and had time on her hands. On 10 February 1562, Lord James married Agnes Keith, daughter of William Keith, 4th Earl Marischal, and Mary hosted a wedding celebration for them at Holyrood. She also promised his long sought request to be made Earl of Moray, the estates of which were in the occupation of the Catholic Huntly, who controlled the North as a personal fiefdom. Moray needed to establish his authority there by cutting Huntly and his overly powerful Catholic allies in northern Scotland down to size. Mary supported him and agreed to travel north with him with 2,000 men. The expedition culminated in Huntly's defeat at the battle of Corrichie, during which he fell dead from his horse after a seizure. His body was now brought to Edinburgh where it was attainted with all the Huntly estates being forfeited. Lord James became Earl of Moray and was able to lay claim to the valuable Moray estates.

It was only on arrival in Aberdeen that Mary received Elizabeth's letter justifying her decision to send an army to France. She provided a graphic account of Catholic butchery, confident that Mary could not ignore her uncles' terrible crimes. Despite claiming that they would have acted out of duty, Mary assured Randolph of her neutrality. Elizabeth ended by saying, 'I would write more, but for the burning fever that now holds me in its grip.'[13] She had contracted smallpox, which could be fatal, and Mary readied herself to claim the English throne. Yet when the English Privy Council discussed the succession at the height of Elizabeth's illness, only a single voice favoured Mary, and Elizabeth recovered.

Despite her meeting with Elizabeth being thwarted, Mary recognised Maitland's efforts by formally appointing him as her Secretary of State and he received the Abbacy of Haddington. After Huntly's defeat, he continued trying to rearrange the meeting, complaining to Cecil that Mary was 'perplexed' and caught in the middle of a conflict between her uncles and England. She required a more secure interest in the succession than relying on Elizabeth's trust after bringing down the leading Scottish Catholic. Randolph told Cecil that, despite loving her uncles, 'yet she loveth better her own subjects', the 'amity' meant more to her than a 'priest babbling at an altar'.[14] Yet Cecil was unyielding.

The war in France was a disaster for the English and they were pushed back to Le Havre. With the Huguenots on the run, there were English fears of a Guise attempt to place Mary on the English throne. When parliament met on 11 January 1563, Cecil tabled a Bill of Exclusion to debar her. When Mary was told, she retired to bed for six days, but sent Maitland to London in a last-ditch effort to stop it from becoming law. He brought a letter from Lord James, seeking to re-ignite a 'love once kindled'.[15] Yet there was vociferous English opposition towards a woman, a Guise, a Catholic and a foreigner. With the Bill being carried, Mary was understandably distraught. She needed a new approach and decided to secure her dynastic rights by finding a suitable husband with or without Guise approval. Maitland was sent on from London to open negotiations in France. It was not lost on Margaret Douglas that it greatly enhanced Darnley's position.

In Elizabeth's eyes, the rival claimants to become her heir all had shortcomings which weakened their position. If Mary were to be overlooked, Margaret and her progeny were next in line. Although they had been born in England, they were Catholic, making them equally unacceptable to parliament, but possibly less threatening despite Margaret's scheming. After them, the next in line, dynastically, was 23-year-old Catherine Grey. As a

Protestant and born in England, she was first in line under Henry VIII's will. Yet her Protestantism was pragmatic, and the Spanish ambassador considered her sufficiently compliant for use to restore England to the Catholic faith, even contemplating arranging her kidnap for marriage to Don Carlos. To keep a close eye on her, Elizabeth retained her as a Lady of the Bedchamber. She had also incurred Elizabeth's enmity. Having married and divorced the Earl of Pembroke's son and heir, Henry Herbert, she clandestinely escaped from Court for long enough to marry and hurriedly bed Edward Seymour, Earl of Hertford (later 2nd Duke of Somerset) without receiving Elizabeth's consent as required by the Royal Marriage Act of 1536. By early 1561, Catherine was obviously pregnant and, after confessing to the marriage, was thrown with her husband into the Tower. Hertford was fined £15,000 by the Court of Star Chamber and the marriage was annulled, making them guilty of 'fornication'. On 24 April 1561, Catherine gave birth to a son, while still in the Tower; she then had three more children, although all were declared illegitimate to debar them from the throne.[16*] Their jailer, Sir Edward Warner, was removed from his post and imprisoned for his leniency. Catherine eventually started a hunger strike to gain sympathy and died on 26 January 1568 aged 27. Her sister, Mary Grey, was never seriously considered; she was almost a dwarf with a curvature of the spine and may have been mentally deficient. In 1565, she secretly married the Sergeant-Porter, Thomas Keyes, a giant of a man, and their disparity in size caused wry amusement. She too was placed in the Tower, where she remained until her husband's death in 1572. They had no children, but she lived on in some poverty until 1578.

The leading Plantagenet claimant was the 25-year-old Henry Hastings, Earl of Huntingdon, a descendant of the Countess of Salisbury, niece of Edward IV. He happened to be Dudley's brother-in-law. Yet, with the Tudors well established, his claim was remote. When Elizabeth was ill with smallpox in the spring of 1562, parliament identified Mary Queen of Scots, Margaret Douglas, Catherine Grey and Huntingdon as the four serious contenders. Quadra reported that there was no certainty about the outcome, but no one wanted Mary, and she would need Elizabeth to recognise her senior dynastic position.

Perhaps the concern that Mary might yet make a dynastic marriage or gain Continental support persuaded Elizabeth that she should reconsider Darnley. In 1563, the return of the Lennoxes to Court was seen as a public statement that the preferences of parliament (the claim of Catherine Grey) would not dictate Elizabeth's policy. According to Quadra:

Many people think that if the Queen of Scots does marry a person unacceptable to this Queen [Elizabeth], the latter will declare as her successor the son of Lady Margaret, whom she now keeps in the palace and shows such favour to as to make this appear probable.[17]

Favouring the Lennoxes might serve as some kind of appeasement of the English Roman Catholics, who,

like the Spanish ambassador, might foresee Elizabeth naming Darnley as her successor ... Such speculation would also distract them from favouring the more alarming claim of the Queen of Scots ... Most significantly, the elevation of the Lennoxes presented an obstacle between the Queen of Scots and the English throne. Thus was Darnley's uniquely 'British' inheritance put to use at last ...[18]

It was this that persuaded Elizabeth to support Lennox's plea for restoration to his Scottish estates. She wrote to Mary in Scotland: 'Having been sundry times requested by her dear cousin the Lady Margaret and her husband the Earl of Lennox to recommend their several suits which have long continued in Scotland,' she now desired Mary to 'give their causes such consideration as in honour and reason they shall merit'.[19] At the same time, Elizabeth showed continuing favour to Darnley and his mother.

Regardless of dynastic entitlement, the English Parliament wanted a Protestant monarch. Elizabeth would be acting against their wishes if she favoured Mary, who was always mistrusted as a member of the Guise family, or Darnley, who was being brought up as a Catholic. In January 1563, Sadler spoke against Mary in the House of Commons, arguing that 'our common peoples and the very stones in the streets should rebel against it'.[20] With English Catholic intrigue always near the surface, a Catholic heir would fuel the continuing doubts over Elizabeth's legitimacy. This would come into even greater focus in 1570, when Elizabeth was excommunicated, although by then Mary was imprisoned in England and Darnley was dead.

Chapter 12

Mary's efforts to find a husband

With Moray dominating her government, Mary settled down to her introspective life at Court, every inch the model queen in her mourning clothes. She made clear that she wanted to marry, but Moray preferred to delay finding her a husband, as it might weaken his own position. She was beginning to find his moralising demeanour irksome, and his 'middle way' to gain her acceptance as Elizabeth's heir had come to nothing. By comparison, Maitland was amenable and Mary began to lean on him for advice. She relied on his diplomatic skills to find her a husband, seeing marriage as the means of providing the 'fortification of her estate' and reinforcing her claim to the English throne.[1] She would not necessarily subordinate herself to her husband, but believed the nobility would be more compliant if dealing with a man. In January 1563, Maitland took charge of her marriage negotiations, in effect replacing Moray as her leading minister. Yet he lacked Moray's authoritative personality.

The choice of Mary's husband, whether Protestant or Catholic, would inevitably disturb the careful balance between her private Catholic and public Protestant affiliation. Any overt Catholic would also jeopardise negotiations for the English succession. She needed a man of appropriate status, but a powerful prince with his own dominions would be seen as a threat by the English. Yet, if he lacked influence, she gained nothing. A Scottish or English subject would be seen as demeaning and would cause jealousy. The choice of suitable candidates was limited, but her principal objectives were to choose someone to promote her claim to the English throne and to avoid having to leave Scotland to reside abroad with a less powerful husband, thereby placing her throne at risk. Darnley must always have seemed appropriate except for his Catholicism.

Widows were not generally the first choice for royal husbands, but, at 20, Mary had youth, beauty and a crown in her favour. She knew that her dynastic claim to the English throne was more of an attraction than her assured possession of the Scottish one. Cecil feared that, if she chose a Catholic husband, the Pope would declare Elizabeth illegitimate, leading to an English Catholic rising in support of Mary's claim. He saw that a Scottish royal family siring children would win English hearts and pass allegiance from the childless Elizabeth to Mary's family, who could unify the two kingdoms. He advised that, if she married without Elizabeth's consent, it would be seen as hostile. He did what he could to delay her making a choice still hoping that Elizabeth would marry before her.

Mary's initial plan was to seek a powerful foreign prince. Yet there was only a handful of suitable candidates available and, as she pointed out to Randolph, they were not falling over themselves to seek her hand. While in London, Maitland met Quadra to reopen negotiations for her to marry Don Carlos, while carefully citing her religious tolerance in Scotland to protect her claim to the English throne. Maitland argued, somewhat implausibly, that Philip would accept the religious *status quo* in both Scotland and England. These negotiations had been continuing since Mary left France, and the marriage suited Moray, as Mary would become an absentee ruler in Spain, leaving him to reassume the Scottish government on her behalf. Quadra was enthusiastic and Maitland saw it as 'such a marriage as would enable her to assert her rights'. He reported from London that the 18-year-old Don Carlos, whose physical and mental shortcomings remained hidden from the diplomatic community, was 'very far in love with her'.[2]

In September 1562, Knox called a Reformist meeting in Ayr, attended by Glencairn, where a bond was signed to protect the Kirk against Mary's rumoured marriage to Don Carlos. He told a large congregation at St Giles's that, if Mary married a Catholic, the realm would be betrayed and she would have 'small comfort'. 'In vehement fume', she demanded: 'What have ye to do with my marriage?' and 'What are ye within the Commonwealth?' He was ready with his answer:

> A subject born within the same, Madam. And albeit I be neither Earl, Lord nor Baron within it, yet has God made me (how abject however I was in your eyes) a profitable member within the same.

He then repeated his sermon, rendering her speechless until she 'howled'. When she had dried her eyes, he told her it was the truth. 'She had no occasion to be offended', and he would endure her tears rather than sully his conscience.

Rumours of the Don Carlos marriage plan resurfaced in Scotland over Easter, and Archbishop Hamilton unwisely celebrated Mass, forcing Mary temporarily to imprison him. Maitland knew that Knox and the hardline Reformers in Scotland would oppose the marriage and tried to neutralise their bigotry by denying any such plans. Yet Mary was not diverted from diplomatic efforts to gain Spanish approval. On 17 April 1563, Maitland arrived in France to seek French support, but Catherine was still trying to prevent an axis of power being formed against France. Despite needing Philip's help against the Huguenots, she was not going to hand him the English throne on a plate. The Guise family was in no position to assist. Two months earlier, while making a routine inspection of his army at Orléans, Guise had been shot three times in the back of his shoulder by a Huguenot. Mary learned this devastating news in St Andrews and, on 15 March 1563, heard that he had died. She 'was marvellous sad, her ladies shedding tears like showers of rain'.[3] She had been widowed for more than two years and was destitute of *confidants* except the four Maries, who knew Scotland no better than she did. Randolph even persuaded Elizabeth to write a much-cherished letter of condolence after Guise's death.

When Catherine de Medici heard the rumour of the Don Carlos marriage negotiation, she immediately suggested that Charles IX, then aged 13, should marry Elizabeth, who was 30, and that his brother Henry, who was 12, should marry Mary, then aged 21. Castelnau was sent to London to make this proposal, but Elizabeth had no desire to be an absentee ruler and politely turned down Charles IX, as being both too big (in terms of power) and too small. Mary believed, incorrectly as it turned out, that Henry, as the second son, provided no advantage, when she had already been married to his brother, the king. She also feared the consequences of leaving Scotland.

Despite Quadra's encouragement, Philip II only played along with the Don Carlos suit to ensure that Mary did not marry the 12-year-old Charles IX, but Catherine de Medici was still vetoing this. With the Guises trying to rebuild their alliance with Catherine, Charles of Guise, Cardinal of Lorraine, wrote to Mary in August, strongly critical of the Spanish marriage and trying to kindle the suit of the Archduke Charles of Austria. Yet Mary did not believe that he offered her the clout to gain the English succession. As she later told the Duchess of Arschot: 'Not that I don't consider it great and honourable, but less useful to the advancement of my interest, as well in this country, as in that to which I claim some right.'[4]

Elizabeth disapproved of Mary marrying the Archduke Charles as much as Don Carlos and told Maitland that she would become her enemy if she chose a husband from the Austro-Spanish Empire. She implied that she would not reject a suit from the Archduke herself. Maitland classified English views on Mary's marriage into three categories: Elizabeth wanted Mary's husband to give her the 'least cause to stand in fear';[5] the Papists wanted a Catholic to put Elizabeth under maximum pressure; and the

Protestants wanted a man to defend their cause. When ambassadors arrived in Scotland on 24 June 1563 from Eric XIV of Sweden promoting the suit of his son Gustavus Vasa, it was peremptorily rejected.

To placate the Reformers, Mary, during 1563, allowed Kirk ministers to occupy manses and glebes of former Catholic priests. Yet Knox remained unimpressed. He equated Catholicism with unbridled sexual lust and, by flaunting her sexuality with dancing and banquets, Mary was unfit to be queen. He claimed that, as a Catholic, she ruled from the heart, but Elizabeth, as a Protestant, ruled from the head. Elizabeth was one of those special women 'raised up by divine authority to be the nursing mothers' of the Protestants.[6] Yet, in reality, she was still at the height of her dalliance with Dudley, whose wife was still alive.

When Condé was captured in March 1563 during the Huguenot defeat at Dreux, a Catholic invasion of England became a realistic threat. The Huguenots sued for peace at Amboise and were forced to join with the Catholics in pushing the English from France. Despite being dug in at Le Havre, plague and bad weather forced Dudley, in July, into ignominious surrender. The garrisons returning to England from France carried the plague with them, resulting in a major outbreak during the winter of 1563 with 3,000 deaths in a week. Elizabeth sought to protect England as an island fortress. She needed to dictate Mary's choice of husband, forcing her to sever her links with France and Spain.

Elizabeth stepped up diplomacy with her sister queen. On 1 September, Randolph told Mary that, if she married the Archduke Charles, the 'amity' with England would be at an end. Although Mary had already rejected him, Randolph bore the full brunt of her fury. She demanded to know what husbands were 'sortable'. Elizabeth knew that she had to clarify 'whom we can allow and whom not; secondly what way we intend to proceed to the declaration of her title', and Mary realised that she had to listen.[7] She could expect no European support and could not afford conflict. Southern Scotland was economically dependent on trade with northern England. To maintain control and to stop Knox's insubordination, she needed recognition as Elizabeth's heir.

On 17 November, Randolph at last delivered Cecil's words defining a husband acceptable to the English. Ideally he should be 'some fit nobleman within the island' committed to the 'amity'. If no one met these conditions, she could seek English consent to marry a foreigner, provided that he resided in Scotland after their marriage. He must be 'naturally born to love this isle', and 'not unmeet'. No one from France, Spain or Austria would be acceptable. Elizabeth had intended that, if Mary followed this advice, her dynastic claim would be reinstated. Yet Cecil changed the drafting to say:

> We do promise her, that if she will give us just cause to think that she will in the choice of marriage show herself conformable … we will thereupon forthwith proceed to the inquisition of her right by all good means in her furtherance.[8]

Although Mary was a foreign head of state, her claim to be Elizabeth's heir would be tried in an English court. This was of course outrageous, but shows Cecil's paranoia following the surrender at Le Havre.

Knowing that Mary would see Cecil's letter as a bitter pill, Elizabeth sent her a diamond ring as 'a token of affection'. Randolph delivered this first and reported that it was 'marvellously esteemed, oftentimes looked upon, and many times kissed'.[9] Yet, when she received Cecil's letter, she was confused at the mixed messages. She was not going to allow the English to nominate her husband and privately renewed her searches. Yet she decided to appear compliant in front of Randolph, while taunting him with help from members of her Court. When she told him that she was expected to marry an Englishman, others asked if Elizabeth had become a man. When asked to suggest a name, he gave no answer, being under instruction not to do so, but said rather lamely, 'Whom you could like best.'[10] When pressed to be more specific, he recommended sending a delegation to ask Elizabeth.

The strain was telling on Mary and, as so often, she became ill from depression, weeping without apparent reason. Having danced late into the night on her twenty-first birthday, she stayed in bed all the next day. Officially she was suffering from a cold, 'being so long that day at her divine service'.[11] Yet she had an abdominal pain in her left side, which is the first record of her gastric ulcer, and her medicines did not initially bring relief.

To promote herself in marriage, Mary continued to maintain the grandeur of her Court. On Shrove Tuesday 1564, she held a celebration that lasted three days. This began with a sumptuous banquet, offering every sort of delicacy. She and her Maries wore costumes in black and white, a style echoed by her guests and staff. Randolph told Cecil that it was the grandest such event ever staged in Scotland, and he shed his puritanical shell to enter into the spirit of it all. He reported that the Scottish Court 'did nothing but pass our time in feasts, banqueting, masking and running at the ring and such like'.[12] Yet Mary had still not replied to Elizabeth's letter setting out the English conditions for her marriage.

Maitland began the marriage debate by suggesting a private meeting between Elizabeth and Mary to discuss alternatives. Although Elizabeth paid lip service to it, a meeting was a non-starter with the English Parliament. Moray and Argyll argued that, as Elizabeth's letter made no mention of a specific candidate and was 'only general', Mary's reply could only be 'uncertain'. They wanted Elizabeth to nominate someone. Mary made clear that, although 'princes at all times have not their wills', she wanted 'nothing more' than Elizabeth's love and was 'without evil meaning' towards her. Randolph affirmed that 'the word of a prince' was to be trusted, but, although her love was genuine, it was not to be presumed upon.[13]

Quite extraordinarily, Elizabeth offered Dudley. She had decided not to marry him herself and was determined to remain a virgin queen. As an ambassador had said to her: 'Madam, I know your stately stomach; ye think if ye were married, ye would be but queen of England, and now ye are king and queen both; ye may not suffer a commander.'[14] Marriage could only breed discord, as Mary was to discover. Elizabeth did not reveal Dudley's name initially, but she had already suggested Dudley to Maitland in an off-the-cuff aside the previous year, but he had not taken this seriously. He replied tongue-in-cheek that she 'had better snap him up herself', but used all his diplomacy in saying that it was proof of the love she bore Mary, 'as she was willing to give her a thing so dearly prized by herself'.[15] He believed that Mary, who had described him as 'Elizabeth's groom' [he was Master of the Horse], would be gravely affronted to be offered Elizabeth's cast-off. Dudley was still under a cloud following the unexplained death of his wife, was only the fifth son of the attainted Northumberland, was not of royal blood, lacked estates or titles and had not redeemed himself in a successful campaign to support the Huguenots in France.[16*]

There was a second problem. Dudley was very unenthusiastic at the thought of being put out to grass in Scotland, even in marriage to Mary, and worked behind the scenes to scupper the plan without offending Elizabeth. He told Melville that he had no desire to marry her:

> he began to purge himself of so proud a pretence as to marry so great a queen, esteeming himself not worthy to wipe her shoes; declaring that the invention of that proposition of marriage proceeded from Mr. Cecil, his secret enemy. 'For if I', said he, 'should have appeared desirous of that marriage, I should have lost the favour of both queens ...'[17]

Cecil undoubtedly saw the negotiation as a delaying tactic, confident that it would come to nothing. Margaret had no idea that Dudley was being proposed as Mary's spouse, and as Elizabeth was showing a 'smiling face' to the Lennoxes, she had every reason to assume the Elizabeth would nominate Darnley, who she was making much of.

In September 1563, Randolph had been told to advise Mary that Elizabeth wanted her to marry an Englishman, but did not officially mention Dudley's name. Randolph visited her at Craigmillar, where she was staying while returning from a trip to the west. She knew he had Dudley in mind, and responded: 'Monsieur Randolph, you have taken me at a disadvantage … Do you think that it may stand with my honour to marry my sister's subject?'[18] Randolph replied that this was 'the means of whom she may perchance inherit such a kingdom as England is'. She asked why this improved her claim, arguing that she had no expectation of the English throne, as Elizabeth 'may marry and is likely to live longer than myself'. She made clear: 'My respect is what presently be for my commodity, and for the contentment of friends, who I believe would hardly agree that I should imbase my state so far as that.' The 'commodity' of princes was their honour and reputation.[19] She believed that she would gain the Scottish lords' respect as she desired, only if her dynastic right to the English throne were recognised. After telling her advisers to leave, she asked Randolph, in the presence of the four Maries, 'Does your mistress in good earnest wish me to marry my Lord Robert?'[20] He confirmed this, and she asked if this meant that she would be recognised as Elizabeth's heir. He said that he thought that she might. 'How would it look', she asked:

if Elizabeth married and had children and I had chosen a commoner as King of Scotland. Would it not be better for England to match me where some alliance and friendship might ensue?

Randolph replied that Elizabeth's chief objective was 'to live in amity with Scotland', but Mary claimed that she had demonstrated her continuing loyalty and should be permitted to marry whom she liked.[21] She made clear that she would choose for herself, but did not rule out completely a member of the English nobility. After dining, the lords rejoined them, and Moray asked Randolph why the English were so anxious to arrange Mary's marriage when they should be focusing on Elizabeth's. Dudley's name was not made public, but Moray privately favoured him, seeing him as a friend, and he wanted to act as his sponsor for the Scottish Crown. Maitland suggested a conference to progress it at Berwick, perhaps with Bedford (the Governor of Berwick) present.

Elizabeth believed she could always rely on Dudley, and was initially happy at the prospect of him marrying Mary, but, being ambitious and arrogant, he would never have remained her puppet. In November, Randolph reconfirmed Elizabeth's opposition to 'the children of France, Spain or Austria'.[22] Then, in March 1564, the Emperor Ferdinand came forward with another offer of his son, the Archduke Charles, undertaking to provide two million francs on marriage with a further five million after his death. He also agreed that he should live with Mary in Scotland, but wanted an answer by the end of May. The Scots warned Randolph in confidence. Randolph concluded that they were trying to force Elizabeth into committing herself. He made Dudley's suit public, but this made Elizabeth realise that she might lose him and she suggested nonsensically that they should live as a *ménage à trois* in an extended Royal family in London. This was not a good example of her ruling 'from the head' as Knox expected, and Mary saw it as unworkable.[23] She needed to be in Scotland with her husband to maintain control.

In July 1564, with marriage negotiations temporarily deadlocked, Mary arranged another summer progress in the Gaelic-speaking Highlands to see and be seen by her subjects, while listening to the harp, bagpipes and bardic poetry. Maitland did not go with her, explaining: 'In the place I occupy, I cannot be spared for voyages, nor do I like it (for it lacks not peril) unless to some good end.' She won hearts and minds by ordering the Court into 'Highland apparel' with Randolph fitted 'in outward shape ... like unto the rest'.[24] Knox complained that she took mass wherever she went and, to Elizabeth's annoyance, Luis de Paz, Quadra's agent, visited her in Argyllshire to continue the Don Carlos marriage negotiations.

In April 1564, Elizabeth at last gained Mary's agreement to receive Lennox to restore him to his Scottish estates. With Margaret Douglas remaining a focus for Catholic intrigue, Elizabeth now kept her under virtual house arrest with Darnley at Court. Lennox's repatriation, which had required him to provide a hefty bribe to the Royal coffers, was not initiated by Elizabeth as a means of promoting his son's marriage to Mary, and her approval of his passport was conditional on him travelling without other members of his family. The advantage of marrying her main rival for the English throne was not lost on Mary however. Although apparently Catholic, he did not seem vehemently so.

As soon as Elizabeth had proposed Lennox's return, she regretted what she had begun. She asked Maitland and Moray to block the passport she had so recently requested, but they wryly advised Mary, who immediately granted it. Even Kirkcaldy, who acted as a spy on behalf of the English by feeding correspondence to Bedford at Berwick, realised the inevitable outcome of Lennox's return, when he suggested that Mary's 'meaning is not known, but some suspect she shall at length be persuaded to favour his son'.[25]

It is perhaps surprising that Darnley had not been put forward before this. For his suit to be acceptable in English eyes, he would need to become a Protestant, but, like his father, he regularly threw his critics off guard by attending Protestant services, which made him seem less threatening in Scotland than Don Carlos. He was now 18 years old, had all the dynastic qualities and courtly graces required, and was very visibly back at Court in London with his mother. It seems clear that although he was being considered as an alternative to Mary as Elizabeth's heir, he was not initially being promoted as her husband. So long as Mary continued to explore opportunities to make a dynastic marriage to a foreign head of state, the English saw their security being threatened and, for a short time, Margaret believed that Elizabeth might nominate Darnley as her heir rather than Mary. This would make his negotiating position to marry Mary very much stronger and might make him king of both Scotland and England. Yet the thought of Mary marrying Dudley was a different matter; Margaret needed to work hard behind the scenes to discourage it.

In June 1564, Elizabeth and Margaret became godmothers to Cecil's infant daughter. This implies that he now saw Margaret as the second lady in the kingdom. In July, Darnley was sent to welcome the new Spanish ambassador, Diego Guzman de Silva on his arrival in London, following the death from the plague of Quadra, whose loss was a great blow for Margaret. Yet Elizabeth did not nominate Darnley as her heir. The most obvious explanation is that his Catholicism made him unacceptable, but it is also reasonable to assume that neither Elizabeth nor Cecil, who were seeing him every day, could take him seriously. Despite a thin veneer of polish, he was seen as reckless, proud and stupid. He was sexually promiscuous, which had left him with syphilis, although this may not have manifested itself by then. He was described as a 'great cock chick', which denoted that he was homosexual.[26] He does not seem to have been seen by the English as appropriate material to be molded as a monarch or as a suitable consort for Mary.

Meanwhile Mary played along with the Dudley suit, while secretly trying to revive negotiations with Spain for a marriage to Don Carlos, but she also planned to meet Darnley. When the English Parliament met again in October, she sent Sir James Melville back to London to propose a conference at Berwick for Bedford and Dudley to meet Moray and Maitland to discuss the Dudley marriage proposal. He was also to renew Mary's claim to the English succession. Elizabeth liked Melville, who was a good linguist, allowing her to practise her French, Italian and indifferent German with him, but she was bitter at some of Mary's recent letters attempting to establish Elizabeth's choice of suitable husbands. She showed him the draft of an acid reply she had prepared. When Melville explained Mary's frustration at not knowing whom Elizabeth preferred for her husband, she tore up the draft and again suggested Dudley, saying that she was proposing to ennoble him. Yet she also showed him his portrait miniature kept in her bedroom, and he saw that it was inscribed 'My Lord's Picture'. When she produced a 'great ruby, as big as a tennis ball', he suggested that she should send it to Mary as a token of her love.[27] Elizabeth was taken aback, but then said that, if Mary did as she wished, she could have both the ruby and the man. In the meantime, she provided a diamond for Mary.

Melville later attended the ceremony for the creation of Dudley as Earl of Leicester, during which Melville saw her tickle his neck. She was having cold feet at the reality of losing him and jealously questioned Melville on Mary's beauty. It was Darnley who carried the sword of state at Dudley's ennoblement, and Melville had to answer Elizabeth's questions on Mary's interest in him. She had already told him that 'ye like better yon long lad', and he replied, 'No woman of spirit would make choice of such a man that was more like a woman than a man, for he was very lusty (lovely), beardless and baby-faced.'[28] This may have been a hint at his homosexuality. Melville did not admit that he had been secretly charged to speak to Margaret Douglas to obtain a passport for Darnley to visit Scotland.

Melville returned to Scotland on the day after the ennoblement ceremony carrying the diamond for Mary from Elizabeth, and Cecil gave him a gold chain. Margaret Douglas needed to move fast. She sent him with other valuable gifts, a 'fair diamond' for Mary, an emerald for her husband, a diamond for Moray, a watch set with diamonds for Maitland and a ring with a ruby for Melville's brother, Sir Robert. He considered her a very wise and discreet matron, but Randolph described her as 'more feared than beloved of any that know her'.[29]

On 22 September 1564, Lennox made an impressive entrance into Edinburgh after an absence of nearly twenty years, riding to Holyrood magnificently attired, supported by twelve velvet-clad horsemen with chains round their necks in front and thirty attendants in grey livery. Mary received him graciously 'in the presence of the most part of the nobility of the realm'[30] and, after making her peace with him, she offered him some of the best rooms. On 16 October, to Moray's dismay, all Lennox's estates around Glasgow and the Clyde were restored. Mary needed to use all her persuasion to induce parliament to agree to this, but she claimed it was 'at the request of her dearest sister Elizabeth'.[31] His restoration cleared another impediment to Darnley's suitability as Mary's husband. Although she was limited to attendance at Catholic services alone, Lennox came to celebrate Mass with her at the Chapel Royal, only adding to mistrust for him among the nobility. Even Mary was suspicious of him despite receiving another valuable gift from Margaret Douglas. This was almost certainly the magnificent Lennox Jewel already discussed on p. 27. Although this originally commemorated Matthew and Margaret Lennox's love, it had been adapted to make it appropriate as a gift to denote Darnley's love for Mary.[32*] After having assisted in arranging Lennox's rehabilitation, Margaret also provided Maitland and Atholl with large diamond rings, and the four Maries received 'pretty things'.[33] Yet when she sought a passport for Darnley to travel north, Elizabeth initially refused, as she was still actively promoting Leicester.

With Moray, Maitland and Knox all favouring Leicester, Moray worked assiduously to assure that Mary was recognised as Elizabeth's heir, in return for forgoing her immediate Catholic claim to the English throne. She would indisputably have married Leicester if the English had agreed to this. In November, Randolph and Bedford arrived at Berwick to meet Moray and Maitland to discuss terms for Dudley to marry Mary, where they were told Elizabeth would never willingly consent to her marrying anyone but Leicester, but they became furious when she refused to confirm Mary as her heir. They considered that Cecil had backtracked and that marriage to Leicester was 'no fit match' unless her right to the succession was agreed.[34] Cecil could not drag out negotiations any longer. He had influenced Elizabeth to refrain from confirming Mary as her heir, knowing that this would end the negotiation. He had to find an alternative. When Maitland suggested Norfolk, whose second wife, Margaret Audley, had recently died, Norfolk politely refused.

On 23 September 1564, Elizabeth wrote to Cecil that she could not decide how to handle Mary's marriage: 'I am at a loss to know how to satisfy her, and have no idea what to say.'[35] Cecil was aware that Throckmorton believed that Mary posed no threat as heir to the English throne if married to an Englishman, and he lobbied for Darnley to replace Leicester as her suitor. This would make Mary's dynastic claim unassailable, avoiding the need for parliamentary consent, and it was a face-saving solution, which allowed

Elizabeth to retain Leicester for herself. Yet Cecil was entirely cynical about Darnley, who was already parading his dynastic claims to both the Scottish and English thrones with arrogance and overbearing conceit. He was insufferably spoilt and a 'political lightweight', making him much less dangerous than a foreign Catholic prince. Mary Guise's uncle, the Cardinal of Lorraine described him as a 'gentil hutaudeau' [agreeable nincompoop].[36] If Elizabeth were to bar Mary from becoming her heir, the objectionable Darnley was next in line. To Cecil, he remained as much of an anathema. Despite a thin veneer of Protestantism, he was at heart a Catholic. His mother had never compromised her faith by attending Protestant services and had endured house arrest for her intransigence. Cecil gambled that if Darnley should marry Mary, he would kill off two birds with one stone, destroying their credibility. He probably considered the suit as another temporary diversion to delay her more serious opportunities, never expecting that Mary would tolerate his bisexual and boorish character for long. He may even have persuaded Moray that Darnley posed no real threat. Cecil shared the English view that, if Mary 'take fantasy to this new guest, then shall they be sure of mischief'. Elizabeth would then realise that they would make inappropriate successors, despite their unrivalled dynastic claim.

With Leicester still harbouring ambitions to marry Elizabeth, he assisted Cecil in promoting Darnley's suit, as a means of extricating himself from his proposed marriage to Mary. They both encouraged Elizabeth to permit his visit to Scotland. Margaret continued to entreat Elizabeth, and Lennox claimed to need Darnley in Scotland to be enfeoffed into their estates as part of their restitution. On 12 February 1565, Darnley was granted a three-month passport to visit his father. Elizabeth later admitted to de Silva that Leicester had turned down the marriage opportunity. By then, she had decided to pull back from letting him go. Cecil's mistake was in failing to appreciate that Mary's marriage to Darnley would destroy Moray's authority, upon which the 'amity' with England depended. Once he had departed, Elizabeth no longer had the means to control him.

Chapter 13

The impact of Lennox's arrival in Scotland

In the early years of Mary's return to Scotland, Moray and Maitland held such a stranglehold over her government that it was perhaps inevitable that she would seek to spread her own wings. She gibed at Moray's constraining influence and, in 1564, she tried to broaden her activity away from 'courtly frippery' by reorganising the Court of Session to assure a proper hearing for the poor. Yet when she grasped the reins for herself, she took decisions of which he strongly disapproved. Whatever else may be concluded about her, when left on her own, she showed political naïvety and a misjudgement of people hard to reconcile with someone apparently so well groomed to govern.

Both Moray and Maitland had a taste for power, but in 1564, several things started to weaken their dominant position in guiding Mary, not least because the choice of her husband would soon be resolved. As their influence declined, their own close working relationship was irretrievably undermined. Moray had not forgotten Lennox's part in leading English forces into Scotland during Mary's mother's regency. He strongly opposed his restoration to his estates and feared the inevitability of him promoting Darnley as Mary's spouse. This would undermine his position as her principal adviser, undoing his considerable achievement in uniting the nobility behind her.

Mary was also wary of Lennox, but recognised the dynastic advantage of marriage to his son. To counter Moray's opposition, she needed a new ally. She had already sought to rehabilitate Bothwell, still being held by Elizabeth in the Tower. In early 1563, she had instructed Randolph to demand his release, saying, 'I do desire that he may be sent hither again into Scotland. So shall the pleasure be great and I will gladly requite the same.' She explained: 'Whatever they say against him, it is rather from hate of his person and love that they bear otherwise than that he has deserved.'[1] Mary had just learned that her dynastic right to the English throne would be subject to trial and did not want Bothwell or any other Scottish lords held in England against her will. She was still angry with him for breaking out of Edinburgh Castle and she wanted him to remain under arrest in Scotland. Yet Randolph reported that he was to be 'reserved, though it were in prison, in store to be employed in any kind of mischief that any occasion may move.'[2] He knew that Bothwell was a threat to both Moray and the 'amity'; he told Cecil: 'One thing I thought not to omit [is] that I know him as mortal an enemy to our whole nation as any man alive, despiteful out of measure, false and untrue as a devil.'[3] It was from Randolph's agent, of course, that Bothwell had waylaid the English money transfer four years earlier.

At the end of June 1563, Bothwell was freed on parole, but was not permitted to leave England. Randolph told Cecil, 'Lock up your wives and daughters!', no doubt a reference to Bothwell having taken Anna Throndssen as a mistress in Denmark, before dumping her after his return to Scotland.[4] He was short of money and petitioned Mary for help. In December, he wrote to Randolph from Northumberland seeking her consent to leave England for France. The passport was granted, but he did not leave immediately. Randolph reported to Cecil that Mary met him secretly at Dunbar in February 1564, and he believed that she planned to repatriate him. For once Bothwell's mission was an act of kindness. They both visited his sister Jean, following the death of Lord John Stewart after only two years of marriage. It was not the start of a romance between them, as Buchanan later suggested. After consoling his sister, he honoured his pledge to go to France, where Mary arranged for him to become Captain of the *Garde Écossaise*.

In February 1565, after a year on the Continent, Bothwell sent another petition to be allowed home, humbly offering to accept reasonable conditions. Randolph reported, 'Of herself, she is not evil affected towards him, but there are many causes why he is not so looked upon as some others are.'[5] Bothwell did not wait for Mary to reply, but arrived in Scotland a month later without her parole. He went to Hermitage Castle, from where he sent William Murray, his chamberlain, to plead his cause, but Moray demanded his arrest and attainder.[6] The theft of the consignment of English money still rankled. Bothwell kept on the move to prevent Moray catching up with him, but Randolph reported that Moray 'followeth the matter so earnestly that Scotland shall not hold them both'.[7] They raked up a story that Bothwell had spoken dishonourably of Mary in France. He had apparently claimed that she and Elizabeth 'would not make one honest woman', and that Mary had been the whore of her uncle the Cardinal.[8] It was also claimed that he had threatened to kill Moray, Maitland and Cecil. Genuinely shocked, Mary agreed that he should face trial. According to Randolph, his return was 'altogether misliked and she had sworn upon her honour that he shall never receive favour at her hands'.[9]

Although Bothwell faced charges for having escaped from Edinburgh Castle, Mary insisted on granting bail. On the date of the trial on 2 May, Moray and Argyll brought between 5,000 and 6,000 troops into Edinburgh. Bothwell did not appear and was found guilty of treason. Yet Mary allowed him to return to France before the verdict and would not forfeit his estates. 'It is to be believed', wrote Randolph, 'that the Queen's Majesty would [do] him good.'[10] Bothwell later supported her marriage to Darnley, and it has been suggested that the real purpose for Moray having troops in Edinburgh was to thwart Darnley's suit to marry Mary by kidnapping them. Yet Mary and Darnley had already left Edinburgh to go hunting before the troops arrived.

After Lennox's arrival in Scotland, he went to stay with his kinsman, Atholl, (Lennox was the grandson of Sir John Stewart, 1st Earl of Atholl, the then Atholl's great-grandfather) to whom he confided his ambitions for Darnley to marry Mary and became 'well friended of Lethington'. Mary Fleming had pushed Maitland into an alliance with Atholl, her brother-in-law, despite their opposing faiths. Maitland was by then expecting Leicester's suit to founder, but could see that Darnley met every objective to strengthen Mary's claim to the English throne. Yet their marriage would reopen all the old factions within the Scottish nobility.

Lennox and Darnley needed allies; they gained support from Hugh Montgomerie, 3rd Earl of Eglinton, George Sinclair, 4th Earl of Caithness, Seton (from France), and William 6th Lord Livingston among others. Eglinton had been a long-standing Lennox ally in their feuding with Glencairn and Robert, 5th Lord Boyd of Kilmarnock. Darnley also became friendly with Riccio and John 5th Lord Fleming, who had succeeded his brother in 1558.

Riccio enjoyed playing music with Mary and was already one of her closest *confidants*. Melville described him as a 'merry fellow' in his extravagant clothing, but 'hideously ugly', being deformed (probably a hunchback). Buchanan claimed spitefully that 'his appearance disfigured his elegance'.[11] Yet he was both loyal, discreet and an amusing raconteur. In December 1564, Mary dismissed Augustine Raullet, her French secretary, ostensibly for accepting English bribes. Yet Raullet was a Guise adherent and was feeding the Cardinal with details of her diplomacy. His trunk full of papers was confiscated as he boarded ship at Leith for France. His departure opened the door for the appointment of Riccio, whose inability to write good French did not seem to deter Mary, despite her regular redrafting of his correspondence. By controlling access to her, he freely accepted bribes, which no doubt financed his extravagant wardrobe. After his murder, £2,000 was found among his possessions and this could not have been amassed from his salary of £80 per year. He was considered a 'sly crafty foreigner' and, as his arrogance grew, he was referred to derogatorily as 'Seigneur Davie'.[12] It was even suggested that he was a papal spy, but no evidence for this has been established among Vatican archives. Melville tried to warn Riccio to be more circumspect, but Mary would not be restrained from showing him favour.

Part 3

Darnley's arrival in Scotland and marriage to Mary

Chapter 14

The complex scheming that led to Darnley marrying Mary

While Cecil's agreement to allow Darnley to visit Scotland can be explained by his cynical assessment that Mary would never put up with his boorish character for long, there has been much debate on why Elizabeth granted Darnley a passport when she knew that the Lennoxes wanted to promote his marriage to Mary. Despite the combined persuasion of Margaret Douglas, Cecil and Leicester, she knew their marriage would make their claim to be her heir irresistible and, in Catholic eyes, both had a better right to the English throne than she did. She knew that they would galvanise Catholic opposition, particularly as they could unite Scotland with England. Yet, despite being critical of the match in public, she agreed to Darnley's visit with its inevitable consequences. She seemed to believe that he would not agree to marry Mary while his mother was under her control, threatened with the loss of the family's substantial English estates. That was to reckon without Margaret Douglas's astute acceptance that the prospect of the Scottish and English thrones for her son was a prize worth any personal inconvenience for herself. Perhaps the consolation for Elizabeth of retaining Leicester was too important. Yet Randolph, who had done so much to promote the match for Mary to marry Leicester, did not relish Darnley's arrival and had heard 'bad things' about him.

The passport was granted in December 1564. It was an extremely cold winter, and Darnley only left after the first thaw on 3 February 1565, travelling up the Great North Road 'accompanied by five of his father's men'.[1] He made good time and arrived in Edinburgh nine days later. He was greeted by Randolph, who had been instructed by Cecil and Leicester to treat him honourably. Despite suffering from a cold, he made a good initial impression. With Mary away hunting in Fife, he spent three days in Edinburgh awaiting letters from his father, who was with Atholl at Dunkeld. He was entertained at Holyrood by Mary's wayward half-brother, Lord Robert Stewart, met his cousin, Morton, and saw Glencairn and 'other gentlemen'. Randolph reported: 'His courteous dealing with all men deserves great praise and is well spoken of.'[2]

As his horses had not arrived from England, Darnley borrowed some from Randolph and set out for Fife, where, on 17 February, he met Mary at the home of Sir John Wemyss of Wemyss. Margaret Douglas had sent her son with further generous presents, this time for Mary, Maitland and Moray. According to Melville:

> Her majesty took well with him, and said that he was the lustiest [loveliest] and best proportioned long man that she had seen; for he was of high stature, long and small [slender], even and erect …[3]

He spent two nights at Wemyss before joining his father at Dunkeld. On arrival, Lennox insisted on him writing to Leicester to thank him for his assistance in obtaining the passport. His letter was most elegant:

> My especial good Lord,
>   Your accustomed friendliness during my continuance in the court, yea, since I first knew your Lordship, cannot, though I am now far from you, be forgotten of my part: but the remembrance thereof constraineth me in these few lines to give your Lordship my humble thanks therefore, and to assure your Lordship that, during my life, I shall not be forgetful of your great goodness and good nature showed sundry ways to me; but to my power shall ever be ready to gratify you in anything I may, as assuredly as your own brother. And thus with my humble commendations to your good Lordship, I wish you as well as your own heart would.
>
>   Your Lordship's assured to command.
>   H. Darnley

> My L. my father sendeth your Lordship his most hearty commendations.[4] (See handwriting on p. 6 of the picture section)

After a brief stay with his father, Darnley then rejoined Mary to take the ferry with her across the Firth of Forth on her return to Holyrood.

Mary gave no initial sign that meeting Darnley was more than a courtesy to her cousin, and Moray saw him 'rather as an enemy than a preferer of Christ's true religion'.[5] With the Court back in Edinburgh, Darnley tried to allay Moray's fears by accompanying him to St Giles's to hear Knox preach. He would happily display Reformist sentiments to help his cause, but also attended Mass with Mary privately. After hearing Knox, he dined at Holyrood with Randolph and Moray, who found him courteous and apparently biddable. Moray suggested that he should partner Mary in a galliard. Even Randolph saw them as outwardly well-suited, reporting: 'A great number wish them well – others doubt him, and deeplier consider what is fit for the state of their country than (as they call him) a fair jolly young man.'[6] It was clear that, despite his effort to charm everyone, he seemed a bit lightweight.

From now on, Darnley was in constant attendance on Mary, being present at banquets and masques arranged by her, feeling at home in the Court environment that she had created. Courtly poets such Alexander Scott addressed verses to her, some of which were set to music, hoping she would soon 'get a Gudeman' as her husband. Although she did not show Darnley undue attention, he shared her pleasures in music and poetry and could converse with her in French and Scots. By chance, violent snowstorms in Edinburgh made travel impossible. Being confined to Holyrood, Darnley enjoyed cards and dice with her and charmed her with his lute playing. This brought him into contact with Riccio, whose friendship he developed. Lennox later claimed that Mary 'was stricken by the dart of love, by the comeliness of his sweet behaviour, personage, wit and virtuous qualities ... as also in the art of music, dancing and playing'.[7*,8] He wooed her with verses that he had written, some in English and some in Scots.

Despite Margaret Douglas's capacity to scheme, no one expected the match to prosper. It seemed clear that Elizabeth would never countenance it, although Mary may have interpreted the granting of a passport as tacit approval. With Randolph still promoting Leicester, he played down any signs of a romance, reporting that her interest 'arose rather from her own courteous nature than that anything is meant, which some here fear may ensue'. Yet he knew Mary's unpredictability, 'seeing she is a woman and in all things desires to have her own will', and he soon had to admit that Darnley's behaviour was 'well liked, and hitherto he so governs himself that there is great praise for him'.[9] She enjoyed his company and courtly skills, and they shared a love of hawking and hunting. Yet he overplayed his hand. Melville reported:

> After he had haunted court some time, he proposed marriage to Her Majesty, which she took in an evil part at first, as that same day she herself told me, and that she had refused a ring which he had then offered unto her. I took occasion ... to speak in his favour, that

their marriage would put out of doubt their title to the succession
… She took ever the longer the better liking of him, and at length
determined to marry him.[10]

Riccio was also persuasive.

In early February, Mary took Randolph aside to make clear that she
intended to remarry: 'Not to marry, you know it cannot be for me. To defer
it long, many incommodities ensue.'[11] At this stage, she would still have chosen Leicester, if she were proclaimed as Elizabeth's heir, but on 16 March,
Randolph was forced to advise her that, if she married him,

> Elizabeth would advance her title to the succession in every way
> that she could, but could not gratify her desire to have her title
> determined and published, until she be married herself, or deter-
> mined not to marry.[12]

This of course might never happen and it brought another outflow of weeping from Mary. Although Randolph was confirming Elizabeth's continued
friendship, Mary realised that the Leicester marriage negotiation had been
fruitless. 'To answer me with nothing,' she replied, 'I find great fault, and
fear it shall turn to her discredit more than my loss.'[13] In reality, Elizabeth
had no choice; neither Cecil nor the English Parliament relished Leicester,
his political opponent, as consort for the Catholic heir to the English throne.

Moray was 'almost stark mad' with rage, seeing his position in danger, as
was Maitland.[14] Randolph blamed Leicester, who had never even met Mary.
He could not believe that he would forgo such a woman of 'perfect beauty'.
He wrote to his friend Sir Henry Sidney: 'How many countries, realms,
cities and towns, have been destroyed to satisfy the lusts of men for such
women.' Leicester had spurned a kingdom and the chance to lie with her 'in
his naked arms'.[15] Eight days later, Mary made a final attempt to revive the
Don Carlos marriage. Yet, by August 1564, Philip had contemplated locking
his son away and ended any thought of him marrying, but it was only now
that Mary had come to accept this. (Within three years, Don Carlos was so
unstable that Philip did imprison him and he died soon after.) She no longer
needed to keep Darnley at arm's length.

When Mary decided to choose a husband for herself, marriage to
Darnley became inevitable. On the day following her discussion with
Randolph, she rode to Leith sands to watch him run at the ring with a
group of companions. Randolph went with her and she asked him to seek

a passport for Maitland to travel through England to France. She did not explain his purpose, but Randolph inferred that she wanted to discuss marriage options with her Guise relations. She had been encouraged by Riccio to believe that marriage would free her from Moray and Maitland. Yet she failed to appreciate its impact on her relationship with Elizabeth, the English government and the Reformers. It would also drive the Scottish nobility back into the factions that Moray had worked so assiduously to end. Mary tried to engineer a formal reconciliation between Lennox and Châtelherault, but the Hamiltons saw their position being threatened if she married Darnley.

Love was in the air at Court with Mary Livingston seeking to marry John Sempill, the illegitimate son of Robert, 3rd Lord Sempill, who was a Catholic, 'a man sold under sin, an enemy to god and all godliness' according to Knox.[16*] John Sempill was one of several illegitimate children by Elizabeth Carlile, an Englishwoman, which resulted in Randolph describing him as 'a happy Englishman'.[17] Mary Livingston was known as 'Lusty' [Lovely] by Mary and her fellow Maries. The Livingstons approved of Sempill, despite rumblings about his illegitimacy, perhaps recognising Mary's wholehearted support for the couple. Despite the Maries having undertaken not to marry before their widowed queen, Mary became bound up in all the arrangements. Randolph, who still had an eye for Mary Bethune, reported, 'at least she will have compassion on her four Maries, who for her sake have vowed never to marry if she be not the first'. The planning went on for two months beforehand, and Mary paid for the rich silk to make the wedding dress and for the banquet, which took place at Forfar on 6 March 1565. She also provided them with estates worth £500 per year. The French ambassador wrote to Catherine de Medici that Mary had 'begun to marry off her Maries, and says that she wishes she herself were of the band'.[18]

Despite Randolph's admiration for Mary Bethune, this seems to have been unrequited, although Mary was well aware of his interest. When Elizabeth would not permit him to attend her marriage to Darnley, Mary tried to entice him by keeping Bethune away from him for a fortnight beforehand, but promising that, if he came, he would be allowed to dance with her. Yet Randolph would not disobey his queen. Mary Fleming was still being courted by Maitland to much incredulity. Kirkcaldy considered her about as suitable for him 'as I am to be pope'.[19] Yet Maitland was obsessed, telling Cecil that his passion brought him at least one 'merry hour' in the day despite the difficulties of state matters, averring 'that those that be in love be ever set upon a merry pin'.[20]

Moray openly opposed Mary's plan to marry Darnley, whose veneer of charm was starting to crack. It was unfortunate that when Lord Robert Stewart showed Darnley a map outlining his half-brother's extensive estates, Darnley unwisely commented that they were 'too much for his needs'.[21] Lord Robert appears to have warned Moray, who complained indignantly to Mary. Although Darnley was made to apologise, Moray realised that he would lose his former authority if Darnley became king. At the beginning of April, he withdrew from Court in disgust at the Catholic ceremony planned for Easter. He needed to assess the English appetite for backing him in taking a hostile step. Yet Mary used his absence as an opportunity to act more independently. With the Court being at Stirling, he was almost certainly behind a Reformist mob that abducted a Catholic priest from Holyrood during Easter. The priest was taken to the Market Cross to be pelted with eggs (the Catholic symbol for Easter) and beaten up. Moray gained initial support from Argyll, Glencairn, Kirkcaldy, William Leslie (who at this time was recognised as Earl of Rothes although he was soon to be demoted by Mary in favour of his younger brother Andrew on grounds of his illegitimacy) and other Protestant lords, who mistrusted Darnley's Catholicism, and from Châtelherault and the Hamiltons, who hated the Lennoxes and saw their position as heirs to the throne being threatened.

Robert Melville, whose family estates had been restored only two years before, also opposed the marriage, despite accepting the gift of a ruby ring from Margaret Lennox. Mary neutralised him by sending him with his brother, Sir James, to seek Elizabeth's consent in London, relying on them to promote it in the best light. Robert stayed on as Mary's envoy in London and was still there at the time of Darnley's murder and Mary's subsequent marriage to Bothwell, whom he also strongly disliked. He eventually returned to Scotland in May 1567, when he retired to his estates at Murdocarney in Fife.

Darnley's friendship with Riccio blossomed out of mutual self-interest. Riccio believed that Lennox and Darnley would protect his position, while he did what he could to promote the marriage. He was admitted to Darnley's 'table, his chamber and his most secret thoughts'. They would even 'lie in one bed together', which could be construed as evidence of a homosexual relationship.[22] With Riccio gaining in influence, he encouraged Mary to wrest control of government from Moray and Maitland, seeing an opportunity to usurp Maitland's position as Secretary of State. According to Buchanan, who was close to the Lennoxes, Riccio 'was also assiduous in sowing seeds of discord' between Darnley and Moray.[23] Those opposing the marriage were shocked by the triangular relationship developing between Mary, Darnley and Riccio, seeing it as a Catholic conspiracy to undermine the Kirk.

By supporting Lennox in his plan for Darnley to marry Mary, Atholl became the focus for opposition to Moray and helped to defeat his ambitions to gain the throne, particularly as Argyll, Moray's most powerful supporter, was also declining in influence. With Moray and Argyll losing authority, Atholl progressively took control of government, and Mary neutralised Maitland by sending him on embassies abroad. From about 15 April to 13 May 1565, he was in London sounding out approval for the marriage. Being friendly with both Atholl and Lennox, he could be relied upon to promote it in the best possible light. With Moray opposing it and developing ambitions to replace Mary on the throne, his relationship with Maitland was irretrievably weakened. Yet Moray was quicker than either Maitland or Atholl to realise that Darnley's arrogance would eventually alienate them all. Being away from Scotland, Maitland could not see Darnley's shortcomings at first hand, or realise that Riccio was usurping his role. Yet he remained nominally as Secretary of State and was astute enough initially to retain a foot in both the Moray and Atholl camps while he judged how the wind blew. He progressively realised that Moray had been right to oppose Darnley. This made him almost schizophrenic about the marriage plan; professionally he saw it as meeting his diplomatic objectives to assure Mary's succession to the English throne, but personally he feared that it threatened his authority.

Although Maitland was practically superseded in his absence by Riccio, he was completely engrossed in courting the fascinating Mary Fleming, fifteen years his junior. Their age disparity caused some mirth and Randolph reported that 'wise as he is he will show himself a fool'. This was a bit rich as Randolph, who was born in 1523, was still playing court to Mary Bethune, some seventeen years younger than himself. With Maitland preoccupied, Riccio was able to use Darnley's influence to fulfil the role of Secretary of State (although he was never formally confirmed in it) during Maitland's absence from Court. Mary can be blamed for her lack of judgement in allowing a Court musician of doubtful integrity to supersede her most trusted and experienced adviser. Maitland may have thought that he could return to influence when he wanted, but, if so, he reckoned without Mary's growing infatuation for Darnley. He would never accept demotion without a fight. This made him devious in the extreme, resorting to every subterfuge to gain reinstatement. It was he who planned Riccio's murder and the removal of Darnley from the throne. Yet he avoided being in the vicinity when crimes were being committed. As a master at hiding his feelings, he was soon mistrusted on all sides.

On 5 April 1565, the Court moved for Easter to Stirling Castle with Mary and Darnley in the early stages of courtship. He partnered her at billiards against Randolph and Mary Bethune. It was agreed that, whoever won, the ladies would share the stake. When Randolph and Bethune triumphed, Darnley settled the debt and presented Mary with a ring and a brooch set with two agates worth fifty crowns. He could ill afford such extravagance, and Lennox had to borrow 500 crowns from Maitland to keep the suit alive.

By some quirk of fate, Darnley became ill at Stirling, suffering a feverish cold followed by skin eruptions. Randolph reported that 'mesels came out on him marvelous thick'.[24] Although Darnley seems to have been treated for measles, it may well be that Mary's doctors failed to diagnose syphilis at this stage. There is no record of the use of 'salivation of mercury' as a cure, nor of halitosis, which was its side effect. Yet, when he suffered a renewed bout at the time of James's baptism, this treatment was applied with resultant reports of his bad breath. He had developed a rash, accompanied by 'sharp pangs, his pains holding him in his stomach and in his head'.[25] These are symptoms of secondary syphilis, which he may have contracted in France on his most recent visit while away from his tutors and parental control. Mary spent much time at his bedside. Although it is often said that she nursed him, it is more likely that 'she cosseted him with kindly attentions'.[26] Any formality between them evaporated and he was given rooms in the royal apartments, where he remained for a month, with Mary visiting him at all times of the day and night, even after midnight. She was suddenly overpowered by the strength of her feelings for him and, as he slowly recovered, royal decorum disappeared, overwhelmed by sensations that she cannot have known she possessed. In the words of a poem of the period it was, 'O lusty May, with Flora Queen.'[27] He made an apparently complete recovery and his face was left unmarked. She did not realise that his tantrums were not just those of a fractious invalid, but symptoms of his disease. She had become enthralled with a 'fantasy of a man, without regard to his tastes, manners or estate'.[28] Concerns about seeking Elizabeth's approval and the need for a powerful marriage connection were suddenly irrelevant. When warned that his shortcomings would alienate the Scottish nobility, she was in no mood to listen. She refused to travel even to Perth while he remained ill, but showered gifts on him and, by attendance on him at night, compromised her reputation.

With Darnley four years her junior, Leslie later confirmed that there was a strong maternal element to Mary's feelings, which caused her to overlook his adolescent shortcomings. He was delighted with all the attention and the success of his family's plan, but was too narcissistic to become infatuated, seeing her only as a trophy. Everyone was caught out by the model queen falling in love out of unbridled passion. The Privy Council was split, with Maitland, who was under pressure from Mary Fleming, Atholl, Ruthven and Riccio, supporting the marriage, and Moray, Châtelherault and Argyll against it. Mary later claimed that Moray had encouraged the suit to annoy Châtelherault and the Hamiltons, thinking that he could change her mind when he needed to. This would explain why he seemed slow in trying to stop the relationship from developing and implies that he accepted Cecil's assumption that she would soon recognise Darnley's shortcomings. Randolph wrote to Cecil belittling his 'behaviour, wit and judgement', and considered Mary 'in contempt of her people'.[29] Yet, after all the favour she had shown to Moray, she expected him to back her marriage. When he opposed it, she let it be known that it confirmed his ambition for the Crown.

The true purpose of Maitland's diplomatic mission to London became clear on his arrival. He had no intention of going to France, but instead demanded Elizabeth's approval for Mary to marry Darnley, who was both a Tudor and an English subject. Elizabeth was suddenly alarmed, realising that it would jeopardise the good working relationship she enjoyed with the Scottish Government. She told the Privy Council that the marriage was 'unmeet, unprofitable and perilous to the sincere amity between the two queens'.[30] In a fury, she refused her consent, claiming to be offended at Darnley's failure to seek permission before leaving England. On 20 April, Margaret Douglas was placed under house arrest at Whitehall, with the Temple Newsam estates being confiscated. Their contents included an ornate bed canopy bearing the royal arms. Two months later, she was moved to the Tower with her confinement made 'hourly more severe'. Her principal offence was that she had deceived Elizabeth by breaking her solemn oath that she would not allow her son to marry without Elizabeth's consent. She was only released to Sheen in March 1567 after her son's murder.[31] Elizabeth signed letters to recall Lennox and Darnley to England, but then countermanded them to avoid being accused of having promoted the marriage by sending them north in the first place. On 24 April, she sent Throckmorton to convey her disapproval and to tell Mary that, if she married Leicester, the succession could be arranged. Cecil spent the whole of

1 May in the Privy Council debating how to prevent the marriage. Mary ignored the English bluster and sought approval from European Catholic heads of state. Maitland followed his brief by meeting de Silva to promote it with Philip II, who saw it as assuring the 'success of her claims and the quiet of her country'.[32] Darnley later wrote to him promising his future services. To Mary's relief, Catherine de Medici also signalled approval, hoping that Elizabeth would seek closer links with France if the 'amity' broke down. She then hedged her bets by telling Elizabeth that she opposed it. Mary also gained support from the papacy, hitherto disappointed at her tolerance of the Reformers. On 22 May, she sought a dispensation needed because she and Darnley were cousins. This was promoted by the Cardinal of Lorraine, despite his earlier disparaging comments, but his envoy only reached Rome on 20 July, though Mary had assumed that it would have been approved prior to her marriage.

Maitland set out back to Scotland soon after Throckmorton, but, on 3 May, Mary received his letter warning of Elizabeth's opposition. She did not waver and immediately fired off a letter to Elizabeth that 'she did mind to use her own choice in marriage'[33] and would not be fed with 'yea and nay', and no longer felt the need for her approval. The messenger carrying it was told to intercept Maitland as he travelled north, telling him to return back south to deliver it after they met near Grantham. Maitland was horrified at Mary's response. He was not prepared to risk the 'amity' and, having pocketed Mary's letter, returned to Scotland. When he reached Alnwick, he caught up with Throckmorton, to whom he explained his predicament; Throckmorton claimed he had never seen him in such a passion.[34] Mary dismissed Maitland from Court for failing to deliver her letter. This undermined their hitherto close working relationship. He now had time to woo Mary Fleming, whose influence over him was such, that he was 'blinded to further and prosecute this marriage' out of love for her.[35]

Mary tried to win over Moray by confirming that, as a minor, Darnley would not be offered the Crown Matrimonial. She summoned him to Darnley's sickroom, but he still refused his support, 'because he feared that the Lord Darnley would be an enemy to true religion'. 'Hereupon between them rose great altercation, [and] she gave him many sore words.'[36] Moray had managed to pass off his objection as religious rather than personal, but Mary neutralised the effect of this by issuing a proclamation that she intended to make no alteration to the religion practised in Scotland. Although she hoped for Argyll's backing, he retired to his estates 'indignant at the overwhelming insolence of Darnley'.

If anyone believed that the marriage would founder through lack of support, they bargained without Margaret Douglas's scheming from imprisonment. She bought Morton's important backing by agreeing to cede her
claim to the Angus earldom. Although he generally supported Moray, he
would not turn down any rich pickings arising out of Moray's decline in
favour. His infant nephew, Archibald, was already established as the 8th Earl
of Angus in accordance with the entail to the 6th Earl's will and, as his guardian, Morton received the income for himself. Angus was also supported by
Morton's close associates, Glamis and the unattractive Lindsay of the Byres,
who had succeeded his father in December 1563. Lindsay was Atholl's uncle
by marriage and Glamis was the grandson of Janet Douglas, Morton's aunt.
Ruthven, who had married Margaret's illegitimate half-sister, Janet, also
offered support, as did her half-brother, George Douglas, 'the postulate'.
Mary overlooked her concerns at Ruthven's use of sorcery by visiting him
at Ruthven Castle for two days starting on 25 June, and he became her chief
councillor to promote the marriage. She could not afford to be too particular
in her allies. Darnley gained the support of William Murray of Tullibardine
and Lord Robert Stewart.

Erskine was persuaded that the marriage was a true love match by his
wife Annabella, Mary's close *confidante*. On 23 June 1565, Mary arranged a
Royal Charter to fulfil his long-held family ambition to be confirmed as Earl
of Mar, a title which had been usurped by James II in 1457. Alexander 5th
Lord Livingston confirmed his support out of loyalty to Mary, despite facing threats from the English under Bedford. Even Glencairn, who disliked
Darnley and supported Moray, overcame his Protestant scruples to attend
the ceremony as Lennox's former ally.

On 15 May, while at Stirling, Mary formally asked the Scottish lords
to support the marriage in the face of Elizabeth's opposition. Although
they were not enthusiastic, they were affronted by English interference and
closed ranks behind her. 'Many consented on condition that no change was
made to the established state of religion.'[37] Only Ochiltree, Knox's father-
in-law, now opposed it on religious grounds, but Moray left before the vote
and Argyll refused to attend. On 21 May, Moray withdrew from Court to
join his mother at Lochleven. He now shunned Council meetings and Atholl
took formal control of government. Mary had shown four years of religious
tolerance. She was popular, and the Scots did not consider it a bad match. It
would not take Darnley long to undo their goodwill.

Throckmorton arrived at Stirling Castle in a final attempt to prevent
the marriage, but, with the gates locked, he was obliged to find lodgings

in the town. When Mary saw him, he handed over Elizabeth's letter and a 'determination' from Cecil signed by a majority of the English Privy Council advising her to drop Darnley in favour of Leicester or another English nobleman. As Leicester had not signed it, its impact was diminished, and Mary confirmed to him that the marriage would go ahead. She had taken Elizabeth's advice in rejecting Continental candidates and choosing an Englishman, who was Elizabeth's 'near kinsman'. Yet she agreed a delay of three months as she was awaiting the papal dispensation to overcome the bar caused by their close kinship. Throckmorton reported back to Leicester that Mary was 'seized with love in ferventer passions than is comely in any mean personage'. Having witnessed their passionate embraces, he commented, 'I cannot assure myself that such qualities will bring forth such fruit as the love and usage bestowed on Darnley shows,'[38] concluding that their marriage was 'irrevocable otherwise than by violence'.[39] Randolph confirmed this, saying, 'Shame is laid aside, and all regard of that which chiefly pertaineth to princely honour removed out of sight.'[40] They were even rumoured to be in bed together, but this seems unlikely, and was later denied by Randolph, who would have been only too keen to report such a scurrilous titbit, but he wrote to Leicester pessimistically:

> I know not how to utter what I conceive of the pitiful and lamentable estate of this poor Queen, whom ever before I esteemed so worthy, so wise, so honourable in all her doings; and at this present do find so altered with affection towards the Lord Darnley that she hath brought her honour in question, her estate in hazard, her country to be torn in pieces! ... The queen in her love is so transported, and he is grown so proud, that to all honest men he is intolerable, and almost forgetful of his duty to her already, that hath ventured so much for his sake. What shall become of her, or what life with him she shall lead, that taketh so much upon him to control and to command her, I leave to others to think.[41]

Throckmorton recommended the 'hardest sequestration' of Margaret, who was already under house arrest. It was now that Elizabeth arranged for her to be moved to the Tower, with all the Lennoxes' English estates being confiscated.

On 10 June, following the vote by the lords at Stirling, Darnley rose from his sickbed to be knighted and created Earl of Ross. As a knight, he swore allegiance to Mary, saying:

> I shall be true and leel [loyal] to my Sovereign Lady, Queen of Scotland, maintain and defend Her Highness' body, realm, lieges, and laws, at the uttermost of my power. So Help me God, the Holy Evangel, by my own hand, and by God Himself.[42]

This confirmed his allegiance to Mary rather than Elizabeth. He was then permitted to create fourteen knights. There were four Stewarts, including Traquair, one Douglas and among the rest was Tullibardine, later Comptroller of the Household.

Despite love tokens being exchanged every day, Darnley started to reveal a violent temper. Randolph reported: 'The passions and furies I hear say he will sometimes be in are strange to believe.'[43] He became progressively more objectionable and hot-headed: 'He spareth not, in token of his manhood, to let blows fly.'[44] When the grant of his earldom was delivered, he threatened Bellenden, the Justice-Clerk, with his dagger, because he was not appointed Duke of Albany as he expected. Mary had held this back while awaiting Elizabeth's reaction. On 23 May, Châtelherault came to offer an olive branch while he convalesced at Stirling, but Darnley threatened to 'knock his pate when he is whole'.[45] 'His pride was intolerable and his words could not be borne except where no man speak again.'[46] He associated with Court reprobates, particularly Lord Robert Stewart, and was often found drunk in Edinburgh bars and brothels. Being unable to keep his mouth shut, he leaked the marriage terms before the Council had approved them. Maitland and Moray saw this as calamitous. It was clear that he saw the marriage merely as a necessary step on his way to becoming king of both Scotland and England.

When the Guises in France heard of Darnley's behaviour, the Cardinal cautioned Mary against the marriage, despite having supported the papal dispensation. Even the four Maries caused a rift by expressing concerns, perhaps coloured by Maitland's rapidly changing opinion. Darnley's allies could no longer defend him. By June, Randolph reported that, 'being of better understanding' of Darnley's shortcomings, Mary was trying 'to frame and fashion him to the nature of her subjects', but with little success as he was 'proud, disdainful and suspicious'. She became ill.[47] Randolph told Leicester: 'Her majesty is laid aside, her wits not what they were, her beauty another than it was, her cheer and countenance changed into I wot not what.' She had become 'a woman more to be pitied than any that I ever saw', and he was 'the most unworthy' to be matched with her.[48] He wrote prophetically, 'What shall become of him I know not, but it is greatly to be feared that he can have no long life among these people.'[49]

Mary was 'bewitched' and would not be diverted from the wedding plan. On 10 June, she summoned a convention of the nobility to meet at Perth to gain formal approval for a Catholic ceremony. Leslie dissuaded Darnley from being more confrontational or from using the opportunity 'to take the final order of religion'. Moray did not go to Perth, claiming that he was ill with diarrhoea at Lochleven, and spread a rumour that the Lennoxes were planning to assassinate him. They in turn claimed that he planned to kidnap Darnley and his father to return them to England. There is no evidence that this was contemplated, but, on 2 July, Elizabeth 'expressly commanded' them to come back and *required* Mary to issue a safe conduct. Mary retired to her rooms in tears. If she defied Elizabeth, she risked her hopes of the English succession. If she capitulated, Darnley would be charged with treason. After delaying her decision for a fortnight, she defiantly instructed them to stay. She told Randolph that Elizabeth had sent Darnley north believing him unworthy of her, but she would choose her own husband and would 'snap her fingers at all who opposed' the marriage. Randolph suggested that Elizabeth would like her better if she became Protestant. Mary was furious at being expected to barter her religion to gain Elizabeth's approval. She told him that, if the 'amity' were now lost, it would be an 'incommodity' as much for Elizabeth as for her.[50]

Cecil threatened war but, with Darnley so much despised, he chose not to interfere with a marriage that might destroy Mary's credibility. Randolph was now aware of Cecil's motive and saw it as a great benefit for Elizabeth, as English Catholics would never support her with Darnley at her side. In June, the English Privy Council secretly agreed to finance Moray in challenging Mary, and Elizabeth sent him £3,000 'to uphold the true religion and to support their queen with good advice'. He met with Randolph, Châtelherault, Glencairn, Argyll and Boyd at Lochleven, and Cecil was approached for troops and artillery, but Elizabeth could not be seen to provide overt support against an anointed queen. Moray had backing from Knox and other Reformist ministers, who condemned Mary from the pulpit. He tried to kidnap the couple as they travelled from Perth to Callendar for the christening of Livingston's eldest son, Alexander. Having been tipped off, Mary left Perth at five o'clock in the morning, escorted by Atholl and Ruthven with 300 horse. They completed the thirty-mile journey without a break, arriving at Callendar an hour before they had been expected to leave Perth.

On 9 July, Mary and Darnley spent two nights at Seton, although Seton himself was still in France. Randolph reported to Elizabeth that they had been secretly married beforehand in Riccio's apartments at Holyrood 'with not above seven persons present', and they consummated their union at Seton.[51] It has been suggested that this was a form of betrothal ceremony, after which it was normal for a couple to have sexual relations. This could explain why Mary brought forward the formal wedding ceremony ahead of receiving the Pope's dispensation and ahead of the three-month delay promised to Throckmorton, so that she limited the risk of becoming pregnant beforehand. Although the papal dispensation had been requested on 22 May, such was the communication difficulty with Rome that it was not granted until early September. Yet, by their wedding day on 29 July, Mary hoped that it would have been approved. The grant, when given, was in fact backdated to the time of the request, so Prince James's legitimacy was never in doubt. Randolph, who was scathing that they had not delayed the wedding for the promised three months, later reported that stories of them consummating their union were merely rumours and 'the likelihoods are so great to the contrary'. His later retraction may have been based on knowing that Darnley was homosexual, but it seems realistic that they would have taken the opportunity away from prying eyes at Court to sleep together. It would have been too much of a temptation for such a besotted couple. Much later when Mary 'was at variance with her husband', Moray wrote to Giovanni Correr, the Venetian ambassador in Paris, 'that the King had boasted to him of having had intimacy with her before she was his wife'.[52] When Mary heard this, she challenged Darnley, but he denied saying it. This only added to Moray's antagonism of him.

After two days at Seton, they returned to Edinburgh, where they walked about the town in disguise before dining at the castle, but this did not prevent them from being recognised. They then 'lay the night' at Holyrood.[53] Wedding plans now proceeded apace. On 22 July, the banns were read at St Giles's. On the following day, Darnley was at last made Duke of Albany and, on the evening of 28 July, Mary issued a proclamation read at the Mercat Cross to confirm that he would be crowned as King Henry. She did not have parliamentary consent for this and later had to attend the vote to assure agreement. She told parliament that she had 'previously been married to one of the greatest kings in Christendom and therefore intended to wed no one unless he were a king'.[54] Yet she refused to grant him the Crown Matrimonial on the grounds that he was a minor. This would have allowed him to succeed her if she died childless. As he was well aware that Francis II had been granted this status at a younger age, it remained a bone of contention thereafter. He had damaged his cause by claiming that he cared more for English Catholics than Scottish Reformers, so that parliament would never have ratified it.

The wedding took place in a Catholic ceremony on 30 July at between five and six o'clock in the morning. Mary still wore 'a great mourning gown of black with the great white mourning hood' as was the custom for Catholic widows. She was escorted by Lennox and Atholl, who then attended Darnley 'clad in splendid garb and glittering gems'.[55] After exchanging vows, he provided Mary with three rings (to symbolise the Trinity) for the fingers of her right hand as was then the custom, the middle one a 'rich diamond' in a red enameled setting.[56] Other than Moray, Châtelherault and Argyll, almost all the nobles attended. John Sinclair, Dean of Restalrig and Lord President of the Council, officiated with prayers over the kneeling couple and was appointed Bishop of Brechin soon after. The couple parted with a kiss while Mary attended a nuptial Mass to symbolise that she could replace her widow's weeds with wedding finery. King Henry remained in his chamber not wishing to give offence to the Protestant lords. Once in her chamber, each of her ladies removed one pin as she changed out of her 'sorrowful garments'.

Although Randolph did not attend, he reported that the couple did not immediately retire to bed 'to signify unto the world that it was not lust moved them to marry, but only the necessity of the country, if she will not leave it destitute of an heir'.[57] At noon, they began a magnificent marriage feast served to them by Atholl and Morton, the only two lords other than Lennox prepared to offer them unreserved support. This was followed by music and dancing. Largesse (small gold coinage) was thrown 'in great abundance' to the sound of trumpets. There was a supper, to which the king and queen were escorted by a procession of nobles. The queen was served by Atholl as sewer (taster of food to be given to the Queen), Morton as carver and David Lindsay, 10th Earl of Crawford as cupbearer, while the king was attended by Cassillis, Eglinton and Glencairn. Before retiring, there was a Latin masque on the triumph of love written by Buchanan. Celebrations continued for three days; on the second day Buchanan provided an equestrian masque with processions of exotically costumed knights offering praises; on the third day, Buchanan called on the four Maries to offer oblations to the Goddess of Health for the future of the royal pair.[58] An *Epithalamium* (a nuptial poem to the bride and groom) by Thomas Craig of Riccarton included the words:

> Thou chiefly, Henry, placed at Scotia's helm
> On whom suspended hangs a powerful realm,
> Thou from those cares thyself canst never free;
> The law which binds on us our loyalty

> Thee too constrains – that none unscathed may dare
> To trample on our rights whilst thou art there ...[59]

Knox saw it as nothing but 'balling and dancing and banqueting', before the couple returned to Seton for their honeymoon.[60]

Praise for King Henry at this time was not limited to Court masques. The French ambassador, Michel de Castelnau, Sieur de Mauvissière, wrote:

> It is not possible to see a more beautiful Prince, and he is accomplished in all courtly exercises. He wishes much ... that he might go and see the King of France ... and professes a sincere desire to render any service in his power to his majesty, and in all things to follow the example of the Kings of Scotland his predecessors.[61]

He came across as a man of culture, writing elegant verses to Mary on the qualities necessary for good government (no doubt in an effort to demonstrate that he was worthy of the Crown Matrimonial). If he had followed his own advice, all might have been well.

On the day after the wedding, Darnley was as proud as a peacock when three heralds appeared at the Mercat Cross and, with a flourish of trumpets, again proclaimed him as king, but only his father echoed support, shouting out, 'God save his grace!' On Mary's instruction, the king's name was given precedence over the hereditary sovereign on state documents and on coinage struck to mark the occasion. The proclamation even bore his signature as king. Yet he remained objectionable, and Randolph reported that 'he looketh now for reverence to many that have little will to give it to him'.[62] Randolph told Leicester:

> All honour that may be attributed to any man by his wife, he hath it wholly and fully ... all dignities that she can endow him with are already given and granted ... She hath given over her whole will, to be ruled and guided as himself best thinketh that she can little prevail with him in anything that is against his will.[63]

Melville reported that she 'did him great honour herself, and desired everyone who would deserve her favour to do the like'. Mary asked him

> to wait upon the King, who was but young, and give him my best counsel, which might help him to shun many inconveniences, desiring me also to befriend Riccio, who was hated without cause.[64]

He seems to have gained the king's respect.

Elizabeth was furious on hearing that the wedding had taken place, particularly after Mary's undertaking not to marry for three months. She feared the restoration of Catholicism in Scotland as a prelude to Mary seeking the English throne. On 30 July, she sent John Thomworth (or Tamworth), a Gentleman of her Privy Chamber, to remonstrate over her 'very strange' and 'unneighbourly' conduct, with instructions to him to address her husband as 'the Lord Darnley' and not as king. She was to be told that 'she forgets herself marvellously to raise up such factions as is understood among her nobility'. Knowing that Moray was about to start his rebellion, which she had financed, Elizabeth told Mary to be reconciled to him, 'who has so well served her'. Mary would have none of it. When Thomworth left Scotland, he refused to accept the safe conduct signed 'Henry R'. After leaving without it, he was arrested and imprisoned before reaching the Border. He was then forced to accept the offending document to gain his release.

Mary and Henry wanted freedom of Catholic worship for all, and Randolph estimated that Papists outnumbered Reformers in Edinburgh. They began converting members of the Court to Catholicism and, when the General Assembly tried to abolish the Mass, Mary claimed that she would not risk

> losing the friendship of the King of France, the ancient ally of this realm, and of the other great princes, her friends and confederates, who would take it in evil part, of whom she may look for support in all her necessities.[65]

Marriage also gave her the confidence to stand up to Elizabeth. She had told Thomworth that she did not 'enquire what order of government her good sister observed within her realm' and that princes were 'subject immediately to God'. She now felt more secure than at any time since leaving France and warned Elizabeth 'to meddle no further with private causes concerning [Moray] or any other subjects of Scotland'.[66] Otherwise she and the king would interfere on behalf of her mother-in-law, Margaret Douglas, who had been unworthily imprisoned. She offered a deal; they would do nothing to enforce their immediate dynastic claim to the English throne and would not assist English rebels against her or seek to change the religion, laws or liberties of England as and when Mary was called to the English throne. In return, they expected Elizabeth not to ally with foreign princes or Scottish rebels against their rule, but to arrange an Act of Parliament to settle the English succession in her favour. This was to no avail. Yet Elizabeth seems to have treated Margaret Douglas fairly leniently, allowing her to lodge in the Lieutenant's quarters with a retinue of staff. Margaret's principal problem was an acute shortage of funds without the income from her Yorkshire estates, and she had difficulty in funding the cost of her food and maintenance in the Tower.

At the time of Mary's return to Scotland, the Crown's traditional supporters had been in disarray. Yet now there was a clearly established group who would back her against Moray, if their interests diverged. They were initially open-minded about Darnley, but he quickly alienated many of them. Support was for Mary alone, although, after the king's murder, even this almost evaporated until her imprisonment at Lochleven. As the senior Catholic among the nobility and head of government, Atholl led Mary's supporters with Maitland's clandestine assistance. They were not all Catholic and were not close-knit. She could always rely on blind allegiance from traditional courtiers like Seton, Livingston and Fleming. Seton returned from France only in August 1565 and was not an enemy of Moray, but would always support her against him. Fleming was a friend of the king, and, as Atholl's brother-in-law, had become Great Chamberlain on 30 June. The powerful Catholic families, such as the Gordons, could always be expected to support the couple as the means of restoring papacy against an increasingly dominant and dogmatic Kirk. Another influential Catholic supporter was John Leslie, who had visited her in France. On 18 October 1565, he was made a Privy Councillor and became her principal adviser in captivity.

The Hamiltons followed Châtelherault's lead in supporting Moray. They hated Darnley and the Lennoxes, but after Darnley's death they reverted to support for Mary. Châtelherault's second son, Lord John Hamilton, born in 1532, went to Italy in 1564, and was not in Scotland at the time of Mary's marriage, only returning in late 1566. His brother, Lord Claud, eleven years his junior, was only 22. Their illegitimate uncle, Archbishop John Hamilton, always supported Mary. He was another worldly prelate, plundering church benefices for his kinsmen and maintaining Grizel Sempill as his mistress.

A number of Protestants placed loyalty to their Catholic queen above their Reformist scruples, but most despised the king. Sir John Maxwell, the second son of Lord Maxwell, was one of those who supported her, or perhaps more particularly opposed Moray, once she was dissociated from

King Henry and Bothwell. His allegiance followed a pattern not dissimilar to Maitland. Despite the considerable power of Mary's supporters, only Lennox could boast acknowledged military skills. She needed to foster the loyalty of Moray's traditional enemies. This meant rehabilitating Bothwell and George Gordon, eldest son of the attainted Earl of Huntly, now deceased. On 19 July, Cecil noted: 'The Earl Bothwell is sent for.'[67]

Chapter 15

Moray's rebellion

Mary moved with admirable speed to isolate Moray and his fellow rebels. She refused to call parliament to meet in July to avoid providing a platform for them to oppose the marriage and portrayed him as petulant at losing power. He may have been illegitimate, but he was well suited to be king with his regal bearing and intellect – and he was James V's eldest son. Unlike Châtelherault and Lennox, he was well respected and had the powerful backing of the Reformers. In 1536, James V had sought a papal dispensation to marry Moray's mother, Margaret Erskine, requesting an annulment of her 1527 marriage to Robert Douglas of Lochleven. Yet this would not necessarily have legitimised Lord James, who was already 4 years old. She had six more children after returning to her husband at the end of her lengthy royal liaison, while Lord James remained at Court to be educated with the king's other illegitimate sons. He was technically legitimised in 1551 to enable him to pass property on to his children, and, being so tantalisingly close to being heir to the throne, he tried unsuccessfully to promote his claim retrospectively.

Despite his obvious qualities, Moray needed general support from the nobility to grasp the Crown and, as Mary's brother, he could not marry her himself. If he could not be king, he wanted to remain the power behind the throne, but the intolerable King Henry now stood in his way and would undo all his good work. Although the Scottish nobility came to recognise the king's shortcomings, there was initial enthusiasm for him. Uncharacteristically, Moray badly misjudged the extent of the support for the Crown.

When Moray tried to build Reformist opposition to the marriage, Mary isolated him politically by exposing the flaws in his propaganda. She had already allayed suspicions by reissuing her 1561 proclamation in the name of both the king and herself to confirm the maintenance of the religious *status quo*. When she heard that people were celebrating Mass in northern Scotland, she told them not 'to do anything as was feared by the Protestants'. She forwent normal Catholic mores by eating meat for the first time in Lent. She attended the Protestant baptism of Alexander, Master of Livingston and heard sermons from approved Reformist preachers. Most Reformers did not believe that their religion was under threat, and even Knox did not back Moray's attempt to gain the Crown for himself. He thus lacked vehement anti-Catholic support.

Moray reverted to inciting the traditional feudal divisions among the Scottish nobility, which he had spent so long trying to heal. He made a personal attack on the Lennoxes by seeking help from their traditional enemies. With Mary so popular, this was never likely to succeed, and it seems that, for once, he allowed self-interest to override more realistic objectives. Despite having covert English financial support, this was minimal, and he failed to realise that taking military action against Mary was doomed to failure.

On 18 July, Moray called a second meeting at Stirling with Châtelherault, Argyll and his senior allies, which sent a plea to Elizabeth to support an armed rebellion. Mary needed to act fast. On 24 July, she wrote to the Pope of her intention to restore Catholicism in Scotland in the hope of him providing a subsidy. On 1 August, she ordered Moray to appear before her within six days and, when he did not come, he was 'put to the horn' (his attainder was publicly pronounced by three blasts of a horn). She warned Châtelherault and Argyll that they would suffer a similar fate if they supported him. By 14 August, the estates of Rothes and Kirkcaldy had also been seized. On 15 August, the rebels left Edinburgh for Ayr, having summoned Glencairn and others to join them there in arms within five days. Although still at Court, Maitland was regarded with suspicion. From Ayr, Moray called 'all good subjects to join them in resisting tyranny, for a king had been imposed on them without the assent of parliament'.[1] His call to arms was not as well received as he had hoped and he set out against Mary with only 600 horse, although probably more than double that number arrived in Edinburgh.

Mary and Darnley were ready to challenge him. By 19 July, ten days before their wedding, Mary had quietly pledged her jewellery to fund a royal army of between 6,000 and 7,000 men. On 19 August, in an effort to appease public opinion, the king attended St Giles's to hear Knox preach. He had arranged for an ostentatious throne to be positioned above the rest of the congregation so that he could listen to Knox's sermons. Yet Knox backed Moray. Not being one to mince his words, he preached a text from Isaiah: 'O Lord our God, other lords than you have ruled over us.' He likened the king and queen to Ahab and Jezebel, demanding:

Did he remove his idolatry? Did he correct his idolatrous wife? No we find no such thing; but the one and the other we find to have continued and increased in their impieties. But what was the end thereof? The last visitation of God was that dogs licked the blood of the one and did eat the flesh of the other.[2]

He ended with a prayer that 'we may see … what punishment he [God] hath appointed for the cruel tyrants …'.[3] Knox preached for an hour longer than expected, with the king grimacing under his invective until he stormed out. He was so furious that he refused dinner and went hawking. Having been summoned before the Council, Knox was suspended for fifteen days, during which he published his sermon.

Three days later, Mary announced that she would face the rebels, who were gathering at Ayr, and by 26 August her troops were mustered from around Edinburgh. The Catholic Sir Simon Preston of Craigmillar replaced the Protestant Archibald Douglas of Kilspendie as Provost of Edinburgh to protect the capital in her absence, and he joined the Privy Council. On 28 August, she set out with between 8,000 and 10,000 men, wearing a steel cap and with a pistol in her saddle holster; King Henry, resplendent in gilt armour, was beside her. They were supported by Lennox, their Douglas kinsmen and the Catholic peers. Many of the rank and file had rallied behind them. Atholl was appointed Lieutenant of the North to deal with Argyll, while Lennox became Lieutenant of the West and later of the South West.

When Charles IX and Catherine de Medici sent their special ambassador, Castelnau, to Scotland to congratulate Mary on her marriage, she had to explain that Moray and his Protestant allies were seeking English help to depose her. If Elizabeth were to support them, there would be no order in the world. She saw them as republicans wanting to usurp government by killing both the king and herself, just as they had deposed her mother. If they succeeded in Scotland, their anarchy would spread to England, the Netherlands and France. She needed French help to nip the rebellion in the bud. Castelnau was not expecting a plea for assistance, having been briefed to persuade her to avoid civil war by being reconciled with Moray and to assure her claim to the English succession by protecting the 'amity'. Yet Mary would not compromise and told him:

> It is incompatible with my honour and with the safety of my person and that of the King my husband, because these rebellious subjects of their bad faith and evil will have decided to kill us both.

She ignored his advice that 'utility, prudence and expediency' obliged her to make concessions. The king was even more determined to risk everything by fighting. Castelnau noted that the grandeur he had seen in him earlier had turned to defiance. He made clear that France was in no position to offer support, with the wars of religion straining financial and military resources. Mary had better success with the papacy; with Moray justifying his attack on religious grounds, she and King Henry portrayed themselves as champions of the Catholic cause. Although she had confirmed the religious status quo in Scotland and had failed to launch a Counter-Reformation since leaving France, she was defending her Catholic throne and, in September, sent an emissary to Rome to seek a subsidy. It is not certain how much the king influenced her to be more confrontational. Up to then she had made a point of trying to diffuse Reformist opposition with her conciliatory stance. He had attended services at St Giles's and had avoided the nuptial mass at the time of his wedding. Their success in gaining support against Moray gave them greater confidence to promote Catholicism at Court and in government. When Mary remained more cautious, King Henry started to promote himself, at Mary's expense, as the Catholic pretender to the English throne, being the more devout Catholic. Yet his personal habits made such a notion grotesque.

In what has become known as the Chaseabout or Roundabout Raid, the two opposing armies never met. Mary and the king set out towards Ayr by way of Linlithgow, Stirling and Glasgow, pushing Moray ahead of them and collecting reinforcements as they went. Lennox commanded the vanguard, while Morton led the 'middle-battle' with the king and queen bringing up the rearguard. Moray marched north to Paisley, where he bypassed her army, and moved on to Edinburgh hoping to join up with Argyll. The Crown's forces followed, through wind and driving rain, giving Moray's troops ahead of them no time to rest. Even Knox could only admire Mary, writing: 'Albeit the most part waxed weary, yet the queen's courage increased man-like, so much that she was ever at the foremost.'[4]

Moray was hopelessly outnumbered, and Mary had hackbutters with her. He reached Edinburgh on 31 August to await Argyll. Although he tried to raise local reinforcements, 'none or few resorted unto them'.[5] Although Châtelherault, Glencairn and William Leslie (by now demoted by Mary as Earl of Rothes on grounds of his illegitimacy) were with him, the combination of Preston as Provost with the townspeople, and Mar's brother, Sir Alexander Erskine of Gogar, at the castle held Edinburgh for the Crown. Sir Alexander sent a message to Mary at Callendar seeking approval to fire the castle's artillery on the rebels, thereby endangering 'a multitude of innocent persons'. When she agreed, it took only six or seven cannon shot to dislodge them. On 1 September, they retreated by way of Lanark to Dumfries. Meanwhile, Mary and the king waited in Glasgow for her northern levies, due at Stirling by the end of September. While readying themselves to face Moray, they doubled back to reoccupy Edinburgh.

On 7 September, Mary sent a strongly worded message to Elizabeth through Randolph warning her not to help Moray. Although this made Elizabeth furious, she feared a French counter-invasion and had cold feet. Supporting Moray was not the same as offering to challenge a foreign queen regent supported by French troops; Mary was an anointed queen, ruling with the support of a majority of her subjects. Elizabeth could not be seen to back the rebels, but promised Moray asylum. It was only if he was able to overthrow the king and queen without her help that she would be able to support him in authority. Moray had insufficient strength to achieve this, but remained a dangerous opponent.

When Lennox and Atholl pursued Argyll back to the Highlands, he retaliated by ravaging their lands as he went. On 6 September, they captured Castle Campbell, forcing Moray to send Sir John Maxwell (who was still sided with him out of his dislike for Darnley) from Dumfries to mediate. He claimed that his actions were true to God, the queen, and the 'Commonwealth'. He complained that Darnley had become king without parliamentary consent, but Mary had not been prepared to listen.

During September and October, Mary and the king went to Fife, Kinross and Perthshire to gather more support and to cut Moray's traditional supply lines from St Andrews. On 6 September, she summoned Glencairn, and others of Moray's supporters to appear there within six days. On 16 September, she issued a manifesto attacking those who 'under pretence of religion' had raised 'this uproar' so that they might 'be kings themselves'.[6] When they failed to appear, they were, on 1 December, found guilty of treason in their absence. Glencairn left for England, but returned home early in the New Year. From St Andrews, Mary and the king travelled to Lochleven, now being used by Moray as a munitions store, threatening his mother and half-brother Sir William Douglas with sequestration if they would not support them. When Mary later told Sir William to surrender the castle, he feigned sickness but agreed to make it available to her at twenty-four hours' notice. Having returned to St Andrews, they travelled through Fife imposing a bond of obedience on the local lairds. They crossed the Tay seeking money in Dundee, but the burgh demanded £2,000 Scots as the price of its loyalty. Being short of funds and with her popularity wavering, Mary returned to Edinburgh, where she was able to borrow 10,000 marks (£6,667 Scots).

Although Mary asked Elizabeth for 3,000 troops, her request was ignored. Seeing that Mary had the upper hand, Elizabeth suggested a truce, if she would pardon Moray and the rebels. Mary told Randolph that she would rather lose her crown than fail to be revenged against them and was in no mood to compromise. She now turned to Moray's traditional enemies for support. Bothwell's journey from France involved taking a fishing boat from Flushing in an attempt to evade English warships commanded by Wilson, a well-known privateer. On 17 September, Wilson caught up with him at Eyemouth, north of Berwick, but Bothwell managed to escape in rowing boats with six or eight men. Although he lost most of his equipment, he joined Mary in Edinburgh with some remaining armour and pistols. His arrival ended any hope of coming to a compromise with Moray, and Maitland immediately retired to Lethington, leaving the post of Secretary of State vacant.

Mary gave Bothwell a great welcome, and the king was 'very gracious and polite' to him.[7] He 'was the most powerful magnate in the Borders, where his anti-English sentiments could be relied upon if the frontier required defending'.[8] On 28 September, he rejoined the Privy Council and was restored as Lieutenant-General of the Borders. From his base at Hermitage Castle, he re-established himself with Border lairds and gained Mary's special trust by bringing many of them into her camp. He was able to deal effectively with their lawlessness and provide a secure defence against English incursions. Yet he was still mistrusted by his peer group. Randolph reported: 'His power is to do more mischief than ever he was minded to do good in all his life.'[9] Yet Randolph took wry delight when Mary upset the king by demoting Lennox to give him command of the royal army. This caused their first open row, but she believed that Bothwell, with his deep-seated hatred of Moray, would display the greater drive. She had to compromise and, although Bothwell retained command, Lennox was to lead the van in battle.

Soon after her wedding, Mary released George Gordon; he had been held for two years at Dunbar following Huntly's defeat and attainder. He presented himself at Holyrood to be restored as Lord Gordon. Although he was soon affirmed as Earl of Huntly, Mary did not immediately restore his estates. As he justifiably blamed Moray for his family's ruin, he became Bothwell's close associate and quickly went north to raise troops, returning on 4 October. Although he had developed Reformist sympathies at Dunbar and refused to take Mass with Mary in the Chapel Royal, this was probably an expedient, and he was soon back in the Catholic camp. His father's body was at last returned for burial in the family tomb at Elgin Cathedral.

On 8 October, he joined the Privy Council, and his estates were freed. Mary ensured that they were now sufficiently dissipated to prevent him from becoming a magnate on his father's former scale. Both the Dowager Lady Huntly and her daughter, Jean, returned to Court and were soon on remarkably good terms with Mary and the king. Bothwell, Huntly and Atholl now became their chief advisers. Despite their devotion, they lacked Maitland's statecraft and Moray's ability to coordinate the nobility. Although Lennox also remained a powerful ally, as soon as Moray went into exile, he started to promote his son, to Mary's detriment.

On 8 October, Mary set out for Dumfries with her forces. Perhaps piqued that Bothwell had been given command, Lennox and the king delayed their departure by going hunting and appeared a week late. This gave time for Moray to give them the slip, causing them Bothwell's lasting antagonism. Dumfries was deserted, with Moray and his allies having crossed over to Carlisle, from where they reached Newcastle eight days later. Although Sir John Maxwell had been instructed to arrest them as they went south, he failed to do so and was accused of treason. Yet he confirmed his allegiance, and Mary absolved him, making him her most loyal supporter. Meanwhile, Bothwell garrisoned Dumfries with 1,500 men to prevent the rebels' return.

Elizabeth was still not prepared to offer Moray overt support, but again sent him money. Randolph delivered 3,000 crowns to Lady Moray, and Bedford handed £1,500 to Moray. With Mary and the king having the whip hand, they would not listen to Elizabeth's pleas for clemency. Moray and his allies were summoned to the Scottish Parliament on 12 March 1566 'to hear and see the doom of forfeiture orderly led against them'.[10] Argyll hid away in the western Highlands, while the remainder stayed in England. When the king left on another hunting trip, Châtelherault came to Mary to apologise for his families' part in the revolt. On 2 January, she pardoned him, but he was exiled to France for five years. With Lennox having hoped to be recognised as Mary's heir, he disapproved of her leniency, but she was starting to mistrust him and needed the Hamiltons held in reserve.

Moray was bitter with Elizabeth for having failed him, but she had to avoid provoking the French. Initially, she refused to allow him to come to London, but relented and 'in a piece of refined deceit' derided him on his knees before the French and Spanish ambassadors. Having made clear that she would never support him against Mary, she secretly granted him a further £3,000 to restore English influence, with instructions to find a way to regain Mary's favour. Despite telling him to leave England, she permitted his return to Newcastle. She asked Robert Melville to intercede on his behalf, but Mary would not barter Lady Margaret's release from the Tower for his pardon. She was taken in by the public humiliation meted out to Moray and agreed to negotiate a new treaty with England, but when she recalled Bothwell from Dumfries to act as one of her Commissioners, the English negotiators angrily withdrew.

With Bothwell now dominating Court, it was agreed that he should wed Huntly's sister, Jean Gordon. By signing their marriage contract, Mary confirmed that this was on her 'advice and express counsel'. They had to wait for a papal dispensation, as Bothwell and Jean were third cousins, placing them within the fourth degree of consanguinity, but Archbishop Hamilton signed the necessary documentation.[11] Huntly provided a dowry of £8,000, which enabled Bothwell to redeem Crichton from his creditors, but Jean astutely retained a jointure over the estate. Mary gave eleven ells [an ell is forty-five inches] of cloth of silver and a taffeta lining for her stunning wedding dress. Although Bothwell insisted on a Protestant marriage service, Mary attended the wedding at the Canongate Church on 24 February 1566, and paid for the banquet and celebration at Holyrood, which included jousting and 'running at the ring'.

The marriage was no love match. Jean Gordon had 'a masculine intelligence', but was 'a cool detached character' lacking beauty and softness.[12] With Seton now back from France, he provided his home with its romantic associations for their honeymoon, but this was not idyllic. Within a week, Bothwell returned to Edinburgh alone, after Jean wore black in mourning for the loss of her sweetheart, Alexander Ogilvy of Boyne. Two months later, Mary arranged for Ogilvy to marry Mary Bethune, who had broken off her long-running attachment to Randolph. Yet, in 1599, Jean eventually married Ogilvy, by when both her second husband, Alexander, 12th Earl of Sutherland, and Mary Bethune, had died. Although Bothwell and Jean were reconciled and lived together 'friendly and quietly', there were no children of the marriage.[13]

The new axis formed between Bothwell and Huntly was extremely disturbing for Moray's supporters. Many shared Maitland's view that Mary and King Henry were trying to weaken the Reformers' hold on power, and Moray soon regained the support of Morton, Ruthven and Lindsay.

Chapter 16

Mary's efforts to govern with her husband without Moray and Maitland

After their marriage, Mary soon became disillusioned with King Henry, who arrogantly and unnecessarily fell out with those whom the Crown needed for support. This caused a breakdown in their warm relationship. On 3 July, Randolph wrote to Leicester:

> He is of an insolent temper, and thinks that he is never sufficiently honoured. The Queen does everything to oblige him, though he cannot be prevailed upon to yield the smallest thing to please her. He claims the Crown Matrimonial and will have it immediately. The Queen tells him that it must be delayed till he be of age, and done by consent of Parliament, which does not satisfy him.[1]

In September 1565, while trying to focus opposition against Moray, Mary was embarrassed by the king's very public visits to bars and male brothels in Edinburgh. When she arrived to try to curb his drinking at an Edinburgh merchant's, he was so abusive that she left in tears. A lady of the court became pregnant by him, and Randolph reported that he was unworthy to be Mary's consort. His performance in government was no better. Although he was required to sign all state documents, he could not keep his mouth shut, so confidential papers could not be shared with him. If he showed an interest, his plans were extravagant and beyond the means of the royal purse. Instead of being concerned with his duties and obligations, he was preoccupied with his rights and privileges, but Mary continued to delay offering him the Crown Matrimonial until he proved himself, knowing that she lacked the power to grant it without parliament's ratification, which would not be forthcoming. King Henry's initial reaction was to try to carry on regardless. Sir John Maxwell (later Herries) reported:

> The king had done some things and signed papers without knowledge of the Queen ... which she took not well. She thought although she had made her husband partner in the Government, she had not

given the power absolutely into his hands ... She thought nothing should be done by him, in relation to affairs of state, without her concurrence and knowledge ... and then, lest the King should be persuaded to pass gifts or any such thing privately to himself, she appointed all things in that kind should be sealed with a seal which she gave to her secretary [Riccio] in keeping, with express orders not to put the seal on any papers unless it be first signed with her own hand.[2]

It has often been assumed that Riccio was given a metal stamp of the king's signature for use when the king was absent, but it is clear that it was to control him from acting independently. This was probably a cause of the king's absences, and he irritated her by going hunting and hawking, often for days at a time. It also caused him to fall out with Riccio.

Mary became pregnant in September, so that she was not always able to work herself and could not join the king on his hunting trips. She had initial doubts about the date of her conception, but it was before 25 September, when the papal dispensation for their marriage arrived from Rome. Fortuitously, this had been backdated to the time of its request on 22 May. There were rumours even then that the king was not the father, but there is no doubt that he was; as a young man, James bore him a striking resemblance. Mary's pregnancy was of huge dynastic importance. A child would provide immeasurable support for her claim to the English Crown and would stand ahead of King Henry, with or without the Crown Matrimonial, as her heir. This was a blow to his ambitions, which were of more importance to him than fatherhood. Mary was still suffering from the recurring pain in her side, which was no doubt aggravated by the early symptoms of her pregnancy. In November, she took to her bed, but the king paid her little attention and went to Fife for nine more days of hunting. On 1 December, she was sufficiently incapacitated to travel to Linlithgow in a litter, rather than on horseback as usual.

Lennox seemed blind to his son's worst excesses. On 19 December, he wrote to Margaret in the Tower:

My Meg, we have to give God most hearty thanks for that the King our son continues in good health and liking, and the Queen great with child, God save them all, for the which we have great cause to rejoice more. Yet of my part, I must confess I want and find a lack of my chiefest comfort, which is you ...[3]

The Spanish ambassador concluded that the king would not have been led astray if his mother had been with him, as she was able to control him. Much to Mary's annoyance, in December he again joined his father for a long hunting trip at Peebles. Although he returned to Edinburgh for Christmas, he then rejoined his father for further hunting until mid-January.

The king's trips with his father may well have been a cover for their Catholic scheming. He was never a devout Catholic, but his parents encouraged him to parade his religion to promote his personal claim at Mary's expense to the Scottish and English Crowns. To cultivate European Catholic heads of state, he arranged for Mass to be celebrated openly at the Scottish Court. The Chapel Royal was like a Catholic parish church. At Christmas 1565, he ostentatiously attended midnight Mass, followed by matins and high Mass, praying 'devotedly on his knees'. He behaved as if he were above the law, as he lacked authority to attend Catholic services as approved for Mary. Yet he was positioning himself as the focus for a British Counter-Reformation. After the Chaseabout Raid, he used Castelnau to seek for him the Order of St Michel, the highest badge of chivalry in France, and requested French help to outlaw the Reformers, but Mary played no part in his scheming. In May and June 1565, Philip II had sent the trusted Alva to Bayonne to reconfirm the terms of the Treaty of Cateau-Cambrésis with France. European Protestants feared the formation of a Catholic league to crush them, but there is no evidence of this, or that King Henry was the object of their attention.

With Moray's revolt at an end, Mary was back in Edinburgh by 19 October. With the majority of the Council being Reformers, the king mistrusted them, and Mary started to appoint middle-class advisers into positions around the Crown. This upset the nobility, who considered such roles as their perquisites. New appointees included Sir James Balfour, Leslie, Riccio, David Chalmers and Francis Yaxley, all Catholic and, initially at least, friends of King Henry. Yet Mary's advisers, particularly King Henry and Riccio, were woefully inadequate as substitutes for Moray and Maitland.

The principal need was to appoint a new Secretary of State, and the two obvious candidates were Balfour and Leslie, both trained in canon law. Balfour had proved a successful Lord of Session. Yet he was treacherous and corrupt, cynically using his experience as a church lawyer to further his own ends. Knox saw him as a notorious blasphemer, claiming that he 'neither feared god nor loved virtue', having reverted to Catholicism after becoming a Reformer at St Andrews.[4] He joined the Privy Council as Clerk-Register in July 1565. After a visit from the king to his wife's home at Burleigh, he became his right-hand man, advising Mary to keep Moray in exile. Leslie, now aged 38, became a conscientious and hard-working Privy Councillor, despite being impulsive and lacking sound judgement. Although the king signed his appointment to become Secretary of State, as the better Catholic, Mary countermanded it. On 24 February 1566 he was appointed Abbot of Lindores, becoming Bishop of Ross two months later. Yet he remained close to Mary, advising and defending her during her later imprisonment.

Mary had a third candidate for Secretary of State in her French Secretary, Riccio, who had become the king's 'only governor', and the man who 'works all' in his counsels.[5] She had trusted him with the steel stamp to confirm her endorsement of the king's signature. He had done much to clear the obstacles for her marriage, and she enjoyed his company. He was sociable, playing cards or making music with her late into the evening. As her relationship with the king deteriorated, that with Riccio grew. He was soon acting as Secretary of State, but as a foreigner was never formally confirmed as such. Randolph became extremely concerned at his Catholic and anti-English influence, writing:

> How she, with the chief of her nobility, can stand and prosper, passes my wit. To be ruled by the advice of two or three strangers, neglecting that of her chief counsellors, I do not know how it can stand.[6]

While Mary may have been misguided in promoting Riccio, it is unlikely that there was anything improper in their relationship. She was pregnant and quite unwell during the autumn of 1565 and spring of 1566, and he was no Adonis, being nearly a foot shorter than she was with an 'illfavoured' face. Yet it suited Mary's enemies to imply that there was more to it than met the eye, and both Randolph and Maitland saw it as dynamite, if the king should learn of it. Randolph, who later described Riccio as 'a filthy wedlock breaker', implied something much darker in Moray's defection from Mary than his personal ambition and hatred of the king, but would not put his thoughts in writing.[7] It has been construed that Moray believed that Mary was involved in an affair with Riccio, but there is no evidence to support this, and it is far more likely she was merely seeking companionship. Maitland also promoted the story, seeing Riccio as having usurped his rightful position as Secretary of State. Yet Mary ignored the criticism and opened herself to scandal by favouring him over her more experienced advisers.

David Chalmers was another lawyer; he had been Balfour's colleague in the Court of Session and in the Admiralty court, over which Bothwell presided as Lord High Admiral. Both were later implicated with Bothwell in King Henry's murder, but carefully covered their tracks. Yet, for now, Chalmers was advising the king. Yaxley had recently been released from the Tower following his involvement in Margaret Douglas's ill-fated efforts to gain Continental European support for Darnley to marry Mary in 1562. She now sent him to Scotland to provide the king with diplomatic advice and a communication link with English Catholics. He was appointed ambassador to Spain, and became the King's Secretary; Mary was unaware that he was conducting diplomatic initiatives purportedly on her behalf. On 13 October, the king sent him to Brussels to tell Philip II that she had lost confidence in her Guise relations and needed Spanish support to achieve a Scottish Counter-Reformation. He claimed that English Catholics 'of good power' would support a Spanish coup to place her on Elizabeth's throne.[8] Although this would need papal ratification, Philip was developing plans to invade Ireland, where Spain was conducting an active trade, as an obvious bridgehead from which to attack England. As Ireland remained predominantly Catholic with many Gaelic chiefs in revolt, Philip discussed with Yaxley his hopes of gaining their support to make Mary their queen in place of Elizabeth.

Mary was unaware of any of these negotiations, but both the Pope and Philip II believed that, with King Henry at her side, she was sincere in seeking to restore Catholicism in Scotland. On 10 January 1566, the Pope wrote to her:

> We congratulate your Highness on having by this notable fact commenced to dispel the darkness which has brooded for so many years over that kingdom and to restore it to the light of true religion – complete what you have commenced.

This was premature because Philip needed to delay providing military support until after his invasion of the Netherlands. He could not risk English interference with his supply lines through the Channel. Yet he sent Yaxley with 20,000 crowns for Mary, but Yaxley was shipwrecked off Holy Island on the Northumbrian coast on his return from Brussels. When his body and document case were washed up, Elizabeth claimed the bounty as treasure trove.

Having been chastened by Elizabeth and told to find a means to return to Scotland, Moray wrote to Riccio from Newcastle offering him £5,000 to obtain a pardon for him. Riccio, who was seeking agreement from parliament to prosecute Argyll for treason and to sequester all the dissident nobles' estates, demanded £20,000. Moray then approached King Henry, who had never been his friend, sending a fine diamond and signing an obligation to be 'his loyal servant'. Again, these overtures failed and, although Mary's attitude towards the rebels had started to soften, she was being encouraged to proceed against them by the newly elected Pius V and by James Bethune, Archbishop of Glasgow, now her ambassador in Paris.[9*] The king was determined to punish the rebels and arranged for their moveable possessions, confiscated by the Crown, to be auctioned off. On 1 December, Glencairn and Moray's other allies were found guilty of treason in their absence. In desperation, they considered trying to kidnap the king and queen.

The strongly Catholic bias among Mary's new advisers seemed particularly suspicious at a time when her Guise relations were stepping up their persecution of French Huguenots. The king no longer attended St Giles's to hear Knox's sermons and persuaded Mary to change her approach to religion. This happened very rapidly. As late as 10 December, she had reconfirmed freedom of Reformist worship and, at Christmas, refused to attend Mass with the king, while deliberately sitting up at cards until late. This enabled him to prick her Catholic conscience by implying that his faith was the more devout. Pushed by her Catholic advisers, Mary resiled from her policy of only attending Mass in private and seemed to stop at nothing in her attempts to charm her most intractable advisers into becoming Catholic. The king provocatively persuaded Mary that the status quo was not equitable. At parliament in the spring, Mary sought to restore 'liberty of conscience', saying 'she will have the mass free for all men that will hear it'.[10] Having masterminded the Scottish Reformation, Knox faced the prospect of all his hard work being undone. When the Kirk would not give ground, parliament became polarised. Randolph reported that she was 'bent in the overthrow of religion'.[11]

On 7 February 1566, the king was invested with the Order of St Michel, which Castelnau had obtained for him. He saw this as a vindication of his strongly pro-Catholic stance. He celebrated with a Catholic festival over Candlemas, which had begun on 2 February. Ambassadors from both the French king and the Cardinal of Lorraine arrived for his investiture, with praise flooding in from Catholic sources abroad. The Cardinal sent a letter from Pius V, congratulating both Mary and the king in glowing terms on the 'brilliant proof of your zeal by restoring the due worship of God throughout your realm'.[12*] This again was premature, but the Pope was encouraging

Mary to weed out the 'thorns and tares of heretical depravity'. With so many foreign dignitaries hoping for progress in restoring papacy, Mary had to be seen to support her husband, with her pregnancy giving her a greater sense of security. She wanted to diffuse the perception that it was the king taking the lead. On 31 January, she wrote to the Pope buoyantly promising to restore 'religion in splendour' in Scotland and later in England. 'In an evil hour' in February, she signed a bond sent by the Cardinal of Lorraine to endorse a new Catholic league between France, Spain and the Empire. She also sent William Chisholm, Bishop of Dunblane as her emissary to Rome seeking spiritual and financial aid.

When the Reformers shunned the king's investiture, he became abusive. He caused a scene by locking Bothwell and Huntly into a room and threatening to throw away the key. Mary tried a different tack, leading them by the hand into Mass, but they refused to attend, preferring to hear Knox at St Giles's. Despite his friendship with the king, even Livingston refused his order to attend Mass. Yet 300 people were present at the services for the king's investiture.

Insensitive as ever, the king would not let matters rest and threatened to restore Mass at St Giles's and in the Council. Randolph reported that Mary was preparing to renew her immediate Catholic claim to the English throne. Yaxley had led her to believe that support for her among English Catholics was 'never so great'.[13] Cecil seemed to have been right; the English were attracted to her and away from Elizabeth by her producing an heir. At the banquet for the foreign ambassadors following the king's investiture, she pointed to a conveniently positioned portrait of Elizabeth and announced that 'there was no other Queen of England but herself'.[14]

Despite Mary showing public support for her husband's pro-Catholic stance, their relationship was not harmonious. She knew that they needed support from European Catholic powers to adopt a Catholic policy. Despite their marriage, English Catholics had made no move to support them to replace Elizabeth on the English throne. She was equally disappointed with Lennox, openly wishing that he 'had not set foot in Scotland'.[15] With his influence being in steady decline, he spent more and more time in Glasgow. Mary had already argued with King Henry over Bothwell's appointment to replace Lennox in command of their forces, and he had been furious when she pardoned the Hamiltons after the Chaseabout Raid. During Christmas 1565, further spats took place in their apartments, and Mary cancelled the understanding that they ruled jointly. State documents that had placed the king's name ahead of Mary's, now placed her name first. Coinage struck at the time of their marriage, showing '*Henricus et Maria*' by the Grace of God King and Queen of Scotland, was changed on the issue to celebrate victory over Moray to show '*Maria et Henric*', queen and king (see picture section p. 11). At the investiture of the Order of St Michel, the king was not permitted to bear royal arms. He reduced Mary to tears when she tried to temper his debauchery at parties with members of the French ambassador's suite and again denied him the Crown Matrimonial.

With the king not playing his part in government, he failed to provide Mary with support in dealing with royal papers. He showed her no affection, preferring liaisons in male brothels or with ladies of the Court. Yet his ostentatious displays of devotion implied that he was the stronger Catholic. Mary probably became aware of his underhand diplomacy in Europe, on which she was not being consulted. They were growing apart. Her pregnancy was another factor; having sired her child, she no longer required him to sleep with her. As he showed no enthusiasm for visiting her bedroom, she saw no reason to go to his, and by all accounts they lived separately.

The Scottish lords, regardless of religious persuasion, ganged up against the new upstarts in government. The threat that Moray and the other rebels in exile would be attainted at the forthcoming Parliament on 13 March seemed to be a precedent for future forfeitures. With the Reformers among them fearing a Counter-Reformation, they looked to Maitland for a solution. Even Mary felt threatened by her husband's plotting, and Randolph was aware of a scheme for Lennox and the king 'to come to the crown against her will'.[16] It was almost certainly Maitland who encouraged Lennox to propose to Argyll that, if Darnley were granted the Crown Matrimonial, he would arrange for Moray and the other exiled lords to be recalled and pardoned and would reverse his religious policy by reconfirming the *status quo*. Moray was being asked to grant the Crown Matrimonial to the person against whom he had rebelled only five months before. With everyone benefiting at Mary's expense, Moray cynically agreed. Yet Riccio would need to be removed, as he was blocking Moray's recall and keeping Maitland sidelined.

Having played on the king's ambition, Maitland implied to him that it was Riccio who was stopping Mary from granting him the Crown Matrimonial. He also suggested that Mary's close friendship with Riccio was more than that of queen and Secretary, and even questioned the paternity of her unborn child. Rumours had reached Catherine de Medici that the king had returned to Mary's apartment late one evening to find the door locked. After shouting to gain entry he had found Riccio in a nightshirt quailing in a cupboard. This seems highly unlikely, as Riccio would never have survived such an encounter, and the king did not report it, even when needing to justify Riccio's murder. Yet Randolph and Bedford, who wanted to make the most of any scandal, claimed 'that David had more company of her body than he, for the space of two months'. Although a sexual liaison may seem unrealistic, there is no doubt that the king was inordinately jealous of their close friendship. It is quite probable that Mary, in her pregnant state, wanted to avoid her husband's sexual overtures. She achieved this by sitting up until all hours with Riccio playing cards. This left the king believing that Riccio had usurped the position of influence that should have been his.

The Reformers needed a scapegoat to blame for the move towards Catholicism, and Riccio was an obvious target. Melville was not alone in believing that he 'had secret intelligence with the Vatican'. Yet, as Mary became isolated, she relied on Riccio all the more. He had 'the whole guiding of the queen and country'.[17] Maitland had long feared the impact of a Catholic circle of ministers surrounding the queen and knew that it would have to be broken if he were to regain his position as Secretary of State. That would require Moray's reinstatement; he had begun to despair of how to achieve it, but Riccio would have to be removed to stop any further deterioration in the Protestant nobles' authority. On 9 February 1666, Maitland wrote to Cecil saying:

> All may be reduced to the former estate if the right way be taken … I see no certain way unless we chop at the very root – you know where that lieth, and so far as my judgement can reach, the sooner all things be packed up the less danger there is of any inconveniences.[18]

He was seeking Cecil's blessing to arrange Riccio's murder.

There has been much debate on precisely what Maitland meant by chopping 'at the very root'. Given his close association with Mary Fleming, it is unlikely that he sought at this stage to topple Mary from her throne. Yet it is more certain that the king had his father's support to use the murder of Riccio as a means of bringing down the queen. When the plan was developed, Randolph wrote to Cecil:

> I know that there are practices in hand contrived between father and son to come by the Crown against her will. I know that if that take effect which is intended, David, with the consent of the King, shall have his throat cut within these ten days. Many things grievouser and worse than these are brought to my ears, yea, of things intended against her own person.[19]

With Châtelherault in exile, it was, of course, an ideal time for the Lennoxes to remove Mary and her unborn child, and to claim the Crown for themselves. All the later actions of the conspirators imply that her downfall was also an objective.

As soon as the king had been hooked into the plan to remove Riccio, he looked to his Douglas kinsmen to manage matters for him, with Morton and Ruthven designated to make the arrangements. Morton saw this as his opportunity to achieve a powerful position, and Maitland persuaded him to play on the apparent slur against Douglas honour caused by the queen's friendship with Riccio. Morton also realised that Moray would need to be rehabilitated to garner more general support among the nobility. Both Randolph and Bedford, who were well aware of the planning, kept Cecil closely briefed. Randolph was in trouble with Mary, who had learned the part he had played in smuggling untraceable coin to Lady Moray to fund his revolt. When he was accused of it, he hotly denied it, but, on 19 February, was given a safe conduct to depart from Scotland at Berwick. With Riccio's assassination still being planned, he remained in Edinburgh until 2 March, a week beforehand, to keep Cecil fully informed. By then he was able to advise that Moray and the exiled lords would leave Newcastle for Berwick on the next day with a plan to reach Edinburgh on the day after the murder. Elizabeth wrote to Mary to complain at Randolph being dismissed and was still objecting to Moray's treatment, despite his all too obvious treasonable activities, which she had financed, and she now sent him a further £1,000.

Most people seemed to know of the plan to murder Riccio. Other than Mary, the exceptions included Bothwell and Huntly, who were bound up in arranging Bothwell's marriage to Jean Gordon on 24 February and would never have welcomed Moray's return. As a Catholic, Atholl was also kept in the dark, despite his close association with Maitland, but he too mistrusted Riccio and was not averse to his death. Cecil knew every detail. This was not simply a plan to remove Riccio, but to discredit the king and restore Moray and Maitland. It might even fulfil his objective of bringing down the queen by associating her with the wayward king.

Chapter 17

Riccio's murder

Failing to see his own shortcomings and 'infatuated by his own arrogance', the king blamed Riccio for freezing him out of government. He wanted revenge and the Crown for himself. The disaffected nobility was only too willing to encourage him to plan Riccio's murder by pandering to his ambitions. 'His youth and inexperience would render him as wax in the hands of the ruthless, power-hungry men who were closing in on him, and as such he would prove their most dangerous weapon.'[1] He believed that the Crown Matrimonial would enable him to dominate Mary. Even without it, the Lennoxes were positioned to claim the Crown for themselves should Mary die without an heir. With Châtelherault in exile, they had only to cite his illegitimacy. The conspirators' objective was to remove Mary's Catholic advisers, thereby regaining liberty of religion and the return of their estates. The king's involvement would provide them with immunity from prosecution, but he would never be allowed to govern.

Having supported the king's marriage, Morton could claim to be affronted at Mary's infatuation with Riccio, but his principal motive was to obtain Moray's rehabilitation. He also made his support conditional on Margaret Douglas withdrawing her claim to the Earldom of Angus, which he still administered for his nephew. He was one of the many nobles who, like Moray, faced sequestration of parts of his estates on Riccio's recommendation at the forthcoming parliament. His murder needed to be undertaken beforehand. Although Maitland had orchestrated the plan, his involvement evaporated. He made a point of dining at Holyrood with peers from the queen's party including Atholl, Huntly, Caithness, Bothwell and Balfour that same evening. This of itself can be seen as suspicious and implies an attempt by him to keep them out of the way. The other conspirators, particularly the king, all confirmed his intimate involvement afterwards, resulting in his attainder.

Morton formulated the murder plan during January and February 1566. He gathered in a number of Douglas connections including Ruthven and George Douglas 'the postulate'. Ruthven was already crippled from inflammation of the liver and kidneys, which resulted in his death in Newcastle three months later. His involvement was conditional on the king solemnly swearing not to reveal the plan to the queen, to which he unhesitatingly agreed. George Douglas was an unsavoury character, who had been involved in Cardinal Bethune's murder. He was Margaret Douglas's illegitimate half-brother, the son of Archibald, 6th Earl of Angus. He joined the Church as a young man, having 'seized the lucrative office of Postulate of Arbroath, despite being a lacklustre preacher, a fornicator, and a devious and violent ruffian'.[2] Melville claimed that it was George Douglas who incited the king by putting into his 'head such suspicion against Riccio'. Between them they gathered together other Douglas connections bent on family advancement. In the main, they were those who had supported the king's marriage to Mary. Ruthven maintained his Douglas affiliation despite the death of his first wife, Janet Douglas (Lady Margaret's illegitimate half-sister), and his remarriage to Jane Stewart, Atholl's eldest daughter. Others included Ruthven's son William, and Sir William Douglas of Lochleven, no doubt out of loyalty to Moray, his half-brother. Sir William was always close to Morton. By the obscure entail to the 3rd Earl of Morton's will, he was to become heir to the Morton title, later becoming the 5th Earl. He had made a miraculous recovery from his apparent sickness during November when threatened with the sequestration of Lochleven with its store of munitions. Lindsay of the Byres, who had supported the marriage and was close to Morton, also joined them. His wife, Euphemia Douglas, was Sir William's sister and a half-sister to Moray. Glamis was the only Douglas kinsman supporting the marriage who does not appear to have taken part in the murder. They had the backing of the Officers of State on the Council, who felt threatened by Riccio's shift towards more Catholic government. There was a group of henchmen, including Andrew Ker of Fawdonside (a cadet branch of the Kers of Cessford), Patrick Bellenden, brother of the Justice-Clerk, and two Ruthven retainers, Thomas Scott, under-sheriff of Perth, and Henry Yair, a former priest. There were about eighty conspirators in all.

The conspirators, other than the king, were seeking to remove the threat of a Counter-Reformation by restoring Moray and his fellow exiles. Lady Antonia Fraser has pointed out that, if they were only seeking to murder Riccio, there were ample opportunities away from Edinburgh, and it was Morton's original plan to seize him clandestinely in his quarters at Holyrood. Yet it seems that the king was not averse to the consequential death of the queen and her unborn child.[3*] By murdering Riccio in her presence, there was a realistic expectation of shock causing a miscarriage and, in mid-pregnancy, this invariably led to the mother's death. Even Randolph

understood that this was part of the plan. Given Maitland's close association with Mary Fleming, he may have remained unaware of this objective
after pulling back from the detail, but Mary came to believe that she was an
intended victim and undoubtedly some of the conspirators tried to terrify
her. It was the king who arranged for the murder to take place at a private
supper party held by the queen at Holyrood, in expectation of being offered
the throne if Mary should die. The other conspirators played along with his
treasonable plan, as it provided grounds for his future deposition to allow
Moray to be swept to power.

The conspirators did not trust the king and insisted on a bond to prevent
him from denying knowledge of the plot afterwards, or to 'allege that others
persuaded him to the same'.[4] On 1 March, he signed a deed acknowledg-
ing that he was the chief author of a plan to murder the 'wicked, ungodly'
Riccio, even though 'the deed may chance to take place in the presence of
the queen's majesty'.[5] He assumed full responsibility for this, despite the
apparent concerns of Morton and Ruthven. The deed was signed by all
those taking an active part, including Morton, George Douglas, Ruthven
and Lindsay. They were not to 'spare life or limb in setting forward all that
may bend to the advancement of his [the king's] honour'.[6] It confirmed that
the king would be offered the Crown Matrimonial in return for pardoning
and protecting the other signatories and permitting the exiles to return to
their estates. He gave an assurance that Protestantism would be maintained,
despite his very public show of Catholicism at Candlemas only a month earlier. Although it was also signed by Ochiltree, Boyd, Glencairn and Argyll,
they were not actively involved, and there were other supporters who backed
it but do not appear to have signed. These included Lennox, Kirkcaldy, Knox,
Archibald Douglas (brother of William Douglas of Whittinghame and the
probable murderer of the king at Kirk o' Field) and, of course, Maitland. A
second copy was sent to Newcastle for signature by Moray, William Leslie
and the other exiled lords, but not every conspirator may have known this.
Despite approving it, Moray was permitted to keep his hands clean and did
not sign it.

If Mary survived, the conspirators had decided to imprison her at
Stirling to await her child's birth. After his failure in the Chaseabout Raid,
her detention would offer Moray an outcome that was probably just as satisfactory. It would certainly suit Cecil if Moray were invited to take the throne,
and he hoped to engineer this. The Douglases had not, in the main, supported his rebellion and may have believed that there were richer pickings
to be gained from promoting King Henry under their close supervision,

but Morton knew that only Moray had the authority to take control. On 8 March, the day before the murder, the king granted Moray a passport to return to Scotland, not realising his intention to usurp control. Home was to escort him, timing their arrival so that they reached Edinburgh immediately following the murder. Yet they reckoned without Mary's quick-wittedness.

It is clear that the English strongly supported the murder plan; the Spanish believed that it had been initiated from England and that Elizabeth had provided funding of 8,000 crowns. Randolph kept Cecil, Bedford and the English Privy Council abreast of the plan as it developed. On 13 February, he sent Leicester full details, including rumours of plans to engineer Mary's death, but told him to keep it to himself for fear of word reaching Elizabeth, who might warn her. Randolph and Bedford advised Cecil of the king's involvement four days beforehand, and Elizabeth was advised that the removal of Mary's pre-eminent Catholic and anti-English adviser was a political necessity. The plan also fitted well with Cecil's efforts to bring down the king and queen. If implicated, the king could be charged with treason and Mary might die from a miscarriage. If she survived, she would be imprisoned with the king, allowing Moray to become regent for her unborn child. If she died, he could aspire to be king. On 8 March, Cecil went to the Tower to advise Margaret Douglas, perhaps hoping to allay any suspicion that he disapproved of her son, but she 'was in great trouble at the news'.[7] It can be no surprise that the plan leaked and, although Mary told Sir James Melville that she was aware of rumours, she dismissed them, claiming 'our countrymen were well-wordy' and asked: 'What can they do? What dare they do?'[8] Melville also warned Riccio, but he distained all danger and despised counsel, claiming: 'They are but ducks, strike one of them and the rest will fly.'[9] Yet he raised a bodyguard of Italian mercenaries for his protection.

Mary later recorded that there was a wider plan, which was abandoned, to murder her close advisers, including Bothwell, Huntly, Livingston, Fleming and Sir James Balfour, but there is no other evidence for such a scheme. Although Bothwell, Huntly and Balfour dined with Maitland that evening and tried to reach the queen, they were told that harm was intended only to Riccio. Balfour's inclusion in her list is surprising, as he was still a close associate of the king, but there may have been doubt of his loyalty, as he was threatened with being 'hanged in cords' if he revealed the king's involvement.

The plot was brought to a head by the opening of parliament on 7 March, when Mary was attended by Bothwell carrying the sceptre, Huntly the crown, and Crawford the sword of state. Still piqued at not being granted the Crown Matrimonial, the king was not present. Despite being nearly six months pregnant, Mary proposed the dissident nobles' attainder, setting a date for the hearing on 12 March. On the morning of 9 March the king played tennis with Riccio, presumably to allay any suspicions, and in the evening Mary held a private dinner in a small room (12ft long by 10ft wide) next to her bedchamber at Holyrood. She was joined by her half-brother and sister, Lord Robert Stewart and Jean, Countess of Argyll, Robert Bethune of Creich, Master of the Household (who had travelled with her to France and was the father of Mary Bethune), Arthur Erskine of Blackgrange, her Equerry and Master of Horse, and Riccio, bedecked in a gown of furred damask over a satin doublet and russet velvet hose. He also wore a cap, which he failed to remove, as he should have done, in her presence. Fleming, as Great Chamberlain, Anthony Standen, Mary's page, Leslie, an apothecary and a groom were in attendance. Although it was Lent, meat was being served in deference to Mary's pregnancy, and the party looked forward to an evening of music and cards afterwards.

The king was not expected at the dinner, as he now rarely ate with Mary, but he admitted Ruthven and an accomplice to his apartment below. They climbed the privy staircase leading to the queen's bedchamber. From here the accomplice went to unlock the outer doors of her presence chamber beyond to provide access for the remaining conspirators led by Morton from the main staircase. Much to the surprise of the party, the king joined them after they had begun eating and sat down beside Mary. He was affable enough and well received, but suddenly Ruthven appeared wearing a helmet with armour under his cloak. He was extremely pale and feverish, but demanded that Riccio, who cowered for protection behind the queen, should be handed over. Mary, who had always mistrusted Ruthven with his reputation for sorcery, demanded to know his offence. He told her, 'He hath offended your honour, which I dare not be so bold as to speak of.'[10] He also accused him of hindering the king's grant of the Crown Matrimonial and banishing many of the lords with a plan to forfeit their estates at the present parliament. Mary replied that, if he had done wrong, he should be tried before parliament. She asked the king if Ruthven was acting at his bidding, but he denied this. The queen then told Ruthven to leave or face arrest for treason. Lord Robert, Bethune, Erskine, the apothecary and the groom tried to seize him, but he drew a pistol, warning them off, and advanced with his dagger on Riccio, who was still hiding behind Mary in the window recess.

The door again opened and Lindsay burst in, followed by six more heavily armed men, George Douglas, Bellenden, the Master of Ruthven,

Ker of Fawdonside, Scott and Yair. There was a violent struggle and the table was overturned with its contents knocked to the floor. The Countess of Argyll managed to save a single candle, which, in addition to the fire in the hearth, provided the only light. Ruthven manhandled the queen out of the way, saying that he had the king's assent, and told the king, 'Sir, take the Queen your sovereign and wife to you.'[11] The king gripped her arm, while Lindsay rammed a chair into her stomach, and Fawdonside held his loaded pistol to her womb. She later claimed he would have killed her, if his gun had not 'refused to give fire'. 'One of Ruthven's followers offered to fix his poniard in the queen's left side', but Standen grabbed it, and was later knighted for saving her life, as he recalled to James VI.[12]

George Douglas seized the king's dagger and thrust it at Riccio, coming so close to the queen that she could feel the cold steel at her throat. Melville claimed that it was left 'sticking in him'. On his knees and clawing at the queen's skirts, Riccio cried out, 'Justice! Justice! Save me, my Lady! I am a dying man. Spare my life!'[13] The king bent back his fingers, so that others could drag him from the room. Ruthven gave orders for him to be taken down the privy stairs to the king's bedchamber. Yet he was dragged through the queen's bedchamber to her presence chamber, where armed men were waiting. They were 'so vehemently moved against David that they could not abide any longer', and Lindsay, Morton and more than a dozen of their supporters stabbed him to death, showing all the hallmark savagery of a ritual killing, with between fifty-three and sixty wounds left in his body, and the king's dagger left embedded in his side.[14] One of the attackers was wounded in the bloodlust, and Yair was so fired up with anti-Catholic sentiment that he stabbed to death a Dominican friar, Father Adam Beck, in his bed. Beck, who had been one of the queen regent's chaplains, was the only other casualty. The king continued to restrain the queen, who later claimed to have been in 'extreme fear of her life'.[15]

After hearing the war cry, 'A Douglas! A Douglas!', Bothwell and Huntly ran with their servants from dinner with Maitland to investigate. They were intercepted by Morton, who had posted twenty men on the stairs to the queen's apartments. Ruthven explained that Riccio had been murdered on the king's command. They were told to return to Bothwell's rooms, but, smelling danger, escaped by a back window 'through the little garden where the lions were lodged', riding first to Crichton and then on to Dunbar.[16] Huntly's mother stayed behind to tell Mary that they would plan a rescue. Mary's servants also came to her aid with staves, but they too were warned off. Morton placed an armed guard round Holyrood and, after seizing the keys from the porter, secured all the gates and doors. Later that evening, Atholl, Tullibardine, Maitland, Fleming, Livingston, Balfour and Leslie were permitted to leave 'in fear of their lives', and Atholl went home to Dunblane.[17]

King Henry was still with Mary in the supper room when Ruthven returned with Lindsay of the Byres and others. Ruthven was feverish and collapsed into a seat, demanding wine, which he downed at a single gulp. In their presence, Mary asked the king how he could betray her so shamelessly. He recited his concerns that Riccio had had too much of her company and even her body, and had persuaded her not to treat him as her equal. She asked what had happened to Riccio. Ruthven explained that he was dead and advised her to pay more attention to her husband and the nobility. Mary later recalled that they

> were highly offended with our proceedings and tyranny, which was not to them tolerable, how we were abused by the said David … in taking his counsel for the maintenance of the ancient [Catholic] religion, debarring of the Lords which were fugitive, and entertaining of amity with foreign [Catholic] princes and nations with whom we were confederate; putting also upon Council the Lords Bothwell and Huntly, who were traitors and with whom he [Riccio] associated himself.[18]

The queen rounded on Ruthven, saying that he had been one of her Privy Councillors throughout and blaming him particularly for her rough treatment. She promised that, if she died in childbirth, her friends would take their revenge, but he merely confirmed that he had followed the king's orders. Mary turned to the king, demanding:

> Why have you caused to do this wicked deed to me, considering I took you from a low estate and made you my husband? What offence have I made you that you should have done me such shame?[19]

He baulked at being treated as inferior and replied:

> Suppose I be of the baser degree, yet am I your husband and your head, and you promised me obedience on the day of our marriage and that I should be participant and equal with you in all things.

She retorted:

> For all the offence that is done to me, my Lord, you have the weight thereof, for the which I shall be your wife no longer nor sleep with you any more, and shall never like well until I have caused you to have as sorrowful a heart as I have at this present.[20]

Still believing that she had been involved in an affair with Riccio, the king complained that Mary had not 'entertained' him since Riccio had come into favour.[21] According to Ruthven, the king said that she 'used to sit up at cards with David till one or two after midnight' and no longer came to his chamber. When he went to her, she 'either would not or made herself sick'.[22] He asked if she found him sexually inadequate, 'Am I failed in any sort?' 'What distain have you of me?' The queen retorted that, under royal protocol, 'it was not a gentlewoman's duty to come to her husband's chamber, but rather the husband to come to the wife's. Her duty was to be chaste, loyal and obedient.'[23]

A messenger then knocked at the door to report that Bothwell and Huntly had escaped. The king immediately departed with Ruthven, leaving Mary alone to make a plan. She feared that she would be held captive or worse, but remained extraordinarily calm, saying: 'No more tears. I will think upon a revenge.'[24] This was not a woman distraught at having lost a lover; she had the presence of mind to send a lady to Riccio's room to recover ciphers used for her correspondence, but she could not communicate with her household, as Douglas men guarded her door and the palace gates. Yet the indomitable Lady Huntly managed to deliver a message from Bothwell that he would attempt to free her. She also knew Moray was about to return and, being unaware of his part in the conspiracy, hoped for his assistance.

When the king returned, he arranged to have Riccio's lacerated body moved from the presence chamber. It was thrown down the stairs and laid across a wooden chest in the porter's lodge. The porter removed the king's dagger and stripped off the rich clothing. On the following day, the remains were quietly buried in the Canongate cemetery near the door to Holyrood Abbey.

After so much disturbance, the 'common bell' had been sounded, resulting in a crowd gathering in the forecourt outside Holyrood. The Provost, Sir Simon Preston, arrived with 400 members of the watch armed with spears. The king dispersed the crowd by confirming from a window that a papal agent had been punished, but Mary was unharmed. When she tried to be seen, Lindsay threatened 'to cut her in collops' if she showed herself.[25] She was later furious with Sir Simon for not investigating further.

The conspirators had agreed that Mary should be sent to Stirling 'under safe keeping' for her confinement and they intended retaining her there afterwards.[26] Lindsay claimed that she would find plenty of time to nurse her baby and sing it to sleep, or shoot with her bow in the garden and do her fancywork. The king was assured that he would receive the Crown Matrimonial and would share the management of the government with the nobles, so long as liberty of religion was confirmed. Yet Ruthven warned:

> If you wish to obtain what we have promised you, you must needs follow our advice, as well for your own safety as for ours. If you do otherwise we will take care of ourselves, cost what it may.[27]

The king was told not to talk to the queen without other conspirators being present. Lennox and the king were suddenly in fear of their lives, and Ruthven warned that, if anyone tried to help Mary escape, they would 'throw her to them piecemeal'.[28] The conspirators now awaited Moray's arrival with William Leslie, in expectation of Moray being returned to power.

Mary knew that the conspirators' weak link was the king. She needed to separate him from them to establish who was behind the plot and to help her escape. She asked him to spend the night with her. Yet Ruthven insisted on him remaining under guard in his own bedchamber. The king now realised that the conspirators had no intention of giving him authority. They had cynically 'made use of him, only that they might involve him in the disgrace and infamy of an act of such atrocity'.[29] During the night, he approached the queen's bedroom by the privy staircase, but the door was locked. He shouted out that he needed to discuss their safety, but the guard would not allow him in. From this, Mary surmised that she had every chance of persuading him to save her and to confirm the child's legitimacy. On the next morning, he was at last permitted to join her 'having passed that night in perplexity, in terror for his own life'. He admitted having signed a bond with the conspirators, which promised him the Crown Matrimonial, being 'young and imprudent and blinded by ambition', but claimed he never thought they would murder Riccio. He told her he was taking a great risk in talking to her and 'that if it were ever known that he had done so he would be a dead man'.[30] He showed her the passport he had granted to allow Moray's return. Mary knew this was not the whole story, and witheringly told him that she would not forget his part in what had happened. She then forced every detail out of him, and warned that the conspirators would never allow him authority and would place his life in danger, which he already realised. She concluded: 'Since you have placed us on the brink of the precipice, you must now deliberate how we shall escape the peril.'[31] He agreed to escape with her, but they quarreled for two hours on how to do so, until he stormed out. Although it has been suggested that she had difficulty persuading him to help her, he knew he had been duped. She cannot be accused of causing his murder by persuading him to disassociate himself from the other conspirators; he took the decision himself. Yet she did persuade him to let her gentlewomen return, giving her a conduit to communicate with her supporters, particularly Bothwell and Huntly. Although Morton and Ruthven quickly removed them, she had already had time to send messages. She warned Argyll, whose wife had been at the dinner, of her predicament and, despite having signed the bond, he set out for Edinburgh to support her, seeking to be returned to favour. She acted cool-headedly, just as in the planning of her marriage and before the Chaseabout Raid.

Mary's first objective was to sow discord between the returning exiles and the murderers, hoping to divide and rule. Never again would she allow her advisers to dominate her as Moray had done 'and so become enslaved'. She needed to balance rival factions; she would pardon the exiles not directly involved in the murder, but would punish those who had taken part, replacing Morton as Chancellor with Huntly. She could not fathom Maitland but, having warned him that she would hold him to account for any actions against her, she decided to attaint him.

Mary's escape plan involved feigning labour pains so that her guards would be removed. When the king returned in the afternoon, she asked for her gentlewomen to be brought back to assist her. The conspirators nominated a midwife, but Mary's ladies primed her to verify the seriousness of her condition and, with the backing of Mary's French physician, she confirmed, conveniently but inaccurately, that Mary was gravely ill, and needed to be released. The conspirators remained suspicious and redoubled the guard. No one was permitted to leave with their face hidden, or anyone whose identity was suspected.

Mary told the king to be reconciled with the other conspirators to allay their suspicions. When he asked her to pardon them, she initially refused out of conscience, but then told him to offer anything he pleased in her name. Having rejoined them, he issued a proclamation dissolving parliament, telling its members to leave Edinburgh within three hours. The exiled lords were unaware of this and, on 12 March, when Moray and his colleagues appeared for trial at the Tolbooth, it was deserted. With the conspirators protected from immediate attainder, they agreed to reduce Mary's guards.

Meanwhile, the Dowager Lady Huntly worked on an escape plan. She was grateful to Mary for restoring the Gordon estates and titles and received a message from her son suggesting that she could smuggle in sheets or a rope ladder under a lidded serving dish. In view of her pregnancy and the presence of guards looking down at her windows from above, Mary vetoed this plan. When Lady Huntly made other suggestions, Lindsay became suspicious and had her removed. Fortuitously, she had by then hidden a message scribbled by Mary next to the skin under her chemise and, although she was searched, it was not found. This instructed Bothwell and Huntly to bring a troop of armed horsemen to Seton on the next evening to escort her to Dunbar, the nearest impregnable royal fortress, which Bothwell's sister still occupied. She also instructed Mar, now the Keeper, to hold Edinburgh Castle on her behalf. Traquair, the Captain of the Guard, was to come on the next evening with Arthur Erskine and Anthony Standen bringing horses outside the walls. In the meantime, she continued to feign labour pains.

Moray, William Leslie and Kirkcaldy had arrived secretly in Edinburgh shortly before Riccio's murder, but remained in hiding until his death was confirmed by the king. They then came to him at Holyrood, where he greeted them thankfully, before they went on to the Canongate to dine with Morton at his home. Mary had refused to see Morton and Ruthven all that day, but, on learning of Moray's arrival, she summoned him. He was still dining with Morton when her message arrived, but hurried to her for an emotional reunion. He expressed shock at Riccio's murder, and denied being the 'chief promoter of the atrocities', as was rumoured.[32] She seemed to accept this, and told him that, if he had been there on the previous evening, he would have protected her. She agreed to a reconciliation, claiming that, but for the king, she would have recalled him much earlier. Yet, when he made an emotional plea for the conspirators to be pardoned, she refused. He then advised her to be reconciled to the king.

Mary tried to gain the king's confidence, appealing to his masculinity by offering to sleep with him. After Moray had departed back to Morton, she again invited him to her bedchamber. This must have raised the conspirators' suspicions that her labour pains were a sham and that she was seeking his help. As they still held the bond in which he had authorised the murder, they were not unduly concerned, but, without this, the coup lost its semblance of legality. To stop the king joining the queen, the conspirators seem to have nobbled him by making him hopelessly drunk, causing him to pass out in a stupor in his bedchamber. At midnight, George Douglas took Ruthven to see him spread-eagled across his bed. Neither Randolph nor Bedford, in their reports to Cecil, could understand why he failed to go to her. At dawn, Ruthven woke him to reprove him for not keeping his assignation, although he had almost certainly played his part in preventing it. The king now climbed the privy stairs to seek a pardon for them.

The king sat beside Mary's bed for an hour while she slept, or feigned to do so. When she awoke, she was understandably off-hand. 'Why did you not come up yesternight?' she asked. He claimed to have overslept, but replied: 'Now I am come, and offer myself to have lyen down by you.'[33] She said she was too unwell for love-making and started to dress, while he sought a pardon for the conspirators to protect his position with them. To give them a false sense of security, Mary sent him back 'very merrily' to confirm that she would grant them a pardon, if they came to her.[34] Despite their scepticism, he swore on his life that she was serious, but, when she sent the midwife and physician to plead for her to be removed to 'some sweeter and pleasanter air', they saw her offer as 'but craft and policy', and asked for her to put her offer of a pardon in writing.[35] When he returned, she set out for him the facts of political life. If she pardoned them, they would not need to give him the Crown Matrimonial, and, in any event, parliament would need to be recalled for its ratification. If he became a Reformer, he would lose any remaining credibility with European heads of state, and, if not, the conspirators would topple him. Realising she was right, he agreed to escape with her that night.

In the late afternoon, Moray came with Morton, Ruthven and Lindsay, and they knelt down before Mary, but she refused to pardon them. When Moray lectured her to show clemency, she scathingly replied that 'ever since her earliest youth, her nobility and others of her people, had given her frequently opportunities of practising that virtue and becoming familiar with it'. To justify her 'blotting out the past', they needed to demonstrate good conduct.[36] Each in turn grudgingly begged forgiveness. When Morton's hose became blood-stained after he had knelt where Riccio had died, he claimed: 'The loss of one mean man is of less consequence than the ruin of many lords and gentlemen.'[37] Mary replied: 'I was never bloodthirsty nor greedy upon your lands and goods since coming into Scotland, nor will I be upon you.'[38] She used her threatened miscarriage to bring the conversation to an abrupt end, but left word with the king that she would 'put all things in oblivion as if they had never been', if they produced written pardons for her signature.[39] Although these would be highly incriminating if left unsigned, they agreed to prepare them, after the midwife again confirmed the serious-ness of her condition.

Mary sent one of her ladies to Melville to ask Moray not to join the other lords for dinner. He came to see her alone with the king, and the three of them walked hand in hand for more than an hour, while she attempted to reconcile them. Being doubtful if she would sign the pardons, Moray took the line that the other conspirators were traitors, in the hope that this would encourage her to make her peace with him. He knew that the king would not protect them, but believed he could arrange their rehabilitation, once back in power. Although the conspirators feared that he was turning his back on them, despite what they had done for him, Morton understood his objective.

At six o'clock, the king collected the pardons from the conspirators for Mary's signature, but she instructed him to delay his return by taking his supper before rejoining them. When Archibald Douglas returned to collect them, it was already late and the king claimed she was unwell, but would sign them in the morning. He then arranged for her remaining guards to be removed, as he would stay with her. Maitland seems to have advised them 'that it would not avail them in law if there were the least appearance of restraint upon her'.[40] Given all that had passed, it is hard to see how this would have improved their legal position, but Randolph believed Maitland wanted to help her, as his own objective of removing Riccio had already been achieved. Ruthven warned the king: 'Whatever bloodshed follows will be on your head.'[41] The conspirators now retired for dinner at Morton's home, unwisely leaving their unsigned pardons behind.

Mary and the king now had the chance to escape. At midnight, they were led by Standen and Margaret Carwood, one of Mary's ladies, down the privy staircase and by the back stairs to the servants' quarters, where her French staff would not give them away. They emerged from the back door of the wine cellar into the Canongate cemetery. On seeing Riccio's newly dug grave, the king exclaimed, 'In him I have lost a good and faithful servant. I have been miserably cheated.'[42] Traquair, Standen and Arthur Erskine were waiting outside the wall of the cemetery. Bothwell and Huntly had sum-moned 'their best friends and most loyal of Her Majesty's subjects' to Seton to await her.[43] At the last minute the king asked that Lennox should go with them, as he feared for his life if left behind. Mary angrily refused, as he 'had been too often a traitor to her and hers to be trusted'.[44]

Mary rode pillion behind Arthur Erskine, while Traquair carried one of the Maries, probably Mary Seton, and King Henry rode Standen's horse, with Standen up behind, but he shook so much that Standen had to steady him. They set off for Dunbar, a distance of twenty-five miles, planning a break at Seton. They trotted through the silent Edinburgh streets, but, as soon as they were out of earshot, they cantered the ten miles to Seton, stopping only when Mary vomited. When the king saw a group of horsemen ahead, he feared it was Morton and Ruthven. He spurred on his horse and whipped up Mary's, shouting, 'Come on! Come on! By God's blood, they will murder both you and me if they can catch us.' Exhausted and in pain, Mary told him 'to have some regard for her condition', but 'to push on and take care of himself'.[45] He disgusted everyone when he did so, but the horsemen turned out to be Bothwell, Huntly, Seton, Fleming, Livingston and Balfour.

At Seton, the royal party switched horses and rode their own to Dunbar, arriving at five o'clock in the morning. Despite exhaustion and sickness after five hours in the saddle, Mary was cock-a-hoop. Atholl, Rothes (Andrew Leslie), Marischal, Glencairn, Home and Sir John Maxwell (later Herries) arrived with a strong force. Glencairn needed to rely on the king not to reveal his signature on the murder bond. There were soon 4,000 men pledged to restore Mary to her throne, and she consulted John Leslie on how to avenge the murder.

Chapter 18

A time for compromise

On the morning of 12 March, the conspirators returned to Holyrood to find that Mary and the king had escaped. Without their promised pardons they were doomed. Furious at being left behind, Lennox galloped to Dunbar to take his son to task. Moray, who had distanced himself from the other conspirators, went to the Tolbooth to announce that they would answer any charges in parliament (where no one would accuse them). Morton, Ruthven and Lindsay sent Sempill, who had not been involved in the plot, to Dunbar to ask the queen to fulfil her promise to sign their pardons. Mary refused, keeping Sempill with her for three days. Despite being wary that Elizabeth was behind the murder, Mary dictated a graphic letter to her explaining her ordeal:

> Some of our subjects and council by their proceedings have declared manifestly what they are … having slain our most special servant in our own presence and thereafter held our proper person captive treasonably.[1]

She warned that it could happen to Elizabeth, but apologised for being too tired to write herself. She told both Bethune in Paris and Charles IX that she was not 'in robust health after the bodily indisposition of our person'.[2]

With the king still terrified, Mary forced him to list the conspirators' names. He named Maitland, but not Moray, Argyll or Glencairn. As Moray had not signed the bond, it is possible that the king could not verify his complicity. The king was now shunned by most of Mary's supporters, with Fleming, his former *confidant*, being particularly critical. When Mary tried to intercede, it was clear that he was regarded with ill-concealed contempt. Their loyalty was to Mary alone.

On 15 March, Mary rewarded Bothwell with the wardship of Dunbar, replacing Sir Simon Preston after his failure to rescue her at Holyrood. Five days later, Huntly replaced Morton as Chancellor, and Balfour took over as Clerk-Register. Mary also confirmed Sir John Maxwell to his wife Lady Herries's inheritance at Terregles. She mustered troops at Haddington with a week's provisions to escort her back to Edinburgh. She thanked Melville for his loyalty, when he brought a letter urgently seeking Moray's rehabilitation. The king asked whether Moray had sent him a similar letter, but Melville claimed diplomatically that he considered the king and queen to be as one. Although the king greatly feared the other conspirators, Melville confirmed that they had fled.

On 17 March, after arriving at Haddington, Mary confided in Melville her bitterness towards King Henry. Melville blamed his youth and the bad counsel he kept with George Douglas among others, but he could see the 'great grudges which she held in her heart'.[3] The next day, she made a triumphant return into Edinburgh, acclaimed on all sides; she was supported by Bothwell, Huntly, Home, Seton, Marischal, Archbishop Hamilton and 8,000 men. She refused to go to Holyrood with its horrific associations, but lodged instead at Sir John Maxwell's home in the High Street with cannon positioned outside, and later at the Bishop of Dunkeld's larger house in the Cowgate. Bothwell policed the streets with trained bands supplemented with Hamilton adherents.

Mary could not accuse the king of treason without prejudicing the legitimacy of their unborn child, but Morton, Ruthven, Lindsay, Ker of Fawdonside, George Douglas and sixty-three others were denounced as rebels by the Privy Council in their absence. On 29 March, they were attainted and their homes were stripped of chattels. Atholl took control of Tantallon, temporarily becoming the young Angus's guardian, which entitled him to the income of his estates. Mary particularly blamed Morton because Ker of Fawdonside, who had levelled a pistol at her, was his adherent.

Morton and the other conspirators headed for England. Morton stayed at Alnwick, while the Master of Ruthven took his sick father on to Newcastle. On arrival, they wrote a grovelling letter to Cecil protesting that they had acted on the king's orders and 'for the preservation of the state and the Protestant religion'. Embarrassed at their failure to detain Mary, Elizabeth witheringly advised Morton to find 'some place out of this realm' where he might hide.[4] Although he tried to go to the Netherlands, Mary had already written to prohibit his entry, so he returned into hiding in England. In May, Elizabeth again told the conspirators to leave, but, as so often, this was for public consumption and they remained unmolested in the north. Before Ruthven's death in Newcastle on 13 June 1566, he wrote for her benefit his 'Relation', which justified the murder on the grounds of Riccio's adultery with Mary.

On 21 March, Knox, who had approved the murder, left for Ayrshire, where he wrote his history of the Reformation in Scotland, beseeching God to 'destroy that whore in her whoredom'.[5] Although Maitland remained behind, he was denounced to Mary by both the king and Bothwell. Although he was warded in Inverness, he preferred to hide with Atholl at Dunkeld, hoping he would intercede for him. Although Atholl attempted this, Bothwell had been granted Maitland's attainted estates and blocked his rehabilitation. When Maitland tried to buy a pardon, Randolph had little hope of him succeeding.

Moray was not convinced that Mary had accepted his assurance that he was not party to the murder conspiracy. He and Argyll retired to Linlithgow, where they worked with Cecil to gain the conspirators' rehabilitation. Mary had to be pragmatic; most of the nobility was implicated, and she needed a government. She absolved those who did not appear to have played an active part, sending Balfour to Linlithgow with a pardon for Moray and the former exiles. She undertook to restore their estates, if they returned home and did not intercede on the conspirators' behalf. Argyll and Glencairn were back at Court in ten days.

Although Randolph spread a rumour that Mary had sent emissaries to Rome seeking a divorce from the king, she would not have considered this before her child's birth. She had to confirm his innocence, so as not to prejudice her child's legitimacy. Their *rapprochement* would dispel lingering doubts over an affair with Riccio. On 20 March, the king signed a declaration before the Privy Council 'upon his honour, fidelity and the word of a prince' that he 'never counselled, commanded, consented, assisted nor approved' Riccio's murder. When this was publicly proclaimed at the Mercat Cross the next day, it was 'not without laughter'.[6] 'Acts of the Privy Council continued to be promulgated in the names of "their Majesties", and Darnley continued to sign State papers, or the stamp of his signature was used in his absence'.[7] Easter was celebrated with full Catholic ritual, allowing the king to be seen as a pious Catholic by the visiting ambassadors. Although Mary was contemptuous of his disloyalty to his fellow conspirators, she had to deflect rumours that he had acted out of revenge, particularly after arranging for Riccio's body to be reburied in 'a fair tomb' at Holyrood Abbey Church.[8]

The king gave orders for the henchmen to be arrested, resulting in Henry Yair, Thomas Scott, Sir John Mowbray of Barnbougle and William Harlaw being condemned to be hanged and quartered. Yet Bothwell stepped in at the scaffold to reprieve Mowbray and Harlaw, who were Lothian lairds. The conspirators in exile were so furious with the king that they sent Mary the bond he had signed, which authorised that the murder should take place in her presence. If they were permitted to return, he would face a blood feud.

Moray provided Mary with the bond signed in Newcastle. This disclosed the king's offers to pardon the exiles and to maintain the religious *status quo* in return for them granting him the Crown Matrimonial. She now knew he had betrayed Riccio, her unborn child, his fellow conspirators and herself. She kept him out of her bed and state affairs, but he remained in residence with her in the High Street, where he could be watched, and to keep up appearances. He was caught trying to go to Stirling to rebuild bridges with Moray and Argyll, but they were already travelling to Edinburgh to see Mary. He was isolated and Randolph reported that he planned to visit Flanders 'to move his case to any prince who' would listen. Although Lennox was banned from Court, he remained at Holyrood, 'sore troubled in mind' and still ill, but the king visited him only once.[9]

With Mary about to move to the royal apartments at Edinburgh Castle to await the birth of her child, she realised it was politically expedient to tolerate Moray, and she remained socially on good terms with him and his wife. Yet she did not trust him, and Bothwell 'now began to be in great favour', becoming, in effect, her chief adviser and the most influential member of the Privy Council.[10] She praised his administrative 'dexterity', which was 'so acceptable to us that we could never to this hour forget it', particularly after masterminding her escape.[11] The captaincy of Dunbar brought him the income of its surrounding lands and he still held the fertile lands of Haddington Abbey and Lethington from Maitland's attainted estates, even though Maitland's father was still residing at Lethington. As a soldier, he combined resource, dependability and the leadership to muster Borderers to his command. Although a Reformer, he had always supported Mary and her mother, despite his imprisonment in both Edinburgh Castle and the Tower.

Bothwell's strongly Reformist stance ended the government's swing towards Catholicism. By an Act of Council, benefices worth less than 300 marks annually were automatically granted to Presbyterian incumbents, and some were taken up. Stipends for ministers were much greater than the pittance previously offered to the priesthood. The Kirk received £10,000 from the Crown out of Catholic Church revenues. Yet, with Mary dependent on papal funding, she could not allow the Catholic powers on the Continent to think that she was abandoning them. She sent the Bishop of Dunblane to Rome to advise the Pope of Riccio's murder, and asked her uncle, the Cardinal, to seek further Vatican aid for her. She hoped that the Pope would understand the delicate balance she had to follow, but he sent the fanatical Nicholas de Gouda as his Nuncio, accompanied by Father Edmund Hay, Rector of the Jesuit College in Paris, to assess her situation. Philip II was shocked, not only at Mary's rapidly changing religious stance, but that the fervently Catholic king had joined with heretics in a murder conspiracy.

Mary's more conciliatory religious stance, coupled with Riccio's removal, encouraged Elizabeth to renew her correspondence with her. Elizabeth was genuinely shocked at the manner of Riccio's murder, sending warnings to both the king and Moray never again to betray Mary. The king feared that reprisals would be taken against his mother in the Tower and wrote to confirm that she was in no way involved. With Elizabeth in sympathy with Mary, she refused to receive his letter. She told de Silva, 'Had I been in Queen Mary's place, I would have taken my husband's dagger and stabbed him with it!'[12] Robert Melville came north to assure Mary of her support, and, on 4 April, to the king's chagrin, Mary invited Elizabeth to stand as godmother to their unborn child. On delivering the message, Melville suggested to Elizabeth that it was an opportunity for them to meet, 'whereat she smiled'. The king asked Charles IX to be a godfather, but Philip II was ignored, perhaps because of his recent coolness, although Mary invited his close ally, the Duke of Savoy.

Despite his administrative skills, Bothwell was not an ideal political adviser and was hated by the English. He lacked the diplomacy of Moray and Maitland, and was out of his depth with Cecil's subtleties. He lacked the patience to use persuasion, preferring differences to be settled with a duel. In Mary's memoirs, written while imprisoned in England, Claude Nau, her secretary, recorded, 'He was a man whose natural disposition made him anything but agreeable or inclined to put himself to much trouble or inconvenience to gain the goodwill of those with whom he was associated.'[13] At the time of her confinement in June, Cecil's brother-in-law, Sir Henry Killigrew, had been sent to Scotland to replace Randolph as British Ambassador. He was always sent north when matters of extreme delicacy needed to be handled, and he reported that Bothwell's influence was greater than all the other lords together, making him 'the most hated man in Scotland'. Despite being a Reformer, Bothwell enjoyed 'a cup too many' with the Bishop of Ross, who, as Mary's ecclesiastical adviser, was writing his *Actis and Constitutionis of the Realme of Scotland from the Reigne of James I* as part of his reform of Scottish law.

Bothwell was now aged 30 and, at 5ft 6ins, was not handsome, despite a string of female conquests. In May 1566, while visiting Haddington with his wife, he enjoyed a fifteen-minute liaison in the steeple of the abbey with her serving maid, 20-year-old Bessie Crawford, a blacksmith's daughter. On a second occasion, Bessie's black hair was in disarray after a tryst in a chamber within the cloister, and he needed help to rebutton his trousers. Jean dismissed Bessie in fury and appears to have received the lands of Nether Hailes from her husband as a peace offering. Mary was not immune to his appeal. As Sir John Maxwell, soon to become Lord Herries, explained:

> He was high in his own conceit, proud, vicious and vainglorious above measure, who would attempt anything out of ambition. His reckless daring appealed to her romantic sentiments, while his strong character and resolute purpose contrasted forcibly with the weakness of her husband Darnley, and his inability to control or protect her.[14]

Yet there is no realistic evidence of impropriety between them prior to King Henry's death, or that they contemplated marriage. Historians have been unjustifiably coloured by the flawed evidence provided in 1568 for the Conferences at York and Westminster, designed to blacken Mary's name.

Chapter 19

James's birth and its aftermath

While awaiting her child's birth, Mary was under the protection of Mar, hereditary Keeper of Edinburgh Castle and Governor of Stirling. She could not face Holyrood, with the nightmare of Riccio's murder fresh in her mind, but she regularly presided over the Privy Council. This now consisted of Bothwell, Huntly, Atholl, Seton, Livingston and Fleming. She wanted sound government during her confinement, but, with Bothwell proving politically inept, needed Moray's reasoned leadership and close English ties. She tried everything to achieve accord. She used Castelnau to appease rivalries, and he gained respect for his impartiality in brokering the return of Moray, Argyll and Glencairn.

On 21 April, Mary recalled Moray and Argyll to Edinburgh and was formally reconciled with them, but she kept them with her at the castle to keep her eye on them. The king opposed their rehabilitation and was supported in this by Bothwell, Huntly and the Bishop of Ross. Mary did not listen. On 29 April, she formally reappointed Moray, Argyll and Glencairn to the Privy Council. She held a feast to reconcile them with Bothwell, Huntly and Atholl, and they joined hands as a symbol that they would work together. Although Bothwell used his influence to keep Maitland sidelined at Dunkeld, when he offered to hunt him down and kill him for his part in Riccio's murder, Moray stepped in to protect him. Despite lacking cohesion, the Council was united in its disaffection for the king, who was almost without friends. Among the nobility, only Atholl and Lennox would talk to him, and Lennox, who had moved to Dunbar after being banned from Court, was much offended with him. The king told Lennox that Mary would not sleep with him and, a few weeks before the child was born, she had recommended that he should take a mistress, saying cynically, 'I assure you I shall never love you the worse.'[1*] Lennox was evidently shocked. He told the king to be a faithful husband to Mary, and the king responded: 'I never offended the queen my wife in meddling with any woman, in thought, let be in deed.'[2] This was a blatant lie as, during her lying in, he was 'vagabondising' in the Edinburgh brothels with his young male friends.[3] If he were to be led astray, Mary would have preferred an aristocratic mistress, who 'might have a civilizing influence on him'.[4] He would also ride off alone along the coast, stripping to swim in lonely lochs and rivers, paying no attention when she told him to avoid such risks. Randolph had reported: 'He is neither accompanied for, nor looked for by any nobleman, attended by certain of his own servants, and 6 or 8 of his guard, he is at liberty to do or go what or where he will.'[5] Although he was cold-shouldered, he was being given enough freedom to plot, but was being carefully watched. He was a marked man.

The king's one supporter of influence was Balfour, who had fallen out with the queen, but even he was soon of doubtful loyalty. The king seemed oblivious of his precarious standing, and, like Bothwell, wanted Maitland kept away from Court, lest he should reveal his part in the murder. He again suggested appointing the Bishop of Ross as Secretary of State, and was furious when Mary turned this down. He sent a message that he had two pistols hanging on the back of his bed, primed and ready to shoot himself. She coolly went to his bedchamber, where he lay in a drunken stupor, to retrieve them. Despite stirring up old factions in an attempt to improve his own standing, he was universally shunned. Although Melville attempted to mediate, Mary told Moray to reprove him for associating with the king.

With Lennox away from Court, the Spanish Ambassador reported that the king did not 'seem bad personally, or in his habits'. He passed his time 'mostly in warlike exercises, being' commended for his horsemanship.[6] With Mary being conciliatory to the Reformers, the king again attempted to improve his flagging image abroad with letters to foreign heads of state to show he was the more ardent papist, hoping to be accepted as the Catholic pretender to the English Crown. He still denied any part in the 'conspiracy whereof he is slanderously and sakelessly traduced', only admitting to having rehabilitated the exiled lords from England without authority. He wrote to Charles IX professing his innocence. To avoid the humiliation of having to return the Order of St Michel, he explained: 'I am greatly wronged by a rumour which makes me guilty of a deed which I truly detest'.[7] He signed his letter as King of Scotland, sealing it with the royal arms. He corresponded with de Alava, the Spanish ambassador in Paris, with whom he became 'an intimate friend',[8] and on 29 April de Silva informed Philip II that he was hearing Mass every day. He wrote to Philip and the Pope that Scotland was 'out of order', criticising Mary for failing to restore Catholicism. Philip acknowledged the letter, which the king interpreted as encouragement. Cecil infiltrated the king's household with a spy named William Rogers, who reported that he claimed to have at least forty English supporters involved in a scatter-brained plan to gain control of both

Scarborough Castle and the Scilly Isles as bridgeheads for a Spanish invasion.[9] Sir Richard Chamberlain, a long-standing associate of the Lennoxes
in Yorkshire, was the Captain of Scarborough Castle, and he had placed it
at Darnley's disposal should he seek to travel to Flanders to elicit Spanish
support. Darnley had also received a map of the Scilly Isles from unnamed
supporters in the West Country. Yet there is no evidence that Philip backed
either plan, as he was relying on Guise assistance for his military objectives
in the Netherlands. It was Mary, not the king, who remained the focus of
English Catholic intrigue to replace Elizabeth. Just as Cecil had feared, her
pregnancy had caused her stock to rise.

One adverse outcome of the king's diplomacy following Riccio's murder was that Philip became wary of supporting Mary. Yet she remained the
papal focus for a Counter-Reformation. On 12 May, the Pope promised
her 150,000 crowns, but wanted to be sure that it would be used to restore
Catholicism. He sent the hardline Jesuit, Vincenzo Laureo, as his Nuncio to
confirm this. Laureo, who had recently been appointed Bishop of Mondovi,
left Rome on 6 June, planning to visit his new see, before travelling to Savoy
and then on to Scotland.

With so much rumour of Catholic plotting, Cecil wanted to test Mary's
loyalty to Elizabeth, and, without telling his mistress, used an *agent provoca-
teur*, Christopher Rokesby, to entice her into a plot to gain the English throne.
Rokesby arrived in Scotland in May, posing as a Catholic fleeing English
persecution. He ingratiated himself with Bothwell, who arranged for him to
meet Mary. He presented her with an ivory crucifix and, after confirming
the strength of Catholic support for her in England, asked her to back an
English plot for Elizabeth's assassination. Mary became suspicious when
he suggested that she should discuss it with her Privy Council. Being eight
months pregnant, she was in no mood for intrigue, but Rokesby returned
to England to build a dossier of purported supporters. On his return, Mary
had him arrested and seized his papers. Among them were Cecil's highly
incriminating instructions in cipher. Killigrew, who knew what was afoot,
wrote immediately to warn Cecil of trouble. With Mary preparing for her
confinement she did not react immediately, but later wrote to Cecil:

> Since our first arrival within our realm of Scotland, We ever had a
> good opinion of you, that you at all times had done the office of a
> faithful minister. Yet these were shaken by the strange dealings of
> an Englishman named Rokesby, ... [and] began a little to suspend
> our judgement, until we receive further trial therein.[10]

She knew that Elizabeth would not tolerate his underhand approach, and he would be embarrassed if she were told. She was trying to buy his loyalty by saving his bacon. When Melville met him in London, he reported that Cecil was 'nothing altered' in his 'good inclination' towards her, to which Mary smugly confirmed, 'of the which we were not a little rejoiced'.[11] Rokesby remained imprisoned at Spynie until she was sent to Lochleven.

Although Bothwell and Huntly remained her most influential advisers, Mary refused their request for Moray to be imprisoned during her confinement to stop him trying to usurp authority. Despite their warnings of his intimate involvement in Riccio's murder, she put him in charge of the government. He promptly refused them lodgings in Edinburgh Castle. This forced her to bar them all from dining with her for a period to keep the peace. She then riled everyone with a show of defiance by appointing Riccio's 18-year-old nephew, Joseph (Giuseppe), who had come to Scotland in Castelnau's train, as her new French Secretary.

Before her confinement, Mary asked the Bishop of Ross to prepare three copies of her will, one for her Guise relations, one for herself and one for her chosen regents. The regency document has not survived, but it is known that she appointed a committee of three, made up of Argyll, Mar and probably the king. The king resented Argyll and Mar's inclusion, but she wanted a conciliatory voice to manage the government with absolute loyalty to the Stewarts. Neither Bothwell nor Moray would have been acceptable, but the lords all signed an undertaking to be bound by it, although she no doubt avoided divulging its contents to them.

The principal part of Mary's will dealt with bequests of her jewellery. An inventory of 250 lots was compiled on sixteen folio pages by Mary Sempill [Livingston] and Margaret Carwood, who were responsible for it. They signed each page, although Carwood's signature is laboriously drawn and she was probably illiterate. Mary annotated her wishes for each item in the margins. If she died, everything except a few specified items was left to her unborn child. If her child also died, there was a range of bequests for those close to her. Her finest gems were to be added in perpetuity to the Scottish crown jewels. These included 'The Great Harry', Henry II's gift on her marriage to the Dauphin. Other principal items were to go to her Guise relations, with a gift of rubies and pearls to pass through successive generations to the first-born of their family. The murdered Duke's children were each to receive rich jewels, particularly his youngest son, Francis, her godson, who was named after her first husband. Anne d'Este, the Duke's widow, was to receive other fabulous items and the Abbess Renée, Mary's aunt, was the beneficiary of several chattels including a portrait of Elizabeth. Other Guise nephews and nieces were each remembered and the Cardinal of Lorraine was to receive an emerald ring. There were twenty-six bequests for King Henry, although these seem to have been the return of gifts he had made to her. One was a diamond ring in a red enameled setting, against which Mary wrote, 'It was with this that I was married; I leave it to the king who gave it to me' – hardly a show of affection.[12] There were smaller items for both Lennox and Margaret Douglas. She remembered her Scottish relatives including Jean, Countess of Argyll, Moray and his wife, and her godson Francis Stewart, son of Lord John Stewart and Jean Hepburn. (He later became Francis Stewart-Hepburn, 5th Earl of Bothwell, and would gain a place in history as the principal thorn in the side of James VI.) There were gifts for her household including her equerry, Arthur Erskine, her ladies-in-waiting, including the four Maries, Margaret, Countess of Atholl, Mary Seton's mother, Marie Pyerres, Mary Bethune's mother, Joanne de la Reyneville, her French Secretary, Joseph Riccio, and other servants. She remembered members of the nobility, including Bothwell, Huntly, Argyll, Atholl and the Dowager Lady Huntly, although none received special treatment. The notable exclusions were Maitland and the Hamiltons, then out of favour. The University of St Andrews was to receive her Greek and Latin books.

By 3 June, Mary had withdrawn for her confinement, still depressed at her husband's shortcomings. She had told Castelnau that she would have preferred to convalesce in France for three months afterwards, but would resist the temptation to return there permanently. With concern for her security, she placed Argyll in an adjacent room to protect her night and day. Margaret Asteane, who was appointed as midwife, was given a new black gown. It was another fifteen days before she began her labour, which proved difficult and protracted. The Countess of Atholl used sorcery to cast the pains onto Margaret, Lady Forbes of Reres, also a Lady-in-Waiting and a member of the ubiquitous Bethune family. She had married Sir Arthur Forbes of Reres and was Mary Bethune's aunt. She suffered magnificently without providing the queen with any apparent relief. Mary was 'so handled that she began to wish that she had never been married', praying for the baby to be saved rather than herself.[13] After twenty hours, a son was born between ten and eleven o'clock on the morning of 19 June. Although Mary was exhausted, James, Duke of Rothesay's abundant health caused great rejoicing, with artillery being fired from the castle and 500 bonfires being lit in Edinburgh alone.

Mary Ogilvy [Bethune] gave the news to Sir James Melville. Within the hour, he set off to tell Elizabeth and to invite her to become a godmother, arriving in London only five days later. Elizabeth, who was at Greenwich, was told of the birth by Cecil. With understandable jealousy, she complained, 'Alack, the Queen of Scots is lighter of a bonny son, and I am but of barren stock.'[14] Yet she received Melville 'with a merry countenance' on the following day, agreeing to become a godmother, but turning down his suggestion that she should visit Scotland. Far from weakening Mary's claim to the English throne, the king had immeasurably strengthened it by siring a male heir. Yet his son was now the heir to the Scottish throne and Mary treated Darnley with disdain. He visited her to see the child and she tried to stop any lingering rumours by making a solemn oath to him before Sir William Stainley that James was 'begotten by none but you'.[15*] With James's obvious Lennox looks, as confirmed by his early portraits, she reportedly said: 'He is so much your son that I fear it will be the worse for him hereafter.'[16] He responded: 'Sweet Madam, is this your promise that you made to forgive and forget all?' Mary answered: 'I have forgiven all, but will never forget! What if Fawdonside's pistol had shot, what would have become of him [Prince James] and me both?'[17] Their relationship had completely broken down, but he never denied the child's paternity and, on the same day, wrote to the Cardinal of Lorraine to announce his birth, requesting that Charles IX should stand as godfather.

On the next day, Killigrew joined the nobility to give thanks at St Giles's for the delivery of an heir. He reported continuing disquiet among rival factions, but went on to visit the queen, who was still weak from her ordeal. She excused a lengthy interview, speaking faintly with a hollow cough, but he saw the prince suckling at Helen Little, his wet nurse, and 'afterwards as good as naked ... well proportioned, and likely to prove a goodly prince'.[18] (There are records that Lady Forbes of Reres was the wet nurse. Buchanan described her as a 'woman very heavy, laith by unwieldy age and fatty substance'. While she had charge of nursery arrangements, it is unlikely that she suckled the prince.) Although James remained with his nurse by day, he slept at night in a cradle by Mary's bed, as she still feared that the king might attempt to kidnap him in the hope of ruling on his behalf.

The birth of a son made Mary more confident to promote her claim to the English throne, but she had no intention of promoting the king. She communicated with Catholics both in England and on the Continent and wrote to the Pope welcoming Mondovi's forthcoming visit on 17 July. This strained her relationship with Moray, who was still seeking the repatriation of Morton and his fellow exiles, and she continued to mistrust him. There was rejoicing in Paris, where Patrick Adamson, a Scottish Presbyterian minister, wrote verses referring to James as the most serene Prince of Scotland, England, France and Ireland. This brought furious protests from Elizabeth, and he spent six months imprisoned for his indiscretion.

Mary recovered only slowly, and the pain in her side recurred, leaving her depressed. In late July, with her doctors advising a change of air, Moray and Mar escorted her by sea down the Firth of Forth, where, as Buchanan reported, 'she joyed to handle the boisterous cables.'[19] She recuperated at Alloa Tower, Mar's home near Stirling, in company with her intimate friends, the Countesses of Mar, Argyll and Moray. As Lord High Admiral, Bothwell arranged the sea trip, but did not travel with them.[20*] The king was not told of the visit in advance, but, when he learned where Mary had gone, rode to Alloa to join them. She could not abide having him near her, and he left in a few hours after a massive row. Castelnau also joined them at Alloa, having been briefed by Catherine de Medici to reconcile the royal couple. He reported the king's arrival, but barely saw him.

Mary relaxed at Alloa for several days, and Mar arranged dancing, masques and sports, which she enjoyed with the Court ladies. John Spottiswood, an acolyte of Knox, was deputed by the General Assembly to visit her to congratulate her on her son's birth and to request a Reformist baptism. Not surprisingly Mary refused. She also received Maitland, who tried to negotiate his rehabilitation, but she would not agree to it. Despite Lady Moray's opportunity to plead for her husband's return to favour, Bothwell remained in authority, and, on 30 June, Mary granted him the Priory of North Berwick. Kirkcaldy claimed that he 'hath now of all men greatest access and familiarity with the queen, so that nothing of importance is done without him'. This made him 'the most hated man among the noblemen of this realm, and it is said that his insolence is such that David [Riccio] was never more abhorred than he is now disliked on every side'.[21] Yet, at this time, there was no hint of him conducting an affair with Mary.

The king's relationship with the Queen continued to deteriorate. Bedford reported:

> The Queen and her husband agree after the old manner, or rather worse. She eateth but very seldom with him, but lieth not nor keepeth no company with him, nor loveth any such as love him … It cannot for modesty nor the honour of a Queen be reported what she said to him.[22]

She did nothing to conceal her contempt for him and used the excuse of wanting to be with her child to avoid having to spend time with him. The king's response to being cold-shouldered was 'a renewed plunge into dissipation'.[23] She 'fell marvellously' out with Melville for having given Henry an Irish water spaniel, saying 'she could not trust him who would give any thing to such one as she loved not'.[24] Later, when travelling back to France, Castelnau claimed to Bedford that they were reconciled, but this was either wishful thinking or an attempt to deceive him. One of Bedford's own spies reported, 'He cannot bear that the queen should use familiarity either with men or women, and especially the ladies of Argyll, Moray and Mar.'[25] When she failed to pay him due attention, he stormed out in a tantrum.

Mary warned Moray that the king was threatening to kill him and, on her return to Edinburgh, she deliberately humiliated her husband before the whole Court by telling him that 'she would not be content that either he or any other should be unfriendly to Moray'. She asked him to admit that his hatred arose from hearsay 'that Moray was not his friend, which made him speak that which he repented'.[26] The king told his father of this lack of respect and her continuing refusal to sleep with him. With his plotting against Moray continuing, he was still being watched. Bothwell also wanted Moray out of the way; he proposed that George Douglas should be offered a pardon in return for providing evidence to incriminate Moray and Maitland in Riccio's murder, but Mary knew their importance in government. Moray retaliated by inciting border lairds, who had English support, into a confederacy against Bothwell; he was forced to leave Edinburgh to deal with them. Moray is also thought to have instigated a story that William Ker, Abbot of Kelso, who was under Bothwell's protection, had revealed Glencairn's involvement in Riccio's murder with 'infamy and words of dishonour'.[27] When the Abbot was murdered, Bothwell, on 28 July, had to travel to Kelso to investigate.

Mary was still depressed and continued to suffer from the pain in her side. On 3 August, she paid another five-day visit to Alloa. Except on social terms, she no longer trusted Moray, although he remained at Court, but she had no other able advisers to assist her in re-establishing her authority. She wanted religious tolerance, but, with Bothwell in control, the Catholic nobility remained marginalised. Recognising his political shortcomings, she increasingly took advice from Atholl, who was guided behind the scenes by Maitland. It was on her second visit to Alloa that Atholl and Moray again requested Maitland's rehabilitation, and he formally submitted to her at Stirling on 4 August. The only evidence that he had masterminded Riccio's murder was the king's increasingly unreliable word; after dining with him alone, she reappointed him as Secretary of State. He immediately advised Cecil and, by 11 August, was back in Edinburgh for an official reconciliation with Bothwell. He could now use his persuasion to gain the exiled conspirators' rehabilitation, but Mary was still not ready to forgive them. His reappointment also heralded the growing prominence of Atholl, causing Argyll, as his long-term enemy, to be left in the wilderness.

Maitland's reappointment shows that Bothwell did not have things all his own way. As Maitland's estates were restored, Bothwell had to relinquish the Abbacy of Haddington, but remained for a considerable period in occupation, leaving them at daggers drawn. There were unverified rumours that Maitland attempted to poison Bothwell, 'who had grown so hated that he cannot long continue', particularly because of his opposition to the exiles' return.[28] Maitland certainly combined with Moray to reduce Bothwell's influence.

While in Alloa, Mary received word that Mondovi was waiting in Paris for the call to visit Scotland, but she replied that his arrival would cause 'great tumults', and she could not receive him with the honour he deserved.[29] Despite her earlier encouragement to the Pope, a Counter-Reformation was out of the question, and Moray had persuaded the nobility to refuse him entry. John Bethune, Master of the Household, was sent to Paris with her apologies, causing Mondovi to send a stern rebuke. He instructed her to restore the Catholic faith, and Bethune returned with a proportion of the promised subsidy as an inducement. On 21 August, Mondovi wrote to the Cardinal of Alessandria in Rome that Mary's difficulties

> might be obviated if the King of Spain should come, as it is hoped, with a strong force to Flanders ... If justice were executed against the six rebels, who were leaders and originators of the late treason against the queen, [their] deaths would effectually restore peace and obedience in the kingdom.

He named them as Moray, Argyll, Morton, Maitland, Justice-Clerk Bellenden and former Clerk–Register MacGill, 'a man of no family and contriver of all evil'. This confirms that Moray was now generally believed to have been behind Riccio's murder. Mondovi described the king as 'an ambitious and inconstant youth, [who] would like to rule the realm'.[30] Yet with Mary being lukewarm, he saw the king as the only means of restoring Catholicism and of bringing the lords involved in Riccio's murder to book.

From the distance of Paris, he had not seen matters for himself, but the Pope naïvely approved of what he was proposing.

Following Maitland's reappointment, the king went hunting and was increasingly ostracised at Court. He seems to have remained in touch with Philip II, now in the final stages of his planned invasion of the Netherlands, and Anthony Standen (the father of Sir Anthony, who had protected Mary during Riccio's murder) left Scotland to assist his Catholic plotting at this time and remained abroad until 1605.[31] It was quite probably Mary's need to keep tabs on the king, which persuaded her to resume sexual relations with him. On 13 August, she made a large payment to him from her Treasury, and provided cloth of gold to furnish caparisons for his horse and a magnificent upholstered bed that had belonged to the queen regent. Although this implies some sort of reconciliation, he was still frequenting Edinburgh brothels.

In mid-August, Mary joined the king for stag hunting at Meggetland, south of Peebles, accompanied by Bothwell, Huntly, Moray, Atholl and Mar. This does not suggest very harmonious company. By then, Buchanan claimed that she was behaving 'capriciously, arrogantly and disdainfully' towards him. On 19 August, she travelled on to Traquair on the Tweed, where the king unexpectedly joined them.[32] The hunting had been disappointing and Mary remained unwell, but at supper he asked her to accompany him for another chase on the following day. Mary later told Nau, 'Knowing that if she did so, she would be required to gallop her horse at a great pace, she whispered in his ear that she suspected that she was pregnant.' Although this seems to confirm that they were back in bed together, it was only two months since James's birth, and she could not have known if she had conceived. Yet it makes Buchanan's suggestion of her conducting a relationship with Bothwell at this stage even less likely. The king's infamously brutal response was: 'Never mind, if we lose this one, we will make another.' Traquair, who had been the king's close ally, having been knighted by him at the time of the royal marriage, 'now rebuked him sharply', saying 'he did not speak like a Christian'. The king retorted: 'What! Ought we not to work a mare well when she is in foal?'[33] It is no surprise that *rapprochement* failed.

On 22 August, Mary interrupted her visit to return to Holyrood for two days after hearing that 'the king, by the assistance of some of our nobility, should take the Prince our son and crown him; and being crowned, his father should take upon him the government'.[34] The prince was still being cared for by Mar and his wife at Edinburgh Castle. Mary decided to move him to the safety of Stirling, the traditional childhood home for royal children. She took no chances and, on 31 August, Lady Reres set out with the prince in a litter escorted by between 400 and 500 hackbutters. The queen personally supervised the security arrangements for the royal nursery at Stirling, appointing Bothwell as captain of the prince's bodyguard. To maintain appearances, she then rejoined the king to hunt at Glenartney near Loch Earn in Perthshire, going on to Drummond Castle near Crieff before returning to Stirling. Although her health had not improved, she was not pregnant.

On 6 September, Mary returned to Edinburgh to plan the celebration for James's baptism. Although she stayed initially at the Exchequer House in the Cowgate, by 12 September, she was back at Holyrood.[35*] The king remained at Stirling, apparently in a foul mood at Maitland's reappointment as Secretary of State. He was visited by Lennox, who wrote to Mary of his son's humiliation and intention to go abroad, as he felt unsafe in Scotland. Morton, who was keeping tabs from England on the king's movements, reported that a ship was waiting for him in the Clyde. The king apparently planned to go to France, hoping to support himself on Mary's dowry, but he was also in touch with Philip II in Flanders; Alison Weir has suggested that this was his destination. It would appear that it was Lennox who persuaded the king not to leave Scotland or to desert his wife, and he warned Mary of what was afoot.

Although Mary visited Stirling to talk through the king's concerns, he refused to return with her to Holyrood. When back in Edinburgh, she showed Lennox's letter to the Privy Council, who resolved to talk to the king. His scheming from abroad would be even more dangerous than at home. A week later, to universal surprise he appeared in Edinburgh, but refused to visit Holyrood until the Council members had been dismissed. This embarrassed Mary and offended them. She tackled him privately about his intentions. Although he confirmed the presence of a ship in the Clyde, he would not divulge his plan for departure. This caused '*une forte belle harangue*' [a big slanging match], witnessed by the new French ambassador, Philibert du Croc, who had replaced Castelnau.[36] She

> took him by the hand, and besought him for God's sake to declare
> if she had given him reason for this resolution [to go abroad]; and
> entreated he might deal plainly, and not spare her. [She had] a clear
> conscience, and that all her life she had done no action which could
> anywise prejudice either his or her honour.[37]

When pressed, he denied that she had given him any justification to leave, complaining only at being shunned as king. As he left, he whispered theatrically, '*Adieu, Madame*, you shall not see my face for a long space'.[38] She was visibly upset, but was advised by both the Council and du Croc to continue her wise and virtuous existence.

Du Croc told Catherine de Medici that the Scots were 'so well reconciled with the queen as a result of her own prudent behaviour, that nowadays there was not a single division to be seen between them'.[39] If Mary had been conducting an affair with Bothwell at this time, the king would surely have cited it to gain sympathy. After leaving for Glasgow with his father, he wrote to Mary confirming his plan to sail, but complained only at his lack of authority. Mary showed the letter to the Council, who confirmed that they would not give him control of public affairs. Melville told Archbishop Bethune in Paris that the king was using the threat of departure to gain the dismissal of Maitland, MacGill and Bellenden. Yet Mary told him that he had only himself to blame and should regain the nobility's respect. She told Lennox that the king had no cause for complaint. The Council took no chances; they wrote to Catherine de Medici with a full account of his behaviour, lest he should attempt to set up a royal court in exile. Du Croc reported to both Archbishop Bethune and Catherine that, although his ship remained in readiness, he was still in Scotland, continuing his hunting and fishing. He explained:

> It is vain to imagine that he should be able to raise any disturbance, for there is not one person in all the kingdom, from the highest to the lowest, that regards him any further than is agreeable to the Queen. And I never saw her majesty so much beloved, esteemed and honoured.[40]

In late September, Moray gained Council support for a second time to refuse Mondovi's visit to Scotland, but Mary failed to tell Mondovi, and he remained in Paris awaiting her call. By now, Pius V believed that the threat of Philip II's delayed invasion of Flanders would be needed for the mission to succeed. By mid-October, Mondovi realised that Mary was stalling, and the Pope recalled him to his see. The Cardinal of Lorraine half-heartedly agreed to intercede, but tried to discourage Mondovi from doing 'something signal for the service of God in Scotland'.[41]

Chapter 20

Mary's illness at Jedburgh and convalescence at Craigmillar

T
o demonstrate her involvement in government, Mary agreed to attend assizes in Jedburgh to deal with the petty offences postponed during her pregnancy. Before leaving Edinburgh, she told Moray, Bothwell, Argyll and Huntly to subscribe to a bond offering each other mutual support, but to ignore the 'King when his orders conflicted with the Queen's wishes'.[1] On 1 October 1566, she ordered the Border lairds to meet her at Melrose. Although the king was invited, he was still threatening to go abroad and did not appear. On 7 October, she left for Jedburgh with an entourage of forty men, including Moray, Huntly, Atholl, Livingston, Seton, Caithness, Rothes, Maitland and the Bishop of Ross, together with judges and court officials.

Three days earlier, as Lieutenant of the Borders, Bothwell had set out for Liddesdale with 300 horse to round up offenders for trial. On arrival at Hermitage, he imprisoned some of the notorious Armstrongs and Johnstones, before going after the Elliotts, who had eluded him. When he caught up with them, he was severely wounded in a skirmish and passed out from loss of blood. He was brought unconscious back to Hermitage with stab wounds to his forehead, thigh and left hand, leading to rumours of his death. Meanwhile, the Armstrongs and Johnstones gained control of Hermitage, forcing Bothwell's officers into releasing their captives.

On 9 October, Mary arrived at Jedburgh to be greeted with the news of Bothwell's injuries at Hermitage, twenty-five miles to the south west. Although the assizes lasted six days, there were fewer cases without the Armstrongs, Johnstones and Elliotts in custody. On 16 October, with the assizes over, Mary rode with Moray and her party to visit Bothwell, believing that he was dying. She wanted a briefing from him as Governor of this border district. After spending two hours with him with Moray and others, she set off back to Jedburgh.[2*] Despite it being a round trip of fifty miles in a day, Hermitage was considered too forbidding for the queen and her attendants to spend a winter night. As she returned, she fell from her horse when it slipped in a bog, losing her watch, and had to stop at a farmhouse near Hawick to dry herself and repair her clothing.

On the next day in Jedburgh, Mary became feverish and the pain in her side was now so acute that she vomited blood 'more than sixty times'. This caused convulsions and she lost consciousness. She lost so much blood and was so cold that her entourage became horrified and she was not expected to recover. The gastric ulcer causing her pain seems to have haemorrhaged.[3*] Matters were made worse by a message from Stirling that the prince was also ill 'and that his life was despaired of'.[4] He, at least, recovered quickly after being made to vomit, but the queen 'had a very severe fit of convulsions', which caused the loss of her vision and ability to speak.[5] Despite his injuries, Bothwell arrived on a horse litter from Hermitage, determined to be on hand if the worst should happen. He had made a remarkable recovery, despite the legacy of a scar on his forehead, and was determined to stop Moray regaining authority. If Mary were to die, he wanted to hear her final wishes.

When, at last, the queen seemed to rally, it proved short-lived. On 24 October, she relapsed and 'all her limbs were so contracted, her face was so distorted [with pain], her eyes closed, her mouth fast and her feet and arms stiff and cold'.[6] She slipped into a coma and again seemed close to death, so that funeral arrangements were discussed. Yet her French doctor, Charles Nau, arranged for her to be 'handled by extreme rubbing, drawing and other cures'.[7] He bound her limbs tightly and forced wine down her throat. This caused her to vomit an amount of 'corrupt blood', which gained some relief. After three hours, she had recovered her sight and speech, and had started to sweat.

Prayers were said in Edinburgh, and Mary made a new will to ensure that the throne passed to James and not King Henry, who she blamed for her illness, and she made a plea for religious tolerance. Despite Bothwell's hopes, Moray was given 'the principal part of the government'.[8] To keep the king out of the picture, she placed 'the special care of the protection of our son' in Elizabeth's hands.[9] This was a masterstroke designed to make her adopt him as his mother. As it now seemed that Elizabeth would remain childless, Mary expected him to be brought up by her as a Protestant in England and to inherit the English throne. Although Elizabeth's reply is missing, on 20 November she acknowledged this obligation, and Mary thanked the English Privy Council for the 'good offers' from her 'dear sister'.[10]

Although the king was recalled from his hunting trip in the West of Scotland, he could not be reached immediately. On 27 October, he set out in haste for Jedburgh, arriving the next day, when the worst was over. He was furious when he was not invited to attend a meeting of the Council and, being unwelcome, returned to Glasgow on the following day. His absence and the delay in his arrival concerned the diplomatic circle in Edinburgh. Du Croc told Bethune that this was 'a fault that I cannot excuse', and it led the Venetian envoy to speculate that he had poisoned her. Mary herself believed poison had caused her illness, but this was not shared by those around her. Maitland considered:

> The occasion of the Queen's sickness is thought and displeasure …
> and the root of it is the king. For she has done him so great honour,
> contrary to the advice of her subjects, and he, on the other part, has
> recompensed her with such ingratitude and misuses himself so far
> towards her that it is a heartbreak for her to think he should be her
> husband, and how to be free of him she sees no outgait.[11]

Maitland was already aware that she wanted to end her marriage.

Mary recovered quickly. On 9 November, she was well enough to move by easy stages towards Edinburgh in a litter. After three weeks, she reached Sir Simon Preston at Craigmillar, just south of Edinburgh. During her illness, European politics had not stood still, and Philip II was preparing for war against the Dutch Protestants. To avoid Scotland being used as a bridgehead for a Catholic invasion of Britain, Elizabeth told Cecil to seek a Scottish alliance, hinting that she would confirm Mary as her heir. On 7 November, she sent Bedford to propose terms, which would confirm Mary's rights to the English succession. She told the Scots:

> Our meaning is to require nothing to be confirmed in that treaty
> but that which directly pertains to us and our children, omitting
> anything in that treaty that may be prejudicial to her title as next
> heir after us and our children, all of which may be secured to her by
> a new treaty betwixt us.[12]

Each would recognise the other as lawful queen. Elizabeth argued that 'this manner of proceeding is the way to avoid all jealousies and difficulties betwixt us, and the only way to secure the amity'. This was merely subterfuge as, two days beforehand, she had told the English Parliament that any recognition of a successor would bring 'some peril unto you and certain danger unto me'. Yet she offered to retract her demand for ratification of the Treaty of Edinburgh, if replaced with a new 'treaty of perpetual amity'.[13]

For once Cecil did not interfere with Elizabeth's efforts to avoid a Spanish-led invasion of Britain. He wanted a secure Protestant government in Scotland and worked assiduously to achieve the repatriation of Morton and his fellow conspirators, knowing that this would trigger a blood feud against King Henry. Despite their estrangement, it might still be possible to implicate Mary in any action taken against the king, thus impairing her claim to the English throne. Cecil avoided becoming personally involved, but pulled all the strings.

Mary recalled Robert Melville to Edinburgh to find a way to overcome the hurdle of her exclusion from the English throne under Henry VIII's will, the validity of which remained in doubt (see p. 24). Elizabeth still preferred the blameless Scottish Queen, if she would agree to the 'perpetual amity'. King Henry did not come into her reckoning. Yet confirmation of Mary's claim was overtaken by events.

Elizabeth needed to develop an understanding with Mary, who was under increasing pressure from the papacy to restore Catholicism in Scotland. Mondovi was using the threat of Philip II's military presence in the Netherlands to insist on Moray and the other Protestant leaders being executed. Yet Mary considered 'the perpetual amity' and her acceptance as Elizabeth's heir to be of overriding importance. She told Mondovi that 'she could not stain her hands with the blood of her subjects, and dared not risk offending Elizabeth'.[14] Cecil tried to resolve the succession by recalling parliament to persuade Elizabeth to marry the Archduke Charles, but she was furious at him raising such a personal matter. Mary's request for her to act as James's guardian had been well timed.

King Henry used the Spanish invasion of the Netherlands as another opportunity to champion his Catholic claims. While Mary was being moved from Jedburgh to Craigmillar, she was warned that he had written to European Catholic heads of state to outline her lack of Catholic commitment. This was Mary's first concrete evidence of his duplicity. If she wanted peace in Scotland, the restoration of Catholicism would need to be deferred. Although the king was trying to improve his own standing, she was mortified at being accused of lacking faith. She immediately wrote to de Silva, and, on 14 November, he reported to Philip II:

> The queen has heard that her husband has written to your Majesty, the Pope, the King of France, and the Cardinal of Lorraine that she was dubious of the faith and asked me to assure your majesty that as regards religion she will never with God's help fail to uphold it with all the fervour and constancy which the Roman Catholic Christian religion demands.[15]

Yet Philip's trust in her was being nibbled away and neither he nor Catherine de Medici offered her further tangible support. The Pope sent Father Edmund Hay to advise her to carry out Mondovi's instructions. This made her furious with the king, and it was in this mood that she discussed ways of ending her marriage.

On arrival at Craigmillar on 20 November, Mary was still being tended by her doctors and was heard to say she 'could wish to be dead'.[16] Eventually on 2 December, 'she vomited a great quantity of corrupt blood, and then the cure was complete'.[17] Much to her chagrin, the king arrived a few days later hoping to restore marital relations, but she would have nothing to do with him. He had never apologised for his part in Riccio's murder, and she told him to return to Stirling. Du Croc told Bethune in Paris that he doubted if they could be reconciled:

> I shall name only two reasons against it: the first is, the King will never humble himself as he ought; the other that the Queen cannot perceive him speaking with any noblemen, but presently she suspects some plot among them.[18]

On 3 December, when the king left, he asked du Croc to ride out from Edinburgh to meet him. When asked to intercede for him, du Croc said there was nothing he could do. King Henry again threatened to leave Scotland, reopening doubts over the prince's paternity, but it was another idle threat and he returned to Stirling for the baptism.

Mary spent almost a fortnight convalescing at Craigmillar. All her senior advisers were with her, apart from Atholl and Glencairn, who were not in Edinburgh. They blamed her recent illness on her disaffection with the king and persuaded her that their separation was a political necessity for Scotland's security. She had originally aired this with Maitland at Jedburgh, and he had been considering how to achieve it. Mary always saw divorce as her preferred course, but it presented difficulties that needed investigation. Maitland was well aware that the only acceptable grounds for a Catholic divorce were adultery or an annulment. Although there was ample cause for separation on grounds of the king's adultery, neither party would be permitted to remarry, and Mary wanted more heirs to protect her succession. There were two grounds for annulment: non-consummation, which could not be argued in this case, or consanguinity where the couple was within the fourth degree (third cousins or closer). Unfortunately, the king and queen had applied for a papal dispensation for their consanguinity beforehand.

The only hope was to argue that the dispensation was invalid because it had arrived after they were married. Even then, annulment meant that the marriage had never taken place, making any child of the union illegitimate. There was precedent for children remaining legitimate, where the couple was unaware of their consanguinity when they married, but this could hardly be argued, as the dispensation had been applied for in advance.

A second problem with divorce was how to control the king afterwards. Far from it improving the security of the realm, it would make him the focus of every Catholic scheme against Mary. Lennox believed that the lords at Craigmillar planned to imprison him after the prince's baptism. There is no evidence for this however, and, if true, the idea must have been dropped. By holding him in custody, Mary would alienate English Catholics, some of whom preferred his claim to the English throne to her own.

The more certain solution was to bring about the king's death, and Maitland considered a prosecution for treason. Yet, under Scottish law, a king could not be found guilty of treason. The Bishop of Ross believed that this could be overcome, as he was a consort subject to the queen, but, even so, a treason trial based on Riccio's murder would implicate Morton and his fellow exiles and bring to light Moray and Maitland's involvement. With so many foreign dignitaries due to arrive for the prince's baptism, the prospect of a trial involving the king and the principal Scottish lords was too scandalous to contemplate. If the king were found guilty, Prince James's legitimacy would again be in doubt. This left murder as the only sure option, although Mary would never agree to it and could not be told. There was a simple means of achieving it without involving anyone at Craigmillar. If the conspirators in exile returned, the king would die in a Douglas blood feud.

Maitland's plan at Craigmillar thus focused on gaining the queen's agreement for the exiles' rehabilitation, and he glossed over the difficulties of obtaining a divorce. He took Moray to broach it with Argyll, Huntly and Bothwell, requesting that each of them should assist in persuading the queen to repatriate the exiles. They all supported this, provided it did not offend her, but Bothwell and Huntly's only reason for wanting Moray's allies to return was to enable them to arrange the king's murder. Maitland then suggested that they could gain Mary's agreement, by offering to arrange her divorce. When Argyll, who had long wanted a divorce from Lady Jean,[19] said that he 'knew not how that might be done', Maitland assured him that a way could be found 'to make her quit of him, so that you and my Lord of Huntly will only behold the matter, and not be offended thereat'.[20] This careful reply does not necessarily imply divorce. Bothwell also requested that, in return for offering assistance, they should have all their estates restored. Despite Buchanan's later claim, Bothwell did not originate the divorce plan to promote his own marriage to Mary, and Moray and Maitland would never have allowed it. He shared the general outrage at the king's behaviour and was not averse to his death.

As their spokesman, Maitland now approached the queen, offering to arrange matters 'as well for her own easement as for the realm', in return for her agreeing to pardon the exiles for their part in Riccio's murder and for restoring all their attainted estates.[21] Despite mistrusting Morton, Mary agreed that he should be rehabilitated to Tantallon. She accepted the proposal for a divorce on two conditions:

> one that the divorcement were made lawfully; the other that it was not prejudicial to her son; otherwise Her Highness would rather endure all torments and abide the perils that might chance her.[22,23*]

With the English succession in mind, she could not countenance an impediment to her son's legitimacy, but, like Argyll, she did not know how to overcome this. Bothwell reassured her that his father had divorced his mother, without prejudicing his legitimacy, when hoping to remarry Marie of Guise. In that instance, Cardinal Bethune had confirmed that he had been unaware of their consanguinity at marriage, and, as *legatus a latere*, did not refer it to Rome.

Although Maitland tried to reassure Mary that the process of ridding her of the king would be conducted legally, he stated rather obliquely that Moray was as scrupulous a Protestant as she was a Catholic and 'I am assured he will look through his fingers thereto, and will behold our doings, saying nothing of the same'.[24] This can only be interpreted to mean that Moray would be allowed to keep his hands clean while a nefarious plot was undertaken. He was still seen by the nobility, other than Bothwell and Huntly, as their natural leader. Mary was given similar assurance that she would be involved in nothing which might tarnish her reputation. Yet she came to realise that, in removing the king, the Protestant lords tried to sully her honour and even to make her son illegitimate, so that Moray could take the Crown. When, in 1569, Moray was challenged to explain reports that he had taken part in the discussions at Craigmillar, he denied any involvement 'tending to any unlawful or dishonourable end'.[25] This, of course, was not a denial of his knowledge of the plans, only that he had not discussed them. His objectives will be discussed later, but if he were allowed to 'look through his fingers', his personal agenda, even then, was to regain control of government.

Although the lords at Craigmillar contemplated the king's murder, they knew Mary would not agree to it, and she was kept aloof from the plan. Two of the depositions for her defence in England show that she knew that means other than divorce were being contemplated but vetoed them. In the first of these, known as the *Protestation of Huntly and Argyll*, she told the lords, while still at Craigmillar:[26]

> I will that you do nothing by which any spot may be laid to my hon-
> our or conscience, and therefore I pray you rather let the matter be
> in the estate as it is, abiding till God in his goodness put remedy
> thereto, than you, believing to do me service, may possibly turn to
> my hurt and displeasure.[27]

Maitland had smoothly replied, 'Madam, let us guide the matter among us, and Your Grace shall see nothing but good and approved by parliament'.[28] The second deposition was prepared in 1568 by her Scottish supporters, including Huntly and Argyll. It implies that she was aware of all the options discussed at Craigmillar, as it states that they had contemplated 'other ways [from divorce and treason] to dispatch him; which altogether Her Grace refused, as is manifestly known'.[29] Despite her veto, she knew murder had been contemplated and that the Douglases would want revenge on return from exile. If she were aware of the full deliberations at Craigmillar, as the depositions suggest, the Lords had to be sure that she would not demand a proper investigation afterwards. When the time came, she was as anxious as they were to huddle up the evidence. She has to have realised that the king's murder was the only safe way to restore her security, even though she vetoed it.

To confirm their agreement, the Lords at Craigmillar will have signed a bond similar to that for the murder of Riccio with the precise objective left ambiguous. Although no such document has survived, there is evidence of it from several sources. Mary later told Nau that, when Bothwell left her at Carberry Hill, he gave her a paper and told her to guard it well, as it was the evidence of the complicity of the other lords in the murder. If this were the bond, as seems likely, it was quickly removed from her and destroyed.[30*] If Casket Letter II is to be believed (and it is the one part of the Casket Letters that appears plausible), the king told her in Glasgow that he was aware that a bond for his murder had been prepared at Craigmillar. In the admittedly suspect deposition of Bothwell's henchman James 'Black' Ormiston before his execution in 1573, he recalls the bond as saying:

It was thought expedient and most profitable for the Commonwealth, by the whole nobility and Lords underscribed, that such a young fool and proud tyrant should not reign or bear rule over them: and that for divers causes therefore, that these all had concluded that he should be put off by one way or another: and whosoever should take the deed in hand, or do it, they should defend and fortify as themselves.[31]

It has to be unlikely that the bond would so overtly have contemplated the king's murder, but the names of the signatories mentioned sound plausible. These were Huntly, Argyll, Bothwell, Maitland and Balfour, who was said to have drafted it. Admittedly, by this time, they had all fallen foul of the government, but, as they include names other than Bothwell and his henchmen, they retain a ring of authenticity, particularly as they exclude Moray, by then deceased, who was allowed to 'look through his fingers'. Of course, those taking the deposition might have edited the names, as Morton is thought to have signed it at Whittinghame after returning from exile. As the king's ally, Balfour's involvement may seem surprising, but as a lawyer he was closely associated with Bothwell, then Sheriff of Edinburgh. His signature denotes one of the many changes in his loyalty during his political career. It has been suggested that he was playing a double game as a friend of the king, by trying to lure the Protestant nobility into a murder plan, which would incriminate them. While his movements over the next few weeks are obscure, we do know that he was part of the plot. With the king isolated, he seems to have chosen this moment, as so often, to change sides, hoping for advantage by backing his enemies.

Just as Morton retained the bond for Riccio's murder, so Bothwell, the soldier among them, agreed to become involved by briefing the returning exiles and offering them assistance, and he was given the bond as his security. Yet it is unlikely that Mary saw it until Carberry Hill.

Chapter 21

The baptism of Prince James

O n 7 December 1566 the queen left Craigmillar for Holyrood to finalise arrangements for the prince's baptism at Stirling ten days later.
This was to be a celebration not only for the heir to the Scottish
throne, but also a future King of England. Three days later, she went on to
Stirling, travelling over two days. The king was already there, but she gave
Bothwell responsibility for the arrangements and for greeting visiting dignitaries. Sir John Forster reported to Cecil, 'All things for the christening
are at his appointment and the same scarcely well liked of with the rest of
the nobility as it is said.'[1] By giving Bothwell such prominence, Mary again
showed a lack of tact with so many English being present, and Sir James
Melville reported afterwards that he 'had a mark of his own that he shot at',
strutting about full of self-importance.[2]

Mary was so concerned at the rumours of the king's scheming that the
Privy Council issued an edict to stop firearms being brought into the castle,
and she dismissed the majority of his servants. Although he replaced them
with Lennox dependants, she remained disconcerted at their number. She
warned their leader, Robert Cunningham, to stop causing trouble and told the
king that any who left the castle would be banned from returning. Du Croc
reported that she kept a wary eye out 'for further contrivances', forbidding the
king from meeting foreign dignitaries unless she herself were present.[3] There
was good reason for this. The town clerk of Glasgow, William Hiegait, had
sent a warning through Archbishop Bethune's servant William Walker that the
king was rumoured to be seeking help to kidnap the prince and to crown him,
so that he could claim the regency. Hiegait had also heard that the king was
threatening to kill Mary's close advisers and was so jealous that either they, or
he, had to go. Yet, even with Lennox's support, he would have needed overseas
help. Hiegait proved an unreliable witness and, when confronted by the Privy
Council to confirm his allegations, he lost his nerve, admitting only to having
heard a rumour that the king was in danger. It was said that he later warned
the king that, if he went with Mary to Edinburgh, she would imprison him.

According to Melville, Mary was 'still sad and pensive', fearing that the
exiles' rehabilitation would lead inevitably to a blood feud: 'So many sighs

would she give that it was a pity to hear her, and few there were to endeav-
our to comfort her.' Despite receiving encouragement from both Moray and
Mar, she would not eat. She walked in the park with Melville, who tried to
console her by saying that 'her friends in England would soon help her to
forget her enemies in Scotland'. Yet he too commended clemency for the
exiles 'to best gain the hearts of the whole people, both here and in England'.[4]

Mary had obtained approval from both Catholic and Protestant Council
members to make the prince's christening a spectacle to rival anything seen
in France. There was to be a three-day fête modelled on one organised in
the previous year by Catherine de Medici at Bayonne to mark French and
Spanish reconciliation. She borrowed £12,000 from Edinburgh merchants,
and raised taxes to pay for it. This was not just a celebration of a baptism,
but of Moray and Argyll's reconciliation with Bothwell. Although they did
not attend the Catholic ceremony, she provided them with new clothing for
the events afterwards. Moray wore green, Argyll red and Bothwell blue,
while many others were magnificently attired 'some in cloth of silver, some
in cloth of gold, some in cloth of tissue, every man rather above than under
his degree'.[5] Banquets with fine wines were prepared to match the magnif-
icence of the costumes, with the food delivered by an elaborate mechanical
'engine' on a moving stage, which eventually collapsed as the final course
was being served. Each course was accompanied by satyrs and nymphs, or
by a child lowered from a golden globe reciting verses. A stage was built for
Buchanan's masques, which extolled Mary's virtues, hardly according with
his later *Detectio*. Mary's valet, the witty Sebastian Pagez, an accomplished
musician from Auverne, prepared entertainments including a ballet, which
caused great offence by depicting the English as satyrs with their tails held
in their hands making obscene gestures! The Scots roared with laughter,
but Bedford had to step in to restore order when an Englishman named
Hatton threatened to stab Pagez through the heart. Despite his puritanism
however, he allowed the English in his train to join in the dancing. Even a
bull hunt was organised. The Comptroller of the Royal Artillery prepared
a spectacular firework display for the finale with cannon from the arsenals
at Edinburgh and Dundee being hauled up the sides of the castle rock at
Stirling to maximise the effect.

The king was highly offended at the attendance of foreign dignitaries, who would see his fall in status. Du Croc had already reported that he
was unlikely to be at the baptism 'as his pride could not brook the insult-
ing neglect'. Even Catholics were generally disillusioned with him. He
was shunned both by Bedford, who had instructions from Elizabeth not to

recognise him as king, and by du Croc, who was advised from France not to allow him an interview as he was not 'in good correspondence' with Mary.[6]

James was carried at his christening by Charles IX's proxy, the Count of Brienne. The Protestant Countess of Argyll represented Elizabeth, who sent her a ruby valued at 500 crowns, but Bedford as a staunch puritan had received permission from Elizabeth to wait outside. With his mother still held in the Tower, the king again objected to Elizabeth becoming a god-mother, but Mary overruled him, although Elizabeth had still not recognised him as king. The Duke of Savoy's proxy, Robertino Solaro, Count Moretta, was expected on 17 December, but was inexplicably delayed and failed to arrive for the ceremony. Mary delayed it for a week, but could wait no longer, and it was only on 1 January that he reached Paris to confer with Mondovi and de Alava before pressing on towards Scotland. Even then he made slow progress, only reaching London on about 18 January. It was suggested that his delay was caused by his negotiations to provide the king with assistance in restoring Catholicism.

The Duke of Savoy sent Mary 'a fan of large size with jewelled feath-ers, of the value of four thousand crowns',[7] while Charles IX provided a necklace of pearls and rubies. On the day before the ceremony, Bedford presented her with a magnificent 'gold font from Elizabeth weighing 333 ounces and decorated with jewels and enamel "designed so that the whole effect combined elegance and value"'.[8] Thieves attempted to ambush it near Doncaster, as it was brought north. It was too small for a six-month-old child, but Bedford was instructed to play down its opulence by suggesting its suitabilty for Mary's next baby. The king did not attend its presentation, as Elizabeth had piqued him by telling him to be obedient to Mary in all matters. When Bedford confirmed that she wanted a conference to discuss Mary's claim to the English throne, Mary promised to send councillors to finalise the arrangements.

The Catholic baptism service was conducted by Archbishop Hamilton, but Mary would not let him spit into the child's mouth, as was the custom, knowing that he suffered from syphilis. The prince was christened Charles James, taking his first name from the King of France. Catholics in attendance included Seton, Fleming, Atholl and Eglinton, while the Protestant nobles waited outside. According to Knox, never slow to belittle Catholic ritual, Seton carried 'the salt, grease and such other things', when others refused and 'brought in the said trash'. Although a Reformer, Sir John Maxwell was created 4th Lord Herries of Terregles, the title of his wife's family, in further thanks for his loyalty.

The queen seemed to put aside her problems and presided in style over the three days of celebration, which Bedford reported as 'great, and great welcome'. Yet she was privately 'pensive and melancholy'. On the next day, when du Croc came for an audience, he found her weeping on her bed. Bedford had at last persuaded her to repatriate the exiles, although Morton also recognised Bothwell's and Moray's part in winning her agreement. On Christmas Eve, Mary formally pardoned Morton and seventy-six other conspirators in their absence, provided that they stayed away from Court for two years. Only George Douglas 'the Postulate' and Ker of Fawdonside were not reprieved, as they had risked the lives of her unborn child and herself. She saw the pardon as another step in appeasing Elizabeth so as to gain recognition as her heir and, on 2 January, wrote to thank her for reviewing Henry VIII's contentious will. Yet the king was now in mortal fear. The exiles saw him as the direct cause of their banishment and the loss of their estates. Although he tried to ingratiate himself with them by personally authorising Fawdonside's pardon following his help to gain him the Scottish Crown, Fawdonside was soon part of the assassination conspiracy.

The king caused great embarrassment by remaining in his apartments at Stirling. Although his absence seems to have been designed to imply doubt over the prince's paternity, in reality he did not want the lesions and suppurating pustules over his face and body to be seen after another outbreak of his secondary syphilis. His affliction has been confirmed by scientific examination of his skull by Karl Pearson at the Royal College of Surgeons in London in 1928. Du Croc followed his instructions and refused to see him, sending a message that his chamber had two doors 'and if he should enter by the one, I should feel myself compelled to go out by the other'.[9] He also reported to Bethune that, even at Stirling, the king was being treated with salivation of mercury and medicinal baths, the standard remedy for syphilis at the time. He continued:

> His bad deportment is incurable, nor can there be ever any good expected from him for several reasons which I might tell was I present with you. I can't pretend to foretell how all may turn; but I will say that matters can't subsist long as they are without being accompanied by several bad consequences.[10]

The king was unhappy at being cold-shouldered and he departed to 'take the air'. While outside he was at last received more deferentially. A member of Bedford's suite, a Mr. Wiseman 'did the king reverence, and, having been very familiar with him in the court of England, used some speeches with him by way of compliment'. Wiseman was reprimanded for failing to adhere to Elizabeth's command not to recognise him as king. Yet he 'stoutly replied that it was a pity that such was her commandment'.[11]

With the celebrations over, Mary left Stirling without the king to spend Christmas as Lord Drummond's guest at Crieff. Bothwell was one of several Councillors to accompany her, leading to further speculation in Buchanan's *Detectio* of his 'filthy wickedness' with her.[12] Yet none of those present corroborated any impropriety.[13*] Mary went on to stay with her Comptroller, Sir William Murray of Tullibardine, brother of Annabella, Countess of Mar. Tullibardine was an ally of the king, so Mary may have seen this as a bridge building exercise. Although Bothwell went with her, it would have been quite impolitic for her to have conducted an affair with him on this visit, as Buchanan later alleged. She remained at Tullibardine until 31 December before returning to Stirling. Bedford spent Christmas as Moray's guest at St Andrews, where he was lavishly entertained for several days before they both rejoined the queen.

Despite the doubts expressed by the conspirators at Craigmillar, Mary still hoped to arrange a divorce from the king and, on 23 December, temporarily restored Archbishop Hamilton hoping to achieve a nullity without prejudicing her son's legitimacy. Although a Catholic divorce could only be granted by the Pope, Mary wanted the Archbishop to mediate on her behalf. As his consistorial role had been removed in 1560, his reappointment was illegal and he was unlikely to succeed. Yet Mary tried to placate the Kirk and, on 20 December, gave the General Assembly a further £10,000. Despite her efforts, his reappointment seemed to presage a Catholic revival, and Moray advised her to comply with their demand for his removal. Before Hamilton stood down on 9 January, he advised her that a Catholic divorce could not be achieved on acceptable terms. The Kirk was in no mood to be conciliatory and the Countess of Argyll was required to do penance for attending the Catholic baptism as Elizabeth's proxy. On 13 December, with unfortunate timing, Hay arrived in Edinburgh on the Pope's behalf with the Bishop of Dunblane. They immediately came on to interview the queen at Stirling, but she probably did not see them, claiming to be busy with the christening arrangements. She knew that they would demand the execution of the senior Protestant lords. This would have been politically disastrous, if not practically impossible. Realising that she would never agree, on 23 December Hay wrote to Mondovi that he would shortly be leaving Scotland.

Thoroughly disaffected, the king crept away to Glasgow before Christmas without taking his leave, hoping for a cure and intending yet again to go

abroad. His affliction only gradually became public knowledge. It was initially reported that he had been poisoned, and later that he had 'the Pox',
which was assumed at the time to mean smallpox, but as soon as he was on
the road, it could no longer be hidden. Buchanan reported:

> Hardly a mile out of Stirling, a violent disorder struck every part
> of his body. Livid pustules broke out accompanied by much pain
> and vexation in his whole body. [He had] black pimples all over his
> body, grievous sweat in all his limbs, and intolerable stink.[14]

A white taffeta mask covered his disfigured face. By 2 January, he needed
proper treatment and was far too ill to go abroad. He sent a message to
Mary that he needed to see her, but she did not go immediately. She was
delayed because she had been thrown from her horse at Seton, having travelled there from Stirling via Edinburgh. Yet she sent her physician to continue his eight-week course of salivation of mercury. This involved sweating
the patient and applying mercury both orally and to anoint the gums. As the
gum tissue died, the teeth were loosened, causing bad breath and copious
flows of saliva. The treatment was then completed with a series of sulphu-
rous baths.

Despite his predicament, the king continued his scheming to replace
Mary on the throne. She still believed that the plot for Riccio's murder was
directed against her, and that he planned to crown Prince James to claim the
regency. He was still demanding the dismissal of Mary's closest Protestant
advisers, particularly Maitland, who was well aware of the king's key role
in arranging Riccio's murder. As late as 20 January, she wrote to Bethune
in Paris that she knew of the king's scheming, 'but God moderates their
forces well enough, and takes the means of execution of their intentions
from them.'

With so much rumoured plotting, it is hardly surprising that Mary
deferred her visit to Glasgow, despite the king's continued requests for her
to join him. Before going, she moved the prince from Stirling to Edinburgh
where he would be out of reach of any kidnap plan launched from Glasgow.
Given Tullibardine's close association with the king, it has also been suggested that she feared leaving the prince in the care of his sister Annabella,
Countess of Mar. If this were a consideration, Mary had no grounds to suspect her loyalty. Despite being a Catholic, Annabella proved the most loyal
and caring guardian of James and, in due course, of James's son. He always
considered her as his surrogate mother.

On 6 January, Mary attended Maitland's marriage to Mary Fleming in the Chapel Royal at Holyrood, but the newly-weds had little time for a honeymoon. Maitland remained at Court and, four days later, accompanied Mary to Stirling to collect the prince. He was still with her on about 12 January, accompanying her while she brought the prince to Holyrood, having spent a night on the way with the Livingstons at Callendar.

With divorce being ruled out, Mary decided to make a new start with the king, while maintaining sufficient supervision over him to limit his plotting against her. His assassination, even without her involvement, would prejudice her hopes of recognition as Elizabeth's heir. It was to achieve his return with her to Edinburgh, where she could keep an eye on him, that she now set out to Glasgow. This leniency was in keeping with her rehabilitation of Moray after the Chaseabout Raid and of the exiles involved in Riccio's murder, despite their treasonable actions. Once the symptoms of his syphilis had subsided, he could be restored to her bed to provide more heirs. It also assured James's legitimacy and enhanced her claim to the English throne. Yet reconciliation was a blow to everyone else, who had seen Mary's disillusionment with him as the means of achieving his removal with the prospect of immunity from prosecution.

Mary sent Bothwell to Dunbar to meet Morton as he returned from England. She wanted Morton's assurance that the exiles would not start a blood feud against the king. She needed the king kept alive. With Bothwell trying to organise them to arrange his demise, he was not the ideal conciliator. Morton crossed the Border on 9 January, after writing from Berwick to thank Cecil for arranging his rehabilitation and offering to do him 'such honour and pleasure as lies in my power'.[15] Cecil probably understood what this meant. The king was a Catholic and a political embarrassment, and would continue to be so as long as he remained alive. The returning exiles in feud with him feared for their lives if he were returned to authority.

Having arrived at Dunbar, Bothwell suffered a haemorrhage, a legacy from his wounds received in Liddesdale, and was laid low for a week. By then, Morton had reached Sir William Douglas's home at Whittinghame about six miles west of Dunbar, where he met Sir William's brother, Archibald, who had acted as the go-between for the nobles surrounding the Scottish Crown with the exiles in England. On 19 January, Bothwell was sufficiently recovered to meet them there, and Maitland appeared from Lethington six miles further on, where he had arrived from Stirling two days earlier to continue his honeymoon.

Chapter 22

Mary's visit to Glasgow to persuade the king to return to Edinburgh

Details of the king's plotting against the Crown are at best shadowy. Yet his plan, however fanciful, was to encourage Catholics in Scotland and northern England to provide support for invading troops, who would install him on the English throne. This shows the deluded grandeur of an unrealistic man, but was extremely dangerous both for Mary, in her efforts to be recognised as Elizabeth's heir, and for Elizabeth and Cecil, well aware of strong Catholic sentiment in northern England. He also seems to have assumed that, by kidnapping James, he could claim the Scottish regency. With an almost total lack of support from among the Scottish nobility, he would have needed foreign assistance, but there is no evidence of either Catherine de Medici or Philip II offering it, despite their continued correspondence with him. There is evidence, however, of secret communication with Philip II and the papacy, which was being kept from Mary, although its objective is not known. This can be pieced together from apparently unrelated information.

Following Yaxley's death, Killigrew reported that his former servant, Henry Gwynn, had arrived in Edinburgh with letters for the king from Philip II in Flanders. It is not clear what they said but he appears to have found them encouraging. Killigrew knew that Rogers was still monitoring the king's activities on Cecil's behalf, having managed to gain the confidence of Sir Anthony Standen. When he was invited to go hunting and hawking with the king, Rogers learned that Gwynn had delivered 2,000 crowns to the king from an English merchant as part of a wider plot, looking for Spanish support, to make him king of both Scotland and England. He received letters from Margaret Douglas and from Arthur and Edward Pole, Yorkist pretenders to the English throne, being held in the Tower. Arthur Pole apparently offered to resign his claim to the English throne in favour of Mary and her husband, although Mary does not seem to have been told.

The king was also plotting to gain the Scottish throne for himself. Although the Pope was impressed by the reports of James's lavish Catholic christening, he knew that Hay's mission had failed and that Mary lacked the zeal to restore Catholicism. When Ker of Fawdonside returned from England after being pardoned by King Henry, Mary was warned that he had claimed 'that within fifteen days, there would be a great change in the court, that he would soon be in greater credit than ever, and then he inquired boldly how the queen was'.[1] She did not understand what this meant, but it alarmed her at a time when she was having such hopeful negotiations with Elizabeth. With the king so well informed of discussions at Craigmillar and elsewhere, she was sure he had spies at Court and she intercepted his correspondence to prevent him from granting passports for his messengers to go abroad. Yet the king's spies in Edinburgh were still able to communicate with him behind her back. Two possible candidates are Joseph Riccio and an Italian Catholic in Mary's service, Joseph Lutini, who also carried Mary's papal messages. On 6 January, Lutini was granted a passport to travel from Edinburgh to Paris. Although this was signed by the queen, Riccio had forged her signature and had given Lutini money to carry a message to Moretta at Berwick. As this lacked the queen's authority, he must have been travelling on behalf of the king, who was by then in Glasgow. The king seems to have used Lutini and Moretta to act as his conduit to communicate with Mondovi, the Vatican and European Catholic powers.

When questioned on the reasons for Lutini's departure, Riccio claimed that he had absconded with money he had lent to him, having agreed to leave horses and clothing in Edinburgh as security. Yet he had taken them as well, and it was then found that he owed money to other servants including Sebastian Pagez. When Mary realised that some of her bracelets were missing, Riccio again blamed Lutini. She immediately instructed Maitland to write to Sir William Drury at Berwick to apprehend him, but Drury was temporarily absent from his post. Being unaware of these accusations, Lutini remained in Berwick awaiting Moretta's arrival.

On 23 January, Drury returned to Berwick, where Mary's letter awaited him. He arrested Lutini, who claimed to be travelling to France on the queen's behalf, but was currently too ill to continue. Drury realised that the passport was counterfeit and sent it with a copy of Maitland's letter to Cecil in London. When Moretta reached Berwick, he was permitted to see Lutini, who told him that he was travelling on Riccio's instruction. Riccio now needed to divert attention from his forgery of the queen's signature, as its discovery would be a capital offence. Furious at having his cover blown, Riccio sent Lutini precise instructions on what to say, if he returned to Edinburgh, but Drury intercepted them, and they too ended up in Cecil's papers. When Lutini eventually returned to Edinburgh, the king was dead and Bothwell dismissed him with enough money to return abroad. By then Riccio had also left, having been branded, unrealistically, as one of the king's murderers.

On 24 January, Moretta moved on from Berwick towards Edinburgh, but met his old friend, du Croc, who rode back with him as far as Dunbar so that they could talk. He reached Edinburgh on 25 or 26 January, taking lodgings at Balfour's house.[2*] With Mary by then in Glasgow, he was greeted by Moray and Maitland. Although they were uncertain of the purpose of his visit, being now more than a month too late for Prince James's baptism, he seems to have been assessing the feasibility of placing the king on the Scottish throne. There is no evidence of military support being offered by the papacy, but there were rumours on the Continent of a plan to assassinate Mary. If these were true, the plan foundered with the king's murder, after which Moretta quickly left Edinburgh. Spanish rumours that she was in danger had reached de Silva in London during December. He had heard from Philip II's aunt, Margaret, Duchess of Parma, in Brussels of a report from de Alava in Paris, that there was a plot for Mary's assassination. As King Henry was de Alava's close *confidant*, it is reasonable to assume that he was behind it. On about 25 January, de Alava warned Archbishop Bethune that 'there be some surprise to be trafficked to the queen's contrary'.[3] His delay in telling the Archbishop has been seen as suspicious, but he would have needed Philip II's sanction to divulge the story. Philip, who was in Brussels, was always well briefed on King Henry's deluded ambitions and must have disapproved of them, because he agreed that Mary should be warned. De Alava gave Bethune no hint of his sources or the nature of the plot, and Mary remained in the dark. Bethune asked Catherine de Medici if she knew of anything and was not entirely convinced by her denial. He sent an urgent warning for Mary to tighten her security and be reconciled with the king, but his letter arrived only on the day after the king's murder.

Even though Mary was unaware of the nature of the king's plotting from Glasgow, he was too dangerous to be left on the loose and she wanted him back under her control. On 20 January, she at last set off on her own initiative to persuade him to return with her to Edinburgh. His removal from Glasgow would, of course, assist any assassination plan, but Mary's objective was to rehabilitate him. She was escorted for the first part of her journey by Bothwell and Huntly with a company of mounted hackbut-ters, and she brought a horse litter on which to transport the king back to Edinburgh. Although she stopped for the night at Callendar, Livingston was not involved in any conspiracy against the king. From here, Bothwell

Mary Queen of Scots, aged fifteen. Painted at the time that she became Queen of France by François Clouet. (Royal Collection Trust © Her Majesty the Queen 2016/Bridgeman Images)

Man in Red, c. 1520–30, thought to be Matthew Stuart, 4th Earl of Lennox (oil on panel). The hilt of the sword depicts a Scottish thistle. Flemish School (16th century). (Royal Collection Trust © Her Majesty Queen Elizabeth II, 2016/Bridgeman Images ROC399152)

The Somerley Portrait, thought to be Lady Margaret Douglas. The cuff links are marked M and D. Attributed to Luca Penni (c.1504-56). (Reproduced by permission of Somerley Enterprises)

The Lennox Jewel

Front

This is a locket initially designed in celebration of the mutual love until 'death shall dissolve' of Matthew and Margaret Lennox.

When Elizabeth was named as Mary Tudor's heir, the Lennoxes focused their ambitions on the marriage of their son, Darnley, to Mary Queen of Scots. Margaret seems to have arranged for the locket to be adapted to make it appropriate as a gift to Mary in contemplation of her marriage to Darnley. It is filled to the brim with symbolism of her dynastic ambition (please see p. 27 for more details).

Images adapted from The Royal Collection ©2012 Her Majesty Queen Elizabeth II.

Reverse

Interior

Darnley's skull and his portraits

In 1928 Karl Pearson, a distinguished biostatistician, was able to measure Darnley's skull, which had been looted from the Chapel Royal at Holyrood in the 18th century, and compare it to known portraits of him. He found that many of them 'were too often a question of relative untruthfulness'. He demonstrated this by drawing in the outline of the skull to copies of the images of Darnley that were known. It is the portrait on the front cover of this book which seems to be the closest likeness.

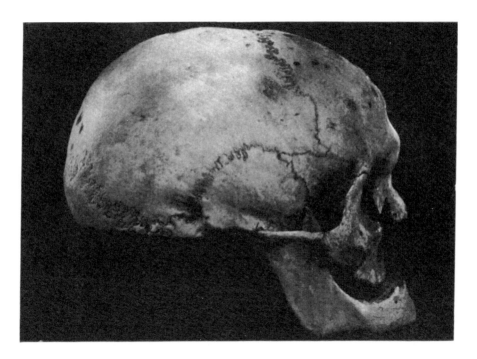

Darnley's Skull. Reproduced with permission from Karl Pearson, *The Skull and Portraits of Henry Stewart, Lord Darnley, and Their Bearing on the Tragedy of Mary, Queen of Scots*, Biometrika (1928) 20B (1): 1–104 (Plate II). Published by Oxford University Press on behalf of The Biometrika Trust.

Detail of Darnley's head from the portrait shown on the front cover of this book. This shows Karl Pearson's outline of his skull with its close correlation to the portrait. (Reproduced with permission from Karl Pearson, *The Skull and Portraits of Henry Stewart, Lord Darnley, and Their Bearing on the Tragedy of Mary, Queen of Scots*, Biometrika (1928) 20B (1): 1–104 (Plate XXX). Published by Oxford University Press on behalf of The Biometrika Trust.)

the remembraunce of yowre accustomed frendlines
constrainethe me in thefs fewe lynes to gene
yowre L. my humble thankes therfore, and to
afsuer yowre L. that dewrynge my lyfe I
shall not be forgetfull of yowre great goodnes
yowre L. afsured to commaunde

H. Darnley.

Darnley Henry (lord)

An example of Darnley's handwriting. Engraving of part of a letter written to Robert Dudley, Earl of Leicester. English school (19th century), Private Collection/© Look and Learn/Bridgeman images LLM978453.

Detail of Darnley's head from the Eworth 1555 portrait. This shows Karl Pearson's outline of his skull with its close correlation to the portrait. (Reproduced with permission from Karl Pearson, *The Skull and Portraits of Henry Stewart, Lord Darnley, and Their Bearing on the Tragedy of Mary, Queen of Scots*, Biometrika (1928) 20B (1): 1–104 (Plate XXVI). Published by Oxford University Press on behalf of The Biometrika Trust.)

Portrait of Henry, Lord Darnley in 1555, aged eight. Oil on panel by Hans Eworth (Flemish). (f. 1520-74 Scottish National Portrait Gallery, Edinburgh/Bridgeman Images NGS6935.)

Detail of Darnley's head from the portrait by Eworth painted with his brother. This shows Karl Pearson's outline of his skull with its poor correlation to his portrait image. (Reproduced with permission from Karl Pearson, *The Skull and Portraits of Henry Stewart, Lord Darnley, and Their Bearing on the Tragedy of Mary, Queen of Scots*, Biometrika (1928) 20B (1): 1–104 (Plate XXVIII). Published by Oxford University Press on behalf of The Biometrika Trust.)

Henry, Lord Darnley with his brother, Charles Stuart (Hans Eworth, oil on panel). It can be seen that the artist's focus is on Darnley's legs. (f. 1520-74 Royal Collection Trust © Her Majesty Queen Elizabeth II, 2016/Bridgeman Images.)

Detail of Darnley's head from the c. 1564 portrait. This shows Karl Pearson's outline of his skull demonstrating that it could not have been a true likeness. (Reproduced with permission from Karl Pearson, *The Skull and Portraits of Henry Stewart, Lord Darnley, and Their Bearing on the Tragedy of Mary, Queen of Scots*, Biometrika (1928) 20B (1): 1–104 (Plate XXVII). Published by Oxford University Press on behalf of The Biometrika Trust.)

Henry, Lord Darnley, c. 1564 (oil on panel). Painted shortly before his arrival in Scotland to meet Mary. It was clearly designed to flatter. Artist unknown. (Scottish National Portrait Gallery, Edinburgh/ Bridgeman Images PG2279.)

Detail of Darnley's head from the double portrait at his marriage to Mary Queen of Scots. This shows Karl Pearson's outline of his skull with its poor correlation to the face in the portrait. (Reproduced with permission from Karl Pearson, *The Skull and Portraits of Henry Stewart, Lord Darnley, and Their Bearing on the Tragedy of Mary, Queen of Scots*, Biometrika (1928) 20B (1): 1–104 (Plate XXIX). Published by Oxford University Press on behalf of The Biometrika Trust.)

Henry, Lord Darnley and Mary Queen of Scots. Painted at the time of their marriage. Scottish School (16th century), Hardwick Hall, Derbyshire. (National Trust Photographic Library/Bridgeman Images USB1161914.)

The silver coin struck to commemorate Darnley's marriage to Mary. This is inscribed 'Henricus & Maria'. (National Galleries of Scotland)

Detail of Darnley's head from the medal commemorating Mary's marriage to Darnley. This appears to be a very good likeness when compared to his skull. (Reproduced with permission from Karl Pearson, *The Skull and Portraits of Henry Stewart, Lord Darnley, and Their Bearing on the Tragedy of Mary, Queen of Scots*, Biometrika (1928) 20B (1): 1–104 (Plate XXXI). Published by Oxford University Press on behalf of The Biometrika Trust.)

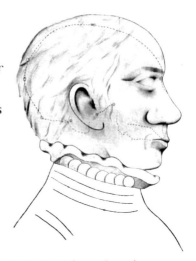

The silver coin struck to commemorate Moray's defeat in the Chaseabout Raid. This is inscribed 'Maria & Henric[us]', after Mary had asserted control over the use of Darnley's signature on Royal papers. (National Galleries of Scotland)

Detail of Darnley's head from the coin commemorating Moray's defeat. This appears to be a good likeness when compared to his skull. (Reproduced with permission from Karl Pearson, *The Skull and Portraits of Henry Stewart, Lord Darnley, and Their Bearing on the Tragedy of Mary, Queen of Scots*, Biometrika (1928) 20B (1): 1–104 (Plate XXXII). Published by Oxford University Press on behalf of The Biometrika Trust.)

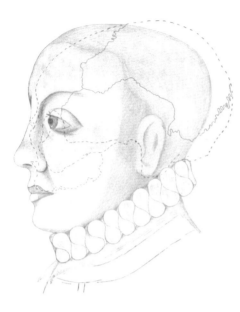

Detail of Darnley's head from Vogelaare's *Memorial*. This shows Karl Pearson's outline of his skull with its lack of correlation to the face in the portrait. (Reproduced with permission from Karl Pearson, *The Skull and Portraits of Henry Stewart, Lord Darnley, and Their Bearing on the Tragedy of Mary, Queen of Scots*, Biometrika (1928) 20B (1): 1–104 (Plate XXXIII). Published by Oxford University Press on behalf of The Biometrika Trust.)

The *Memorial of Lord Darnley* (oil on canvas). The bone structure of the images of Lennox and Margaret Douglas appear similar to those in the 'Man in Red' and in the 'Somerley portrait'. The artist will not have met Darnley and makes no attempt to provide a likeness. Livinus de Vogelaare (Flemish). (Royal Collection Trust © Her Majesty Queen Elizabeth II 2016/Bridgeman Images ROC753015.)

The placard of the Mermaid and the Hare. An example of a more
sophisticated form of propaganda, intended to undermine Mary. Here
Mary is depicted as a mermaid, a well-recognised synonym for a prostitute,
next to a hare, which was the Bothwell crest. Note the sea anemone,
a symbol for female genitalia, and the phallic positioning of the sword.
(The National Archives/Photolibrary.com)

The murder scene at Kirk o'Field. This has been drawn by one of Cecil's spies. Note the courtyard area behind the rubble of the destroyed buildings

where deliveries could be made relatively unnoticed. (The National Archives/Photolibrary.com)

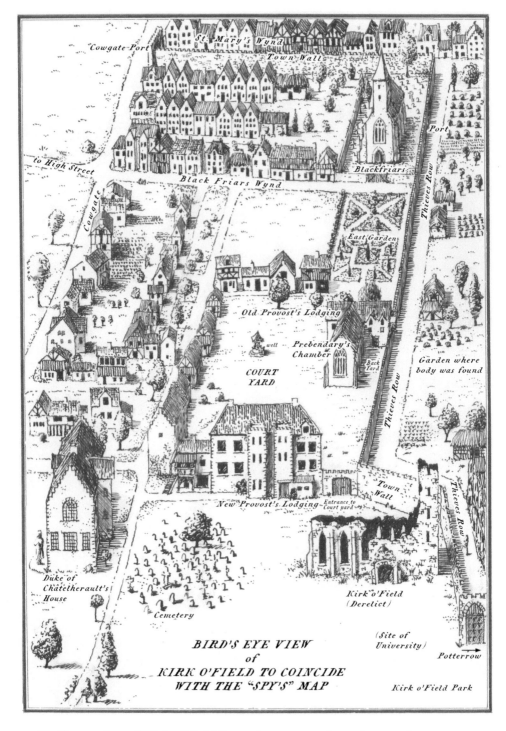

Bird's eye view of Kirk o'Field from the same angle as the one drawn
by the spy. This gives some idea of the layout of Kirk o' Field and its
surrounding area, and demonstrates the accuracy of the spy's narrative
drawing. (©David Atkinson, Handmade Maps Ltd.)

returned with Huntly to Edinburgh, as he had pressing business in the Borders. Mary now arranged for a party of about forty Hamiltons, including Archbishop Hamilton and Sir James Hamilton of Luss, to escort her to Glasgow. As long-standing Lennox adversaries, they were not the most conciliatory group with which to enter Glasgow on 22 January, but she needed protection and would require all her guile to persuade the king to come back with her.

The king had been at death's door over Christmas but was back in the care of his father, who could see no wrong in him. 'He was brought so low that nothing but death was expected; yet the strength of his youth did at last surmount the poison.'[4] Even so his face remained disfigured by pustules, and he was losing his hair (both symptoms of syphilis). He retained a Gentleman of the Bedchamber in Glasgow, Captain Thomas Crawford of Jordanhill, who had been a distinguished mercenary on the Continent before returning with Mary in 1561. He later provided evidence both to Lennox and the Commissioners at the Conferences at York and Westminster of the conversations between Mary and the king in Glasgow.

On Mary's arrival, Lennox sent Crawford to apologise for not coming personally to greet her, as he was unwell. Casket Letter II confirms that he was suffering from nose bleeds, an indication of fear in sixteenth-century France. On hearing this, Mary retorted that 'he would not be afraid if he were not culpable', but Crawford assured her that Lennox's only fear was to know what she might have planned for him.[5] Mary curtly told him to hold his peace. The king also asked to defer his meeting with her until the following day, as he was still suffering skin eruptions on his face. Doubtful of her security at Lennox Castle, she stayed in Glasgow for the night, probably at the Episcopal Palace, where she retained Hamilton protection.

It was then that Mary was said to have written the first of the so-called Casket Letters to Bothwell. Their origin and intent to incriminate her in her husband's murder will be discussed in detail later, but the individual letters are dealt with in the period of the text to which they apply. They were numbered I to VIII for their use as evidence at the Conferences at York and Westminster in 1568, placing them in rough chronology. In addition to the letters, there were two purported versions of Mary's marriage contract with Bothwell, and a long love poem made up of twelve sonnets. Together these amounted to twenty-two documents. As none of the originals now exist, their content is known only from French or English language transcripts made for the Conferences and, in a few cases, from translations included as Appendices to the Scottish edition of Buchanan's *Detectio*, where the first sentence only is in the original French. Without the originals, the handwriting cannot be authenticated. Yet most of them seem to have been genuine letters, but either taken out of context or manipulated with false additions, although at least one seems a complete forgery. None of the transcripts is dated, addressed or signed. Yet Mary's letters were always addressed and included a carefully constructed phrase before her signature. Each has textual shortcomings, suggesting inexpert and hurried manipulation. A great deal of ink has been expended on them over succeeding centuries and the purpose here is to outline only the most plausible outcome of this research.

Casket Letter I was almost certainly written from Mary to Bothwell and may be a postscript to an official letter. At the top of the transcript there is an annotation in an English hand reading, 'Proves her disdain against her husband'. Although it is headed 'From Glasgow this Saturday morning' it is much more likely that it was written from Stirling on Saturday 11 January, a fortnight earlier. In this context it is clear that Mary was unaware of Bothwell's haemorrhage at Dunbar and was annoyed that he had not confirmed Morton's undertaking not to seek revenge against the king. As she had been in Stirling with the infant James, whom she had not seen for some while, she mentioned him in the letter. She wrote:

> It seemeth that with your absence forgetfulness is joined, considering that at your departure you promised to send me news from you; nevertheless, I can learn none. And yet did I yesterday look for that [i.e. Prince James] [which] shall make me merrier than I shall be. I think you do the like for your return, prolonging it more than you have promised. As for me if I hear no other matter of you according to my commission, I bring the man [i.e. James] [on] Monday to Craigmillar, where he shall be upon Wednesday; and I go to Edinburgh to be let blood, if I have no word to the contrary. He [i.e. James] is the merriest that ever you saw, and doth remember unto me all that he can to make me believe that he loveth me. To conclude, you would say that he maketh love to me, wherein I take so much pleasure that I never come in there but my pain of my side doth take me: I have it sore today. If Paris doth bring back unto me that for which I have sent, it should much amend me. I pray you send me word from you at large, and what I shall do if you be not returned when I shall be there; for if you be not wise, I see assuredly all the whole burden [i.e. protecting the king from a vengeful Morton] fallen upon my

shoulders. Provide for me and consider well. First of all I send this present to Lethington to be delivered to you by Beaton, who goeth one day of law of Lord Balfour.[6*] I will say no more unto you, but that I pray God send me good news of your voyage.[7]

If from Stirling, Casket Letter I is an innocent rebuke to Bothwell for not keeping her informed. It is certainly not a love letter to him. Her description of the 'man' only makes sense as a reference to her son and his apparent affection for her. This was a common description for a male child used by the Guise family, and Mary always referred to her husband as the king. She plans to move James from Stirling to Craigmillar, a favourite retreat, to provide security close to Edinburgh while she is being let blood, and we know that James arrived there with her on Wednesday, 15 January. Yet there is strong evidence that the letter has been manipulated by adding the words, 'From Glasgow, this Saturday morning' (implying it was written on 25 January, the only Saturday that Mary was there). As James never went to Glasgow, the immediate implication is that the 'man' being discussed is the king, and Mary is bringing him to Craigmillar as part of her plot with Bothwell to murder him. Yet the king was still extremely unwell and could not have left Glasgow for Craigmillar two days later, and he arrived at Kirk o' Field only after a further week's recuperation. To describe the king as 'the merriest you ever saw', when he was sulking in Glasgow and covered with pustules is absurd and conflicts with Casket Letter II.

The timing of Paris's journey with Mary's letters is also problematic.[8*] We know that she arrived in Glasgow only on 22 January and that Casket Letters I and II were purportedly written during the next three days. Thus Paris could not have reached Edinburgh, a hard day's ride away, with packages for Maitland and Bothwell until the evening of 25 January at the earliest. Yet Moray's journal recording Bothwell's movements confirms that he left Edinburgh for Liddesdale on the evening of 24 January. This is corroborated by Henry, Lord Scrope, who kept a watching eye on his activities from Carlisle.[9*] Neither Paris nor Bethune would have had time to follow Bothwell to Liddesdale and, as Paris went straight back to Glasgow, he could not have met him. Yet a fortnight earlier, on 13 January, he could easily have ridden from Stirling to meet Bothwell at Dunbar, near Maitland at Lethington. By suggesting that Casket Letter I was written from Glasgow, it implies that Mary thought Bothwell should have been planning the king's murder, or she would find 'all the whole burden fallen upon my shoulders'.[10] Yet at that time he was actively involved in policing Liddesdale.

On 23 January, the morning after arriving in Glasgow, Mary met up with the king. The gist of their conversation is recorded in Casket Letter II. In its English translation, this amounts to 3,132 words purportedly written by her on 23 and 24 January, although the transcript is undated and unsigned. It is annotated by the English, 'The long letter written from Glasgow from the Queen of Scots to the Earl of Bothwell.'[11] Mary's official record of her meeting with the king, which forms the principal part of this document, is almost certainly genuine and may have been the one letter originally found in the silver casket, and we know that Paris did carry a letter from Glasgow on her behalf. In the Scots version, Bothwell is referred to in the third person and in other parts so are Moray and Maitland. This implies that it was originally addressed to several of her advisers, including Bothwell. This official report is corroborated by Crawford's evidence prepared in late 1568 for the English Commissioners at the Conferences at York and Westminster. He claimed that the king had told him of the conversation immediately afterwards, but, as his report is almost word for word identical to the English translation of Mary's original in French, he must have copied it. It was important to keep both pieces of evidence consistent, and, although their similarity may seem suspicious, the content appears plausible.

According to Crawford (and, to a great extent, Casket Letter II), the king claimed to have been cruelly treated by Mary, who would not accept his repentance for having 'failed in some things, even though such like greater faults have been made to you sundry times, which you have forgiven. I am but young ...' He used the excuse that they were not living as man and wife, which 'bringeth me in such melancholy as you see I am in'. When she asked why he had a ship waiting to take him abroad, he blamed his lack of money. She queried Hiegait's report of his plot to imprison her, so he could rule in James's name. At first he denied knowing of it, but then admitted being told of Hiegait's story by John Stewart of Minto, Provost of Glasgow and that 'the Council had brought me a letter to sign to put him in prison, and to kill him if he did resist'. He told her that he was aware of a bond prepared at Craigmillar that she had refused to sign. (He seems to have learned of this from Lord Robert Stewart.)[12*] He again asked her to 'bear him company, for she found ever some ado to draw herself from him to her own lodging, and would never remain with him past two hours together at once'. She seemed to doubt his assurances of loyalty, and did not reply immediately, but was 'very pensive, whereat he found fault'.[13]

The conversation then moved into safer territory. The king said he had heard that Mary had come with a litter, and she replied that she hoped he would use it to travel with her to Edinburgh, as he did not appear well enough to ride. He complained 'that it was not meet for a sick man to travel that could not sit on a horse, and especially in so cold weather'. She explained that she had arranged for him to convalesce at Craigmillar, 'where she might be with him and not far from her son'. He agreed to go in the litter, if 'he and she might be together at bed and board as husband and wife, and that she should leave him no more'. Realising that his principal objective was to renew sexual relations, she confirmed that this was why she had come, but insisted that 'before they could get together, he must be purged and cleansed of his sickness, which she trusted would be shortly, for she minded to give him the bath [for his cure] at Craigmillar'. She told him not to divulge their discussion, as 'the Lords would not think good of their sudden agreement considering he and they were at some words' before; he accepted their need to placate them.[14]

The wording of the official letter confirms Mary's intention to be rehabilitated with the king. Whether she was genuinely prepared to live with him again as man and wife once his cure was complete may seem unlikely, but their later conversations at Kirk o' Field show that she had led him to believe this. She remained disillusioned with him and probably intended to keep him under house arrest in Edinburgh to prevent him from trying to usurp the throne or from kidnapping Prince James. There is no hint that she was bringing him to Edinburgh to facilitate his murder, as both Cecil and Moray would imply. She was trying to gain Morton's assurance that he would be protected.

Although Mary was able to persuade the king to return with her to Edinburgh, he did not divulge details of his scheming against her. His rather meek agreement to go with her suggests that he hoped his objectives would prove more practicable, once they were reunited. Yet his decision to go was taken against the advice of both his father and Crawford, who objected to Craigmillar being used for his recuperation. It was well fortified and seemed better suited as a prison or a murder location. If Mary genuinely sought his rehabilitation, Crawford believed that she should have brought him to Holyrood.

Surrounding the official report, which forms the main part of Casket Letter II, there is evidence of manipulated insertions. These are principally at the end, but also where there may have been spaces in the original text. In Cecil's transcription, there are two double-lined gaps in the printed text and John Guy has suggested that these mirrored those in the original. At both these points further incriminating words seem to have been added, which perhaps failed to fill the available space, and result in *non sequiturs*. In the middle of the document there is a list of headings, presumably to remind Mary of matters to report. All these are covered in the text. Yet immediately before and after it, the letter becomes absurdly personal and incriminating. The traditional view had been that the letter was written over two days and the headings were at the break between two sessions. Yet, as Mary records that she was short of paper, it is more likely that the original report spanned the headings with a gap on either side, later filled by a manipulator with falsified additions. In some instances, these are in Mary's idiom, perhaps culled from earlier passionate letters to the king. Others seem to be drawn from letters written by Bothwell's lovers, suggesting that the perpetrator had access to all their correspondence. The second section is followed by another list of headings: 'Remember you of the purpose of Lady Reres, of the Inglishman, of his mother, of the Earl of Argyll, of the Earl of Bothwell and of the lodging in Edinburgh.' These are not covered in the preceding text and seem to be incriminating falsifications.[15] If the letter were addressed only to Bothwell, it is unlikely that Mary would have referred to him in the third person. The lodging in Edinburgh is assumed to refer to Kirk o' Field, although it had not by then been chosen as the king's residence. On page 301, reference 20 to Chapter 19 shows that Lady Reres is depicted as a go-between in the purported romance between Mary and Bothwell, although this is improbable.

The official report begins: 'Being gone from the place where I have left my heart', hardly the way to open a document for general consumption.[16] If there were space at the top of the opening page, someone could have added these words to imply Mary's infatuation for Bothwell, but, if genuine, they probably apply to the infant James at Stirling. Immediately before the first list of headings are the words:

> We are tied to each other by two false races. The good year untie us
> from them. God forgive me and God knit us together for ever for
> the most faithful couple that ever he did knit together. This is my
> faith. I will die in it.[17]

This implies that Mary is tied to the king and Bothwell to Jean Gordon, whose families are each acting 'falsely' against them. Yet, at this stage, Huntly was still loyal to Bothwell, only turning against him after his sister's divorce. It also implies that Mary was already involved in a relationship with Bothwell. Perhaps the words come from a letter that she wrote after their marriage, but they are more likely to be from one of Bothwell's former mistresses distraught at his arranged marriage to Jean Gordon. Immediately afterwards, the letter continues: 'I am ill at ease and glad to write unto you when other folk be asleep, seeing that I cannot do as they do, according to my desire, that is, between your arms my dear life ...'[18] This could also have been written by one of Bothwell's former mistresses. The letter continues: 'Cursed be the pocky fellow that troubleth me thus much ... I thought I should have been killed with his breath, for it is worse than your uncle's breath ...'[19] If not written by Mary, this shows an intimate knowledge of what was happening. The perpetrator knew that the king was receiving 'salivation of mercury' for his syphilis with its side effect of bad breath, and was aware of Bothwell's 'uncle's' similar affliction. This is assumed to refer to Bothwell's kinsman, Patrick Hepburn, Bishop of Moray, who was known to have syphilis.

Immediately after the first headings, the letter refers to Livingston teasing Mary about Bothwell's infatuation for her while drinking her health at Callendar in the presence of Lady Reres. Yet again the perpetrator seems to have known all the circumstances, but the wording does not imply that Mary was already involved in an affair with Bothwell. It is then claimed that she was secretly sewing her lover a bracelet: 'In the meantime take heed that none of those that be here do see it, for all the world will know it.'[20] Again, this could have been written by one of Bothwell's former lovers, and the wording is inconsistent with the previous section, where the writer has confirmed that Bothwell's infatuation has been noticed by Livingston. The letter then says:

> You make me dissemble so much, that I am afraid thereof with horror, and you make me almost to play the part of the traitor. Remember if it were not for obeying you I had rather be dead.[21]

Although this is incriminating, it is not consistent with the surrounding wording, which reverts to her agreement to resume sexual relations with the king. In the next apparent gap, the letter states:

> To be short he will go anywhere upon my word; alas! And I never deceived anybody, but I remit myself wholly to your will ... Think also if you will not find some invention more secret by physic, for he is to take physic at Craigmillar and the baths also. And shall not come forth of long time ... but I shall never be willing to beguile one that putteth his trust in me. Nevertheless, you may do it all, and

do not esteem me the less therefore, for you are the cause thereof. For my own revenge I would not do it.[22]

This implies that she is encouraging Bothwell to poison the king, as she cannot bring herself to deceive him after he has put his trust in her. Yet it is unthinkable that Mary would append a murder proposal onto an official account of her discussion with her husband to be shown to others. If these are her words taken from another letter, then the original source would surely have been submitted. Although Buchanan had access to the Casket Letters to enable him to write his *Detectio*, he does not refer to the proposal to use poison. He would surely have done so if it were in the version shown to him, and it would seem that the original evidence had to be modified to make it less ambiguous and more incriminating.

The letter continues in an implausibly intimate manner, again referring to Mary secretly sewing a bracelet. It then says:

Burn this letter for it is too dangerous, neither is there anything well said in it ... Now, if to please you, my dear life, I spare neither honour, conscience nor hazard, nor greatness, taking it in good part ... Love me always as I shall love you.[23]

Yet she would hardly have put such an instruction in writing, and the letter was not burned. As Lady Antonia Fraser has reasoned, although Casket Letter II offers the only incriminating evidence against Mary, the authenticity of the incriminating parts is very doubtful.

Although parts of Mary's correspondence used in evidence seem to have been forged, this does not of itself show her as innocent of the murder. Yet we know that, when divorce could not be achieved on acceptable terms, her preference was to have the king rehabilitated. Despite the risk of his continued plotting and her distaste at resuming sexual relations with a syphilitic, he strengthened her claim to be recognised as Elizabeth's heir, as now seemed so tantalisingly close. As late as 8 February, the day before the king's murder, Mary sent Melville to London to renegotiate the Treaty of Edinburgh and wrote to Cecil asking him to accept her good opinion of him, despite their differences. On the evening of the murder, she was showing the king great affection, hardly likely if she were a party to it. Yet rehabilitation overlooked two crucial matters. It assisted those wanting the king's demise and it was unacceptable to the Scottish nobility and the English government led by Cecil.

Part 4

KING HENRY'S MURDER

Chapter 23

The planning of the murder of the king

If Moray were to be permitted to 'look through his fingers' to avoid being implicated in the king's murder, it was even more important for those planning it to keep Mary in the dark, as she would have to call for an investigation afterwards. She had consistently affirmed that she did not want her name to be sullied. Although one of Bothwell's kinsmen, John Hepburn of Bolton, confessed under torture that he believed Mary had consented to the murder, her passionate behaviour with the king at Kirk o' Field beforehand makes it highly unlikely that she knew of it.

Bothwell saw the king's murder as a political necessity. Although he hoped to discuss it with Morton at Dunbar, his haemorrhage prevented them from meeting there. He knew the exiles would want revenge on the king for failing to protect them after Riccio's murder, and, as their leader, Morton was the obvious man to organise it. As soon as he had sufficiently recovered, Bothwell came to meet Morton at Whittinghame, hoping to pass responsibility for it onto the planner of Riccio's murder. Morton certainly wanted the king dead, but was in no position to arrange it. In accordance with the terms of his rehabilitation, he was not permitted within seven miles of the Court at Holyrood. He had also been told by Moray to persuade Bothwell into organising it. Cecil and Moray wanted Bothwell as the scapegoat, so that they could perhaps implicate Mary with him in a crime of passion. This involved engineering a tale of a romance between them, when none existed. They had three objectives: Moray would be restored as regent of Scotland; Cecil would remove two unacceptable claimants to the English throne; and England's northern border would be protected by an anglophile Protestant government in Scotland. This may sound like being wise after the event, but there is evidence of all these objectives being pre-planned. Even Mary came to accept this herself. In Nau's *Memorials*, written on her instruction while in captivity in England, he recorded that the queen's enemies 'having used [Bothwell] to rid themselves of the king, designed to make [him] their instrument to ruin the Queen'. They thus signed a bond to induce her to marry Bothwell 'so that they might charge her with being in the plot against her late husband and a consenting party to his death … this they did shortly after, appealing to the fact that she had married the murderer'.[1]

When Bothwell realised that he would need to organise the king's murder himself, he was determined to cover his tracks so completely that he could not be implicated. The complication for those investigating the murder is in sifting through all the concocted depositions, particularly of Bothwell's movements to show that the evidence of him being present at the murder is unrealistic. Immediately beforehand, he was residing at Holyrood with his wife, where arrivals and departures would have been noted by the Guard. He remained in the queen's company for the whole of the day of the murder, for much of it attired in fancy dress. He was at the palace shortly before it took place, holding a late meeting with the queen and Stewart of Traquair, Captain of the Guard, almost certainly to discuss the prince's future protection. He was in his bed at Holyrood with his wife, when woken to be told of the explosion. There is no plausible evidence that he left Holyrood to involve himself in the murder after his late meeting with the queen, and the Guard was never asked to verify his movements. He wanted to demonsrate that he slept in his bed at Holyrood.

Yet Bothwell was deluded if he thought he could avoid being implicated. Too many of his enemies knew he had planned it. Moray's allies could plant rumours without infringing their bond, and they fanned them to good effect. Within a week of the murder, the public learned from placards posted in Edinburgh that he had organised it and, absurdly, the queen was implicated with him in a crime of passion, despite there being no hint of impropriety between them beforehand.

There is little doubt that the detailed murder plan was conceived by Bothwell, Morton, Balfour and Douglas with a few trusted henchmen. In his deposition, John Hay of Talla, another Bothwell associate, claimed that, on 7 February, two days beforehand, Bothwell said to him: 'John, this is the matter. The king's death is devised. I will reveal it unto you for if I put him not down, I cannot have a life in Scotland. He will be my destruction!'[2] Morton, Maitland and Balfour later admitted becoming aware of the detailed plan on about 7 February as did Moray. It was probably only then that it was finalised, and it is known that the gunpowder was moved into position only on the evening of 9 February, shortly before the explosion. Yet they all knew well before this that murder was contemplated.

On 19 January, the day before escorting the queen as far as Callendar, Bothwell had come to Whittinghame to meet Archibald Douglas. Despite being a Lord of Session and a minister of the Kirk, Douglas was a devious character, having been on the fringes of Riccio's murder plot. He had already agreed to assist with the king's assassination; he was associated with Bothwell through the courts and later married his sister Jean. (Following the death of Lord John Stewart, Jean had remarried John Sinclair, Master of Caithness, from whom she was divorced in 1575. It was then that she married Archibald Douglas.) It is often suggested that it was Morton who persuaded his 'cousin' Archibald to take his place in the conspiracy. Yet he was only a remote connection, being a second cousin of his wife's grand-father the 2nd Earl of Morton. He was there because he had acted as the communication link between the Craigmillar bond signatories and the exiles in England and had been recruited by Bothwell.

Morton arrived at Whittinghame to find himself at a meeting with Bothwell, Douglas and Maitland, who had arrived from Lethington. The official purpose was to ensure, on the queen's behalf, that he would not reopen old scores with the king. Yet Bothwell briefed him on the murder objective and privately asked him to arrange it, 'seeing it was in the queen's mind that the king should be taken away'.[3] Morton later claimed that Douglas and Maitland added their persuasion (although Douglas denied this and Maitland was then out of favour). In all probability, Maitland was assisting Morton in trying to persuade Bothwell to arrange it himself. Morton testified that he asked to see the queen's warrant approving it, but they became evasive. He claimed that, even if the queen had sanctioned it, he would have preferred to return to exile. This, of course, was a blatant attempt to demonstrate his innocence. Although he later implied that he could not become involved after being so recently pardoned, he certainly provided henchmen. John Hepburn of Bolton's deposition says that the original plan was for each of the nobles to send two of their servants 'to the doing thereof in the fields' (meaning some out-of-the-way place).[4] Paris implied the use of a ritual blood feud, similar to that devised for Riccio. He claimed under torture that Maitland, who at that point was out of favour with Moray, was Bothwell's chief accomplice, supported by Argyll, Huntly, Morton, Ruthven and Lindsay among the nobility. When asked if Moray was involved, Paris claimed he was neutral. Given the careful manipula-tion of the depositions, it is surprising that these names were not expunged, but each could probably demonstrate that he was not present, and there is no other evidence of Argyll, Huntly, Ruthven and Lindsay's involvement. Although Douglas and Balfour are known to have taken part, Paris did not mention them. The principal organisers were Bothwell and Morton, but they avoided being there on the night. Bothwell was with the queen, where his absence would have been noticed, and Morton faced arrest if seen within seven miles of Edinburgh. To cover their tracks completely, they arranged to blow up the Kirk o' Field at night, having encircled the building to prevent the king's escape.

As Moray intended to leave Edinburgh beforehand, he wanted Morton to organise the nobility in his absence. Morton was told to ingratiate himself with Bothwell, so that they could share the government afterwards. Although they were never natural allies, he might be able to entice Bothwell into setting his cap at the queen, which could implicate her in a crime of passion. To return to power, Moray needed Bothwell destroyed and the queen discredited. He could then arrange for Morton, Maitland and Balfour's involvement to be airbrushed out, although Maitland avoided becoming involved in the detailed arrangements. Balfour did not come to Whittinghame, but he bartered olive oil to acquire a barrel of gunpowder and arranged its positioning in the cellar of the Old Provost's Lodging. Although his movements remained shadowy, he later sought a pardon, which he would have needed only if he were involved. By 9 February, he had left his Edinburgh home, where Moretta was staying, and was busy unnoticed at Kirk o' Field. Yet it was Douglas who coordinated the arrangements on the night, relying on the protection of Moray and Cecil in return for his silence. He was ultimately found innocent of a crime, for which several others were executed. Without realising it, Bothwell was being isolated with his henchmen, allowing Moray, who had always hated him, to claim that he had organised the murder alone. Morton told the truth in 1581, when he admitted under oath that he knew of the plot, but had not taken part in it. Yet he will have signed the Craigmillar bond with Douglas at Whittinghame and took no steps to warn his kinsman, the king, of the plan for his murder.

Bothwell and Morton soon had enough adherents to 'take the deid in hand'. With Bothwell 'ruling all at court', there is evidence of him recruiting help by claiming that the murder had the queen's approval.[5] There is a report that, after meeting at Whittinghame, Bothwell and Maitland went with Douglas to Holyrood to obtain the queen's sanction, which she refused. Douglas, who was apparently acting only as a messenger, was instructed 'to show to the Earl of Morton that the Queen will have no speech of the matter'.[6] This story seems a conveniently devised fabrication to implicate Maitland and Bothwell and to exonerate Morton and Douglas. It also suggests that Mary was aware of the murder plan, even if she did not approve it. As she failed to arrange a full investigation afterwards, any foreknowledge would have implicated her. Yet in all probability there was no such meeting.

If the conspirators wanted her kept in the dark, they would hardly have asked for her approval.

To give credence to a crime of passion, Buchanan's *Detectio*, not written until 1568, recounted numerous liaisons between Mary and Bothwell before the king's murder, but none of them stand up to critical examination (see many of the endnotes). Both had been at death's door, hardly an aphrodisiac for a romance. In a Court full of rumour, the ambassadors' grapevine would have jumped at any juicy impropriety. With Mary actively seeking recognition as Elizabeth's heir, she would have wanted to avoid any scandal prejudicing her hopes. The king, with his close bloodline to both thrones, was far more appropriate as a consort than the unacceptable Bothwell.

Even though the *Detectio* can be shown to be fabricated, it has been suggested that Bothwell undertook the king's murder as part of a personal agenda to marry the queen. From the doubtful evidence of Casket Letter II, we have seen that Livingston hinted at Bothwell's infatuation at Callendar before Mary's visit to Glasgow. Yet Bothwell had no reason to believe that she would agree to marriage if freed from the king, and he was already married. If marriage were his motive, he would have sought assurances of support from the other signatories of the Craigmillar bond. There is no verifiable evidence of a rumoured discussion at Dunbar at which the nobility bargained with him for personal benefit in return for their backing. They hated him and would hardly promote him to replace the king. It was Moray whom they wanted as the power behind the throne. If Bothwell married the queen, Moray would be left out in the cold. Yet once the king was dead, Morton cynically enticed Bothwell into a marriage for Scotland's security. It was only then that the crime of passion scenario became plausible.

Chapter 24

The demise of the king

Although Mary remained depressed and unwell, she had been able to persuade the king to return from Glasgow. She reasoned that Edinburgh offered him protection, and she could keep watch on his plotting. The returning exiles were not permitted within seven miles of Court, and she believed that Bothwell had gained Morton's undertaking not to harm him.

On 27 January, Mary left Glasgow with the king, who travelled in her litter. The lesions on his face were healing, but he was still wearing a taffeta mask. They spent a night at Callendar followed by one or two nights at Linlithgow, before heading on for Craigmillar. Although Bothwell returned from the Borders, he only reached Edinburgh on 30 January. He could not have been planning the murder while in the Borders as Buchanan claimed, and the lodging at Kirk o' Field had not yet been chosen.[1*] Although he was back in time to escort Mary and the king to Craigmillar, shortly beforehand, the king announced that he would not stay there, perhaps heeding Crawford's concerns that he could be imprisoned. Instead, he chose to recuperate at Kirk o' Field, just inside the Town Wall, where he was to make a rapid recovery in fresh air on a hill overlooking the Cowgate (see map of Edinburgh pp. xii–xiii). This location was undoubtedly chosen at the last moment by the king himself. One of his servants recorded:

> It was devised in Glasgow that the king should have lain first at Craigmillar, but because he had no will thereof, the purpose was altered and the conclusion taken that he should lie beside the Kirk o' Field.[2]

He did not want to be seen with his taffeta mask at Holyrood, three-quarters of a mile to the north-east. With Châtelherault still exiled in France, the king seems to have assumed that he could occupy his new mansion there. Archbishop Hamilton was in residence however, and with the Lennoxes being traditional Hamilton enemies, it was not made available. Balfour then proposed the Old Provost's Lodging nearby, as it was available for lease from his brother.

To gain a full understanding of events at Kirk o' Field, it is necessary to understand its layout. The Old Provost's Lodging faced onto a small quadrangle measuring 86ft by 73ft with a well at its centre, just within the Old Town Wall in the south-east corner of Edinburgh. (This wall is often referred to as the Flodden Wall, but modern research shows that no new wall was built after the battle of Flodden.) Until the Reformation the quadrangle had been surrounded to the west by the collegiate buildings of the church of St Mary-in-the-Fields. This was now in ruins, damaged first by the English in 1544 and then by the Reformers in 1558, so that the buildings in the quadrangle had been converted into residential accommodation. The old Friars' Hospital outside the quadrangle to the north-west had been rebuilt as the three-storey Hamilton House. To the east, there were gardens with orchards sloping downhill, and beyond these, about 200yds to the north-east, was the ruined Blackfriars Monastery with its gate through the Town Wall behind (see bird's eye view of Kirk o' Field on page 16 of the pictures section).

Sir James's brother, Robert Balfour, had taken a lease over three of the buildings in the quadrangle in the previous year. He occupied the New Provost's Lodging himself and let out the Old Provost's Lodging for short-term rent, employing John Hepburn of Bolton as its warden. The Old Provost's Lodging was adjoined by the single-storey Prebendaries' Chamber, built over a cellar to provide a *salle* of 45ft by 15ft, where tenants could entertain their guests. Robert Balfour held several properties for rent, and the lodging had been used by Bedford in the previous month, before attending the prince's baptism at Stirling.

The New Provost's Lodging was on the west side of the quadrangle, with an adjoining wall running from its southern end to the Town Wall, which ran at right angles behind the quadrangle's southern side. The adjoining wall completed the quadrangle's enclosure, but there was a gateway through it to provide its main access. The south side of the quadrangle to the right of this gateway housed the Prebendaries' Chamber and, beyond that, was the Old Provost's Lodging, backing onto the Town Wall. This had a door on its east side at cellar level, opening onto the gardens and orchards sloping away beyond. The narrower Prebendaries' Chamber had a secluded little courtyard behind it, adjacent to the Town Wall. (This can be clearly seen on the spy's narrative drawing of the murder scene – see illustrations section pp. 14–15.)

The Old Provost's Lodging was on three floors. On each of the upper two levels, there was a bedroom measuring 16ft by 12ft, with a window facing north onto the quadrangle, with a *garde-robe* behind measuring 7ft by 12ft. The two bedrooms were connected by a turnpike stair in a turret. At the rear, there was a galleried staircase area that extended over the top of the Town Wall to provide sleeping quarters for servants. The drop from the galleried area to the ground on the far side of the wall was about 14ft. The wall was 6ft thick at its base, tapering to 1ft at the top. The main entrance of the lodging was approached from the quadrangle to the lower of the two bedroom floors, which also provided access at the same level to the *salle*. The cellar, reached by a stone stairway, was a vaulted stone undercroft, in which there was a kitchen with its door opening onto the garden to the east. On the kitchen's west side, a second door opened into a passage, leading back through the Town Wall, where there was a postern gate opening into an alley known as Thieves Row. The passage must have had access on its opposite side to both the cellar under the Prebendaries' Chamber, and to the little courtyard behind. The cellar of the Prebendaries' Chamber started at head height by the passage, but tapered to 2ft high at its west end. Outside the Town Wall to the south of Thieves Row were further gardens, next to which were two small cottages.

There is no plausible evidence that Kirk o' Field was chosen as a suitable place to murder the king, although this was to be alleged by Buchanan. The detailed murder plan could not have been developed until his arrival on 1 February, and there is evidence that it was not finalised until a week later. Neither Bothwell nor Morton was involved in choosing it, although they could only have approved of its layout and location, as it could be approached almost unnoticed through the postern gate from Thieves Row and from the side door to the kitchen.

Although adequate by the standards of the time, the king was disappointed at the accommodation's lack of grandeur, and 'in no wise liked of'.[3] It took all Mary's persuasion for him to agree to occupy the rooms, which were 'more easy and handsome'. She explained that there was 'a privy way between the palace and the lodging, where she might always resort to him till he was whole of his disease'.[4,5*] This ran along the outside of the Town Wall from Holyrood to the gate at Blackfriars Monastery, from where there was access through the east garden. To make the lodging more amenable, Mary arranged for six tapestries, together with a turkey carpet and furniture, to be brought from Holyrood to improve the interior. Further tapestries depicting 'the hunting of the conies' were hung in the *garde-robes*. The king agreed to sleep in the upper bedroom, but did not consider the black velvet bed, which had been used by Bedford, to be adequate. His own bed, hung with violet-brown velvet and richly decorated with cloth of gold was brought in. This had previously belonged to the queen regent. A bath for his medicinal treatment was placed beside it, covered by the door removed from the upper entrance to the internal turnpike staircase. To implicate Mary in her husband's murder, Moray claimed that she arranged for his bed to be returned to Holyrood to prevent it from being destroyed in the explosion, saying that she used the pretext of wanting to save it from damage by soiled bathwater. This was another of his fabrications, as both the bed and the rich tapestries were included in the inventory of items destroyed. Mary was to occupy the lower bedroom, from where she could nurse him and keep a watchful eye on any scheming. This was also elaborately furnished with a bed, covered in yellow-and-green damask with a furred coverlet, and a leather chair of estate on a dais, upholstered with watered silk of red and yellow. Five more tapestries were hung on its walls. These were all destroyed in the explosion.

Mary slept at Kirk o' Field on 5 and 7 February having administered the king's medicinal baths. She also considered staying there on the night of the murder, again demonstrating that she was unaware of the detailed plan. She visited him daily and, by all accounts, good relations were restored. They would sit up playing cards until midnight, or listening to music. Knox wrote that 'everyman marvelled at this reconciliation or sudden change'.[6] This has been seen as a deception by Mary to avoid suspicion, but, to rehabilitate the king, she needed to regain his confidence. Such was their apparent rapport that he warned her of attempts being made to sow discord between them. In a tone of injured innocence, he even reported that there were claims that he planned to take her life. She was not taken in and, despite her outward showing of affection, was aware of his continued plotting. On 7 February, she again wrote to Drury in Berwick to demand Lutini's arrest, and on the next day forbade Moretta from coming to visit the king. She must have enjoyed using the excuse that she feared his master the Duke of Savoy's resentment at the part played by the king in the murder of his former servant, Riccio. Despite her doubts about him, the king appears to have accepted her friendly overtures, writing to Lennox that she 'doth use herself like a natural and loving wife'.[7]

It was about now that Mary is purported to have written Casket Letter III, for which a transcript survives in the original French. It is annotated by an English clerk, 'To prove the affections'. It starts:

> Monsieur, if the displeasure of your absence, your forgetfulness, the fear of danger so promised by everyone to your so-loved person may give me consolation, can console me, I leave it to you to judge, seeing the unhap that my cruel lot and continual misadventure has hitherto promised me, following the misfortunes and fears, as well of late as of long time by-past, the which ye do know.

It carries on in this uncharacteristically submissive vein, saying:

> I will in no wise accuse you ... of the coldness of your writing, since I am so far made yours that that which pleases you is acceptable to me ... and to testify to you how lowly I submit me under your commandments, I have sent you, in sign of homage, by Paris, the ornament of the head [probably a locket of hair] ... In place whereof, since I have always left it unto you, I send you a sepulchre of hard stone [thought to have been a *memento mori* – a jewel designed to remind the wearer of his mortality], coloured with black, strewn with tears and bones ... The enamelling that is about is black, which signifies the steadfastness of her who sends the same. The tears are without number ... of your absence, that I cannot be in outward effect yours ... My only wealth receive therefore in all good part the same, as I have received your marriage with extreme joy, the which shall not part forth my bosom till that marriage of our bodies shall be made public ... I have shown unto the bearer that which I have learned, to whom I remit me, knowing the credit that you give him, as sure does that will be for ever unto your humble, obedient, lawful wife ...[8]

The reference to Paris (although Mary generally referred to him as Joachim and this could of course be a forged addition) is really the only evidence that this is a passionate message from Mary to Bothwell when she cannot be with him. The letter's humble tone with its grammatical inconsistencies makes it quite implausible as one she would have sent to him. He was purported to be making suit to her, not her to him. Although Bothwell could be cruel, there is no evidence of any unkindness to her before her abduction from Almond Bridge to Dunbar. If written by Mary, it is much more likely to be a letter to the king before their official marriage. As Paris was Bothwell's servant before entering royal employment, it is also possible that it is a copy, forged in Mary's writing, of a letter to Bothwell from a former mistress, perhaps Anna Throndssen. It is quite unrealistic to consider it as a love letter from Mary to Bothwell. She could not claim to be his lawful wife, as neither of them was free to marry and, as both were for most of this time at Holyrood, she could hardly complain of his absence. Also it is difficult to envisage, during her recent hectic schedule, that she would have had time to commission an elaborate jewel for him.

When the king arrived at Kirk o' Field, Mary appears to have tried to arrange for him to be reconciled with the nobility as part of his rehabilitation. They would have none of it, warning her that he would put a knife to her throat and theirs. According to Buchanan, only Bothwell made any show of friendship, apparently to deflect suspicion from his involvement in the murder plan. Yet the king used this friendlier atmosphere to discuss Maitland with her privately, warning that he 'was planning the ruin of the one by the means of the other, and meant in the end to ruin both of them'.[9] Maitland certainly wanted the king's ruin, but, as Mary Fleming's husband, he is unlikely also to have sought to destroy the queen. Yet he backed Moray, who wanted them both removed.

The king had several of his own servants at Kirk o' Field. His valet, William Taylor, slept on a pallet in his room, with Taylor's page, Alastair (or Andrew) McCaig, sharing the galleried anteroom outside his *garde-robe* with two other chamber servants, Thomas Nelson and Edward Symonds. The lodging provided up to six others, supervised by Hepburn of Bolton. They slept with the king's four grooms, including Master Glen, on the lower floor. Bonkil, the cook, returned home at the end of each day, as did Sandy Durham, Master of the King's Wardrobe. There were no guards, indicating that the king was oblivious to the rumours of plotting against him. Melville recalled that 'many suspected that the Earl of Bothwell had some enterprise against' the king, but Melville did not personally believe it and said nothing.[10] On 8 February, Lord Robert Stewart arrived to warn the king that 'if he retired not hastily out of that place, it would cost him his life'.[11] The king immediately told Mary, who interviewed Lord Robert with Moray and Bothwell in front of the king. When Lord Robert denied giving the king a warning, the king drew his sword and started to fight, causing Mary to ask Moray to intervene. By now, both Moray, as he subsequently admitted, and Bothwell knew that the story was true, but said nothing. This again confirms Moray's intimate knowledge and approval of the murder plot. By arranging for Bothwell and Moray to interview Lord Robert, it might be implied that Mary also knew of it, but it required her two most senior advisers to question her half-brother.

At the Conference at York, a letter was produced in Mary's 'own hand', placing a different slant on Lord Robert Stewart's row with the king. Far from Mary asking Moray to prevent the fight, it claimed that she incited it to provoke Lord Robert into killing the king to save Bothwell the trouble. Yet the letter was quickly withdrawn and was not seen or mentioned again. Perhaps it was too obviously a forgery. If genuine, it would surely have provided compelling evidence for her prosecution. Casket Letter IV, purportedly written to Bothwell on 7 February, two days before the murder, seems to corroborate the missing letter's assertion that Lord Robert was incited by Mary to murder the king. Yet it is completely implausible as a missive from Mary to Bothwell, and is so long that it is unimaginable that she would have needed to write it, when she was seeing him every day. There is a French transcript and an English translation made for the Conference at Westminster, for which it was annotated somewhat obscurely: 'Letter concerning Holyrood House'.[12] It seems to be an amalgamation of at least two letters with a forged addition. It contains an obscure metaphor from Greek mythology and a quotation from an early version of a sonnet from *Le Second Livre des Amours* by Ronsard. Mary, the king, Maitland, Buchanan and Cecil might reasonably be expected to have understood the analogy, but, despite Bothwell having some Classical learning, it would surely have been over his head. Yet the king employed reference to the sonnet in his own verses. Its use in confirming that Mary incited Lord Robert into killing the king is entirely conjectural, as neither is mentioned by name. Furthermore, it only takes on its intended purpose in the English version used at Westminster, which mistranslates what is recorded in the French transcript. Cecil, who knew the poem, spotted the error and corrected his copy, but did not draw attention to the obvious shortcoming. It is more likely to be a letter written from Mary to the king, using analogy with which he was familiar. In that context, she is jealous of some new mistress, and threatens a separation if he does not return to her. A more detailed analysis is given in endnote 13 to this chapter.[13]

On 8 February, Lennox left Glasgow intending to visit his son at the end of his convalescence. He wanted to use the king's warmer relationship with the queen to seek his own reconciliation with her. It was reported that he was attacked in a Glasgow street before leaving and was saved only by Sempill's intervention, but Lennox never mentioned it and arrived safely at Linlithgow. It has also been suggested that his visit was timed to congratulate the king on achieving a successful coup against Mary. Yet nothing is known about how this would have been achieved.

With the murder imminent, on the morning of Sunday 9 February, Moray came to the queen to seek consent to leave Edinburgh to see his wife, who had suffered a miscarriage at St Andrews. This seems a convenient excuse, as he did not return immediately his wife had recovered. As he later admitted, he knew that the king was to be murdered that night.

Mary is reputed to have taken time out of an almost impossibly busy schedule on Sunday 9 February to write Casket Letter V to Bothwell. This concerns the dismissal of an 'unthankful' servant, and is endorsed: 'Anent the dispatch dismissal of Margaret Carwood; which was before her marriage;

proves her affection.' Yet the letter itself does not refer to Margaret Carwood by name and she was certainly not a servant that Mary dismissed. She had been granted a handsome pension on the previous day in contemplation of her marriage, and Mary paid for her wedding dress and reception, which took place on 11 February, despite the king being murdered the day before. For Mary to attend her service was thus a mark of signal favour. The letter begins:

> My heart, alas! Must the folly of one woman whose unthankful-
> ness to me ye do sufficiently know, be occasion of displeasure unto
> you, considering that I could not have remedied thereunto without
> knowing it. And since that I perceived it, I could not tell you, for
> that I knew not how to govern myself therein.

This seems to refer to an unnamed servant, known to have become pregnant out of wedlock. While this was not infrequent, it was much frowned upon by both the Kirk and Mary. Margaret Carwood was certainly not unthankful and was not pregnant before marriage. The only known slur against her is Buchanan's dubious assertion in his *Detectio* that it was 'Margaret Carwood, who was privy and helper of all their [Mary's and Bothwell's] love'. She was never called to give evidence to provide a proper understanding of the letter, which shows that Mary is just as angry with the servant as the recipient.

Without knowing the context in which it was written, the letter's mean-ing is ambiguous, but it can be conjectured that the recipient has blamed Mary for continuing to employ a servant against his will. Mary is responding that she only wants to do as he wishes. If he can find an alternative she will be rid of the servant, as soon as she has been married off. She says:

> For neither in this, nor in any other thing, will I take upon to do
> anything without knowledge of your will, which I beseech you let
> me understand; for I will follow it all my life more willingly than
> you do declare it to me.

The recipient seems particularly angry at the servant gossiping about his unfaithfulness to Mary. The French transcript continues:

> And if ye do not send me word this night, what ye will that I shall
> do, I will unburden myself of it [dismiss her], at the risk of mak-
> ing her attempt [reveal] something that could be harmful to what
> we are both aiming at [the English throne]. And when she shall be

married, I beseech you give me one [a new servant], or else I shall
take such as shall content you for their conditions; but, as for their
tongues, or faithfulness towards you, I will not answer [for them].

If she is to choose the new servant, she cannot be responsible for them being
loyal to the recipient. Yet the first sentence of this quotation has been maliciously mistranslated. Taken out of context in the English version, it reads:

And if ye do not send me word this night, what ye will that I shall do, I
will rid myself of it, and hazard to cause it to be enterprised and taken
in hand, which might be hurtful to that whereunto both we do tend.[14]

This implies that Mary is planning the king's murder with Bothwell,
even though the sentence makes no sense as part of a discussion about
the servant. Mary then denies complaining about the recipient's lack of
fidelity, by continuing:

I beseech you that [the alleged infidelities] are opinion of other person, be not hurtful in your mind to my constancy. [You now] mistrust me, but when I shall put you out of doubt and clear myself,
refuse it not my dear love, and suffer me to make some proof of my
obedience, my faithfulness, constancy, and voluntary subjection,
which I take for the pleasantest good that I may receive, if ye will
accept it, and make no ceremony at it, for ye could do me no greater
outrage, nor give me more mortal grief.[15]

This is clearly a letter from Mary to the king, who is concerned at gossip
about their marital difficulties at a time when they are being reconciled. She
is trying to dissuade him from causing a scene when they are both hoping
for her to be recognised as Elizabeth's heir. It is the king who is referred to as
'my heart' and 'my dear love' in a spirit of reconciliation, although this may
be a forged addition. It is hard to imagine that Bothwell would have been
worried about the dismissal of Mary's servant, and, as they were together all
that day, a letter would have been unnecessary.

On the morning of Sunday 9 February, the king attended Mass before taking his last medicinal bath. Mary attended the Chapel Royal for the wedding
of her French valet, Sebastian Pagez, who married another favourite servant,
Christina (or Christily) Hogg. Mary provided her richly embroidered wide-
sleeved wedding dress, made from thirteen and three-quarter ells of black

satin, with a velvet lining. She also gave thirty-two ells of green ribbon to make her skirt and hood. At noon, she attended the wedding breakfast as guest of honour. The guests wore carnival clothes with masks, and Pagez had prepared a masque for the evening celebration, which the queen had promised to attend. As a Reformer, Bothwell will have excused himself from the Catholic marriage service, but in carnival clothes he attended the wedding breakfast. At four o'clock, without changing, he came with the queen to the Canongate to a dinner for Moretta at the home of John Carswell, Bishop of the Isles (or Argyll), with most of the nobility, other than Moray and Maitland, in attendance. It is not known why Maitland was absent, as he joined the queen at Kirk o' Field later and was not involved in the detailed murder plan.

At about seven o'clock, with the dinner over, the queen, still in costume, rode to Kirk o' Field, where she was joined by 'the most part of nobles then in this town', including Bothwell, Huntly, Argyll, Maitland and Cassillis.[16] It was later claimed that she had intended spending the night there on the last day of her husband's convalescence, and he certainly tried to persuade her to stay. The king entertained her with music, and she chatted to him 'more cheerfully than usual for a few hours' and 'often kissed him'. The guests at Kirk o' Field showed no apparent concern at the royal embraces, with Bothwell, Huntly, Argyll and Cassillis playing dice. Yet she had always planned to return to Holyrood for the wedding masque and her horses were waiting to take her back. It was after eleven o'clock when she was reminded that she needed to leave. Before her departure, she gave the king a ring as a token of her promise to be permanently reunited by sleeping with him on the following night. Moray, who was not there of course, later claimed to de Silva that she 'had done an extraordinary and unexampled thing on the night of the murder in giving her husband a ring, petting and fondling him after plotting his murder', which was 'the worst thing' about the deed.[17] This is yet more of his scurrilous rumour-mongering.

To the king's disappointment, Mary immediately set out for Holyrood with her entourage, telling him she would remain there for the night, as it would be too late to return afterwards. Bothwell had reminded her that she was going to Seton the next morning and would want an early start and it is alleged that Maitland also discouraged her return. It had been a long day and there was a light frosting of snow. As she mounted her horse to leave, she saw Paris with his face all blackened, saying, 'Jesu, Paris, how begrimed you are!'[18] He did not respond, but she would hardly have drawn attention to him, if she had known that he had been moving gunpowder into the cellar under cover of the babble above.[19*]

When the queen arrived at Holyrood, she saw the end of the masque and attended the bawdy ceremony to put the bride and groom to bed. At around midnight, she held a private conference with Bothwell and Stewart of Traquair, the Captain of the Guard. After fifteen minutes, Traquair left, but Bothwell stayed with her 'for a considerable time'.[20] It has been conjectured that Traquair and Bothwell were reporting knowledge of the king's alleged plot against her, implying that she saw this as the last straw for her marriage, but there is no evidence that she faced imminent danger requiring such an urgent discussion. With the gunpowder already packed into the cellars of the Old Provost's Lodging and Prebendaries' Chamber, it was too late to abort the explosion. It has also been argued that Bothwell needed Mary's blessing to light the fuse. Yet it would have been unrealistic to seek it when they were already committed, particularly as neither she nor Traquair were aware of the plan. Yet Traquair knew the king's shortcomings, and might have had sympathy with the conspirators. Given the late hour, their lengthy conversation must have had another urgent purpose, perhaps the arrangements for the prince's security while Mary was at Seton. Bothwell may have prolonged the discussion to demonstrate his non-attendance at the murder scene, particularly as Traquair, as Captain of the Guard, could be asked to confirm his movements.

Apart from some extraordinarily dubious depositions taken from his henchmen under torture, there is no evidence of Bothwell leaving Holyrood that evening to supervise the explosion, and the guard was never asked to confirm his movements, as there would have been none to report. Without being involved in the movement of the gunpowder, he could hardly have lit the fuse. If he had wanted to give his final authority, with or without the queen's sanction, it would have been less conspicuous to send Paris or another servant. As Sheriff of Edinburgh, he would be woken immediately after the explosion and needed to be in his rooms. If he had only returned to Holyrood afterwards, he would have had some explaining to do. When he went to investigate on the next day, he did not seem to know what had happened. This again suggests that he was not there on the night before.

After the queen's departure from Kirk o' Field, Sandy Durham also retired for the night. It was later suggested that he seemed over-anxious to get away and may have been a spy for the conspirators, but this seems unlikely. The king arranged for his 'great horses' to be ready to leave for Seton with the queen at five o'clock the next morning. According to Nelson, as reported in the *Lennox Narrative,* he then ordered wine and sat up for about an hour with the remaining servants. Although Taylor had asked him to play his lute, he had said that his hand was tired but they sang a psalm unaccompanied from a book that Taylor produced.[21] They had no forewarning of what was to happen.

At about two o'clock in the morning there was a huge explosion, resembling a volley from twenty-five or thirty cannon, which woke people all over Edinburgh. According to Herries, 'the blast was fearfull to all about, and many rose from their beds at the noise.' It was followed by 'the confused cries of the people'.[22] Paris was later to say that every hair on his head had stood on end. The Old Provost's Lodging and adjacent Prebendaries' Chamber were destroyed,

> not only the roof and floors, but also the walls to the foundation, so that no one stone rests on another.[23] It was said that great stones, of the length of ten foot and of breadth of four foot, were found blown from the house far away.[24]

Mary recorded that all was 'either carried far away or dashed in dross to the very groundstone'.[25]

Several depositions were taken on 11 February, the day after the murder, from those in the vicinity of the explosion. Barbara Martin in Blackfriars Wynd testified that she had heard running footsteps passing immediately beforehand. She looked from her window to see thirteen armed men emerging from Blackfriars Monastery to the south and hastening up the High Street. Her neighbour, Meg Crokat, who had been in bed with her two children, ran naked to the door of her cottage to see eleven men, one wearing silk, emerging from Blackfriars Gate, where they split into two groups as they hurried away. She asked them what the 'crack' was and, after hearing Barbara Martin calling them traitors, concluded that they were up to no good. Women lodging in cottages by the south garden and orchard outside the Town Wall heard a plaintive voice crying, 'Pity me, kinsmen, for the love of him who had pity on all the world!'[26] This was followed by silence.

The town watch arrived and arrested Captain William Blackadder, the first man they saw. He happened to be a friend of Bothwell, but came running after hearing the explosion while enjoying a drink with a friend. A large crowd gathered at the scene of devastation, some with lanterns. They found an empty barrel of gunpowder by the side door to the east garden and spotted the blackened figure of Nelson crying for help from the top of the Town

Wall. He was only superficially injured, either having being thrown clear by the blast or, more likely, having escaped beforehand by climbing out from the gallery. People started digging frantically, knowing that the king was staying there, but it was dark and cold with intermittent snow.

At Holyrood, Mary was also woken by the explosion and sent messengers to establish the cause. They returned to report that Kirk o' Field was destroyed. Bothwell, as Sheriff of Edinburgh, was woken by his servant George Halket, although in reality it is inconceivable that he could have slept through such a blast. He was told that the king was believed to have been killed. He shot up shouting: 'Fie! Treason!'[27] He sent men to investigate before returning to bed with his wife to await news.

Two bodies were found in the rubble; one was McCaig, but two more servants survived (probably including Symonds, who, like Nelson, was on the upper floor). There was no sign of Hepburn of Bolton or the lodging servants, suggesting that they had all been involved in moving the gunpowder and had left before the fuse was lit. There was still no sign of the king or his valet, Taylor, but, at about five o'clock in the morning, a search of the south garden and orchard beyond the Town Wall revealed their nearly naked, but unmarked, bodies more than fifty yards from the lodging. There was no gunpowder on their clothing or evidence of strangulation. It was later established that one of the king's ribs was broken, but that was the only sign of a struggle. Beside them, laid out in a row, was a chair, a piece of rope, a dagger, the king's furred nightgown and a quilt. These were carefully positioned, and the king's hand modestly covered his genitals. A backless velvet slipper, thought to have belonged to a conspirator, lay nearby.

A surgeon, John Pitcairn, was called to remain with the king's body. A message was sent to tell the queen of the king's death, and Bothwell, who was still in bed, was woken by Huntly. He dressed quickly and, with Huntly, Argyll, Atholl, Maitland and the Countesses of Atholl and Mar, went to console the queen. He reported that she was 'greatly afflicted by it all'[28] and Clernault, the Cardinal of Lorraine's agent, wrote that she was 'one of the most unfortunate queens in the world'.[29] Moretta added that she was 'in great fear of a worse fate'.[30] She seemed unable to deal with her correspondence, but sent Bothwell with men to make a diligent search. He held several suspects, until they could provide alibis for their movements. He also arranged with Sandy Durham for the king's body to be laid out in the New Provost's Lodging with a guard of honour, before it was carried back to Holyrood to be embalmed. The Court was ordered into mourning and, in accordance with French custom, Mary retired into forty days' seclusion.

Huntly suggested that the Privy Council should be called to 'deliberate about the means of apprehending the traitors who committed the deed' and it met at the Tolbooth shortly after noon with Argyll, as Lord Justice-General, presiding.[31] Many of its members were parties to the conspiracy, but Tullibardine represented Lennox interests. To bring some order to all the rumours, it prepared a detailed account to be sent with Clernault to Catherine de Medici. This stressed that it was

> engaged in an enquiry and, having once uncovered the matter, Your Majesty and all the world shall know that Scotland will not endure that such a cause for shame should rest upon her shoulders.[32]

It reported Mary's belief that it was only good fortune that prevented her and a great many of the nobility being killed with her husband. It offered a reward of 2,000 crowns for information, but professed the Council's ignorance. It interviewed Thomas Nelson, but when he was asked who held the key to the building, he replied that it was the queen. Realising his state of shock, Tullibardine asked for an adjournment until the next day.

Chapter 25

A review of what happened

The henchmen involved in the king's murder were provided by Bothwell, Morton, Archibald Douglas and probably Balfour. They included Bothwell's relative, Hepburn of Bolton, the warden of the Old Provost's Lodging, who is likely to have provided the duplicate keys. Other Bothwell men included John Hay of Talla, whose mother was a Hepburn; James 'Black' Ormiston, Bothwell's bailiff; Robert 'Hob' Ormiston, Black Ormiston's uncle; James Cullen, a captain of the Royal Hackbutters and explosives expert, who had been a mercenary in France, Denmark and Poland, but was now a 'creature of Bothwell's';[1] Patrick Wilson, a merchant who had arranged Bothwell's tryst with Bessie Crawford and who provided a barrel of gunpowder; and three of Bothwell's servants, who were to move it into position, William Powrie, his porter, George Dalgleish, his tailor, and the reluctant Paris. It is probable that some of them were seconded as the lodging's 'downstairs' servants. Archibald Douglas, Bothwell's close associate, came with a dozen or so Douglas adherents provided by Morton and himself. Ker of Fawdonside, forgetful that he owed his return from exile to the king, was outside Kirk o' Field with a detachment of mounted men. There were probably about thirty men involved, but the depositions vary.

Balfour's name was linked with Bothwell's on billboards in Edinburgh shortly after the murder. He purchased and supervised the movement and packing of the gunpowder, and presumably arranged its storage close to Kirk o' Field, possibly at the New Provost's Lodging. He may not have been involved thereafter as there were enough servants to heave it into position, but his movements on the day of the murder are not known. He was closely associated with Bothwell (but not a kinsman as is sometimes suggested) and several of the depositions link him to the plot without identifying his role. There is also a reference implicating Huntly, Bothwell's closest ally among the nobility, but this is not corroborated and appears unlikely.

Archbishop Hamilton, who had accompanied Mary to Glasgow, was much later accused of being part of the conspiracy, perhaps because the Hamiltons were the Lennoxes' traditional enemies. He was staying at Châtelherault's house from where a light was seen in an upper window before the murder.

After the explosion the light had been extinguished, hardly surprisingly, but this was deemed to be a signal.[2]*

There is no doubt that Bothwell masterminded the murder plan, even though he was not present. While in captivity in England, even Mary came to accept (if she did not already know it) that he was 'one of the murderers of the king'. He detested King Henry, but also seems to have developed an infatuation for Mary in the weeks beforehand. This was mentioned by both Melville and Livingston, not people with reason to falsify it. Yet it is very unlikely that he arranged the murder hoping to marry her, as he was already committed to Jean Gordon. Nevertheless, once the murder had been undertaken, Morton seems to have given him encouragement to marry Mary.

Most of the evidence for the murder arrangements comes from the manipulated depositions of Bothwell's associates, almost all taken under torture. Not unnaturally each was trying to protect himself, but there is a common thread implicating Bothwell and, where possible, the queen. They almost completely erase the involvement of Morton, Balfour, Douglas and other conspirators, except where they had fallen foul of Moray at the time of preparation.

The manipulators went to great lengths to avoid unhelpful depositions being made available. Paris was only most reluctantly involved and admitted going to the docks at Leith beforehand to find a boat on which to escape, but none was ready to sail. As he had carried messages between Bothwell and the queen and had helped in the movement of the gunpowder at Kirk o' Field, his evidence might have seemed crucial. He later escaped with Bothwell to Denmark, where the lords sought his extradition. This was not as one might expect to procure him as a witness, but to make certain he kept his mouth shut. He was handed over in Denmark on 30 October 1568, but it was only three weeks later, shortly before the Conference at Westminster, that Cecil was told. No urgent effort was made to repatriate him to give evidence, and he was not brought back to Scotland until June 1569. He was then imprisoned at St Andrews until, on 9 and 10 August, he secretly made two conflicting depositions under torture before Thomas Buchanan, George Buchanan's nephew, and George Wood, Moray's private secretary. It is clear that these were manipulated. In the first, he claimed that, while acting as the queen's messenger, he had tracked Bothwell down at Kirk o' Field on 25 January 1567. Yet at that time Bothwell was indisputably in the Borders. He also claimed that Bothwell said to him: 'Commend me to the queen and tell her that all will go well. Say that Balfour and I have not slept the night, that everything is arranged, and that the king's lodgings are ready for him.'[3]

Yet we know that Kirk o' Field had not been chosen by 25 January, and the murder plan had not by then been agreed. The deposition implies that Balfour, who was by now out of favour, knew of the plot before 25 January. Yet he was much later to confirm that he learned of it only on 7 February, the most likely date for it to have been finalised. Paris claimed that Maitland, also by then out of favour, had told him to advise the queen to use Kirk o' Field as the king's lodging, but we know that Maitland was not involved in choosing the location. In his second deposition, Paris slightly contradicts his earlier one. He says that he came to Edinburgh on 25 January and found Bothwell dining with Balfour (although we know that Bothwell was still in the Borders) and Bothwell told him to tell Mary that he was sending her a diamond in place of his heart (although there is no plausible evidence of a romance between them before the king's death). He then visited Maitland, who told him that the king would be better off at Kirk o' Field (still highly unlikely as at that time Craigmillar had been chosen for the king's recuperation). On 27 January, he arrived back in Glasgow, just as Mary and the king were leaving for Craigmillar. According to his deposition, he accompanied them as far as Linlithgow, from where he was sent off by the queen with two bracelets for Bothwell, now apparently returning from Liddesdale (and not in Edinburgh as stated earlier in the deposition). Reference to the bracelets seems designed to corroborate Mary's gift as reported in Casket Letter II, prepared two years earlier. In addition to Balfour and Maitland, the deposition also implicates Huntly and Argyll in the murder plot. By then, all four were seeking Mary's restoration, and Moray was using every means to try to discredit them. Paris had to be silenced as he knew too much and his depositions were never published. He was not brought to trial, but was taken straight to the gallows to be hung, drawn and quartered. From the scaffold, he bravely shouted out, denying having carried letters between Bothwell and the queen as was recorded. Buchanan never included Paris's evidence in updated versions of his *Detectio*. It conflicted with what he had already tabled.

It was Bothwell who developed the plan to use gunpowder to blow up Kirk o' Field and its occupants. With the king having several loyal servants on the premises, Bothwell did not believe he could maintain secrecy if he were stabbed or poisoned. By blowing them up, he hoped to destroy the evidence. The claim that the lodging had been undermined before the king's arrival can only be a fabrication. John Hay of Talla recorded, probably correctly, that Bothwell did not finally decide on using gunpowder until 7 February and it was delivered only on the evening of 9 February. By then,

Bothwell could not have supervised its positioning as he was with the queen and in costume.

All the depositions confirm two sources of supply of the powder. The main part appears to have come from the arsenal at Dunbar, while a second delivery came in a barrel purchased from Patrick Wilson in Edinburgh. According to Drury, this was valued at £60 Scots and appears to have been acquired by Balfour in a barter transaction for olive oil. During his imprisonment in Denmark, Bothwell recorded that the gunpowder went to 'Sir James Balfour's house', where a mine was prepared.[4] With Moretta staying there, it is quite unlikely that Balfour would have received it at his main residence, but it could more logically have been taken to the New Provost's Lodging, from where it was a short step to the little courtyard behind the Prebendaries' Chamber with its access to the cellars below the king's accommodation.

Robert Balfour would not have agreed to the destruction of his letting accommodation without compensation. Little is known about him, but he was one of several younger brothers of Sir James, without the means to bear its loss, and it is suggested that Sir James acquired his leases shortly before the explosion. If so, the New Provost's Lodging could justifiably be described as Sir James's house. The propaganda afterwards accused Sir James, not Robert, of involvement in the conspiracy. An almost complete absence of evidence against either of them demonstrates Sir James's part in putting the official story together.

The depositions weave very different and sometimes conflicting tales to show how the gunpowder arrived at Kirk o' Field. They are all totally unrealistic, but were designed to involve Bothwell and his men in every stage of its movement and to implicate the queen. If accepted at face value, there was insufficient powder, inadequately contained, to achieve the explosion that occurred. Paris claimed that Bothwell told him of his intention to use gunpowder on 5 February, while they were attending the queen at Kirk o' Field. Bothwell had been suffering from 'the bloody flux' [dysentery] for some time and sought his old servant's help for a place to relieve himself from his 'usual illness'.[5] Paris helped him to undress and stayed with him at a place between two doors, while Bothwell divulged his plan and Paris reluctantly agreed to help him. Two days later, Bothwell apparently asked him to provide a key to the queen's room, but as he did not have one, Paris arranged for a copy to be made. When he produced it on the next day, Bothwell already had a complete set and told him to retain it. Bothwell could presumably have obtained the set of keys from Hepburn, who was later to drop them down a hole in a quarry. The need to access the queen's bedroom fits with the unlikely story that the powder was placed under her bed, implying that she knew of the planned explosion.

According to the depositions, the main gunpowder supply left Dunbar on 7 February. Paris reported that it arrived on the evening of 9 February packed in 'polks' (leather bags) in two trunks, one of leather and one of wood, to be stored in the back hall of Bothwell's lodgings at Holyrood. This implies that Bothwell had arranged its delivery and perhaps that the queen knew about it. Yet we know that Bothwell was not available to receive it at Holyrood on 9 February, and it is implausible to suggest that such dangerous material should have been brought to a royal palace full of lighted candles and open fires, risking its discovery by the guard on arrival. It would have been delivered to an agreed location close to Kirk o' Field. Yet every deposition is consistent on it going to Holyrood and from there to Kirk o' Field. John Hay of Talla confirmed the second source of supply. His servant went to Patrick Wilson to collect the barrel, estimated to be the size of a 54-gallon cask. If so, the servant would not have been able to move it by himself. Yet he apparently brought it openly through the Edinburgh streets to Holyrood.

According to Hay's deposition, from four o'clock in the afternoon until dusk on 9 February, he attended a two-hour meeting at Holyrood with Bothwell and Hepburn. As soon as it was dark, they walked to Black Ormiston's house in Blackfriars' Wynd to discuss final details with Black and Hob Ormiston. Then, from about half past eight to ten o'clock at night, Bothwell stood in the Canongate to supervise the gunpowder's movement from Holyrood to Kirk o' Field. Yet we know that from four o'clock Bothwell was with the queen at the dinner for Moretta, and the idea of his involvement in moving gunpowder wearing carnival costume in the very public Canongate is unthinkable. If it were being brought from Holyrood, his men were all aware of the shorter more secluded route through the old Blackfriars Monastery gate.

Hepburn's deposition claims that Bothwell remained at the banquet held for Moretta until a quarter to eight. From here he apparently went with Paris to visit his mother and then walked to Black Ormiston's lodging, leaving there at half past eight to join the queen at Kirk o' Field. While this timing may seem more plausible, his absence from the queen for this forty-five-minute period would not have gone unnoticed. Paris claimed to have walked with Bothwell from the dinner for Moretta to join the Ormistons, going on with them to the Cowgate to meet Hay and Hepburn. After discussing the murder plan, Bothwell and Paris came on to Kirk o'

Field. This is largely corroborated by Black Ormiston, who claims to have met Bothwell in the Cowgate, walking from the dinner to Kirk o' Field. They then agreed to move the gunpowder by the secret way, and he apparently went to open the old Blackfriars Monastery gate to let them in.

Between half past eight and ten o'clock, Powrie, Dalgleish and Wilson apparently moved the trunks and the barrel containing gunpowder openly through the streets from Holyrood to the Blackfriars Monastery gate about 200 yards from Kirk o' Field. Powrie originally claimed that they completed the task with two horses in one journey, but later amended this to using one horse on two journeys, with the trunks carried on the first and the barrel on the second trip. Whichever version is accepted, it is estimated that only two hundredweight of powder could have been moved, insufficient to achieve the explosion that occurred, and it would have seemed extraordinarily suspicious to the guards at Holyrood. Black Ormiston and two others (not recognised by Powrie, Dalgleish or Wilson) wearing cloaks and velvet slippers, met them at the gate. (This unsubstantiated reference to their footwear seems designed to explain that the single velvet slipper found near the king's body belonged to one of Bothwell's men.) Both Hepburn and Powrie claimed that Bothwell came to the gate to tell them to hurry (which is unlikely, but it gives the impression that the powder was being moved at his instruction). The depositions are consistent that the powder was delivered to the side door of the kitchen, but do not make it clear how it arrived. The obvious way from the Blackfriars gate would have been through the east garden, a distance of 200yds. Hepburn claimed that Powrie was sent to buy candles and that by the light of one of them the polks were unpacked from the trunks and were carried with the barrel by Powrie, Dalgleish and Wilson to a wall surrounding the east garden. From here, Hepburn, Hay and Black Ormiston heaved them over it to the side door. Yet there does not seem to have been anything more than a low wall in the east garden (none is shown in the drawing sent to Drury immediately after the murder) and there would have been access through any garden wall, as it formed part of the secret way from Holyrood mentioned by the queen. Another version says that the polks were taken by Powrie, Dalgleish and Wilson outside the Blackfriars gate and round the back of the Town Wall into Thieves Row. At a point opposite the east garden Hepburn, Hay and Black Ormiston lifted them over the 14ft wall (although the barrel would have been too heavy to lift). To move them this way seems nonsensical and risked making a noise. A much more probable and less obtrusive route would have been to use either the postern gate from Thieves Row or the little courtyard behind the Prebendaries' Chamber.

These both led to the cellar passage, giving hidden access to the kitchen and the cellar below the Prebendaries' Chamber. As the empty barrel was found by the side door to the east garden it has been assumed that it was too wide to go through it, suggesting that it could have arrived there only from the Blackfriars gate. Yet there is no absolute evidence that the barrel was too large, and this is only assumed because it provides an explanation for it being found there. It could have been emptied within the cellar, perhaps to fill a mine, after which it would have been moved through the side door out of the way. The manipulators certainly tried to show that the gunpowder arrived in the east garden and that Paris provided access by unlocking the side door (although it had no lock and needed to be unbolted from the inside). There are two reasons for them wanting to demonstrate that it came in that way. The kitchen had access by stone steps to the floor above, where the queen's bedroom was located. To implicate the queen, it was claimed that the powder was placed under her bed. If it came in this way, it could hardly have come from the New Provost's Lodging, making Balfour's involvement less likely. From there, the shorter and more convenient route was into the little courtyard behind the Prebendaries' Chamber with its access to the cellar passage. Whichever route were chosen, it was only the lodging servants who could have transported it unobtrusively.

Once inside the lodging, the Ormistons positioned the gunpowder. This could not have been until Bonkil had gone home for the evening and the kitchen embers had been extinguished. The royal party, arriving from the dinner for Moretta, was not in need of food. Powrie and Wilson seem to have become worried and were apparently sent back to Holyrood with the empty trunks. Yet this also seems nonsense, and the trunks were more likely to have been destroyed in the explosion.

The depositions claim that loose gunpowder was piled under the queen's bed. This is also implausible. Any of the guests could have visited her bedroom, which was on the same level as the *salle* to leave coats or use the *garde-robe*. This would have disturbed those moving the powder. Loose powder would have covered the room in dust, risking ignition from a naked light, and, if not contained, powder would burn rather than explode. An explosion in the bedroom could never have destroyed the lodging and Prebendaries' Chamber completely. Yet the depositions all confirm that, after positioning the powder, Paris locked the queen's bedroom giving the key to Hepburn, even though Hepburn had his own set.

The only realistic way to achieve the damage that occurred was for the gunpowder to be packed into mines in the cellars under both the Old

Provost's Lodging and the Prebendaries' Chamber. These were accessible from the passage to the postern gate and to the little courtyard, where its movement would have been concealed from view. Yet Bothwell apparently again found it necessary to appear to tell them to make less noise.

With the gunpowder in place, Paris apparently left the side door unbolted and the cellar door unlocked. The Ormistons went home after establishing that others would prepare the fuse. Although access was apparently to be provided through the side door, they would have had to rely on the king's servants not bolting it before they retired. It is more likely that those lighting the fuse entered through the postern gate. It was claimed that George Dalgleish acquired a yard of lint from the guard at Holyrood to make a fuse. Perhaps this information was intended to implicate Traquair and even the queen, or to corroborate the gunpowder being moved from Holyrood in the first instance. When the queen was leaving for Holyrood from Kirk o' Field late in the evening, she saw Paris all 'begrimed' while he went to advise Bothwell that all was ready. He claimed that Argyll patted him on the back, implying that Argyll was also in the know. By the time of Paris's deposition, Argyll had only recently submitted to Moray after supporting Mary.

With everything apparently prepared, Bothwell returned to Holyrood with the queen. After holding their late meeting, it is alleged by Buchanan that he 'passed to his chamber and there changed his hose and doublet and put his side cloak about him and passed up to the accomplishment of that most horrible murder'.[6] His alleged movements then become absurdly public for a soldier expert in covert operations. Carrying his sword and with at least eleven men, including Paris, Powrie, Dalgleish and Wilson, they apparently walked to Kirk o' Field, making themselves known to the guard, before taking the open route down the Canongate. They woke the porter to open the Netherbow Port 'to friends of Lord Bothwell's' (although elsewhere it is implied that they crossed through the wall only at the Blackfriars gate), but when asked why they were out so late, they did not reply.[7] They then marched openly up the High Street and into Blackfriars Wynd. This conveniently explains why Barbara Martin saw a party of men shortly before the explosion. Although they stopped at Ormiston's lodgings, he was not there and later claimed to be drinking with a friend, Thomas Henderson, no doubt a convenient alibi. They then took the secret way through the monastery grounds to gather in the east garden. It is reported that Bothwell told them not to stir, while he and Paris went forward with Cullen. Cullen had apparently advised Bothwell to strangle the king, as it was more certain than powder, and he scaled the Town Wall to hide in the south garden to block the king's escape. This implied that it was Cullen, acting on Bothwell's instruction, who suffocated the king, explaining away any Douglas involvement. If Cullen did scale the wall, it is more likely, as an explosives expert, that he entered the lodging by the postern gate in Thieves Row, from where he lit the fuses in the cellars before joining the Douglases.

All the plausible evidence shows that Archibald Douglas and about a dozen followers were hiding in the cottages near the south garden, where they were joined by Cullen to block the king's escape route. Douglas's servant, John Binning, testified under torture in 1581 that his master was 'art and part' of the murder and 'did actually devise and perpetrate it'.[8] It is known that the Douglas men wore clothing over their armour and slippers to deaden the sound of their boots. This would explain a velvet slipper being found. As a voice was heard shouting: 'Pity me my kinsmen!', it can be implied that the king recognised his Douglas assassins, and they were seen afterwards leaving by Blackfriars Wynd. None of the depositions suggest that Bothwell's men went that way.

The depositions tell a different story. When Bothwell and Paris allegedly returned to the east garden, Paris escorted Hay and Hepburn to the side door (still apparently unbolted) and opened the door to the queen's bedroom for them to light the slow-burning fuse. They then locked all the doors to prevent the king's escape (although the side door only bolted from the inside), and returned to the east garden. The depositions all report a long delay. Fearing that the fuse had failed, Bothwell apparently pulled Hepburn behind him to investigate, but Hepburn held him back from looking through the queen's bedroom window (which faced onto the quadrangle at the front of the building). At this moment, there was reportedly a flash from a window facing the garden, followed by a violent explosion. The lodging lifted behind them as they scrambled back to rejoin Dalgleish and Powrie. From here they ran through the old Blackfriars Monastery into the Cowgate.

There are shortcomings in all this evidence. Although a flash was reported from a window before the explosion, there was no window facing the east garden. The explosion was too great for the powder to have been in the queen's bedroom, and the conspirators could not have hoped to light a fuse there without disturbing the sleeping occupants in the rest of the house. A seasoned soldier like Bothwell would never have returned to check the fuse by looking through a window. The only purpose of this evidence is to demonstrate Bothwell's part in lighting it.

The reported route taken by the conspirators on leaving Kirk o' Field is also ridiculous. Having allegedly returned down the Cowgate to the

Netherbow Port, they again had to wake the porter, despite the explosion. They could just as easily have gone through the old Blackfriars Monastery gate or climbed over a broken down piece of wall further on. It is claimed that they split into two groups, with Bothwell and Paris continuing down the very public Canongate to Holyrood, while the remainder took St Mary's Wynd. Only Bothwell needed to return to Holyrood, but they all apparently gave his name when challenged by the guard, by when the palace was in a state of alarm. Neither the porter at the Netherbow Port nor the guard was ever asked to confirm these movements.

With the plans to destroy Kirk o' Field already finalised, Bothwell had no reason to return to supervise the lighting of the fuse. His only justifiable motive would have been to bring the queen's sanction, but she would not have been aware of the plan and it was too late to abort it. If he did return, he did not need eleven men with him. He could have gone alone or perhaps with Paris, who knew the interior. There is no evidence that his other companions helped in lighting the fuse, but they could have been there to block the east garden as an escape route. Only Cullen of Bothwell's party crossed the Town Wall, but could not have sealed off the south garden and Thieves Row alone. Although they must have seen them, neither Hepburn nor Hay mentioned the presence of Douglas men. This evidence can only have been expunged.

Bothwell apparently lost patience with Paris, who was reportedly panicking as he returned to Holyrood. Hay had to threaten him with a pistol to shut him up, but claimed to have taken him to his house for the night. It seems nonsensical that Hay and Paris should have returned to Holyrood, where their movements would be recorded, only to leave again. A claim that the queen saw Paris and told him 'not to worry' can only be seen as another effort to incriminate her.

The final twist is that the gunpowder did not kill the king. His servant Nelson, who had been sleeping in the gallery, was calling for help after the explosion from the top of the Town Wall. The king must have been disturbed, probably by those lighting the fuse and, with his valet, Taylor, had tried to escape. The servants who survived seem to have been in the upper gallery, from where they scrambled onto the Town Wall with the king, who had grabbed his dagger, a nightgown and quilt before leaving. He and Taylor lowered themselves on the far side with a rope and chair, but the king seems to have fallen and cracked a rib. They ran through the south garden and orchard, but were accosted by Archibald Douglas and his henchmen, now including Cullen, who emerged from the cottages. The king pleaded for his life, before both he and Taylor were suffocated. Cullen, who admitted being there, said 'the king was a long time a-dying, and in his strength made debate for his life'.[9] With the explosion imminent, they had no time to move the corpses nearer to the lodging, but laid them out with their possessions, before escaping up Blackfriars Wynd, leaving behind a velvet slipper. When Bothwell arrived the next morning to inspect the bodies, it was not clear how the king and Taylor had died. Having assumed that they had been killed in the explosion, he was amazed to find their bodies unmarked.

Chapter 26

The immediate aftermath of the murder and Mary's reaction to it

On the morning after the murder, Bothwell visited Kirk o' Field in his capacity as Sheriff of Edinburgh. He arranged for the king's body to be moved to the New Provost's Lodging for examination and he stopped the public from searching for clues in the rubble. Having returned to Holyrood, he went with Huntly to see the queen. He told Sir James Melville that 'the thunder came out of the sky and had burnt the king's house' and that the queen was 'sorrowful and queet'.[1] She also went to see the body, but showed no emotion. In the afternoon it was brought on a board to Holyrood to be embalmed before lying in state at the altar in the Chapel Royal. There was no state funeral, but the body was interred in the tomb of the kings in the old Abbey Kirk at Holyrood 'quietly in the night without any kind of solemnity or mourning heard among all the persons at Court'.[2] Cecil noted that the king's private burial caused great indignation in London, where it was felt that a state funeral would have been more appropriate. Buchanan's *Book of Articles* (the English translation of his *Detectio*) later claimed that the body was 'without any decent order, cast in the earth without any ceremony or company of honest men'.[3] Yet the location was magnificent and the quiet ceremony was ill-attended principally because it was conducted with Catholic rites. In accordance with normal custom for a consort, the queen did not attend. Lennox, who had been in Linlithgow, returned to Glasgow without being present, probably concerned for his own safety or in fear that his part in his son's plotting might be leaked.

Although Mary was extremely shocked and no doubt frightened at her husband's death, she was expected to face up to it cool-headedly. In her letters written immediately afterwards to Elizabeth and her French relations, she confirmed her belief that she was also intended as a victim to make way for a regency for her son. Only by complete chance had she not spent the night of the explosion at Kirk o' Field. This implied that she thought that Moray sought the regency or even planned to usurp the throne for himself. Nau later recorded her belief that Moray had left Edinburgh after finalising his plan to gain the Crown by ruining her. Either he had arranged the murder himself, or it had been done on his behalf by the returning exiles as a blood feud against the king. Mary never varied from her view that the returning exiles wanted her dead. It was to be expected that she would deal severely with their treasonable actions.

Mary's initial reaction to her husband's murder was identical to that following Riccio's death eleven months before. It was only by chance that she had not slept that night at Kirk o' Field. She wrote to Elizabeth and her French relations:

> We hope to punish the same with such rigour as shall serve for example of this cruelty to all ages to come. Always who ever have taken this wicked enterprise in hand, we assure our self it was dressed always for us as for the King.[4]

On 11 February, Clernault left for Paris with the Council's letter to Catherine de Medici and one from Mary to Archbishop Bethune. She told him: 'The matter is so horrible and strange, as we believe the like was never heard of in any country.'[5]

Mary seemed too distraught to take control. Although she wrote to Lennox promising justice for the king, she took no immediate action to set up an enquiry, and the Council's efforts were half-hearted. A reward of £2,000 Scots was offered for information with 'an honest yearly rent' and a pardon to anyone giving evidence, but no one came forward. A proclamation signed by Argyll was affixed to the Mercat Cross confirming that 'the Queen's majesty, unto whom of all others the case was most grievous, would rather lose life and all than it should remain unpunished'.[6] Yet no proper investigation was undertaken. On 11 February, Barbara Martin and Meg Crokat became intimidated under cross-examination and the judges dismissed them as fools. They may have said too much, because their evidence was suppressed. Pitcairn, the surgeon, was also interviewed, but could add very little.

While the Council was deliberating, Mary went into seclusion in darkened rooms and, on the Council's advice, moved for security with Prince James into Edinburgh Castle. It took 100 mules to transport her clothing, furnishings and papers from Holyrood. Yet, on 11 February, she attended the wedding ceremony of Margaret Carwood to John Stewart of Tullipowreis, honouring a pledge to her faithful retainer. Although she was not at the banquet afterwards, Mary's involvement drew scathing comments from Buchanan for leaving her mourning chamber so soon. Otherwise she remained in her rooms, apparently too upset to see anyone. Believing that she was endangering her health, her physicians advised the Council that she needed fresh air. Yet again she chose to go to 'Seton to repose there and take some purgations', arriving on 16 February with Maitland, Livingston, Archbishop Hamilton and about 100 attendants.[7,8*] Although Bothwell, Huntly and Argyll escorted her there, Bothwell and Huntly immediately returned to act as James's official guardians at Holyrood. She also needed to return to Edinburgh after three days, as will be explained, but she remained distraught and, by 21 February, was back at Seton, this time with Bothwell in attendance. By now her grief seemed illusory. On 26 February, she dined with Robert, 2nd Lord Wharton, at Trenant, where, according to Drury, she partnered Bothwell to beat Huntly and Argyll at archery with the losers paying for dinner. Although other reports claimed that she was too unwell to play, the damage was done.

From Mary's viewpoint, the one person who could hardly have been involved in the king's murder was Bothwell. Although he remained a loose cannon politically, he had been her saviour after Riccio's death, and she could always rely on him. She knew at first hand that he could hardly have murdered the king, as he had been with her for the whole of the day before-hand, and she had seen him, until he assuredly went to bed with his wife at Holyrood, shortly before the explosion. Yet his attitude afterwards was unexpected. While it would be thought that he too would want his arch-enemy, Moray, and the returning exiles investigated, he was advising Mary, like everyone else, not to investigate too thoroughly. Even more surprisingly, there were rumours of his involvement, and Lennox was telling her that he was the culprit. On 16 February, only a week after the murder, the first placards appeared which accused Bothwell and, quite absurdly, implicated Mary.

Despite Bothwell being mentioned as the likely perpetrator of the crime, only he, in Moray's absence, had the prestige to manage the government, and Mary pinned her hopes on his guidance by putting him in charge. Unlike King Henry, he could not be treated as a wayward youth of 20, and, at 32, he soon dominated her with his assuredness and vigour, becoming the virtual ruler of Scotland with command of the Royal Bodyguard. After Argyll, he was Scotland's most powerful magnate with his own Border militia. He now enjoyed an apparently close alliance with Morton, leader of the powerful Douglases; and he also had the availability of military support from the Gordons. He negotiated with a German mercenary to provide Mary with

3,600 crack troops, although it is not clear that they ever reached Scotland. As hereditary Lord High Admiral, he received the proceeds of treasure taken from all wrecks on the Scottish coast. As Sheriff of Edinburgh, he maintained a close association with the legal profession, holding coveted preferments in his gift. He could be suave, despite a rough and lawless nature and an uncontrollable temper. Although Mary feared him, his attraction was in being Moray's deadly foe.

To the shock of the Guise family and European heads of state, Mary's European correspondence dried up and she seemed completely distraught and dazed, retiring to a darkened room to cry. It has been argued that her lacklustre demeanour was caused by illness. Yet, she had always been courageous in a crisis, even when unwell. Only eleven months earlier, when five months pregnant, she had shown extraordinary resource after Riccio's murder to save her throne. She had been to Glasgow since her haemorrhage at Jedburgh and with considerable guile had single-handedly persuaded the king to return with her to Edinburgh, writing a detailed and logical report of their conversation to her advisers. After marrying Bothwell, she would again show great bravery in escaping from Borthwick Castle and in trying to garner support for their cause. Yet now she collapsed. This was not out of remorse for her husband, who, as she knew, was continuing to plot her overthrow, but she did not want him dead. Regicide was an unpardonable crime, and his death weakened her hopes of being accepted as Elizabeth's heir. If she had sought a proper investigation, she would have retained her Crown, and the king's murder would have been seen as the necessity it was for her security.

If illness were not the cause of Mary's indecisiveness, it can only be assumed that she had come to realise that the king's murder did not just involve Moray, Morton and the returning exiles. Perhaps the lords at Craigmillar, including Argyll, Huntly, Bothwell and Maitland, had taken the law into their own hands to free her from her husband. When divorce and a trial for treason could not be achieved on an acceptable basis, her options were either to make the best of her marriage, perhaps with the king under some form of house arrest, or to condone a plan for his assassination. We can be sure that she never gave approval for his death, but the nobility would never accept their reconciliation. Perhaps she felt guilty at them having to take action to remove a man, over whom she had made a complete fool of herself. She knew murder had been discussed, and was aware from the king in Glasgow of a bond prepared at Craigmillar. If the nobility had acted collectively, none of them would want a detailed investigation, and Bothwell would have been best suited to have organised the deed.

Like Mary, the Privy Council was making very little serious effort to seek out the murder culprits, and there were concerted efforts at a cover-up. Almost all the depositions used as evidence were taken under torture and are hardly credible, even though corroborated from several sources. They were not made public at the time and were attested by Justice-Clerk Bellenden, who was not present when they were taken. When their evidence was eventually tabled it implied that Bothwell and his henchmen had undertaken the king's murder unassisted by the rest of the nobility, and even that the queen had enticed him into it. Her motive for wanting her husband's death was being explained by her being involved in a passionate romance with Bothwell.

Bothwell relied on the Craigmillar bond for protection, and only Lennox and his close allies were showing any remorse at the 20-year-old king's death. To assure that his accomplices kept quiet, Bothwell provided them with bribes and promises of future protection. Hay and Hepburn were rewarded with fine horses. Powrie, Dalgleish and Wilson were promised positions at Hermitage and were assured, if they held their tongues: 'They should never want so long as he had anything.'[9] Paris remained for a time in Mary's employment, carrying confidential messages between her and Bothwell. Bothwell arranged for Sir James Cockburn of Skirling to be appointed Governor of Edinburgh Castle. This alienated Mar, the former Governor, with his vital control of Prince James. Skirling also became Comptroller of the Household to replace Tullibardine.

Although his power was growing, Bothwell needed a guard to travel through the streets and 'held his hand on his dagger' when meeting opponents.[10] Yet he brazened it out and, on 14 February, attended King Henry's funeral. On 7 March, he arranged Morton's formal rehabilitation. After making a humble apology for his part in Riccio's murder, Morton was restored to his estates and returned to Court as Lord Chancellor. Bothwell tried to assure his loyalty by agreeing to share government with him, but was not above circulating rumours that Morton had arranged the murder, leading Drury to believe that he had been involved. In late April, Drury advised Cecil: 'Morton is noted to have assured friendship with Bothwell, which, to be the thankfuller now for his favour showed him in his absence and trouble, he intendeth to continue.' Sir James Melville also confirmed that Bothwell had 'packed' up a quiet friendship with Morton.[11]

On 16 February, the first of a number of placards appeared. This accused Bothwell, Balfour, David Chalmers and 'Black' John Spens, the Queen's Advocate, who was described as 'the principal deviser of the murder, the queen assenting thereto, through the persuasion of the Earl of Bothwell and the witchcraft' of Janet Bethune (Bothwell's former mistress and widow of Sir Walter Scott of Buccleuch). It went on to say: 'And if this is not true, [ask] Gilbert Balfour [another brother of Sir James].'[12] Chalmers was Bothwell's recent appointee as Common Clerk of Edinburgh and, according to Buchanan, had provided his garden for trysts between Bothwell and the queen. Although Spens was later arrested, any part that either he or Chalmers played in the murder is unknown. Balfour kept out of sight and, on 26 February, returned home with an escort of thirty men by a secret way, remaining there with armed protection. On the next night, the placards accused Mary's foreign servants, Pagez, Joseph Riccio and Francisco Busso. It was to scotch this unlikely tale that Mary temporarily returned from Seton. Bothwell threatened to wash his hands in the blood of the placards' creators, if he could find them, but this did not silence them and, after a few nights, voices in the streets were calling out that he had murdered the king.

By dawn on 11 February, the day after the murder, the news had reached Drury at Berwick some sixty miles away, and he forwarded a message to Cecil, inadvertently reporting that Lennox's body had been found beside his son. By then Drury knew from his spies in Edinburgh that the king had not been killed in the explosion, but had been suffocated. He organised agents to establish what had happened. One of them prepared a narrative drawing of the murder site, which Drury forwarded to Cecil in London (See p. 14–15 of the pictures section.). By the end of February Drury had heard that Hepburn of Bolton was one of the murderers and had lit the fuse, that Balfour had purchased the gunpowder, that it had been Cullen's idea not to rely on gunpowder alone, but to strangle the king for greater surety, and that Fawdonside was with a group of horsemen in a nearby alley ready to help if called. Fawdonside later carried messages for Bothwell and was still with him at Carberry Hill. As an explosives expert Cullen was almost certainly responsible for positioning the gunpowder and preparing the mine on Balfour's behalf. He was arrested after Carberry Hill, when he apparently confessed to his part in the crime, but was released, presumably because he knew too much. He escaped by ship with Bothwell but was recaptured at Lerwick in Shetland. He was bribed to silence by being offered a position as an officer in the Edinburgh garrison. He later joined Kirkcaldy in Edinburgh Castle, but was shot in a cupboard, when the castle fell in 1573.

On 14 February, Cecil was able to advise Elizabeth of the king's murder. The French ambassador in London immediately sent an express messenger to du Croc, who was in Dover awaiting a ship for France, asking him with all speed to advise the French Court. Still believing that Lennox had been a victim, Lady William Howard (Margaret née Gamage), wife of the Lord Chamberlain, and Lady Cecil (Mildred née Cooke) were instructed by Elizabeth to advise Margaret Douglas in the Tower. She was inconsolable, and Elizabeth sent her physician with the Dean of Westminster, who was maintaining Charles Stuart in his care, to comfort her. On 20 February, Cecil went to the Tower himself to advise Margaret that Lennox could not have died in the explosion as he had assuredly been in Glasgow at the time. Yet Margaret remained in fear that Lennox would be next on the list and that the 'heretics' would gain control of her grandson. On 21 February, Elizabeth asked her cousin, Thomas Sackville, Lord Buckhurst, to take Margaret into his care and to permit her son Charles to join her. Buckhurst was the son of Sir Richard Sackville, who had died in the previous April. They moved to Sackville Place in London, but were eventually released to the run-down royal palace of Coldharbour belonging to George Talbot, 4th Earl of Shrewsbury. The Lennoxes were in great financial difficulty with their Yorkshire estates being attainted and mismanaged by Elizabeth's commissioners. Although Elizabeth retained control, the Lennoxes were permitted to draw on its revenue, although there was very little available.

With the king being dead, Moretta's mission (whatever it had been) could be forgotten. He quickly left Edinburgh, travelling with Father Edmund Hay to Paris to advise Mondovi. He provided two differing reports. In the first, he claimed that the king had heard a noise and looked out to see a group of armed men attempting to enter the lodging, but they found the doors locked with the keys on the inside. Having run downstairs to escape, he was intercepted and strangled on reaching the garden. The fuse was then lit to hide the evidence. Moretta changed this report when it became known that the king had climbed over the Town Wall. His second version claimed:

> The King heard a great disturbance, at least so certain women who live in the neighbourhood declare, and from a window they perceived many armed men round about the house. So he, suspecting what might befall him, let himself down from another window looking on the garden, but he had not proceeded far before he was surrounded by certain persons.[13]

After being strangled with his nightshirt, his body was dragged into the garden. This suggests that he climbed out of the window in the servants' antechamber opening onto the far side of the Town Wall. Clernault reported that the king and Taylor were found *mort et étendu* [dead and laid out], as if they had been moved from where they died.[14] He also said that McCaig's body was found dead nearby (and not in the rubble of the building as reported elsewhere). It thus seems that all the servants in the upper antechamber escaped the blast.

On 17 February, de Silva sent a report from London to Philip II in the Low Countries. He had delayed it for three days in the vain hope of hearing of the perpetrators' arrest. On 18 February, Sebastian Pagez left Edinburgh with letters from Mary to Archbishop Bethune, to Mondovi in Paris and to Elizabeth in London. René Dolu, the treasurer of Mary's French dowry, went with him. She acknowledged the Archbishop's warning of a plot against her, which had arrived after the king's death. Pagez must have overplayed the strength of Mary's faith to Mondovi, who reported to Rome that she was now ready to execute the six leading Protestant lords. Yet there is no other evidence that she contemplated this. Robert Melville heard the news while travelling to London to negotiate Mary's claim to the English succession. He immediately returned to Edinburgh, but she was too distressed to receive him and 'ordered him to continue his journey as he had been previously instructed'.[15] He returned to London with the Council's official account of the murder for the English government.

The news was greeted with horror across Europe. By March, Moretta had told Giovanni Correr, the Venetian ambassador in Paris, who reported:

> It is widely believed that the principal persons of the kingdom were implicated in this act, because they were dissatisfied with the King ...[16] This assassination is considered to be the work of the heretics, who desire to do the same to the Queen, in order to bring up the prince in their doctrines and thus more firmly establish their own religion to the exclusion of ours.[17]

Suspicions fell on Moray. Mondovi reported from Paris that he

> has always had the throne in view although he is a bastard. He is persuaded by the [Protestants] that it is his by right, especially as he maintains that his mother was secretly espoused by the King his father.[18]

Following the arrival of Moretta and Father Hay in Paris on 15 March, Mondovi added that Moray

> desires upon this occasion to murder the Earl of Bothwell, a courageous man much trusted and confided in by the Queen, with the

intention of being afterwards able to lay snares for the life of Her Majesty with greater ease.

He also claimed that Moray sought

the governorship of the Prince and, by consequence, the whole realm. If he should gain this, which may God avert, he may be able to accomplish the wicked end he has set before himself, and herein the favour of England will not be wanting. The English Queen is jealous of the Prince as the legitimate heir of both those realms, and will not omit to favour the said Moray, being bound to her by many obligations as well as religion.[19]

Although his insight into Scottish affairs was not always reliable, on this occasion he seems to have been fairly close to the truth. Yet the Edinburgh propaganda soon took effect, and Bothwell became the most likely perpetrator with Mary being seen to have connived in it. Melville reported that 'everyone suspected the Earl of Bothwell and those who durst speak freely to others said plainly that it was he.'[20] Yet de Silva realised that no one would dare to accuse him openly.

Rumours of Mary's involvement in the murder continued to grow. Even the Cardinal of Lorraine ignored her, believing what he had heard in France. He wrote secretly to Moray, suggesting that they should unite to restore order and decency in Scotland. On 24 February, unaware of Cecil's scheming, Elizabeth wrote in the strongest terms to advise Mary to seek

to preserve your honour [having heard that] instead of seizing the murderers, you are looking through your fingers while they escape ... if it be the nearest friend you have, to lay your hands upon the man who has been guilty of the crime.[21]

She knew of the rumours that accused Bothwell and wanted to avoid the ugly precedent of a queen being deposed. When faced with a similar situation, she had insisted on a proper investigation after Leicester was implicated in the death of his wife, Amy Robsart. Although he was exonerated, she gave up all thought of marrying him to avoid further political embarrassment. If Mary failed to distance herself from Bothwell, Elizabeth could never confirm her to the English succession. Renegotiation of the terms of the Treaty of Edinburgh was now forgotten; Elizabeth wanted its ratification in full.

Mary was too insulted to reply. Catherine de Medici told her, through her ambassador, to 'do such justice as to the whole world may declare your innocence'.[22] Although privately she believed Mary was well rid of her foolish husband, she recognised that culprits needed to be brought to justice. When Mary failed to take action, Catherine wrote again, on behalf of both Charles IX and herself, to confirm that

> if she performed not her promise of seeking by all her power to have the death of the king their cousin revenged, and to clear herself, she should not only think herself dishonoured, but to receive them for her contraries, and that they would be her enemies.[23]

Even Archbishop Bethune, her most loyal supporter, told her 'to preserve that reputation in all godliness you have gained of long' by prosecuting those who committed the crime.[24]

In the light of all this forthright advice, Mary's failure to arrange an independent investigation was inexcusable. Yet she seemed to believe that, if she probed too far, she would be at personal risk and so chose to gloss over what had happened. She forgot that, unless justice was seen to be done, rumours of her involvement would continue to grow. The lords realised this and, as soon as they gained power, were quick to appease public opinion by bringing Bothwell's henchmen to book.

On the Continent, opinion of Mary's involvement was mixed. Some thought that she had acted out of revenge for Riccio's murder. De Alava in Paris reported to Philip II that many believed she had acted in self-defence before the king killed her, although he did not personally believe this. As he had initiated the warning of the king's scheming to Bethune, he was in a position to judge whether this posed a serious threat. He was inclined to Archbishop Bethune's view that the murder was controlled from England and aimed against the queen as well. Cecil faced a lot of awkward criticism and, after suffering Margaret Douglas's strident demands for vengeance, confessed to Drury that he wanted nothing more than to resign.

Lennox was grief-stricken and wrote to Cecil offering to collaborate with him to avenge his son's murder. Although the king had repudiated his allegiance to Elizabeth and had opposed her appointment as James's godmother, Lennox assured Cecil that he had always been her most loyal subject and 'acquaintance'. Lennox did not come to Edinburgh 'on account of the overweening power and licence of Bothwell', but he bombarded Mary with letters.[25] Despite her protestations to the contrary, he complained that she was not doing enough to bring the murderers to book and asked her to cross-examine those mentioned in the placards. As she was unaware of any evidence that would stand up to examination in court, she wrote to him on 1 March from Seton that there were so many names

> that we wot not on what ticket [placard] to proceed. But if there be any names mentioned in them that you think worthy to suffer a trial, upon your advertisement we shall stand with the cognition taking, as may stand with the laws of this realm; and, being found culpable, shall see the punishment as rigorously executed as the wickedness of the crime deserves.[26]

She was telling him that, if he brought a private prosecution, she would punish anyone found guilty. Yet Lennox had no evidence. Disillusioned, he asked Cecil for Elizabeth's help to press for a trial. He told Mary to prosecute those on the first two placards, which included Bothwell, Balfour and her foreign secretaries. Perhaps he hoped to disassociate himself from the secretaries' part in his earlier plotting.

Part 5

THE CONSPIRACY TO FORCE MARY TO ABDICATE

Chapter 27

Pawns in a game of chess

In a sense, the murder of the king was the beginning, not the end, of the story. No one other than the Lennoxes, and perhaps Mary, was sorry to see his demise, and even Mary wanted a divorce. It was not King Henry's death that forced Mary off her throne, it was her decision to arrange Bothwell's trial as a white-wash and subsequently to marry him.

Mary and Bothwell failed to appreciate that they were pawns in a much more sophisticated game of chess being played out around them. Although Moray organised it, Cecil did everything he could to support him without becoming personally involved. Elizabeth was facing a build-up of Catholic hostility fueled by Philip II. Mary, even though she might not be aware of it, was the focus of every Catholic plot against her, whether from home or abroad. Cecil urgently needed to re-establish a secure Protestant government in Scotland to protect England's northern border. Mary's marriage to King Henry had reinforced her dynastic claim if Elizabeth should die childless, and, although Elizabeth had advised parliament, immediately before the king's murder, that she would not recognise the Scottish queen, she was still dangling the English throne before her, despite it being an anathema to Cecil.

Cecil had supported Moray in repatriating Mary from France in 1561, but she had not proved as compliant as they had hoped. Since then, her threat to English security had only increased. Moray had not been able to mould her into following his Protestant leadership. Despite showing tolerance, she remained determinedly Catholic. The English Parliament had become vociferous in its view that it would never accept a Catholic monarch, even on terms that permitted freedom of Protestant worship, and Mary had chosen a Catholic husband against English advice. Most importantly, Elizabeth had failed to resolve the succession by marrying and producing heirs of her own and was unlikely to do so.

Cecil needed a more drastic solution. If Mary could be implicated in the plot to kill her husband, she would lose prestige as a Catholic icon, and Elizabeth would find her unacceptable as her heir. Cecil's role was to protect his mistress and secure her government. Elizabeth was unaware of his scheming and initially took steps that contradicted his objectives. She wanted the appropriate dynastic succession, even if that meant a Catholic queen, and played no part in his underhand game of chess. Yet she was eventually persuaded of the danger posed by Mary and supported her astute and loyal Secretary.

Cecil was always fully informed on events in Scotland and his detailed records are the principal source of evidence for the king's murder. He had to stop a Scottish Counter-Reformation. He had persuaded Elizabeth to fund Moray's rebellion in the Chaseabout Raid and to approve Riccio's murder. He continued to see Moray, his close *confidant*, as the obvious choice for Scottish regent: trustworthy, shrewd, Protestant, a proven leader and an Anglophile. When an anonymous letter arrived in Scotland reporting that Archbishop Bethune believed Moray was 'the author of the king's death', Moray admitted to Cecil: 'I am touched myself' (meaning that there were rumours of his involvement). This suggests that they trusted each other. Archbishop Bethune was well informed; he 'affirmed that the assassination was controlled from England, where the intention had been to kill the queen as well'. With great prescience he wrote from Paris: 'I fear this to be only the beginning of the tragedy, and all to run from evil to worse, which I pray God of his infinite goodness to avoid.'[1]

Moray had spent much time with Cecil in England after the Chaseabout Raid planning how to restore his authority. Following the prince's birth, he could not claim the throne, but the regency met his thirst for power just as well. After Riccio's murder, he had hoped to use the king's involvement to justify Mary's arrest, if she did not die from a miscarriage. With James yet to be born, he may have hoped to gain the Crown. It was only her resourcefulness that had put paid to this. When it came to the king's murder, he advised Morton and Maitland to ensure that Bothwell organised it, to make him the scapegoat. If Bothwell could then be persuaded to become the queen's protector by marrying her, a crime of passion scenario to implicate Mary might become plausible. If he had not thought this through at Craigmillar, his plan was fully formulated by the time of the king's death, when it was put into effect. Cecil's close involvement in the scheme can be inferred because he did nothing to discourage the hated Bothwell from taking control of government or from contemplating marriage to Mary, even though, on the face of it, their marriage could only be to Moray's and England's disadvantage.

Maitland supported Moray in seeking the king's removal and in wanting Bothwell out of the way. Yet they did not always see eye to eye, and Mary Fleming, who by all accounts continued to twist her husband round her little finger, might have been expected to keep him loyal to the queen. Immediately after the murder, Maitland continued his official brief to gain Mary the English succession. On 13 March, he wrote to Cecil accepting that this would only be realistic if she became Protestant. He promised to discuss this with her, believing that she could be persuaded after her recent financial support for the Kirk and coolness to Mondovi. Yet he had been so closely involved in the plans for both Riccio's and the king's murders that for a fatal period, starting in late March 1567, Moray was able to blackmail him into providing assistance and Maitland later claimed that he would have been at great personal risk if he had not. He single-handedly persuaded Mary to marry his arch-enemy, Bothwell, to make the crime of passion story seem plausible. Yet he knew that the English would consider Bothwell to be unacceptable as Mary's consort on the English throne. Perhaps he hoped that later he could dissuade her from the marriage, as he would try to do at Dunbar. He also provided the Casket Letters by manipulating their correspondence as evidence of a crime of passion. He was as much the cause of Mary's downfall as Moray and Cecil, despite later supporting her in captivity. His position was impossible and, although he temporarily remained at Court, he kept a low profile. Moray's allies doubted his loyalty, even after his departure from Mary's service to join them at Stirling.

Despite Morton sharing the government with Bothwell, he was never his natural ally, but was dominated by Moray and told Cecil that he would do 'anything in my power to gratify you as your assured friend'.[2] Morton's role was to marshal the Scottish nobility to enable Moray to 'look through his fingers' from abroad as events unfolded. Moray had learned during the Chaseabout Raid that he could not be seen to promote himself and had to wait to be called. Although Morton had sent henchmen to assist Bothwell at Kirk o' Field, he had personally kept his hands clean. His first task was to entice Bothwell into believing he should marry the queen for Scotland's security. He was then to galvanise support for Moray from members of the Catholic nobility by shocking them into believing the crime of passion story. If this brought Mary down, Moray would become regent. Moray and Cecil did not have to promote the story themselves; it was fed to the Lennox faction.

Argyll remained close to Mary, providing stability by helping Bothwell in government. He too may have been acting on Moray's instruction as the means of keeping the Catholic Atholl, with whom he remained at loggerheads, away from direct contact with the queen. Yet Argyll's loyalty was to Mary alone and, when Bothwell sought to marry her, he temporarily joined those seeking to oust him. As soon as Bothwell had lost power, he reverted to being a Marian supporter, thereby alienating Moray and Morton. Atholl is an enigma, as he had been kept in the dark by the conspirators and was likely to seek a proper enquiry. After his initial backing of her marriage to the king, he had fallen out with Lennox over his son's shortcomings. Yet, as a leading Catholic, he was distressed by his death and, on the night afterwards, heard sounds as if the foundations of his Holyrood apartment were being undermined. After a sleepless night, he moved with his family into the town taking Tullibardine with him. Buchanan claimed that Bothwell thought they were probing too far, so 'it behoved them, for fear of their lives, to leave the court'.[3] As a Catholic, Atholl certainly wanted Mary to remain on the throne as she was the bastion against the spread of the Scottish Reformation, but he would not support her marriage to the Protestant Bothwell, who seemed to have masterminded King Henry's death.

Moray had to carry the factious Scottish nobility with him and to provide incontrovertible evidence against Bothwell and Mary, who remained popular despite her Catholicism. Although most of the lords at Craigmillar had wanted to be rid of the king, neither Bothwell nor Huntly and the Catholics would have seen advantage in Moray replacing her. Knowing that he lacked universal support, Moray gave no hint of his intentions to the bond's signatories. His failure to overthrow her in the Chaseabout Raid and her escape after the murder of Riccio had been calamitous. Her Catholicism alone did not provide acceptable grounds for her deposition, but her involvement in a crime of passion to murder her husband fitted the bill.

Given Bothwell's part in the king's murder, it might have seemed logical for Moray to encourage a detailed enquiry, feeding into it sufficient information to implicate him. Yet this would incriminate most of Moray's allies as signatories of the Craigmillar bond, which Bothwell held. Other than the bond, there was very little verifiable evidence against him and none against the queen. If Bothwell were accused, Mary would protect him. He had always been loyal, and it was Moray and his allies whom she mistrusted. To give veracity to the crime of passion story and to remove the evidence of the part played by others, he needed to demonstrate Bothwell's involvement in every stage of a murder plan that had Mary's blessing. He had to show that Bothwell and his henchmen had organised the provision of gunpowder, the lighting of the fuse and the suffocation of the king with his servant outside the Town Wall. This had to be backed with incontrovertible evidence. His allies tortured witnesses into falsifying their depositions, but, despite every effort, they often conflicted or did not follow the required line, making them implausible.

It was only in anticipation of the English Conferences that Moray and his allies began to put together evidence to back their assertions of the part played by the queen in a crime of passion. While she was being held without trial at Lochleven, he had been able to avoid producing it on the apparent grounds of protecting her honour, but after she escaped to England there had to be an enquiry. It was only on 27 May 1568, more than fifteen months after the king's murder, that Buchanan, now aged 62, was commissioned by Moray to prepare his *Detectio*, a highly fanciful but damning account written in Latin, designed to colour public opinion against her. Buchanan followed the line of the Edinburgh posters that she had formed an attachment out of lust for Bothwell, such that they had worked together to bring the king back from Glasgow to Edinburgh, where Bothwell murdered him, leaving them free to marry. He provided page after page of scurrilously readable tittle-tattle against the queen written in a vitriolic style. As he had not been present, he relied on 'closed writings', which Moray sent to him. His first version became available only in early June 1568, when he referred to its hasty preparation.

At first glance, Buchanan seems an unlikely choice to be the author of a condemnation of Mary and Bothwell. It has resulted in him being castigated as 'the basest hireling scholar of all the ages'.[4] A classicist, poet and Calvinist, educated in Paris, Buchanan had helped Mary with her Latin when she returned to Scotland, had assisted her in composing verses to be sent to Elizabeth and had written masques to entertain the Court. He had eulogised on the beauty of the Maries and had recently written a masque extolling Mary's virtues for Prince James's christening celebrations. Yet he had been brought up near Glasgow of impoverished parents, owing his education to Lennox philanthropy. While he would support Mary as the wife of a Lennox son, the king's murder made her his deadly enemy. He also owed a favour to Moray, by whom he had been appointed Principal of St Leonard's College at St Andrews University. He now used his platform as Moderator of the General Assembly to back Moray and his adherents. He was also a political theorist who advocated the republican ideals of a free state as espoused by Greece and Rome. He linked Classical ideas with Calvinist doctrine to develop a far more sophisticated thesis than Knox's *Monstrous Regiment of Women* for opposing the divine right of monarchy. Rulers were chosen to fulfil defined roles and were not above the law. If they proved inadequate, they could be replaced, even by tyrannicide.

Buchanan trusted Moray and may genuinely have believed that Mary had connived with Bothwell in the king's murder. In mid-1568, without close examination, people grasped at his *Detectio* as the evidence needed to incriminate her. Yet, on publication, he described it only as 'an information of probable and infallible conjecture and presumptions'. Obvious errors have been cited in the endnotes, but he believed the ends justified the means. He painted the king as a saintly paragon to match the Lennox image of him and cunningly blended fact with scurrilous gossip to create a tissue of lies. It would never stand up to scrutiny to find Mary guilty of conspiracy, and it provided no credible evidence of her having advance knowledge of the plot to kill her husband.

Moray still needed incontrovertible evidence. In the summer of 1567, with Mary already imprisoned at Lochleven, there is the first mention of a letter written by her being found in a silver casket in Edinburgh. This rapidly grew to a total of twenty-two documents. The lords argued that it was these that justified them rising against their anointed queen. Yet there is conflicting evidence for the timing of the discovery. In November 1567, the lords confirmed in parliament that they took up arms against the queen on 15 June, as a result of seeing 'divers her privy letters'.[5] Yet in his sworn statement to Elizabeth and Cecil at the Conferences, Morton says that the letters were found only on 19 June, four days too late to justify the action taken at Carberry Hill. While Moray was returning to Scotland from France in early July, he told de Silva in London of a single letter written to Bothwell by Mary from Glasgow implicating her in the murder. De Silva was also aware from du Croc of the lords' assertion that Mary was an accomplice to her husband's murder 'proved by letters under her own hand'. The casket became the purported source of all the falsified correspondence used to justify Mary's detention in England.

Modern research shows that there are obvious shortcomings in the Casket Letters, but, at the time, they seemed sufficiently plausible to justify keeping Mary under arrest, and they have fooled generations of later historians. The English Commissioners at York and Westminster, who knew they were flawed, never permitted their cross-examination. Elizabeth's limited objective was to justify retaining Mary under house arrest in England, without finding her guilty of her husband's murder. The result was that Mary was indisputably wronged.

After being openly hostile to King Henry and in the face of rumours linking him to the murder, Moray went to great lengths to clear his name. On 13 March, he advised Cecil that he had been in St Andrews when the blast occurred. Yet Mary became very suspicious when he asked her for a passport to visit England, apparently en route for France. If innocent, he had no reason to leave. Yet he had to avoid taking part in the struggle for power that was ahead. He would not challenge Mary for the throne for a second time. As her half-brother, he could not make the perfect political alliance by marrying her. Yet he was of royal blood, had held the reins of power before and had English support. He was not walking away, but would wait for the call to become regent for James. He knew only too well that, without general support, this role was a poisoned chalice. If his departure allowed Bothwell to gain control by marrying the queen, he had evidence of his part in the king's murder with which to bring him down later. He countered rumours of his own involvement by isolating Bothwell and his henchmen as the perpetrators of the crime and by orchestrating the crime of passion story to implicate the queen.

Moray did not leave Scotland immediately, but stayed away from Edinburgh, despite Mary's requests for assistance. He used the excuse of his wife's miscarriage to remain at St Andrews, but she was not too ill to prevent him, on 26 February, travelling to meet secretly with Morton, Lindsay of the Byres, Caithness and Atholl at Dunkeld, where this cross-party group will have focused only on a mutual desire to bring down Bothwell. With Atholl present, Moray will have glossed over the Craigmillar bond and Mary's future. Morton's attendance demonstrates that his friendship with Bothwell was illusory. They agreed to form a coalition of Protestant and Catholic 'Confederate' lords to work for the good of Scotland. Yet, as rumours against Mary started to mount, Moray had to be seen to be supportive. He did not need her brought down before Bothwell had sought to marry her. He returned to Edinburgh for a short period before 8 March to provide a steadying hand. More importantly, he was able to meet Killigrew.

Elizabeth had reappointed Killigrew, Cecil's brother-in-law, as her ambassador in Scotland, ostensibly to express her concern at Mary's loss. He arrived in Edinburgh on 7 March and delivered Elizabeth's stinging letter of 24 February demanding a thorough investigation into the murder. She now addressed Mary as 'Madame' rather than more customarily as 'Sister'. After returning from Seton, Mary received Killigrew at Holyrood in a darkened room. Yet his main purpose was to establish from Moray how the crime of passion story was being received. After dining with Moray and his allies, he provided an official report indicating that every effort was being made to find the murderers. 'Despite great suspicions, there was no proof', but he needed to ensure that the Scottish lords would rebel against Mary, who was showing favour to Bothwell, England's enemy. Until her abduction on 24 April, the only evidence of an amorous relationship between them was in the placards, and news of her abduction could not have reached London before Killigrew had set out. In all probability, he brought Cecil's sanction for Mary's deposition, but this could only be achieved if she married Bothwell. With Cecil maintaining such detailed records, the lack of an explanation for Killigrew's visit is suspicious. Moray wrote a letter to Cecil, which Killigrew carried south, ending it by saying that Killigrew 'hath heard or seen more than I can write'.[6] This implies that Cecil and Killigrew both had an intimate understanding of Moray's plan and trusted him.

Jean Gordon had been so ill at the end of February that one ambassador reported her death and Bothwell began to think that he might be free to remarry Mary. By 20 March, Jean had recovered and took the first step in seeking a divorce. It is not clear what prompted her to do this, although Buchanan's *Detectio* alleges that her agreement formed part of the negotiation for the return of Huntly's estates. As these were not formally restored by parliament until 19 April however, she is unlikely to have jumped the gun and, according to Drury, Huntly was reluctant to agree to the divorce (although this may not have been correct). It has also been suggested that Jean was in fear for her life, believing that her illness had been caused by poison. She had never loved Bothwell and, whatever her motive, the documentation cited his adultery with Bessie Crawford in May 1566, ten months earlier (Jean might have been expected to ignore adultery with her serving girl, but it provided an adequate motive). Her action only added to speculation that Mary planned to marry Bothwell. Rumours started to circulate among Edinburgh stallholders and, when Mary rode past the Lawnmarket, women cried out: 'God save your Grace if you be innocent of the king's death.'[7] Drury could soon tell Cecil that 'the judgement of the people' was that they would marry, and even the English ambassador in Paris heard this.[8]

The campaign of placards in Edinburgh gathered pace and focused against Bothwell. There were crude portraits of him with the words: 'Who is the king's murderer?' or 'Here is the murderer of the king.' It was almost certainly Tullibardine who initiated the campaign in Edinburgh with help from his brother, James Murray of Pardewis, and they were to be accused of it by Bothwell. Tullibardine had always remained loyal to the king and was one of the few seeking justice for him.[9] If Mary were not involved in a crime of passion with Bothwell beforehand, the rumours broadcast on placards only five days after the king's murder need an explanation, when there was no evidence by then to suggest any amorous attachment. Tullibardine had already left Edinburgh, and they were not close enough to verify the story for themselves; it must have been fed to them by someone who wanted also to implicate Mary. The only realistic candidates are Moray and Cecil, with assistance on the ground from Morton and Maitland. This implies that there was a well-formulated plan to promote this scenario before the king was murdered.

There was a second, more sophisticated, source of propaganda. Both Maitland and Buchanan are plausible candidates for initiating it, but it was more realistically Cecil, who was, at the same time, employing Sir Francis Walsingham in anti-Papist propaganda in England. This new campaign was meticulously planned and, as each placard appeared, those involved made sure that the content was fed to Lennox, while Drury kept Cecil closely advised of its impact. On 1 March, Mary was depicted as a mermaid, a well-recognised synonym for a prostitute, next to a hare, which was the Bothwell crest. It is full of scurrilous Classical metaphor. (See p. 13 of the pictures section.) In her right hand, Mary holds a large sea anemone, the symbol for female genitalia. In her left is a folded net with which to snare her prey. The hare is surrounded by swords to denote Bothwell's military standing, with one suggestively positioned as a phallic symbol. Mary and Bothwell were mortified and tried to establish who was behind it. They interviewed the minister of Dunfermline, who could give no help, but made Bothwell laugh by suggesting that it must have been a Papist canon who had sired three children in adultery! The Council was asked to silence it. On 14 March, a warrant accused Murray of Pardewis of having 'devised, invented and caused to be set up certain painted papers upon the Tolbooth door of Edinburgh, bending to her majesty's slander and defamation'.[10] He fled to England, but offered to return to defend himself. Although he seems to have been behind the initial campaign, aimed at bringing Bothwell to book, as a Catholic, it is unlikely that he would have used the smutty innuendo of the mermaid to depict Mary.

As criticism grew, Mary became increasingly concerned. On 19 March, with Bothwell's agreement, she arranged for James to be escorted by Argyll and Huntly to Stirling, where Mar had been newly reconfirmed as Governor. Before this, she had discussed with Killigrew the possibility of sending the prince for his upbringing to England. Yet Elizabeth believed that this would cause Mary 'anxiety, as any little illness it might have would distress her'.[11] Elizabeth's only concern was to avoid the potential heir to the English throne being sent to France. Although Mary had considered returning there, Catherine de Medici wanted her to clear her name.

If the public was beginning to believe that Bothwell had murdered the king to marry Mary, there is no plausible evidence that Mary even remotely considered marriage until her abduction. Nevertheless, he was the one person she trusted and, without his help, she believed the Reformers would want Moray to replace her. On 12 March, at the end of her mourning period, Mary was in tears while attending a requiem Mass for the king at Holyrood. She was completely distraught at a further requiem Mass on Palm Sunday, 23 March. On 30 March, Drury reported: 'She has been for the most part either melancholy or sickly ever since [the murder], and … often swooned … the Queen breaketh [weeps] very much.'[12] She was too stricken to correspond and, as her letters were in Scots not French, she will not have drafted them. Although she replied to Elizabeth's letter of 24 February demanding action to clear her name, this is lost. According to de Silva, who discussed it with Elizabeth, it 'contained only lamentations for the troubles she had suffered in her life, and a request that the Queen would pity her'.[13] This was no way to impress her sister queen. Her extraordinary show of sorrow continued, when she was accompanied by two of her Maries to pray for four hours on Good Friday, 28 March. Yet by Easter she was back to her old self again, returning to Holyrood for dancing and banquets. It was now that Bothwell started to court her, and no one was discouraging him.

The game of chess had to be played most carefully, always thinking several moves ahead. It would be incredibly hard to circumvent the pitfalls looming almost every step of the way. The most important thing was to ensure that everyone involved in the murder plan kept their mouths shut. Given that they were also implicated, this might not seem too hard a task. It was particularly important to silence Bothwell, as he held the bond incriminating most of the conspirators. They also had to blacken Mary's name. By using placards in Edinburgh to plant rumours that she was involved with Bothwell in a crime of passion to murder the king, they hoped that Elizabeth would be turned against her and her Catholic allies, both on the Continent and among the Scottish nobility, would be neutralised. If Mary's part in the murder were to be investigated, evidence would be required which would stand up in a court of law, when she had not been involved. The innuendo of the placards and Buchanan's *Detectio* would not be enough.

If the crime of passion scenario were to appear plausible, Mary needed to agree to marry Bothwell. To achieve this, several almost insuperable obstacles had to be overcome. Bothwell had to be found innocent of the king's murder, which he had organised in collaboration with those who signed the Craigmillar bond. If the prosecution produced evidence, the existence of the bond, which incriminated almost all of Moray's close allies, might become known without Mary being implicated. Revelations arising out of an investigation into Bothwell's part in the murder might deter Mary from marrying him, particularly as he did not meet her objective of gaining recognition as Elizabeth's heir. He was hated by the English, who would find him totally inappropriate as a consort for the heir to the English throne, despite his Protestantism. Mary's Continental Catholic allies were likely to try to dissuade her from an inappropriate Protestant match with the man generally thought to have murdered her husband. Another danger of Mary marrying Bothwell, was that she might learn the names of those involved in the murder plan and would have to be persuaded not to prosecute them. Bothwell had to be free to marry Mary. As he was married to Jean Gordon, their divorce would need to stand up to Catholic scrutiny. It was helpful, at least, that Jean seemed equally anxious to end their marriage.

Once Bothwell was married to Mary, he would become the most powerful man in Scotland. Without concerted opposition against him, he would have sufficient military support to make his position unassailable. Elizabeth would never authorise overt assistance to depose an anointed queen and she wanted a dynastic succession to the English throne. This would make Mary her heir, regardless of her Catholicism. Mary was likely to retain the support of Scottish Catholics. Would the dubious tale of a crime of passion to murder King Henry seem sufficiently plausible to turn them against the couple? While it was reasonable to hope that they would take up arms to be rid of the Protestant Bothwell, they were unlikely to agree to Mary being deposed. Yet without Catholic support, or at least their assurance of neutrality, Moray and his allies would struggle to gain the upper hand.

Once Mary and Bothwell had been defeated, the conspirators would have to decide what to do with them. They could not execute an anointed queen. Their plan was to imprison Mary and for Moray to become regent for Prince James. They needed her held securely in a place where she could not communicate with her supporters. They could perhaps avoid a prosecution on the grounds of protecting her honour, but, if it became necessary, they needed evidence. So long as Mary remained alive, her allies in Scotland were likely to take up arms to seek her release. Once separated from Bothwell, she would receive support both from Catholics and those who hated Moray, such as the Hamiltons. If Bothwell were imprisoned, he would need to face trial, which risked the production of evidence against the other conspirators. It would be much better if he escaped to an out of the way place, where it might be possible to arrange his assassination or incarceration. Heaven forbid if either of them should be set free; the genie would be out of the bottle.

With all these problems unresolved, Moray left Edinburgh on 7 April with Elizabeth's safe conduct to travel to England. Bothwell was overjoyed at his departure. Yet Moray's objective was to implicate Mary and, to this end, Morton and Maitland maliciously encouraged Bothwell to marry her. This suited Cecil perfectly. While in London, Moray justified his departure from Scotland to de Silva by saying that

> he did not intend to return until the Queen had punished the persons concerned in her husband's death, as he thought it was unworthy of his position to remain in a country where so strange and extraordinary a crime went unpunished. He believed that the truth might certainly be ascertained if due diligence were shown.[14]

This unctuous stance did not impress Archbishop Bethune, who warned de Alava that, despite his show of loyalty, in reality, he was Mary's deadly enemy. Before his departure, he appointed Mary as guardian for his infant daughter; he would not have chosen her if he believed her guilty. He must have been confident that his supporters in Scotland would challenge Mary and Bothwell if they married, and he knew he could rely on Cecil.

Chapter 28

Bothwell's exoneration and marriage to Mary

For those who argue that Mary had no advance knowledge of the conspiracy to murder her husband, the most difficult issue is to explain why she condoned a whitewash for Bothwell's trial with no evidence being presented. All the early commentators accepted the view of the propaganda that she had been involved with him in an amorous attachment and wanted to avoid a proper investigation. They thought she was completely in his thrall and was involved in a crime of passion. Yet this is unrealistic. It is also argued that she was suffering a mental breakdown caused by her earlier illness and depression, but this was not in character and conflicts with her behaviour when Riccio was murdered, when in Glasgow in the previous month, and at Borthwick a month later.

We know from Mary's correspondence that she thought the king's murder was also aimed against her, and Moray was behind a conspiracy to bring her down. He was most suspiciously leaving Scotland at a time when he had everything to gain if she were removed from the throne. The murder was much more likely to involve Moray or the returning exiles than Bothwell, who had been with her for most of the day beforehand. She was aware of the Reformers' long-standing objective of creating a Scottish republic. Their action to depose her mother as regent had begun a pattern of events, which continued with the Chaseabout Raid, the murder of Riccio and now the death of the king, all aimed at bringing down the Scottish Crown. The nobility had another reason for acting against Mary. In December 1567, she would be 25, the age when Scottish kings could revoke grants of land given during their earlier years. Most of the nobility had benefited, and she believed that they wanted her removed from the throne to avoid their recall.

The only man Mary trusted to support her was Bothwell, but she had been warned from several sources, including the placards in Edinburgh, that he had organised the murder. An enquiry might implicate the one man capable of protecting her throne, although, from what she knew, she would expect him to be exonerated. Instead of investigating further, she unwisely provided him with church vestments to make clothing, and reduced the forfeitures on a number of those who had been at Craigmillar. This implied that she was involved in a pay-off. All her close advisers were discouraging her from holding a trial and, when Lennox forced her into it, she condoned the Privy Council's decision to arrange Bothwell's acquittal without evidence being presented. Mary really had no choice in the matter and did not feel able to stand up to her Council, who were unified in wanting an acquittal. The Council, with Bothwell present, met on Good Friday, 27 March, to assure this. Only Lennox, whom Mary despised and mistrusted, actively sought evidence against him, and it was on his insistence that Mary at last set 12 April as the trial date. The outcome was bound to be a whitewash. In his memoirs, Bothwell claimed to have called for it to silence the innuendo in the placards. Yet, Lennox's lack of evidence made the result inevitable. The court recorder wrote that 'Bothwell was made clean of the said slaughter, albeit that it was heavily murmured that he was guilty thereof.'[1] This was particularly unsatisfactory because, if Bothwell were not the murderer, no alternative culprit was put forward. The mud continued to fly, and Buchanan recorded that after 'this jolly acquittal ... suspicion was increased and retribution seemed only to be postponed'.[2] To endorse Bothwell's innocence, Mary granted him Dunbar Castle to reward his 'great and manifold services', and he also received the principal estates of the Earldom of March.[3] More naïvely, she also provided him with horses and rich clothing previously belonging to the king. The tailor making the alterations remarked that 'it was but right and according to the custom of the country for the clothes of the deceased to be given to the executioner'.[4]

Lennox was too nervous to come to Edinburgh for Bothwell's trial. Although he had sought a delay to enable him to gather more evidence, he left Glasgow beforehand, having received Mary's permission to travel to England after visiting Prince James at Stirling. After sending a letter to Margaret in London via Drury, he boarded a ship in the Gairloch on 29 April. He arrived at Portsmouth on 10 May. While awaiting permission to disembark and a safe conduct from Elizabeth, his ship was driven by a storm across the Channel to the Brittany coast, from where Margaret had to send another ship to collect him. After being detained temporarily in Brittany, he was back at Southampton by 7 June, from where he wrote to Elizabeth seeking forgiveness for his past disloyalty. Elizabeth promised to help the Lennoxes avenge their son's death, as they had now lost faith in gaining Mary's support. Both Leicester and Cecil, who claimed credit for Margaret's release, also promised every assistance. Elizabeth offered money and men against the Confederates, but could not be seen to take up arms against a fellow queen. The Scottish Lords sent Margaret's half-brother, George Douglas 'the Postulate' to London to explain why they were taking up arms and to seek Elizabeth's support against Mary and Bothwell. Elizabeth's response was to send Throckmorton to Scotland to establish what had happened, little realising Cecil's duplicity. Although Moray visited Margaret in London to offer assistance, Margaret was suspicious of trusting a heretic.

The next stage of the game of chess was hugely assisted by Bothwell. Once it had been hinted to him that he should consider marrying the queen, he was determined to do so, not least because he believed that it would provide him, as the queen's consort, with immunity from prosecution. Their marriage did not become a realistic possibility until after his acquittal. Although the Casket Letters included two versions of marriage contracts purportedly signed on 5 April, a week before the trial, it was the Lords' objective to show that Mary had agreed to the marriage before Bothwell's acquittal, thereby implicating her in a crime of passion. Yet they were demonstrably predated even if not outright forgeries.

Following his trial, Bothwell took control of government and did much to reconcile the nobility. Huntly was secretly promised the Lord Chancellorship in thanks for assuring Bothwell's acquittal. To smooth the divorce from Jean Gordon, he was granted other parts of the March estates at Dunbar. Eleven forfeitures on dissident Protestants, including those on Morton and Argyll, were reduced. Argyll was granted estates previously belonging to the king. On 17 May, Boyd became a Privy Councillor and also received areas of the Lennox estates. It all seemed like a pay-off. With his estates being usurped, Lennox, who was now in England, realised that his position was precarious. As late as 13 March, Maitland, who was still trying to promote Mary's claim to the English throne, was advising her to marry a Protestant husband such as Leicester, who was acceptable to the English. Yet most Scots, particularly the Catholics, believed a fellow Scot would assure their independence. This played into Moray's hands. With a Catholic being unacceptable to the Reformers, he persuaded them that the Anglophobe Bothwell was the next best thing.

On 19 April, at the end of the sitting of parliament, Bothwell entertained twenty-eight members of the nobility to dinner at Ainslie's Tavern near Holyrood, ostensibly to celebrate his acquittal. With his guests well wined and dined, he produced a document intended as a bond. In addition to confirming his innocence, it suggested that the queen was 'now destitute of a husband, in the which solitary state the commonwealth of this realm may not permit Her Highness to continue and endure'. It proposed that she should marry him, but he will have needed tacit encouragement from

Morton (and probably even from Moray, who was still in Scotland despite his non-attendance) to make this proposal. The bond called for signatories to provide backing for the sake of the realm. In return, they would be protected from prosecution for any past offences. Although Morton signed the bond, his relationship with Bothwell was already strained, with the Chancellorship having been offered to Huntly. His signature has to be seen as further evidence of the game of chess. With Bothwell falling into their trap, the signatories helped to snare Mary. It is known that these included Morton, Huntly, Sutherland, Caithness, Rothes, Cassillis, Seton, Fleming, Sinclair, Boyd, Glamis, Sempill, Ross, Herries, Archbishop Hamilton and six bishops. Neither Maitland nor Atholl attended the dinner, but Atholl seemed to accept Moray's cynical assertion that Bothwell offered the best means of assuring Scottish independence. Yet Morton insisted that Bothwell should not become king or wield royal powers on marriage.

Armed with the Ainslie's Tavern bond and accompanied by Maitland, Bothwell went to see Mary, who had returned to Seton at the end of parliament. He showed her the signatures in support of their marriage, but she turned down his suit. While she relied on Bothwell, she did not always follow his advice. She knew that their marriage would fatally prejudice relations with England and there were continuing rumours of his part in her husband's murder. Although he seemed to accept her refusal with a good grace, Morton ensured that the Council still provided active support. Mary told Nau that she was

> circumvented on all sides by persuasions, requests, and importunities; both by general memorials signed by their hands, and presented to her in full council, and by private letters.[5]

Acting on the Privy Council's instructions, on 20 April Maitland was sent to speak to Mary privately to add his persuasion for the marriage, despite his hatred of Bothwell and his knowledge that it would destroy Mary's ambition to be recognised as Elizabeth's heir. It seems hardly credible that he should have encouraged her to marry the man who had kept him out of favour after Riccio's murder and had refused to hand back his estates after their release from attainder. Much has been made of Mary Fleming's influence on retaining his loyalty to Mary, but he was forced into the role of promoting the marriage, which would implicate her in a crime of passion. When Moray put pressure on him, he felt sufficiently threatened that he also undertook to prepare the Casket Letters as evidence. When he met Mary, he cited her recent lack of leadership, advising that 'it had become absolutely necessary that some remedy should be provided for the disorder into which public affairs of the realm had fallen for want of a head'. He explained that it had been

> unanimously resolved to press her to take Bothwell for her husband. They knew he was a man of resolution, adapted to rule, the very character needed to give weight to the decisions and actions of the Council. All of them therefore pleaded in his favour.

When she expressed concern at the continuing rumours of his part in the king's death, he responded 'that Lord Bothwell had been legally acquitted by the Council. They who made this request to her did so for the public good of the realm'. This was persuasive and she 'began to give ear to their overtures, without letting it be openly seen'.[6] Bothwell had been loyal, was a brave leader, a good administrator and powerful personality. Their marriage would strengthen the government, but, contrary to the propaganda, it was never an insatiable love match.

On 21 April 1567, Mary returned to Edinburgh to sign papers. Later that day, she set out secretly for Stirling to visit James, now aged 10 months, for what would be their last meeting. Maitland, Huntly and Sir James Melville escorted her with thirty armed horsemen. Bothwell did not go with them, but remained in Edinburgh, where he raised a force on the pretext of going after Borderers, who had recently despoiled Biggar. His real plan was to kidnap Mary as she returned from Stirling. Buchanan claimed that Mary went to Stirling intending to move control of the prince from Mar to Bothwell, but Mar thwarted this by retaining the prince under his control at all times. It seems unlikely that Mary had planned this, as on her departure the next morning without him, she pressed Mar 'to be vigilant and wary that he was not robbed of her son'.[7] The crime of passion story would become much more credible however, if it could be demonstrated that Mary had colluded in her abduction, with or without the prince.

Bothwell assembled 800 horse at Calder Castle, south-west of Edinburgh, from where he rode to Linlithgow to ask Huntly for help in abducting the queen. Huntly's refusal implies that Mary was unaware of Bothwell's plan. Yet Moray's allies spread rumours that Mary had agreed to it. Casket Letters VI, VII and VIII and the French love poem were produced as evidence of Mary's collusion. Casket Letter VI records her mistrust for Huntly and is endorsed, 'From Stirling afore the ravissement – proves her mask [pretence] of ravishing [seizing].'[8] It says:

Alas, my Lord, why is your trust put in a person so unworthy to mistrust that which is wholly yours? … You had promised me … that you would send me word every day what I should do. You have done nothing thereof. I advertise you well to take heed of your false brother-in-law. He came to me … to say what he was to write on my behalf to explain … where and when you should come to me, … and thereupon hath preached unto me that it was a foolish enterprise, and that with mine honour, I could never marry you, seeing that you being married, you did carry me away … he is all contrary … I told him … that no persuasion nor death itself would make me fail of my promise. As touching the place … Choose it yourself and send me word of it … And seeing that your negligence doth put us both in danger of a false brother, if it succeed not well, I will never rise again … I wish I were dead. For I see everything is going badly. You promised something very different in your prediction, but absence have power over you that have two strings to your bow.[9]

The letter is intended to imply that Bothwell has failed to tell Mary where he planned to kidnap her. She believes that, by sending Huntly who disapproves of the marriage, he is risking it becoming known that she has agreed to it. She fears that Bothwell is not getting on with it, as he still has 'two strings' (Mary and Jean Gordon). Yet Huntly had by then already given approval for Bothwell to divorce his sister and did not criticise Mary until an argument with her at Dunbar. There is no record that he left her at either Stirling or Linlithgow to carry messages to Bothwell. It was Bothwell who came to him. Buchanan's *Detectio* also differs from Casket Letter VI as it claims that Mary had agreed with Bothwell the place of her abduction before going to Stirling. It seems to be a transcript of a later genuine letter, which Mary wrote to Bothwell from Dunbar, predated to make it look as if it were from Stirling. By then Jean's divorce papers had been filed, and Huntly had quarrelled with Mary, as confirmed in her later correspondence. The letter shows her agitation that she is risking everything. Even Cecil's clerk realised that the English version had been predated as he corrected present to past tenses in a couple of places to show that it was written after her abduction, and headed it: 'Copie from Stirling after the ravissement'. Yet, if sent after the abduction, it lost its point as evidence of a crime of passion. Even Cecil showed he was not above a little manipulation of his own, as he changed 'after' to 'afore'.[10]

The transcript of Casket Letter VII shows that it was intended as the second in a sequence of letters written by Mary from Stirling. It continues in a vein similar to Casket Letter VI, saying:

> Of the place and time, I remit myself to your brother [Huntly] and to you. I will follow him and will fail in nothing on my part. He finds many difficulties. I think he does advertise you thereof and what he desires for the handling of himself. As for the handling of myself, I heard it once well devised. Methinks that your services, and the long amity, having the good will of the Lords, do well deserve a pardon, if above the duty of a subject you advance yourself, not to constrain me, but to assure yourself of such place near to me, that other admonitions or foreign persuasions may not let me from consenting to that that ye hope your service shall make me a day to attend. And to be short, to make yourself sure of the Lords and free to marry, and that you are constrained for your surety, and to be able to serve me faithfully, to use a humble request joined to an importune action. And to be short, excuse yourself, and persuade them the most you can, that you are constrained to make pursuit against your enemies. You shall say enough, if the matter or ground do like you, and many fair words to Lethington. If you like not the deed, send me word, and leave not the blame of all unto me.[11]

If genuine, the letter confirms that Mary knew of her abduction in advance and, by proposing that Bothwell should be pardoned, implicates her in the murder. Yet it seems certain that Casket Letter VI was written after the abduction. As this is intended to be before it, it can only be a complete forgery attempting to overcome the shortcomings of the earlier letter. It avoids the mention of any row with Huntly at this early stage, but demonstrates Mary's collusion in her abduction by telling Bothwell how to react. As a forgery, it shows remarkable insight. It is aware that there are 'other admonitions and foreign persuasions' disapproving of the marriage.[12] It knows that Bothwell has enemies, who need to be placated. As it singles out Lethington to receive 'many fair words', it must be concluded that Maitland wrote it. He hated Bothwell and wanted those seeing it to understand his behind the scenes efforts to oppose the marriage.

Casket Letter VIII was deemed to be the third in the same sequence of letters sent to Bothwell by Mary from Stirling, although she was not there for long enough for a third delivery. It refers to Huntly as 'your brother-in-law that was', who has come to her 'very sad' and in fear that he is acting treasonably.[13] Yet Bothwell had not by then divorced Jean Gordon. As it also mentions Sutherland being there, it fits as a genuine letter, written to Bothwell – by then her husband – at Melrose while she was at Borthwick. It will be discussed in that context.

It was also claimed that Mary wrote a long love poem to Bothwell from Stirling. Its twelve verses each take the form of a sonnet on a separate page. They show her infatuation for a man to whom she has pledged her son, her honour, her life, her country and her subjects. Yet Mar had prevented James being pledged to Bothwell. In line seventeen, it describes Scotland as 'my country', but Mary would always have referred to 'my Kingdom' or 'my Realm'.[14] Buchanan claimed that it was composed 'while her husband lived, but certainly before [Bothwell's] divorce from his wife', and he admired its 'tolerable elegance'.[15] Yet both Brantôme and Ronsard considered its French too unpolished to have been written by Mary, who was well trained in courtly phrasing and analogy, and its scansion is faulty. Buchanan probably wrote it himself and, despite its short-comings, would have been one of the few in Scotland capable of it.

On 24 April, the royal party left Linlithgow, but when they approached the River Almond six miles from Edinburgh, Bothwell appeared from Calder with his 800 men with swords drawn. They halted and Bothwell rode forward to take the queen's bridle, as if she were captive. He told her that an insurrection was threatened in Edinburgh and he would take her to Dunbar for safety. Neither Mary nor her entourage seemed to believe this, but, when her escort made ready to defend her, she agreed to go with him 'rather than bloodshed and death should result'.[16] Huntly, Maitland and Melville went with her. Mary's lack of resistance was a critical argument for those claiming that she was involved in a crime of passion, but she did not resist as she trusted Bothwell and wanted to avoid conflict.

Those seeking to exonerate Mary claim she was raped by Bothwell at Dunbar and agreed to marriage only because of the resultant risk of her being pregnant. She certainly wanted to give this impression. In two letters to France, she claimed to have been taken by force. *The Diurnal of Occurrents* records that Bothwell 'ravished her and took her to his castle'.[17] Yet the word 'ravish' at this time meant 'seize'. She was certainly seized, but was she raped? With Dunbar full of people, she could have screamed for help. She was there for twelve days with her servants and advisers, and Bothwell was not always there. On 26 April, he returned to Edinburgh with Mary's encouragement to assist in Jean Gordon's Protestant divorce petition. By then they had agreed to marry – hardly likely if she had been raped.

According to Nau's Memorials, dictated by Mary while in captivity in England, she complained to Bothwell at her treatment after arrival at Dunbar, and he retorted that

> she was in one of her own houses, that all her domestics were around her, that she could remain there in perfect liberty and freely exercise her lawful authority. Practically, however, all happened very differently, for the greater part of her train was removed, nor had she full liberty until she had consented to the marriage, which had been proposed by the Lords of the Council.[18]

Bothwell explained to her privately that, although everyone claimed to be his friend, in reality they hated him without reason and he needed her protection. He wanted to marry her before his rumoured participation in the king's murder became a public outcry. His intentions were entirely honourable and he would 'serve and obey' her for the rest of her life.[19] Yet she again refused him, even though he again produced the Ainslie's Tavern bond, confirming the nobility's support. This does not imply that she was raped.

Sir James Melville, who remained at Dunbar for the night, claimed that, despite being rebuffed, Bothwell dismissed her servants and raped her. Given the risk of pregnancy, she was left with no choice but to marry him. In her letter to the Bishop of Dunblane, she wrote:

> Seeing ourselves in his power, sequestered from the company of our servants, and others of whom we might ask counsel … already welded to his appetite, and so we left alone, as it were a prey to him … [he] ever pressing us with continuous and importunate suit. In the end when we saw no hope to be rid of him, never man in Scotland making a move to secure our deliverance, we were compelled to mitigate our displeasure, and began to think upon that he propounded.[20]

She is saying that, although Bothwell put her under huge pressure, he won her round. With so many people in the castle, even though most of her servants had been dismissed, this has to be more likely than rape. They agreed to consummate their relationship, as there would be strong efforts by the rest of the nobility to separate them. Her pregnancy would enable them to push through with their marriage. Mary was taking a high-stake gamble. She did become pregnant, but could not have known this at their wedding three weeks after her abduction, and rape would have been a good defence if she had wanted to extract herself. Yet she did not bargain on the adverse effect of the marriage on her popularity.

This was no love match. Bothwell is known to have had a predilection for anal sex with both male and female partners. Although it is difficult to judge, she provided later hints that she found her sexual experience with him distasteful. While her infatuation for King Henry is in no doubt, Bothwell's rugged methods may not have appealed. For a man who relished his sexual pleasures with the lusty Bessie Crawford in a church tower, Mary may have seemed slightly tame.

Both Maitland and Sir James Melville were soon doubting whether the marriage plan would succeed. Sir James told her that marriage to 'a man commonly adjudged her husband's murderer would leave a tash [slur] upon her name and give too much ground for jealousy'.[21] Even Huntly, still Bothwell's closest supporter, showed no enthusiasm for it. Despite having argued the Privy Council's case in support of it, Maitland remained hostile to Bothwell and only wanted to get away from Dunbar, particularly after Bothwell threatened to murder him. He told Cecil that he survived only because the queen intervened on his behalf. (Drury's record says that it was Huntly who attacked Maitland, but the queen shielded him from his drawn sword with her body, threatening 'that she would cause him to forfeit lands and goods and lose his life unless he desisted'.[22] As Drury was not present, Melville's report that Bothwell was the assailant seems more likely.) Furious at the opposition of Maitland and Melville, Bothwell imprisoned them both, although Melville was permitted to leave with Huntly the next day. Pragmatic as ever, Maitland probably acted on Moray's instruction by playing along with the marriage plan and he accompanied Mary and Bothwell to Edinburgh for their wedding.

Despite rumblings of opposition, nothing would stop Bothwell from marrying Mary and he moved forward with all speed, believing that a queen's consort could not be prosecuted for the king's murder. It took only three weeks from the abduction until the wedding ceremony. The biggest hurdle was the divorce from Jean Gordon, who willingly colluded in the civil proceedings on grounds of adultery with Bessie Crawford, so that the decree was confirmed on 3 May. Yet this would not allow a Catholic to remarry, and Bothwell asked Sir James Balfour to fix it for him. The only acceptable form of Catholic divorce was an annulment on grounds that they were within the fourth degree of consanguinity. Archbishop Hamilton, who had conducted their wedding, was approached and, on 7 May, signed the papers, conveniently forgetting that he had granted a dispensation for consanguinity before their wedding in the previous year.

While Bothwell was in Edinburgh to resolve the divorce, Huntly stayed in Dunbar, where he had a row with Mary over her marriage plan. This is mentioned in Casket Letter VI, which, as explained, was written by Mary from Dunbar and not prior to her abduction. Although Huntly had agreed to the divorce and was formally restored to his estates, he was becoming isolated by supporting them, and later failed to provide his promised military backing. This would become the nail in the coffin for Mary and Bothwell at Carberry Hill.

Bothwell's abduction of Mary and his scarcely credible divorce proceedings alienated the Catholic lords, and Mary was now in Moray's trap, as their marriage implicated her in a crime of passion. On 27 April, Morton met at Stirling with Argyll, Atholl and Mar, who all believed that Mary was being held against her will. Morton's presence shows that his alliance with Bothwell and his support for the marriage at Ainslie's tavern had been illusory. It was the first time that he had made his opposition public. As it was three days after Mary's abduction to Dunbar, he was assured that they were now committed. He no longer needed to encourage a marriage, which would leave Moray out in the cold. A gathering, which included all the rival factions, met at Stirling on 6 May with the common goal of bringing Bothwell down. In Moray's absence, Morton had the task to 'manage all', and a letter was written to Moray seeking his return.[23] The group also signed a bond as Confederate lords to 'pursue the Queen's liberty, preserve the Prince from his enemies in Mar's keeping, and purge the realm of the detestable murder of our king'.[24] They stopped short of accusing Mary of conspiring with him, despite a general belief that she had done so. They wanted her released from Bothwell's cruel 'tyranny and thralldom'.[25] Yet Mary still saw Bothwell as offering her the best hope of powerful leadership, and his control of the munitions at Dunbar and Edinburgh Castles seemed to prevent his opponents from mounting a challenge. She found it hardly credible that support for him had evaporated, given the signatures on the Ainslie's Tavern bond.

The Confederates were now made up of a powerful cross-section of both Catholic and Protestant nobles. They were joined by Mar, who had control of the prince and by Moray's half-brother, Sir William Douglas, who offered Lochleven as a stronghold to imprison Mary when the time came. The Catholics among the Confederates always remained loyal to the queen, believing that she was being held by Bothwell against her will. Moray's mainly Protestant supporters had the broader objective of deposing Mary and appointing him as regent. Most importantly, the Confederates mustered

3,000 troops at short notice and, having overwhelming public support, were in a position to make a stand against Bothwell.

Maitland failed to attend the meeting at Stirling, as he was still at Dunbar, and his non-appearance caused the Confederates to 'muse much'. He was probably not being held strictly against his will at this point, but pragmatically chose to sit on the fence. It is likely that he was still trying, with the help of Mary Fleming, to protect Mary's position by dissuading her from marrying Bothwell, but failed to do so. Although this was at odds with Moray's plan, he later concocted the Casket Letters, and it would seem that he was blackmailed by Moray, who could reveal his part in the two murders. His duplicitous stance left him mistrusted on all sides.

The Confederates worried that Huntly still supported Bothwell and, with Châtelherault abroad, were unsure of Hamilton affiliations. Balfour seemed to be in Bothwell's camp after having been installed by Bothwell as Governor at Edinburgh Castle, an unlikely role for a lawyer, in an effort to assure his allegiance. Yet his loyalty remained in doubt, and Melville later admitted having secretly asked him to hold the castle for the Confederates in order to protect the prince and the queen 'who was so disdainfully handled'. His change of allegiance passed control of the ordnance and royal treasure to the Confederates. Yet he treacherously let Bothwell believe that he held the castle on his behalf.

Cecil provided the Confederates with all the help he could without alerting Elizabeth to what he was doing. Yet she was 'greatly scandalised' by events at Dunbar and would no longer accept Mary as her heir.[26] She promised to help Lennox avenge his son's murder, hoping that James would be brought to England into his grandmother's care.

Well aware of the opposition building against him, Bothwell raised troops in the Borders, and with his control of the munitions at Dunbar and, as he thought, at Edinburgh Castle, his position seemed unassailable. On 6 May, he set out with Mary for Edinburgh accompanied by Huntly and Maitland, and, on arrival, the castle guns fired a salute 'most magnificently' despite the sullen crowds.[27] He tried to limit external communication with her, so that she would not realise the hostility they faced, but both Herries and Sir James Melville came in an attempt to stop the marriage. Maitland told Melville that 'he had done more honestly than wisely' and warned him to keep out of sight 'till [Bothwell's] fury was slaked; because I was advertised there was nothing but slaughter in case I had been gotten'.[28] Drury reported that Bothwell's efforts to keep Mary away from her traditional advisers caused them to quarrel. He concluded that they would not long agree after their marriage.

On 8 May, a proclamation was issued that Mary would marry Bothwell. On 12 May, she was escorted by the Lords of Session to the Tolbooth where Bothwell, in a scarlet robe edged with ermine, was created Duke of Orkney and Mary placed the ducal coronet on his head. On Morton's insistence, he was not made king and all official documents required her signature. The next day, Mary and Bothwell signed the marriage contract, which described her as a young widow, 'apt and able to procreate and bring forth more children' to maintain the Stewart dynasty, having been encouraged by the 'most part of her nobility' to marry. To appease the mainly Protestant lords that opposed him, Orkney insisted on the wedding taking place in the Great Hall at Holyrood in accordance with Reformist rites, and not in the Chapel Royal. This resulted in a Catholic boycott. At the marriage ceremony on 15 May they were 'handfasted' as an exchange of rings was considered Popish. Although it demonstrated her desire to be seen to act for the good of her realm, Mary's participation in a Protestant service later caused her great distress, and lost her the last vestiges of papal support.

The marriage service was not well attended, despite some of the Confederate lords feeling duty bound to be there. Huntly was a witness and those attending included Maitland, the four Maries, a few nobles and the couple's servants. There were members of the Catholic clergy, including Archbishop Hamilton and the Bishops of Ross and Dunblane. It was a pathetic little event compared to the glittering pageantry of her earlier marriage celebrations.

On the evening of the wedding, a further placard appeared in Edinburgh quoting from Ovid, '*Mense malas maio nubere vulgus ait* [As is commonly said, wantons marry in the month of May]'.[29] Cecil rubbed his hands in ill-disguised glee, writing that Scotland was 'in a quagmire; nobody seemeth to stand still; the most honest desire to go away; the worst tremble with the shaking of their conscience.'[30] The game of chess was going to plan.

Chapter 29

The confederate alliance challenges
Mary and Orkney

After her wedding, Mary and Orkney sent messages to Elizabeth and to her Continental allies to justify their marriage. Mary claimed that 'she had been very content to take him for our husband. From his first entering into his estate, he dedicated his whole service to his sovereign.'[1] She explained that he had been cleared by parliament of all suspicion of murder and had the support of the other lords, although, with their factious nature, they were now trying to put him down. This lacked conviction, when the other lords, speaking with one voice, were already seeking Elizabeth's help. Elizabeth was convinced that Orkney had murdered the king and posed a threat to James. The English had always disliked him and believed that he would colour Mary against them. Elizabeth's main objective was to gain control of the prince, by placing him in Margaret Douglas's care. Mary found herself shunned by her Guise relations and severely criticised by both European heads of state and the papacy. She was without a shoulder to lean on.

Immediately after the wedding Mary seemed greatly distressed; friction with Orkney now became open hostility. This seems to have been caused by her realisation that her marriage was extremely unpopular. Having been able to do no wrong since her return from France, public opinion was suddenly against her and she realised that the rumours of his part in murdering King Henry were likely to be true. She may have seen the Craigmillar bond, which he eventually gave to her at Carberry Hill, and was by then aware that most of the lords lining up against her were also implicated. It was Mary's remarriage, not the king's murder, which was now the focus of international scandal, and would prove her undoing. The broadsheets in Edinburgh had a field day, likening her to Delilah, Jezebel and Clytemnestra. In Catholic Europe, she was seen to have entered into a bigamous marriage with a heretic in an unlawful ceremony.

At some point shortly after the wedding, Mary must have realised that she was pregnant and there were already speculative rumours of this in England.

This was an insuperable barrier to her ending the marriage and she stood firmly behind her new husband. If he should be found guilty of treason, their child's legitimacy would be questioned. The only matter of importance to her was providing a second heir to the throne; despite James's robust health, life was fickle. Without her children, her death would result in anarchy in Scotland, with the Hamiltons and Lennox Stuarts, neither of whom offered decisive leadership, fighting it out. The Confederates had no inkling of her pregnancy and could not understand her ignoring their advice to leave her husband.

With Orkney presiding over the Council, he provided strong and intelligent leadership with 'a latent talent for diplomacy'.[2] There was to be a rota of councillors, including Morton, in permanent attendance at Court. To win over the Reformers, he blocked Catholic efforts to restore the Mass, annulling Mary's dispensation for Catholic nobles and her servants to worship with her in private. To ameliorate the nobility, he restored Morton to Tantallon; Fleming, who remained continuously loyal, was made Governor of the seemingly impregnable Dumbarton Castle and would continue to hold it for Mary until 1571. Yet Orkney's lack of general support left him with no opportunity to demonstrate his qualities.

On 6 June 1567, Huntly requested leave to visit his estates. Mary refused permission for him to depart from Court and accused him 'with many bitter words' of plotting treason against her as his father had done.[3] On the same day, Maitland had a furious row with Orkney and, without taking leave of the queen, left Court with Mary Fleming. Mary was distraught to lose her chief Marie. He joined up with the Confederates, but they remained suspicious at him for having stayed so long with Mary. Yet his arrival proved a rallying point for them. The Hamiltons and Home, hitherto Mary's supporters, also joined, but the Hamiltons wanted assurance that, after James, they were recognised ahead of the Lennoxes as heirs to the throne. (There must be considerable doubt whether either Archbishop or Lord John Hamilton genuinely supported the Confederates at this stage, although the elderly Châtelherault, who was still in exile, may have done. All contemporary references suggest that they remained strong adherents of the queen. Yet for a short period after Moray became regent, he bought their loyalty in return for recognising their prior claim after James to the Crown, but they soon mistrusted Moray's own ambitions and rejoined Mary's supporters.) Even Mar favoured Mary's deposition. Yet, she still trusted him, saying: 'He hath assured me to be mine and faithfully ever', so that James remained in his care.[4] Although Orkney made repeated demands for the prince to be handed over, Mary sent the Bishop of Ross to Stirling to forbid it: 'But my

Lord of Mar was a trew nobleman, and would not delyuer him out of his custody, alleging that he could not without consent of [parliament].'[5]

The Confederates were united in their desire to bring Orkney down and signed another bond confirming, as common ground, their intention to liberate the queen. Those whose sole objective was to topple Orkney expected her to desert him when she realised the extent of the public opinion against her, but others saw the marriage as the opportunity for removing her as their Catholic monarch. They feared that if Orkney gained control of the prince he would proclaim himself as king.

By 25 May, Orkney knew that he faced a rebellion. Mary had to raise 5,000 crowns and sent table silver and gold to be converted to coin at the Mint. Even Prince James's christening font was handed over, although it was so large that the furnace failed to generate sufficient heat to melt it. The queen's lieges were summoned to attend her on 15 June at Melrose, but she was shocked at the opposition to her.

With Holyrood unfortified, Orkney planned to move with Mary into Edinburgh Castle, but Balfour managed to discourage this, while assuring them of his continuing loyalty. On 7 June, Orkney took her to Borthwick Castle, twelve miles south-east of Edinburgh to await the muster of their levies at Melrose. The castle belonged to the Catholic William, 6th Lord Borthwick, Orkney's adherent. It was a fine fortress built in about 1425, impregnable without cannon, but difficult to provision in a siege. After installing Mary in the keep, Orkney left to link up with Home, not knowing of his defection to the Confederates. He returned to Borthwick on 9 or 10 June, but although Mary brought her muster forward, her 'proclamation was not so well obeyed, and so many as came had no heart to fight in that quarrel'.[6]

Casket Letter VIII was indisputably written by Mary from Borthwick on 8 June, while Orkney was at Melrose, notwithstanding that it is annotated as being from Stirling before her abduction. Having asked to return to his estates three days earlier, Huntly feared that Mary would accuse him of treason, but he arrived from Edinburgh with 300 horse raised by Livingston and himself, aware that the Confederates planned to attack Borthwick on the following day (10 June). Mary's letter refers to him as 'your brother-in-law that was', and reports that he has promised his backing, supported by

> many folks here, and among others the Earl of Sutherland, who would rather die, considering the good they so lately received of me [in being restored their estates], than suffer me to be carried away, they conducting me, but wants advice on what to do after tomorrow.

Yet, she worries that Huntly's support is half-hearted and he

> hath abashed me to see him so unresolved at the need. I assure
> myself he will play the part of the honest man; but I have thought
> good to advertise you of the fear he hath that he should be charged
> and accused of treason, to the end that, without mistrusting him,
> you may be the more circumspect.

By predating the letter, as if written from Stirling, the manipulator has used Mary's words of being 'carried away, they conducting me' to imply that she colluded in her abduction, although this makes no sense in the surrounding context.[7]

Orkney sent an urgent request for support from Balfour, Lord John Hamilton and Huntly, who had returned to Edinburgh. On the evening of 10 June, Home joined Morton and Mar at Liberton Park, four miles south of Edinburgh, from where they advanced on Borthwick with between 700 and 800 mounted hackbutters to be joined by many of their Confederate allies. Although Drury tried to persuade Cecil to send English troops to support Home, Elizabeth was still not prepared to be seen to oppose a fellow sovereign. Still trying to gather troops, Orkney did not risk becoming holed up at Borthwick with an inadequate force. Leaving Mary in command of a small garrison, he escaped from a postern gate to seek reinforcements at Haddington, hoping that the Confederates would not attack her on her own.

Unaware of Orkney's escape, the Confederates lined out 2,000 men before Borthwick, taunting him with cries of, 'Traitor! Murderer! Butcher!' Late in the evening, Mary shouted back that he was not there. They called on her to return to Edinburgh to assist in finding the king's murderers, but she refused. This brought insults 'too evil and unseemly to be told, which the poor princess did with her speech defend'.[8] Being without artillery, they withdrew, claiming that their sole objective was to avenge the king's murder. On 12 June, a secret Council at the Tolbooth declared Orkney 'to be the principal author and murderer of the king's grace of good memory and ravishing of the Queen's Majesty'.[9] This had the effect of reversing his acquittal and gave legal substance to their call to arms. Morton's men plundered the gold collected at the Mint, including the still unmolten christening font. He now offered twenty shillings per month, a substantial rate, to anyone taking up arms to deliver the queen from Orkney. When Argyll arrived with a substantial force, the Confederates boasted 3,000 men.

Although Huntly and Archbishop Hamilton's attempted to generate support for Mary in Edinburgh, they were forced to seek refuge in the castle. Huntly apparently hastened north to raise more troops, but his willingness to support Mary and Orkney was evaporating. Hamilton headed south-west, but his family was also ambivalent about providing assistance. Despite receiving another urgent call to bring support, they were fearful of the Confederates' substantial build-up.

At midnight on the following evening Mary escaped from Borthwick Castle by a postern gate 'dressed in men's clothes, booted and spurred'. After travelling a mile, she was met by Orkney's servants, who took her to him and then on to Dunbar, where Seton greeted their arrival at three o'clock in the morning. Orkney's main objective was to regain control of Edinburgh, but he needed more men and left to gather troops in the Borders.

By focusing only on executing justice on 'the murderer of the king and the ravisher of the Queen', the Confederates outwitted Mary and Orkney in their call to arms. They soon had 4,000 men and the backing of the Reformist clergy. By 14 June, Orkney had returned with 1,600 men, but they were inferior troops provided by minor Border lairds. Drury had bribed the Elliots of Liddesdale to intercept and harry smaller contingents attempting to join him, so that much of his hoped-for support failed to materialise. Although Mary wanted to look the part, her clothing had been left at Borthwick and she had to borrow garments from a countrywoman, 'a red petticoat' that barely covered her knees, 'sleeves tied with bows, a velvet hat and a muffler'.[10] Despite lacking the trappings of royalty, she left Dunbar to link with Orkney at Haddington, burning with defiance and supported by 200 hackbutters, sixty cavalry and three field guns. On arrival, she had 600 cavalry, but was dismayed at the disappointing level of support. Unaware that they were hopelessly outnumbered, she and Orkney marched on, and the Confederates, with their numerical superiority, were anxious to confront them before rumours of her pregnancy started to attract sympathy. Balfour showed his true colours by enticing them into a trap. On 13 June, he encouraged them to march on Edinburgh, where he promised his support. Even though they still awaited troops, they set out immediately, unaware that they were outnumbered. They billeted at Prestonpans, from where they rode to Seton for what would be their last night together. The Confederates had taken no chances over Balfour's loyalty. Maitland interviewed him for three hours to gain assurance that Edinburgh Castle would be held for them and promised to back his retention as Governor.

Early on 15 June, Mary and Orkney moved forward to Carberry Hill overlooking the River Esk, seven miles east of Edinburgh, where they were strategically positioned in an earthwork dug by Somerset prior to Pinkie Cleugh. Having left Edinburgh at two o'clock in the morning, the Confederates camped at the foot of a hill, two miles to the south-east. They carried banners between two spears, showing the infant James before his father's body praying, 'Judge and avenge my cause, O Lord.'[11] Morton and Home, with Ker of Cessford and Kerr of Ferniehirst, led the main body of cavalry, while Atholl, Mar, Glencairn, Lindsay, Sempill and Ruthven commanded the foot. Kirkcaldy controlled a smaller contingent of horse to block Mary from withdrawing to Dunbar.

Mary and Orkney played for time, vainly, as it turned out, having heard that Huntly and Archbishop Hamilton were on their way with 800 men. Although their troops set out to support Mary, they seem to have received word that a compromise had been reached and did not continue. This may have been a convenient excuse. The day was long and hot, and the Confederates had access to water from a stream. With neither side being inclined to fight, the time was spent in negotiation. Glencairn sent a message to the queen that the Confederates had no quarrel with her and, if she handed over Orkney, the murderer of King Henry, they would 'restore her to her former authority as their natural sovereign'. She angrily refused, telling them to 'yield or take their chance in battle'.[12] Orkney seemed to offer her better prospects than the likes of Morton, Ruthven and Lindsay.

Du Croc offered to mediate to prevent the Confederates from engaging their anointed queen in battle. Morton explained that their complaint was against the king's murderers, not her. If Mary would not leave Orkney, one of the Confederates would face him in single combat. Du Croc crossed the open ground to put this to Mary. After kissing her hand, he told her what the Confederates were proposing. She retorted in fury:

> It looks very ill of them to go against their own signed bond, after they themselves married me to him, having already acquitted him of the deed of which they would now accuse him.[13]

She told him to offer them a pardon for their offences, if they would submit. When Orkney arrived to ask what they proposed, du Croc loudly assured him of their loyalty to Mary, but told him quietly that they were his mortal enemies. Orkney complained:

> Is not the bond they gave to me well known to everyone? ... I have never meant to offend any of them, but rather to please them all, and they only speak of me as they do out of envy of my high estate.

In swashbuckling fashion, he affirmed: 'Fortune is free to those who may profit from it, and there is not a single one of them who would not gladly be in my place.'[14]

The Confederates now sent a herald to Orkney with a written statement of their reasons for taking to the field. He later claimed: 'These were, firstly, to set the queen free from the captivity, in which I was holding her, and also to avenge the death of the king, of which I had been accused.' He replied that he

> was not holding the queen in any captivity, but that I loved and honoured her in all humanity as she deserved. There had not been any question of my participating in, or consenting to, the murder of his Majesty,

having been cleared by parliament. He was ready to defend his honour against any comer, claiming, 'My cause is so just, I am quite sure that God is on my side.'[15] With typical bravado, he called on a Confederate to take up his challenge. James Murray of Pardewis immediately stepped forward, but the queen vetoed him because of his inferior rank. Orkney then offered to fight Morton. As both of them had taken part in the murder plot, this was a macabre jest. Morton was now aged 47, some fifteen years the elder, and was no longer considered proficient in armed combat, so Kirkcaldy offered to fight on his behalf. Wary of his awesome reputation, Orkney refused to fight with 'one who was only a baron', and suggested Moray's father-in-law, the reclusive Marischal. Despite his appropriate rank, Marischal was not fit, and Lindsay claimed the right to fight, as a closer kinsman to King Henry than Morton, and took off his armour to limber up. (In fact he was only remotely connected to Darnley.) Lindsay was no mean challenge and the queen intervened in tears to prevent the fight. She knew she was pregnant, and feared her protector being killed. Du Croc backed her and returned to the Confederates with Mary's offer of clemency, but Glencairn retorted that they wanted revenge for the king's death.

Time had elapsed, and, with the day hot, the Confederates had the advantage of shade in the valley in addition to water. Mary's troops on the hill became extremely thirsty in the full sun. When Orkney sent scouts in search of water, they were captured. Wine arrived in casks from Seton, but this only caused dehydration. As the day progressed, raw Border troops slipped away, causing others to disappear or even to desert to the Confederates.

Despite Orkney facing unassailable numerical odds, du Croc had grudging respect for his management:

> I am obliged to say that I saw a great leader, speaking with great confidence and leading his forces boldly, gaily and skilfully. I admired him, for he saw his foes were resolute, he could not count on half his men, and yet was not dismayed. He had not on his side a single lord of note. Yet I rated his chances higher because he was in sole command.[16]

Mary would not surrender her throne lightly, but, with her army reduced to less than 400 men, the military outcome was not in doubt. She tried to leave the field, but found her way blocked by Kirkcaldy. When one of Orkney's men took aim at him, she immediately told the man not to shame her, knowing that Kirkcaldy was an ally at heart. When she sought terms, Maitland and Atholl were too embarrassed to negotiate, but Kirkcaldy assured her that, if she went with them, Orkney could leave with a safe conduct. Orkney begged her to retreat with him to Dunbar to raise another army: 'I told her they would take her prisoner and strip her of all authority.'[17] As so often when faced with a crucial decision, Mary took the wrong one and overrode her husband. She wanted him free to fight again, after lying low while she arranged a proper review of the king's murder. Kirkcaldy heard her telling him that

> she owed a duty to the late king her husband, a duty which she would not neglect. Most willingly therefore would she authorise everyone to exercise the fullest liberty of inquiry into the circumstances of his death. She intended to do so herself, and to punish with all severity such as should be convicted thereof.[18]

She made clear that she would investigate both her enemies and her husband, which implies that she had seen the Craigmillar bond. She probably expected another whitewash. She told Orkney that, if found innocent,

> nothing would prevent her from rendering to him all that a true and lawful wife ought to do, but, if guilty, it would be to her an endless source of regret that, by her marriage, she had ruined her good reputation, and from this she would endeavour to free herself by all possible means.[19]

By distancing herself from him, she hoped to demonstrate her own innocence.

Orkney left Mary with the Confederates. His safe conduct suited them, as they did not want his evidence revealed in an investigation. Mary wept as they embraced. (The Confederates claimed that they kissed passionately in front of both armies, but this was no doubt for public consumption. Du Croc's eyewitness report says that they clasped hands. This seems more likely as they were both on horseback.) He gave her what seems to have been the Craigmillar bond, implicating many of their opponents, telling her to 'take good care of the paper'.[20] Seton and Fleming with between twelve and thirty horsemen accompanied him to Dunbar with a plan to raise reinforcements. He never saw her again.

Always chivalrous, Kirkcaldy assured Mary that

> he had been sent, at the unanimous consent of the rebels, for the sole purpose of offering to the Queen, as their rightful superior, their true allegiance, and to give her a guaranteed safe conduct to come amongst them. Furthermore, that each single one of them wanted no more than to accord her all honour and obedience in whatever way she wished to command them.[21]

Mary very quickly learned that this was not the general intention, and Kirkcaldy considered her subsequent treatment and imprisonment in Lochleven to have breached his honour. He led her on horseback to join the other Confederate lords. She was still in the clothes she had borrowed at Dunbar, begrimed from her day in the saddle. Yet she held her head high, and Mary Seton, who had remained with her on her pony, was in attendance. She was received with 'all due reverence' by Morton, Home and the other lords, who assured her that she was now in her rightful place among her own true and faithful subjects.[22] Yet their deference was short-lived. According to Drury, they produced the banner showing the dead king's body, which she later admitted 'she wished she had never seen'. Troops jostled her, shouting: 'Burn the whore! Burn the murderess of her husband!'[23] Kirkcaldy and other lords struck out with their swords at those taunting her, but to little effect. According to du Croc, she 'talked of nothing but hanging and crucifying them all'.[24] She rounded on Morton: 'How is this, my Lord Morton? I am told that all this is done in order to get justice among the king's murderers. I am told that you are one of the chief of them.' He answered: 'Come, come, this is not the place to discuss such matters,' but was sufficiently disconcerted to move out of earshot.[25] She was escorted to Edinburgh under guard, with the banner showing the king's body ahead of her, reaching the gates after eight o'clock in the evening. The Confederates had packed the streets with people screaming: 'Burn the whore! Kill her! Drown her! She is not worthy to live!' 'All disfigured in dust and tears, she rode past amid execrations of the people from the windows and stairs.'[26]

Mary was not taken to Holyrood but, at Maitland's suggestion, to the Black Turnpike, a luxurious but fortified house on the High Street, the official residence of the Provost. After arriving at eleven o'clock at night, she was placed under guard in a sparsely furnished upper chamber. The banner depicting the dead king was positioned in the street opposite her window with the mob continuing to shout abuse.[27] She was without servants and, with guards in her bedroom, could not undress even when she wanted to relieve herself. Although she was invited to join her captors for supper, she refused, perhaps in fear of poison. She had no chance to escape.

Mary had no one to turn to. She realised that the Craigmillar bond signatories would want her dead or removed from the throne. She was too exhausted to sleep, but lay down fully dressed for the night with the clatter of guards outside her door. The next morning, in a desperate bid for help, she appeared in hysterics at her window with her tangled hair hanging loose. She opened her bodice to expose her breasts and, with 'piteous lamentations', appealed to those below. Although some continued to insult her, many were 'moved to compassion' until the guards pulled her out of view. Independent witnesses reported that the crowds were soon supporting her, but when the lords promised to return her to Holyrood 'to do as she list, she was so pacified that the people willingly departed'.[28] Yet Home, with his cavalry, spent three hours clearing the streets to prevent a rescue attempt.

Afterword

Whatever else may be concluded about Mary, she was a poor judge of character. Her choice of King Henry was disastrous, and by failing to conduct a proper investigation into his murder, she lost her throne. Her cosseted upbringing in France had left her ill-prepared for the intransigence of either the Scottish nobility or the Kirk. Both were questioning the divine right of her rule, but she lacked Elizabeth's political astuteness. Her naïvety led her to embrace unrealistic goals. She never understood that she had no expectation of being accepted as heir to the English throne by an English Parliament so long as she remained personally Catholic. Yet she would never suborn her faith to meet her political ambitions. She had hoped that once accepted as Elizabeth's heir, she would be able to rely on the English to protect her Scottish throne. Yet it was unrealistic to expect them to protect a Catholic queen on their northern border, particularly when she was a member of the belligerent and ultra-Catholic Guise family. The English were only interested in Scotland maintaining secure Protestant government.

Mary lost her throne, not because she may have had some knowledge of the conspiracy to murder King Henry, but because she organised Bothwell's trial so that it was seen to be a whitewash and then agreed to marry him, even though he was generally thought to have murdered her husband. It is really very difficult to show her in a good light. The claim that she married Bothwell because she was completely under his thrall, the result apparently of her dangerous illness and acute depression, is questionable. At considerable personal risk, she had protected Maitland and Melville from his violent temper. She was in sufficient authority to quarrel with him immediately before their marriage. Her determination to go ahead with it can be explained by her fear of being pregnant and her belief that the signatories of the Ainslie's Tavern bond supported him. Yet she knew from Elizabeth, Catherine de Medici and Lennox, and more recently from Herries, Melville and, almost certainly, Maitland, that she would be marrying her husband's murderer. She could hardly claim that she did not believe it, as she was aware of a bond being signed at Craigmillar. She also knew that marriage to Bothwell would preclude her from succeeding to the English throne and from any future Catholic support. Yet she was cajoled by him into believing that it provided them with mutual protection. If her first sexual encounter with him was in Dunbar on 24 April, she could not have known that she was pregnant by 9 May when the banns for her wedding to him were published. She had only to claim rape, as everyone assumed, to explain her pregnancy. She always maintained that she married Bothwell for reasons of state. This was no love match and she made no effort to provide him with assistance after Carberry Hill. Yet, with muddle-headed logic, she spurned all rational advice and seemed to believe that marriage to the most powerful Scotsman available was the only way to protect her throne and, if she were pregnant, would legitimise another heir to secure her dynasty. She brought about her own downfall and it is hard to make a case that she deserves to have been treated better by history.

The villain was Moray, who was encouraged by Cecil and had the support of Morton and Maitland (in his effort to save his own skin). Their conspiracy to persuade Mary and Bothwell to marry to enable them to bring down a Catholic monarchy was underhand in the extreme. History has exonerated Cecil, perhaps because his loyalty was to Elizabeth, but he was the *eminence grise* behind Mary's undoing. The Protestant Lords needed his blessing to seek her abdication, and his meticulous records show the extent of his involvement.

Yet the game of chess was not yet played out. The first bit of good luck was that Orkney escaped, but was unable to raise support to come to Mary's aid. Realising that he needed to be seen to be brought to book, Morton sent Kirkcaldy and Tullibardine after him. Kirkcaldy was not an experienced sailor and was probably chosen to marginalise his continuing opposition to Mary's imprisonment. They had orders to seize Orkney and to execute him without trial. As Lord High Admiral, he had gone to Dundee, where he fitted out four men-of-war, considered the fastest in Scotland, and, on 19 August, set out to sea supported by several of his Kirk o' Field henchmen with cannon and 400 hackbutters. He sailed north and, from a base in Shetland, pirated English and Danish shipping to raise money. Kirkcaldy and Tullibardine surprised him at Lerwick, where they were able to arrest Cullen, Hay of Talla and Hepburn of Bolton, but Orkney managed to escape with two of his ships, taking Paris with him. They sailed to Bergen in Norway, then part of Denmark, where he was well entertained by the Governor, until Anna Throndssen, who, most unluckily for him, was living there, sued him for breach of promise to marry her. To stop the action, Orkney promised her an annuity from Scotland and handed over one of his ships.

Seeing Orkney as a potentially lucrative political hostage, Frederick II moved him to 'honourable confinement' at Copenhagen Castle. While there, he prepared his fanciful memoirs *Les Affaires du Conte Boduel*. From here, he was taken for greater security to Malmö Castle (now in Sweden), where he remained decently housed. Moray was anxious to isolate him, as Mary had been able to send him messages from Lochleven, and had authorised him to offer the Orkney and Shetland islands to Frederick II, if he would send Danish troops and ships to her assistance. Moray, as regent, would never have agreed to this. When Mary escaped from Lochleven, Moray was fearful that the Danes might free Orkney to enable him to provide evidence at an enquiry into King Henry's death. He pressed Frederick for his extradition to Scotland. Yet the Danish king still saw Orkney as a bartering counter and refused, but released Paris back to Moray's control. In 1573, when Frederick realised that he had no hope of receiving a ransom for Orkney's release, he transferred him to the forbidding Dragsholm Castle on the Jutland coast, where he saw out his remaining days. He lived on there in alcoholic excess until 1578.

Mary was moved from Edinburgh over night to the island fortress of Lochleven in Kinross-shire, crossing the Firth of Forth by ferry. It was imperative that she should be stopped from communicating with her allies to reveal what she knew, particularly as Orkney, who was still at this stage in Scotland, was bent on a rescue attempt. She was guarded by Sir William Douglas with the unsavoury Lindsay and Ruthven, but there was no groundswell of sympathy for her. She was exhausted and hardly ate until, on about 24 July, she miscarried twins losing a great deal of blood. While she was recovering, Lindsay came to her to seek her abdication, threatening to cut her throat if she did not sign the papers appointing Moray as regent. On Moray's arrival to take control, Mary was given no opportunity to clear her name. She always considered that her signature given under duress was invalid.

There was soon an upwelling of 'Marian' support from Catholics and from those who opposed Moray, particularly the Hamiltons. Despite disapproving of Mary's marriage to Orkney, Elizabeth strongly resented an anointed queen being incarcerated and wrote letters of sympathy to her. She sent Throckmorton to see her, but there was little that he could do. Despite promises of help from her supporters, it was Mary's personal charisma that melted hearts at Lochleven to assist her escape. With the aid of Willy Douglas, an orphaned cousin of Sir William, she was spirited away in a rowing boat wearing a mantle with a hood. She was met on the shore by Seton and John Bethune, her Master of the Household. The genie was out of the bottle, and Moray was 'sore amazed'.[1] She was cheered on by the people as she rode with her auburn hair flowing to join Seton and the Hamiltons. She soon had 6,000 troops behind her, with Argyll, who had provided the largest contingent, being placed in command.

Moray moved fast. He positioned himself at Glasgow to stop Mary from reaching Dumbarton to join a ship to take her abroad, and he sent Ruthven to block the passes of the Tay to prevent Huntly coming south to support her. Morton, Home and Kirkcaldy all arrived to join him and, although he had less troops, Scotland's best generals were now at his side. He decided to challenge the Marians two miles south of Glasgow at Langside. With Morton in command, he appointed Kirkcaldy to have 'special care as an experimented captain to oversee every danger'. The Hamiltons were spoiling for a fight and Mary's troops approached Langside up a street from the south, where Kirkcaldy had installed 200 hackbutters behind garden walls. They picked off the advancing Marians as they approached. Although her troops fought their way forward bravely, Moray's rearguard was brought up to push them back. Although they were in desperate need of support from Argyll's highlanders, at this critical point, Argyll suffered an epileptic fit, and the field was left in disarray. To avoid bloodshed, Moray sought to capture those he could, but it was a rout.

Mary's fate was sealed. She left with Livingston, Fleming Bethune, Herries, Maxwell and Lord Claud Hamilton for a nightmare journey to Dumfries and on to Herries's stronghold of Terregles. Moray did not follow her, but returned to Edinburgh, seizing the properties of her supporters as he went. Mary's most obvious course was to go to France, where she had lands and income; Herries promised to rally support for her on her return. Yet, believing Elizabeth's recent promises of assistance, Mary chose to throw herself on her mercy by going to England, against the advice of everyone with her. She later wrote to Bethune in Paris: 'I commanded my best friends to permit me to have my own way.' On the next day, 16 May 1568, a fortnight after her escape from Lochleven, Mary's party embarked on a fishing boat at Abbeyburnfoot (near Maryport) for the four-hour journey across the Solway Firth to Workington in Cumberland. She would never see Scotland again.

On Mary's arrival in England, the management of the game of chess was transferred from Moray to Cecil. Elizabeth confirmed that she should be received honourably with her restoration to be discussed. Yet Cecil had no desire to see the Scottish government he had worked so hard to install overthrown, and strongly opposed any sympathy for Mary. The Lennoxes hurried to Court, begging Elizabeth on their knees to seek justice for their son. Margaret's face was 'all swelled and stained with tears', but Elizabeth lost patience with their cries for vengeance and sent them away.

Mary's situation was summarised by Cecil in a note that he wrote to clarify his own thoughts. She had been accused of being an accessory to murder and of having married the murderer. Yet she had come to England of her own accord, having trusted Elizabeth's frequent promises of assistance. She was illegally condemned by her subjects, having been imprisoned without trial in front of parliament. As a queen she was subject to no one, but had offered to justify her behaviour personally to Elizabeth. He argued somewhat disingenuously that, as Darnley had been king, he was a public person and her superior. This placed her open to a public investigation, but neatly overlooked that the king had never received the Crown Matrimonial and was not her equal. Furthermore, Elizabeth would never approve the deposition of an anointed queen, but she might not fight for her restoration against her subjects' will.

With an eye to English security, Elizabeth's views started to move more closely into line with those of Cecil. Moray's Regency offered greater security on her northern border. With a Protestant government in Scotland and Mary being held in England, she felt secure. Yet European governments were watching her, and she needed to justify retaining Mary in custody. There had to be an investigation, but it suited Elizabeth to prevaricate. For once Cecil approved of her indecisiveness. She gave the impression of offering assistance by arbitrating with the Scottish government for Mary's restoration. Yet, when Mary approached the French to send 2,000 foot and 500 horse to Dumbarton, to be paid for out of her French estates, Elizabeth made clear that this would be regarded as a renewal of old quarrels, fearing a rekindling of the *Auld Alliance*.

While being held in the north of England, Mary behaved like a model queen, preferring to be treated as a guest rather than a prisoner, and she was joined by Mary Seton and other members of the Scottish Court with a substantial household. She was warned that Elizabeth would not meet her until 'the great slander of murder' had been 'purged', and Cecil told Moray that an English review of the murder was inevitable. Convincing evidence would be required if the English were to protect him in government. Cecil knew that, if Mary returned to Scotland, the Regency would be untenable. Yet Moray was surprised to find himself as the defendant for having forced an anointed queen to abdicate. Yet it soon became clear that it was an investigation of Mary. Mary was under house arrest at Bolton Castle, but when she realised that she was in effect the defendant, she refused to attend the Conference, sending Herries to lead commissioners in her place. Her absence suited Moray and Cecil who were short of evidence.

Moray sent his secretary, Wood, to London to blacken Mary's name and it is clear that Elizabeth was shocked by his revelations. Yet proper evidence was required. It was only now that Moray commissioned Buchanan to write his *Detectio* (see p. 190). Maitland was probably producing the Casket Letters while Mary was at Lochleven, but their number was increased and they were amended after Mary's escape to England. Moray wanted to know what would happen when the Conference ended. If she were to be returned to the Scottish throne regardless of the outcome, he would rather not provide evidence (particularly as she would know that it had been falsified). Cecil gave him a secret assurance that she would not be returned to her throne. He also sought evidence from Lennox, which was ultimately produced as his *Narrative*, blending authentic fact with fabrication. This sometimes contradicted the depositions provided by Bothwell's henchmen under torture.

The conference at York was chaired by Thomas Howard, 4th Duke of Norfolk, supported by Thomas Radcliffe, 3rd Earl of Sussex, and Sadler. There was to be no judgement because Elizabeth had no authority to try the Scottish queen and wanted to avoid finding her guilty. She just wanted Mary sufficiently tarnished to justify retaining her in England. It is clear that Norfolk, who had Catholic sympathies, and his colleagues knew what was expected of them. Yet Norfolk was not a close ally of Cecil, who he considered an upstart. On arrival in York on about 1 October 1568, Moray privately, and quite improperly, provided Norfolk with transcripts of the evidence. He wanted assurance that the Casket Letters were sufficient to find Mary guilty. Norfolk and his colleagues recognised immediately that, if they were genuine, they would incriminate her, but, if fraudulent, she would be exonerated. Neither of these outcomes was what Elizabeth wanted. They concluded that the letters should not be tabled, and Sussex wrote to Elizabeth that the best solution was for the whole matter to be 'huddled up with a show of saving [Mary's] honour'. He went on to comment on his poor opinion of the Scottish nobility, a view he shared with Norfolk. He believed that if Mary were to confirm Moray as regent, Moray would withdraw his accusations against her and repeal the Scottish Act of Parliament declaring her guilty of the king's murder. He added that the Hamiltons wished to see her restored only because they hated Moray. He concluded:

> Thus do you see how these two factions, for their private causes, toss between them the crown and public affairs of Scotland, and care neither for the mother nor child, but to serve their own turns.

While Elizabeth's reply was awaited, Maitland approached Norfolk to suggest that he should consider marrying Mary. This was hardly likely to appeal to Moray, for whom Maitland was ostensibly working. Norfolk did not reply, but it is clear that he was receptive having earlier turned down the proposition made at Berwick, although it would need Elizabeth's blessing. This suggests that he realised that the Casket Letters were fraudulent. Mary was also made aware of the proposal. As the recently widowed senior English peer, she was hopeful that Elizabeth would approve, and secretly wrote to Dragsholm to seek a divorce from Orkney. Although Orkney agreed to it, the Pope refused its ratification, fearful of the outcome for Mary of Elizabeth's wrath. When Elizabeth tackled Norfolk on the rumours of their marriage plans, he was obliged to deny them.

When Elizabeth was briefed on events at the Conference at York, she annoyed Norfolk by ending the proceedings there and moving them to Westminster, where she and Cecil could control the outcome. Before they began, Cecil wrote himself a note. If they wanted to keep Mary imprisoned,

> this matter must at length take end, either by finding the Scotch Queen guilty of the crimes that are objected against her, or by some manner of composition with a show of saving her honour. The first, I think, will hardly be attempted for two causes: the one, for that, if her adverse party accuse her of the murder by producing her letters, she will deny them, and accuse most of them of manifest consent to the murder, hardly to be denied, so as, upon trial on both sides, her proofs will judicially fall best out, as it is thought. I think the best in all respects for the Queen's Majesty [Elizabeth], if Moray will produce such matter [privately] as the Queen's Majesty may find the Scotch Queen guilty of the murder of her husband, and therewith detain her in England at the charges of Scotland.

This was a proposal for everything to be 'huddled up' as Sussex had recommended. It was most important that Mary should not be permitted to attend. By now, Elizabeth was closely sided with Cecil on how to deal with Mary, whatever she might still say for public consumption. She must have known that the evidence against her was fraudulent, but needed an excuse to retain her under house arrest. She also saw Mary's proposed marriage to Norfolk as threatening.

On 30 October, Elizabeth authorised the Council to advise Moray that Mary would not be returned to the Scottish throne if found guilty. The plan was to retain her in England and to confirm Moray as regent. This at last persuaded him to produce his evidence, but with a show of great reluctance. The outcome was prejudged well before the London proceedings began. Without Mary or her Commissioners being present, Moray tabled Buchanan's *Book of Articles* (the *Detectio* translated into English), Lennox's *Narrative* and an Act of Parliament confirming her abdication. Although he tried to avoid having to produce the Casket Letters, they were eventually provided with a sworn affidavit of their authenticity signed by Morton, together with some of the henchmen's depositions. Having had them copied, the English commissioners returned the originals to Moray without conducting a check of the handwriting.

Elizabeth now brought the Conference to a close without any conclusions being reached. Mary was not found guilty and Elizabeth 'saw no cause to conceive an ill opinion of her good sister of Scotland'; nor was she found innocent and, to the world at large, she remained tainted with suspicion. The matter was 'huddled up' exactly as Sussex had proposed. Elizabeth achieved a whitewash, but while Moray was free to return to Scotland and privately received £5,000 from her to help him to defeat Mary's supporters there, she remained incarcerated at Bolton, but refused to confirm her abdication. The English Commissioners were sworn to secrecy, and the existence of the Casket Letters was not made public. Elizabeth retained a hold over Moray. She could still restore Mary to the Scottish throne whenever she wished. This spectre kept the Scottish government closely allied to English foreign policy, just as it had previously been allied to France.

Mary was now moved south under the control of George Talbot, 6th Earl of Shrewsbury and his wife Bess of Hardwick, with whom she was to remain almost continuously for fifteen years. Yet, even now, Mary posed a threat each time a new Catholic intrigue sought to achieve a Counter-Reformation, and she reinvented herself as a Catholic icon. Furthermore, Cecil had not resolved the problem that she remained the dynastic heir to the English throne. If he could not incriminate her in Darnley's murder, he would try a new tack: he would implicate her in one of the many Catholic plots aimed at her replacing Elizabeth on the English throne.

Mary saw marriage to Norfolk as an opportunity and she became secretly betrothed to him by letter. As the proposal involved her repatriation to

Scotland, Moray was horrified, but Cecil encouraged Norfolk in his suit in the certain knowledge that Elizabeth would never condone it and it might incriminate them. Norfolk contemplated a full-scale rebellion to be supported by the Spanish from the Netherlands and by a group of Catholic Earls in the North of England. Yet English support was not widespread. Elizabeth threw Norfolk in the Tower, but the Catholic Earls continued their plan in what became known as the Northern Rising. This was doomed to failure from the start and never moved south of Yorkshire, and an attempt to rescue Mary petered out before it had begun. Yet the rebellion was very dangerous for Mary and Norfolk and it ultimately resulted in Norfolk's execution. Elizabeth refused to prosecute her sister queen, as there was no evidence that she had supported it.

Cecil encouraged Moray to hunt down lingering Marian support in Scotland. The Hamiltons and the Scottish Catholics gained assistance from a few Protestants, who were naturally supportive of Mary against Moray, now that she was separated from Orkney. These included Kirkcaldy and Maitland. They gained control of a number of strategic castles. Fleming still held Dumbarton, which allowed supplies from Continental allies to be delivered. Most importantly, Kirkcaldy took control of Edinburgh Castle. The Marians were now a force to be reckoned with. In November 1569, Moray went to Dumbarton in an attempt to persuade Fleming to give up his struggle, but Fleming refused. As he was returning, Moray was assassinated by the Hamiltons at Linlithgow.

Despite Moray's demise, his Reformist allies remained in the ascendancy, having control of James, still under Mar's care at Stirling. Although Morton took effective control, Elizabeth insisted on Lennox coming north to become regent for his grandson. She had realised that the alternative of sending James to England for his upbringing would cause offence in Scotland. Lennox's regency was confirmed on 13 July 1570. He was quite unsuited to such a political role. He sent all his official correspondence to Elizabeth through his wife, explaining:

> I cannot well commit the handling of those matters, being of such weight, to any other than yourself, neither am I assured if other messengers should be so well liked of, nor if the personages with whom you have to deal would be so plain and frank with others as they will be with you.

He was acutely short of money and Margaret had to pawn her jewellery to fund him while he sought Elizabeth's financial assistance. Yet Elizabeth reasoned that she could influence him by continuing to detain Margaret and their son, Charles, in England.[2*] Mary and Elizabeth were on common ground in wanting King James to be sent to England to be brought up by his grandmother, but Lennox respected the devoted care provided by Mar and his wife and left him where he was.

No one could fault Lennox's bravery in facing Mary's adherents head on. He sent troops, which regained control of Dumbarton, arranging the execution without trial of Archbishop Hamilton who had taken refuge there. The Hamiltons were determined on revenge. On 4 September 1571, they arranged a coup at a parliament called at Stirling, during which Lennox was assassinated. His bleeding body made a lasting impression on his 6-year-old grandson. Margaret Douglas was distraught, but had come to realise the Mary was not involved in the king's murder and started to show great sympathy for her. She suffered 'a languishing decline' but lived on until 1578, dying in great poverty.

It was Mar, not Morton, who became regent to replace Lennox. As a neutral, he 'enjoyed such a general respect' in the desire for peace that he gained universal support. He was not to prove astute as a leader.

> Though actuated always in the discharge of his public duties by a high sense of honour, he had neither the force of character nor the power of initiative to enable him to carry out an independent policy in difficult circumstances.

He was unwell and died on 29 October 1572 within a year of his appointment. The way was now open for Morton's regency, despite Elizabeth's misgivings.

Notwithstanding his key part in Mary's undoing, Maitland was by this time working hard to secure her release with support from Mary Fleming. Although suffering from a wasting disease, he was determined to make a final stand on her behalf. He arranged to be carried on a litter into Edinburgh Castle to show solidarity with Kirkcaldy. On becoming regent, Morton was determined to regain control of the castle. He called in Drury's English artillery to undertake a devastating cannonade. Maitland had to be carried to the vaults below St David's chapel as his frame 'could not abide the shot'. On the following day, with Maitland at his side, Kirkcaldy surrendered. Although the Marians offered bribes to save Kirkcaldy's life, Morton was determined to stamp out lingering opposition, and saw his sacrifice as essential to the regency's security. On 3 August, Kirkcaldy was executed 'as a stern necessity as he had exasperated public feeling'. On 9 July, Maitland, who had been imprisoned at Leith, took poison to kill himself 'after the old Roman fashion'. He was 45. Mary kept her feelings to herself, when she heard of his death. Shrewsbury reported that she made 'little show of grief, and yet it nips her near'. She may have realised that, at the last, he had become truly loyal to her.

Morton proved an efficient organiser. He was a conciliatory force in Scottish politics, holding together the Confederates, despite their many differences. He systematically stamped on petty rivalries to restore peace between differing factions. He streamlined Scottish government, fostering closer ties with England to simplify the merger between the two countries when James came to inherit the English throne. Yet his dictatorial approach gained him enemies. James was terrified of him and this pushed him into the company of a group of favourites led by his Lennox cousin, Esmé Stuart, 5th Seigneur d'Aubigny. They turned on Morton and, on 23 May 1581, he was found guilty of being 'art and part' of the murder of King Henry and was executed on the following day.

What of the henchmen at Kirk o' Field? To provide scapegoats for the murder, Moray had rounded up most of Orkney's men. Some of these, like Paris, had escaped with him on his ships, but, when captured, they were brought back to Edinburgh. It was most important that they kept their mouths shut, but they were tortured to provide a sanitised version of what had happened that did not conflict too glaringly with Buchanan's *Detectio* and the Casket Letters. To deflect attention from himself, Moray brought them to trial, where their manipulated depositions were read out. They were not permitted to give evidence, but were hung drawn and quartered. From the scaffold, they shouted out the names of the Lords involved, causing a clamour that they should 'suffer for their demerits', with uncomfortable rumours that their servants were being used as scapegoats.

Balfour arranged to have his part in the murder air-brushed out, although rumours persisted. Mary considered him an 'arch traitor' for double-crossing Orkney and herself while at Edinburgh Castle. He continued to switch sides and was one of those who supported Mary's marriage to Norfolk. This resulted in Moray accusing him of taking part in King Henry's murder, but Balfour bribed Moray's secretary, Wood, to drop the charges and he was freed. It is clear that he knew too much. By the time of Lennox's appointment as regent, Balfour was openly supporting Mary, and, in September 1571, his estates were forfeited at the Stirling parliament. He immediately did a *volte face* to protect himself and threw in his lot with the regency.

He was still seen as chiefly culpable and retired to France. In January 1573, he received a remission, but his forfeiture was not lifted and he remained under a cloud in France until 1580. In June 1579 he was again accused of taking part in the murder; he was confirmed as a traitor and his forfeited estates were divided up. In March 1580, he agreed to act as a prosecution witness against Morton, if permitted to return to Scotland unmolested with his estates restored. His evidence was not very incriminating, and he did not produce the Craigmillar bond, although he may have had a copy of the one signed at Ainslie's Tavern. He was not restored; in July 1581, he appealed, but was again turned down. Surprisingly, he died in his bed in Paris in 1584 after years of double dealing.

It was Archibald Douglas who murdered the king in the garden behind the town wall. Yet he remained for a time on the justice bench in Edinburgh, reliant on his part having been expunged from the evidence, and he married Orkney's sister Jean in about 1580. When his name was mentioned at the time of Morton's trial however, he fled to England, from where Elizabeth refused to hand him over. In his absence, his lands were forfeited and his servant, John Binning was imprisoned. Binning was tortured and, before being hanged, drawn and quartered, revealed Douglas's part in the murder. Douglas left England for France from where, between April and November 1583, he corresponded with Mary seeking assistance for his rehabilitation. She confirmed that 'if he is in any way connected with the death of the late king my husband, I will never intercede for him'. He told her that, in 1566, Moray, Atholl, Bothwell, and Argyll had signed a bond at Craigmillar to support Morton and the other exiles in having nothing to do with King Henry and to work for the exiles' return. It is not clear why he mentioned Atholl rather than Maitland and Huntly, but in other respects it was a half-truth. He did not refer to the murder plan, but confirmed having acted as the intermediary for the lords in exile. Eventually, in May 1586, he was tracked down in Scotland and accused of taking part in the murder. Yet, like Balfour, he knew too much. He was aware of the English government's involvement, and Elizabeth bribed James to ensure that he was cleared, even though it was by then well known that he had murdered the king. He argued that he could not have lost a velvet slipper at the murder scene, as the road was too rough for slippers, and he was not wearing one. He was pronounced 'clean and acquit of being in company with Bothwell, Ormiston, Hay and Hepburn in committing the crime'. With his estates restored, he became the Scottish ambassador in London and was for a short period Elizabeth's agent at the Scottish Court.

With Elizabeth being excommunicated by the Pope in 1571, Cecil redoubled his efforts to find evidence to incriminate Mary in a Catholic plot against the English crown. With help from Sir Francis Walsingham, his master spy, he provided conduits for communicating with her, enabling him to infiltrate her correspondence. He also planted *agents provocateurs* to promote conspiracies against Elizabeth. One of his agents was Roberto Ridolfi, but Walsingham planted other 'moles' in the offices of Archbishop Bethune in Paris, where most of the plotting was being instigated.

Throughout Mary's detention in England, she continued to pose a threat to English security. At last Walsingham's agents developed a plausible plot against Elizabeth designed to place Mary on the throne with Spanish help. Other agents provided a delivery service for Mary's correspondence and a code-breaker was brought in to decipher her letters. When Sir Anthony Babington, a wealthy, intelligent and romantic 25-year-old English Catholic squire from Derbyshire walked into Bethune's office in Paris, Walsingham's agents persuaded him to lead the plot. Once Mary had established his credentials, she wrote letters in code in support of the plan. At last, Cecil had the evidence he needed.

Mary was executed at Fotheringhay on 8 February 1587, not because she was implicated in King Henry's murder, but because she indisputably supported a fabricated plot for Elizabeth's assassination. Even now, Elizabeth was very reluctant to authorise Mary's execution. She needed to assess the reaction of the Catholic powers on the Continent and the young King James. James paid lip service to wanting his mother protected, but he had gained a taste for government and preferred her to be kept out of the way. Although he came to recognise that she had been grossly wronged, the genie had been pushed back into the bottle, and Cecil had won his game of chess.

Cecil lived on with a clear conscience providing advice to Elizabeth until his death in August 1598. He had protected her on her throne for all but the last five years of her reign. She told him: 'You are in all things my *Alpha* and *Omega*.' They were of course lucky. In the year after Mary's execution, Philip II had launched a Spanish Armada to avenge her death and to place his daughter the Infanta Isabella on the English throne. Philip's huge fleet was scattered by a storm in the Channel and its massive men-of-war were outmanoeuvred by far smaller English frigates. King Henry may have been long forgotten, but his murder nearly changed the course of British history.

Genealogical tables

1. The English succession

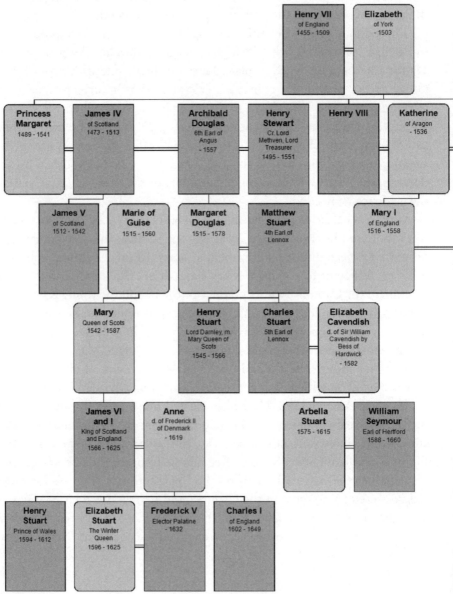

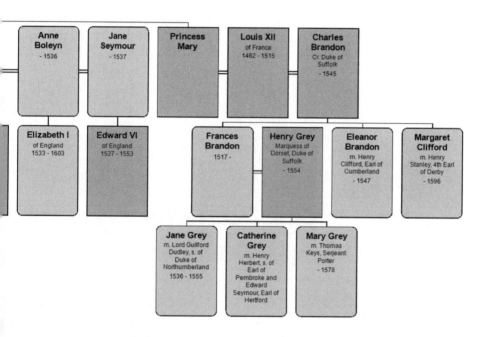

2. The Scottish succession

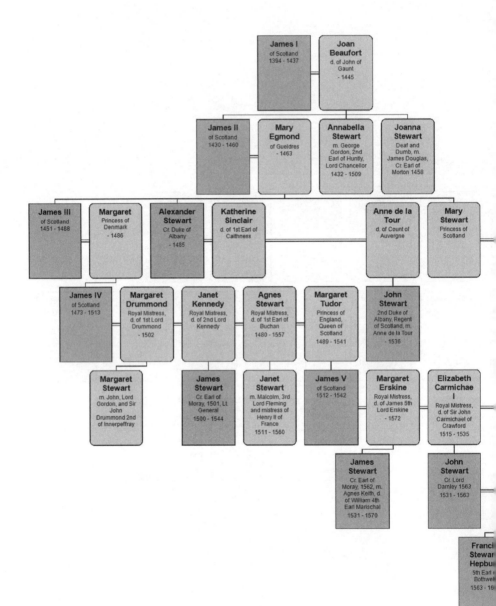

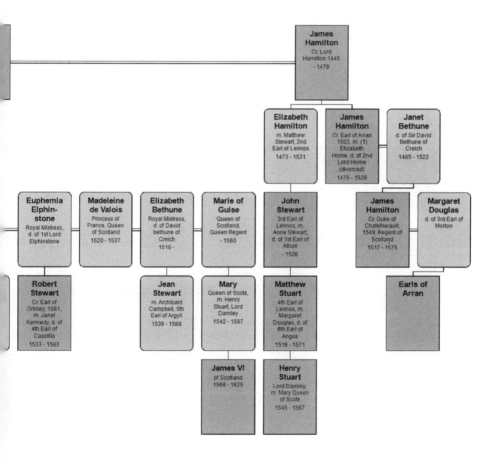

3. Stewart (Stuart) of Lennox

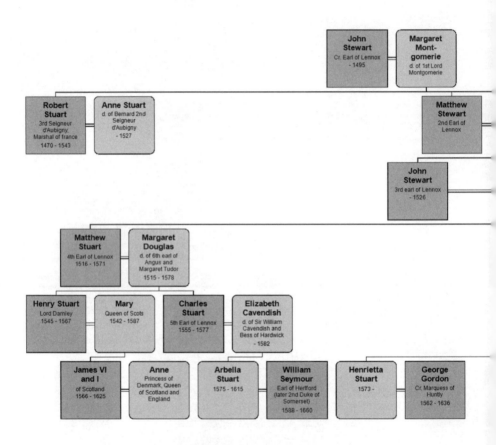

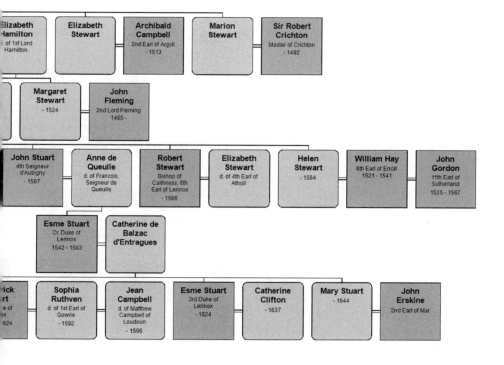

4. Douglas of Angus

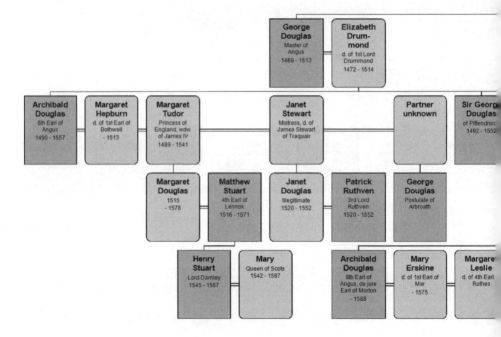

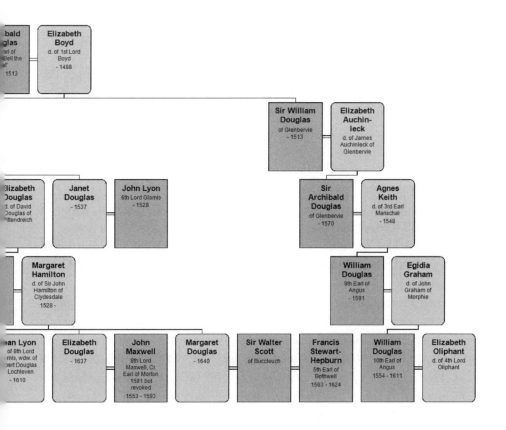

...bald ...glas
...arl of ...Bell the ...t ...1513

Elizabeth Boyd
d. of 1st Lord Boyd
- 1498

Sir William Douglas
of Glenbervie
- 1513

Elizabeth Auchin-leck
d. of James Auchinleck of Glenbervie

...lizabeth ...ouglas
...of David ...ouglas of ...ittendreich

Janet Douglas
- 1537

John Lyon
6th Lord Glamis
- 1528

Sir Archibald Douglas
of Glenbervie
- 1570

Agnes Keith
d. of 3rd Earl Marischal
- 1548

Margaret Hamilton
d. of Sir John Hamilton of Clydesdale
1528 -

William Douglas
9th Earl of Angus
- 1591

Egidia Graham
d. of John Graham of Morphie

...an Lyon
of 8th Lord ...mis, wdw. of ...bert Douglas Lochleven
- 1610

Elizabeth Douglas
- 1637

John Maxwell
8th Lord Maxwell, Cr. Earl of Morton 1581 but revoked
1553 - 1593

Margaret Douglas
- 1640

Sir Walter Scott
of Buccleuch

Francis Stewart-Hepburn
5th Earl of Bothwell
1563 - 1624

William Douglas
10th Earl of Angus
1554 - 1611

Elizabeth Oliphant
d. of 4th Lord Oliphant

Bibliography

Anderson, James, *Collections Relating to the History of Mary Queen of Scots,* Edinburgh, 1727 ("Anderson").

Armstrong-Davison, M. H., *The Casket Letters,* The University Press of Washington, DC, 1965 ("Armstrong-Davison").

Bannatyne, R, *Bannatyne Manuscript* ed. and intr. by W. Tod Ritchie, Vols. I to IV, Scottish Text Society, 1934 ("Bannatyne Manuscript").

Bannatyne, R, *Bannatyne Memorials of Transactions in Scotland,* ed. R. Pitcairn, Bannatyne Club, Edinburgh, 1836 ("Bannatyne Memorials").

Bingham, Caroline, *Darnley: A Life of Henry Stuart Lord Darnley Consort of Mary Queen of Scots,* Constable and Company, London, 1995 ("Bingham").

Birrel, Robert, *Diary 1532-1605, from Fragments of Scottish History,* ed. D. J. Dalyell.

Blackwood, Adam, *History of Mary Queen of Scots: A Fragment;* cited in Weir, p. 39 ("Blackwood").

Bothwell, Earl of *Les Affaires du Conte de Boduel,* ed. H. Cockburn and T. Maitland, Bannatyne Club, Edinburgh, 1829 (*"Les Affaires du Conte de Boduel"*).

Brantôme, Pierre, *Discours de la Reine d'Escosse,* from *The Lives of Gallant Ladies* ("Brantôme").

Buchanan, George, *Book of Articles,* 1568 ("Buchanan *Book of Articles"*).

Buchanan, George, *Detectio Mariae Reginae: Ane Detection oth the Doings of Marie, Queen of Scots, touching the Murder of her Husband and her Conspiracy, Adultery and Pretensed Marriage with the Earl of Bothwell, and the Defence of the True lords, Maintainers of the King's Majesty's Action and Authority,* Edinburgh, 1958 ("Buchanan's *Detectio"*).

Buchanan, George, *The Tyrannous Reign of Mary Stewart,* ed. and trans. W. A. Gatherer, Edinburgh, 1958 ("Buchanan").

Diurnal of Occurrents, Bannatyne Club, Edinburgh, 1833 ("Diurnal of Occurrents").

Ellis, Henry, ed. *Original Letters illustrative of British History,* 2nd series vol. 2, (1827) ("Ellis").

Fleming, David Hay, *Mary Queen of Scots from her birth until her flight into England,* London, 1897 ("Fleming").

Fraser, Lady Antonia, *Mary Queen of Scots,* Weidenfeld & Nicolson, 1969 ("Antonia Fraser").

Fraser, Sir William, *The Lennox,* 1874 ("Fraser *The Lennox*").

Goodall, W, *Examination of the [Casket] Letters Said to be written by Mary Queen of Scots to James, Earl of Bothwell,* Edinburgh and London, 1754.

Gordon, Sir R, *Genealogical History of the Earldom of Sutherland,* Edinburgh, 1813 ("Gordon").

Gore-Browne, R, *Lord Bothwell,* London, 1937 ("Gore-Browne").

Guy, John, *My Heart is my Own,* Harper Perennial, 2004 ("Guy").

Henderson, T. F, *The Casket Letters and Mary Queen of Scots,* Edinburgh and London, 1890 ("Henderson").

Herries, Sir John Maxwell, Lord, *Historical Memoirs of the Reign of Mary, Queen of Scots,* Abbotsford Club, ed. R. Pitcairn, Edinburgh, 1836 ("Herries").

Hosack, J, *Mary Queen of Scots and her Accusers,* Edinburgh, 1969 ("Hosack").

Hume, Martin *The Love Affairs of Mary Queen of Scots: A Political History,* Eveleigh Nash, 1903 ("Hume").

Jebb, S, *De Vita et Rebus Gestis Serenissima Principis Marie Scotorum Reginae, Franciiae Dotariai,* 1725 ("Jebb").

Keith, Robert, *History of the Affairs of Church and State in Scotland from the beginning of the Reformation to 1585,* ed. J. P. Lawson and J. C. Lyon, Spottiswoode Society, Edinburgh, 1844, 1845, 1850 ("Keith").

Klarwill, Victor von, *Queen Elizabeth and Some Foreigners: etc.* John Lane and The Bodley Head Ltd., 1928 ("Klarwill").

Knox, John, *History of the Reformation,* ed. And trans. W.Croft Dickinson, 1949 ("Knox").

Knox, John, *Works of John Knox,* ed. D. Laing, Edinburgh, 1895 ("Laing, Knox").

Labanoff, Prince (A. I. Labanoff-Rostovsky) *Lettres de Marie Stuart,* London, 1844 ("Labanoff").

Leslie, John, Bishop of Ross, *The Historie of Scotland,* ed. Fr. E. G. Gody and William Murison; Scottish Text Society ("Leslie").

Levine, Mortimer *Early Elizabethan Succession Question from Tudor Dynastic Problems,* California 1966 ("Levine").

Macaulay, Sarah, *Lennox Crisis,* in *Northern History, vol. 41.2,* 2004 ("Macaulay").

MacNalty, Sir Arthur Salusbury, *Mary Queen of Scots: The Daughter of Debate,* London, 1960 ("MacNalty").

Mahon, Major-General R. H, *Mary Queen of Scots: A Study of the Lennox Narrative*, Cambridge University Press, 1924 ("Mahon").

Marshall, Rosalind K, *Queen Mary's Women*, John Donald, 2006 ("Marshall").

Melville, Sir James of Hallhill, *Memoirs of his own Life, 1549-1593* London 1683, ed. Thomas Thomson, Bannatyne Club, Edinburgh, 1827, reprinted 1872; ed. Gordon Donaldson, The Folio Society, 1969 ("Melville").

Mumby, Frank Arthur, *The Fall of Mary Stuart: A Narrative in Contemporary Letters*, Constable, 1921 ("Mumby").

Nau, Claude, *Memorials of Mary Stewart*, ed. J. Stevenson, 1883 ("Nau").

Neale, Sir J. E., *Elizabeth I and her Parliaments*, Jonathan Cape, 1934 ("Neale").

Ovid, *5th Book of Fasti.*

Pearson, Karl, FRS, *The Skull and Portraits of Henry Stuart, Lord Darnley, and their bearing on the Tragedy of Mary Queen of Scots* Biometrika, July 1928 Cambridge University Press, 1928 ("Pearson").

Philippson, Martin, *Histoire du regne de Marie Stuart, 3 Vols., Paris, 1881-2* ("Philippson").

Phillips, John, *A Commemoration of the Right Noble and virtuous Lady Margaret Douglas's good Grace, Countess of Lennox* London 1578 ("Phillips").

Pitcairn, R, *Ancient Criminal Trials in Scotland*, Vol. 1, Bannatyne Club, Edinburgh, 1833 ("Pitcairn").

Pitscottie, Robert Lindsay of, *History and Chronicles of Scotland*, Vols. I and II, Scottish Text Society, ed. A. J. Mackay, 1899, 1911 ("Pitscottie").

Plowden, Alison, *Two Queens in One Isle*, Brighton, 1984 ("Plowden").

Pollen, J. H, *Papal Negotiations with Mary Queen of Scots*, Scottish History Society, 1st Series, Edinburgh, 1901 ("Pollen").

Prebble, John, *The Lion of the North: One Thousand Years of Scotland's History*, London, 1971 ("Prebble").

Protestation of Huntly and Argyll ("Protestation").

Robertson, Joseph, *Inventaires de la Royne d'Escosse, Douairière de France, 1556-1569*, Bannatyne Club, Vol. III, Edinburgh, 1863 ("Robertson").

Ruthven, Lord, *The Murder of Riccio, being Lord Ruthven's Own Account of the Transaction*, Holyrood Series, 1891 ("Ruthven").

Sadler, Sir Ralph, *The State Papers and Letters of Sir Ralph Sadler*, ed. A. Clifford, Edinburgh, 1809 ("Sadler").

Sanderson, Margaret, *Mary Stewart's People*, Edinburgh, 1987 ("Sanderson").

Schutte, Kim, *A Biography of Margaret Douglas, Countess of Lennox, 1515-1578; Niece of Henry VIII and Mother-in-Law of Mary, Queen of Scots*, New York, 2002 ("Schutte").

Sitwell, Edith, *The Queens and the Hive*, London 1962 ("Sitwell").

Spottiswood, John, *The History of the Church and State of Scotland* London 1655 ("Spottiswood").

Stow, John, *The Chronicles of England, from Brute [Brutus] unto this present year of Christ, 1580* Ralph Neberie, London, 1580 ("Stow").

Strickland, Agnes, *Lives of the Queens of Scotland and English Princesses connected with the Regal Succession of Great Britain* (William Blackwood, Edinburgh and London, 8 Vols., 1850-59) ("Strickland").

Teulet, A, *Papiers d'État Relatives à L'Histoire de l'Écosse au 16e siècle*, Paris, 1862 ("Teulet").

Tytler, P. F, *History of Scotland*, Edinburgh, 1841 and New Enlarged Edition, 1870 ("Tytler").

Weir, Alison, *Mary Queen of Scots and the Murder of Lord Darnley*, Jonathan Cape, 2003 ("Weir").

Weir, Alison, *The Lost Tudor Princess, A Life of Margaret Douglas, Countess of Lennox*, Jonathan Cape, 2015 ("Weir – Margaret Douglas").

Wormald, Jenny, *Mary Queen of Scots, Politics, Passion and a Kingdom Lost*, Tauris Parke Paperbacks, 2001 ("Wormald *Mary Queen of Scots*").

Papers

British Library Manuscripts ("BL MMS").

including:

Egerton MMS.

Cecil Papers, Hatfield House ("Hatfield House").

Cotton Manuscripts, British Museum ("Cotton MMS").

Cotton Manuscripts, Caligula B X 16 ("Caligula").

CSP Foreign: *Calendar of State Papers, Foreign Series*, Elizabeth, ed. J. Stevenson, 1863.

CSP Scottish: *Calendar of State Papers relating to Scottish affairs*, ed. J. Bain, 1898.

CSP Spanish: *Calendar of State Papers, Spanish*, Elizabeth, ed. M. A. S. Home, London, 1892.

CSP Venetian: *Calendar of State Papers, Venetian*, ed. R. Brown and G. C. Bentinck, 1890.

Hamilton Papers, ed. J. Bain, Edinburgh, 1890 ("Hamilton Papers").

National Archives, State Papers.

Public Records Office ("PRO").

Register of the Privy Council of Scotland.

Sloane Manuscripts, British Museum ("Sloane MMS").

State Papers in the Public Records Office ("*State Papers* in the PRO").

Zurich Letters, or the Correspondence of Several English Bishops and others with the Helvetian Reformers during the Reign of Queen Elizabeth, Vol. 1, ed. Hastings Robinson, The Parker Society, Cambridge, 1846 (Zurich letters 1).

References and endnotes

PART 1: THE LENNOXES' BACKGROUND AND SCOTTISH HERITAGE

Chapter 1: The Marriage of the Earl of Lennox to Lady Margaret Douglas

1. Pitscottie, p. 182; cited in Weir – Margaret Douglas, p. 111.
2. Spottiswood, p. 257; cited in Weir – Margaret Douglas, p. 111.
3. Pitscottie; cited in Guy, p. 30.
4. Phillips; cited in Weir – Margaret Douglas, p. 111.
5. Phillips; cited in Weir – Margaret Douglas, p. 115.
6. Strickland, Vol. 2, p. 320; cited in Bingham p, 37.
7. The contention that Arran was illegitimate was highly convoluted, but had been propounded by the devious David Bethune (or Beaton), Cardinal Archbishop of St Andrews, who as leader of the wealthy Scottish Catholic Church was trying to stem the tide of the Scottish Reformation, for which the dithering Arran was demonstrating support. Arran's father's first wife, Elizabeth Home, had received a divorce from her former husband, Sir Thomas Hay, Master of Yester, to enable her to marry him on 28 April 1490. Fourteen years later, on 15 November 1504, the 1st Earl had received papal authority to divorce Elizabeth on the grounds that her original divorce from Sir Thomas Hay was invalid and she had not been free to remarry him. This had been reconfirmed on 11 March 1510. Despite this, Bethune now argued that Elizabeth Home had in fact received a valid divorce from Sir Thomas Hay and had thus been repudiated by the 1st Earl without cause. If Bethune's view were upheld, it invalidated the 1st Earl's second marriage to the Cardinal's 1st cousin Elizabeth Bethune, who was Arran's mother. He also argued (entirely against his own interest) that if papal authority were rejected because Scotland was becoming Reformist, then the Pope had no right to grant the divorce. This left Elizabeth Bethune's children illegitimate. With Arran falling for this somewhat doubtful ruse, he reverted to Catholicism, opening the door for Lennox to promote himself as the Protestant claimant to the Scottish throne.

Chapter 2: Matthew Stuart, 4th Earl of Lennox

1. The Lennox Stuarts had been mercenaries in France for several generations, and were traditional captains of the *Garde Écossaise*. The French title of Seigneur d'Aubigny had been granted by Charles VII on 26 March 1423 to John Stuart, grandfather of Sir John, 1st Earl of Lennox. When the Lennox earldom was granted in 1475 (although it was subsequently revoked and reconfirmed in

1488), the French title was carried by the junior branch of the family. Robert, 3rd Seigneur d'Aubigny had inherited from his cousin, Bernard, who died in Scotland in 1508. Bernard was an illustrious mercenary for the French, known as 'the father of war' and 'the prince of knighthood and the flower of chivalry', who had supported Henry VII against Richard III at Bosworth Field in 1485. This made the Lennox Stuarts historic allies of the Tudors. Robert had married Bernard's daughter, Anne, but had no children. On his death, Lennox's brother, John, inherited as 4th Seigneur and was the father of Esmé Stuart, later Duke of Lennox.

2. Wormald *Mary Queen of Scots*, p. 43.
3. Pitscottie, *Chronicles 2*, p. 8.
4. Antonia Fraser, p. 22; Guy, p. 25.
5. Sadler to Henry VIII, Sadler v. 355.
6. Hamilton Papers II, p. 33; cited in Antonia Fraser, p. 24.
7. Cited in Guy, p. 29.
8. The marriage was annulled on the grounds of consanguinity. Agnes Sinclair was the daughter of Margaret Hepburn, sister of Patrick, 1st Earl of Bothwell. Patrick, the 3rd Earl, was thus her first cousin once removed.
9. Cited in Guy, p. 30.
10. Cited in Guy, p. 31.

Chapter 3: Lady Margaret Douglas

1. Cited in Bingham, p. 16.
2. Bingham, p. 15.
3. Captain Strangeways to Cardinal Wolsey, 26 January 1529, cit. Strickland, Vol. 2, p. 279; cited in Bingham, p. 17.
4. Cited in Bingham, p. 26.

Chapter 5: Efforts to secure a Protestant succession for the English throne

1. Third Act of Succession, 1544; cited in Guy, p. 279.
2. Bingham, p. 56.
3. Zurich letters 1, p. 125.
4. Bingham, p. 63.

Chapter 6: The upbringing of Lord Darnley

1. In accordance with normal Scottish practice, Darnley should have been known as the Master of Lennox, but being in England he became Lord Darnley, a name taken from one of the forfeited Lennox estates.
2. Bingham, p. 58.
3. Cited in Bingham, p. 52.
4. Cited in Bingham, p. 53.
5. Ellis, Henry, ed. *Original Letters illustrative of British History, 2nd series vol. 2*, (1827) pp. 249-51; cited in Bingham, p. 53.

6. Bingham, p. 56.
7. Bingham, p. 59.
8. Bingham, p. 52.
9. Knox II, p. 174; cited in Antonia Fraser, pp. 275-6, and in Weir, p. 101.
10. Melville; cited in Weir, p. 57.
11. Melville; cited in Weir, p. 57.

Chapter 7: The Scottish Reformation

1. Guy, p. 39.
2. Antonia Fraser, p. 29.
3. Wormald *Mary Queen of Scots*, p. 88.
4. Laing, Knox, IV, p. 373; cited in Antonia Fraser, p. 177.
5. Wormald *Mary Queen of Scots*, p. 94.
6. Cited in Antonia Fraser, p. 115.
7. Melville, p. 51; cited in Antonia Fraser, p. 115.
8. Cited in Antonia Fraser, p. 120.
9. The financial structure of the Catholic Church remained untouched. There was no suppression of the monasteries as in England, but they were left to decline through a lack of support, and the Catholic clergy and bishops continued to receive their stipends. Church funds were already controlled by the Crown, and no one wanted to upset the lucrative benefices enjoyed by members of the nobility. In 1562, it was at last agreed that two-thirds of the income should remain with them, with the balance being provided to finance the Court of Session and the Kirk.
10. Blackwood; cited in Weir, p. 39.
11. CSP Foreign III, p. 409; cited in Guy, p. 220 and Antonia Fraser, p. 149.
12. *Les Affaires du Conte de Boduel*, p. 7; cited in Guy, p. 222 and Antonia Fraser, p. 149.
13. Anna Throndssen reappeared in Scotland in 1563 to seek recompense from Bothwell, but he does not appear to have assisted her, although she was still alive in 1607. The Throndssen family claimed that she had married Bothwell, after they had offered a dowry of 40,000 silver dollars, but she never claimed to be the Countess of Bothwell and there is no record of the marriage. It has been suggested that his only known child, William, was Anna's son and certainly Bothwell's mother left her estate to him.

PART 2: COMPETING AMBITIONS TO BE RECOGNIZED AS ELIZABETH'S HEIR

Chapter 8: Mary's marries the Dauphin and becomes Queen Consort of France

1. Jebb, p. 671.
2. Cited in Antonia Fraser, p. 87.
3. Cited in Antonia Fraser, p. 87.

4. CSP Venetian; cited in Guy, p. 88.
5. Guy p. 94.
6. Bingham, p. 67.
7. Macaulay.
8. CSP Foreign, Elizabeth Vol.1.
9. Fraser *The Lennox* Vol 1, p. 469; cited in Bingham, p. 6.
10. Bingham, p. 69.
11. Bingham, p. 71.
12. Guy, pp. 115-6.
13. Antonia Fraser, p. 142.
14. Brantôme; cited in Antonia Fraser p.151 and Guy p. 133.

Chapter 9: Margaret Douglas's initial efforts to promote Darnley as a husband for Mary

1. Bingham, p. 75.
2. PRO SP/12/13 No. 33 Confession of Arthur Lallart; cited in Bingham, p. 76.
3. Bingham, p. 77.
4. National Archives State Papers, 12/23, f. 78; cited in Weir – Margaret Douglas, p. 203.
5. Lieutenant of the Tower to Cecil, 20 September 1562 PRO SP/12/24 No. 49; cited in Bingham, p. 78.
6. Bingham, p. 78.
7. Schutte, p. 182; cited in Marshall, p. 114.
8. Macaulay, p. 287.

Chapter 10: Events following Mary's arrival in Scotland

1. Knox II, p. 13 et seq.; cited in Antonia Fraser, p. 177.
2. CSP Scottish, I, p. 551; Knox, II, p. 20; Laing Knox, VI, p.132; cited in Antonia Fraser, p. 178.
3. Cited in Guy, p. p. 148 and in Wormald *Mary Queen of Scots*, p. 127.
4. Buchanan, p. 53, cited in Antonia Fraser, p. 219.
5. Weir, p. 31.
6. Cited in Weir, p. 29.
7. Cited in Guy, p. 149.
8. Knox, II, p. 43; cited in Antonia Fraser, p. 209.
9. CSP Scottish, II, p. 148; cited in Antonia Fraser, p. 209.
10. CSP Scottish, I, p. 582; cited in Antonia Fraser, p. 196.
11. Cited in Antonia Fraser, p.199.

Chapter 11: Rival efforts to be established as Elizabeth's heir

1. Cited in Guy, p. 116.
2. Lord Robert Dudley had been a childhood friend of Elizabeth. His father, Northumberland, had failed in his attempt to install Lady Jane Grey on the English throne, resulting in his attainder and execution (see Chapter 12,

reference 16 on p. 294), leaving the family in a parlous financial position. Yet by selling land they had helped to support Elizabeth in captivity during Mary Tudor's reign. Elizabeth had fallen passionately in love with the attractive Dudley, resulting in a rumoured affair between them. Despite his father's position as Protector for Edward VI, Dudley was associated with the conservatives in English politics, including Norfolk and some of the powerful Catholic families in the north, who wanted to break Elizabeth's close association with the 'low-born' Cecil. Cecil feared that his carefully planned efforts to secure a Protestant succession in England would be jeopardised if Elizabeth married this fifth son of the attainted duke, and it would open up petty jealousies within the English nobility. He initiated a rumour that Dudley was offering to restore Catholicism in England, if Philip II would support his marriage to Elizabeth. Yet he had already been married for ten years, although his wife, Amy Robsart, was extremely ill. Cecil hinted that Dudley was poisoning her, but she died after breaking her neck in a fall downstairs at the home of friends. With Dudley at the height of his romance with Elizabeth, the natural question, no doubt fueled by Cecil, was to ask if her fall was an accident. Had she committed suicide or was she pushed? Although the investigation exonerated Dudley, the rumours persisted and Elizabeth realised that she could never marry him. She needed the love of her people, and this marriage would bring only dissent. When faced with a similar choice, Mary would fail to show such political sensitivity.

3. Cited in Guy, p. 156.
4. Cited in Guy, pp. 129, 255.
5. Cited in Guy, p. 129.
6. Cited in Guy, p. 146.
7. Levine, pp.117-8; cited in Antonia Fraser, p. 186.
8. Cited in Guy, p. 148.
9. CSP Foreign, III, p. 573; cited in Antonia Fraser, p. 189.
10. Cited in Guy, p. 160.
11. Philippson, III, p. 457; cited in Guy, p. 161.
12. Sidney to Cecil, 25 July 1562, CSP Scottish, 1547-1563, p. 641.
13. Cited in Guy, p. 166.
14. Cited in Guy, p. 168.
15. Cited in Guy, p. 168.
16. Hertford and Catherine Grey spent nine years in the Tower. Despite their children's illegitimacy, Edward, their heir, was reconstituted as Earl of Hertford, and his son, William, was restored by Charles II as 2nd Duke of Somerset, later being created Marquess of Hertford in his own right. He too made an unwise alliance in 1610, when he secretly married Arbella, daughter of Charles Stuart, Margaret Douglas's second son. With so much Tudor blood coursing through their veins, James VI, like Elizabeth before him, was to consider them hostile to his position on the throne.

17. Quadra to Philip II 16 June 1563, CSP (Spanish) Vol. I, p. 339; cited in Bingham, p. 83.
18. Macaulay, pp. 267–287.
19. Elizabeth to Mary 16 June 1563 CSP (Scottish) Vol. 2, p. 14; cited in Bingham, p. 83.
20. Cited in Antonia Fraser, p. 188.

Chapter 12: Mary's efforts to find a husband

1. Cited in Guy, p. 170.
2. Cited in Guy, p. 174.
3. CSP Foreign, VI, p. 211; cited in Antonia Fraser, p. 237.
4. Cited in Guy, p. 181.
5. Cited in Guy, p. 175.
6. Cited in Guy, p. 177.
7. Cited in Guy, p. 182.
8. Cited in Guy, p. 183.
9. Cited in Guy, p. 185 and in Antonia Fraser, p. 191.
10. Cited in Guy, p. 186.
11. Cited in Guy, p. 186.
12. CSP Scottish, II, p. 8; cited in Antonia Fraser, p. 216.
13. Cited in Guy, p. 189–90.
14. Cited in Wormald *Mary Queen of Scots*, p. 134.
15. Cited in Antonia Fraser, p. 245.
16. John Dudley, Earl of Warwick, had been created Duke of Northumberland in the reign of Edward VI following the attainder of Sir Thomas Percy, who would otherwise have been heir to the Percy Earldom of Northumberland. The Duke was attainted and beheaded in 1553, after his ill-fated attempt to place Lady Jane Grey, married to his fourth son Lord Guildford Dudley, on the English throne. In 1557, Sir Thomas Percy's son, Thomas, was restored as 7th Earl of Northumberland, but was later attainted following the Catholic-inspired Northern Rising in 1569, after which the Northumberland earldom passed to his brother.
17. Melville, p. 40; cited in Bingham, p. 86.
18. Randolph, 5 March 1564, Cotton MMS; Caligula B X f. 265.
19. Randolph, 5 March 1564, Cotton MMS; Caligula B X f. 265.
20. Cited in Guy, p. 192.
21. Cited in Guy, p. 192.
22. Cited in Antonia Fraser, p. 245.
23. Guy, p. 193.
24. Knox, II, p. 85, note 6; cited in Antonia Fraser, p. 248.
25. Cited in Guy, p. 194.
26. Guy, p. 198.
27. Cited in Guy, p. 197.

28. Melville, p. 35; cited in Wormald *Mary, Queen of Scots* pp. 150-1 and in Antonia Fraser, p. p. 254.
29. Melville, p. 40; cited in Marshall, p. 115.
30. Bingham, p. 86.
31. Cited in Guy, p. 198.
32. The jewel is of a type generally given as a love token at marriage, and it is not unreasonable that the inscription reading 'Death shall dissolve' which originally related to the love between Matthew and Margaret was now being used to promote Darnley's suit.
33. Cited in Guy, p. 199.
34. Cited in Guy, p. 200.
35. Cited in Guy, p. 202.
36. Teulet, II, p. 42, cited in Antonia Fraser, p. 256.

Chapter 13: The impact of Lennox's arrival in Scotland

1. Cited in Guy, p. 225.
2. Cited in Guy, p. 224.
3. Gore-Browne; cited in Guy, p. 225.
4. Cited in Guy, p. 225.
5. Cited in Guy, p. 227.
6. *Les Affaires du Conte de Boduel*; CSP Scottish.
7. Cited in Guy, p. 228.
8. CSP Scottish, II, p. 139; cited in Guy, p. 228 and in Antonia Fraser p. 270.
9. Cited in Guy, p. 228.
10. Cited in Guy, p. 228.
11. Buchanan, p. 93; cited in Antonia Fraser p. 272.
12. Cited in Weir, p. 51.

PART 3: DARNLEY'S ARRIVAL IN SCOTLAND AND MARRIAGE TO MARY

Chapter 14: The complex scheming that led to Darnley marrying Mary

1. Stow, p. 1126; cited in Bingham, p. 88.
2. Randolph to Cecil, 12 February 1565, CSP (Scottish) Vol. 2, pp. 124-5; cited in Bingham, p. 89.
3. Melville, p. 45; cited in Bingham, p. 222 and in Guy, p. 225.
4. BL Add. MSS 19401, fol. 101; cited in Bingham, p. 90.
5. Randolph to Cecil, 8 May 1563, CSP Scottish, II, p. 156.
6. CSP Scottish, II, p. 126; cited in Antonia Fraser, p. 257.
7. It is thought that Darnley and Lennox were responsible for introducing the Hudson family, a father and four sons, from Yorkshire to play their viols at the Scottish court. They were provided with liveries for Darnley's marriage to Mary.

8. *Lennox Narrative*, para. 2; cited in Mahon, p. 120; cited in Bingham, p. 92.

9. Cited in Guy, p. 205, Antonia Fraser, p. 258 and Weir, p. 57.

10. Melville, p. 45; cited in Bingham p. 96.

11. Cited in Guy, p. 203.

12. Cited in Weir, p. 60.

13. Cited in Guy, p. 206.

14. Cited in Guy, p. 206.

15. Cited in Guy, p. 207.

16. Lord Sempill had a reputation for lawlessness, generally taking sides with his mother's family, the Montgomeries, in feuds against the Boyds and Cunninghams. In 1549, Archbishop Hamilton had to intercede to save him from execution for slaying William, 3rd Lord Crichton at Châtelherault's house. In addition to John and several other illegitimate children, he also fathered a substantial family of legitimate children by his wife, Isabel, daughter of Sir William Hamilton of Sanquhar. Sempill acted as bailiff at Paisley Abbey, and one of his daughters, Grizel, lived openly as the Archbishop's mistress, providing him with at least three children, whom he later legitimised.

17. Cited in Antonia Fraser, p. 258.

18. Teulet, II, p.52; cited in Antonia Fraser, p. 258.

19. CSP Scottish, II, p.75; cited in Antonia Fraser, p. 257.

20. CSP Scottish, II, p. 129; cited in Antonia Fraser, p. 257.

21. Keith; cited in Weir, p. 60 and in Guy, p. 208.

22. Guy, p. 207.

23. Antonia Fraser, p. 258.

24. Randolph to Bedford, 7 April 1565, CSP (Scottish) Vol. 2, p. 141; cited in Bingham, p. 98.

25. Cited in Guy, p. 208.

26. Cited in Bingham, p. 98.

27. Bannatyne Manuscript; Oxford Book of Scottish Verse, p. 176, cited in Antonia Fraser, p, 261.

28. CSP Scottish; cited in Weir, p. 63.

29. CSP Scottish, cited in Weir, p. 63, 65.

30. CSP Scottish; Keith, cited in Weir, p. 64.

31. CSP Spanish; cited in Weir, p. 77.

32. Cited in Guy, p. 208-9.

33. CSP Scottish; cited in Weir, p. 66.

34. Throckmorton to Leicester and Cecil, 11 May 1565, CSP (Scottish), pp.158-9.

35. Cited in Guy, p. 209.

36. CSP Scottish, cited in Guy, p. 209 and in Weir, p. 66.

37. *Les Affaires du Conte to Boduel;* cited in Weir, p. 67.

38. CSP Scottish; cited in Weir, p. 68.

39. Throckmorton to Queen Elizabeth 21 May 1565, CSP (Scottish) Vol. 2, p. 163; cited in Bingham, p. 99 and in Guy, p. 213.

40. CSP Scottish; cited in Weir, p. 68.

41. Randolph to Leicester 21 May 1565, CSP Scottish, Vol. 2, p. 166; cited in Bingham, p.101, in Guy, p. 211, in Wormald *Mary, Queen of Scots*, p. 155 and in Weir, p. 68.
42. BL Cott. Caligula BX (16) fol.295, '*The Oath of an Earl that the said Henry made*'; cited in Bingham, p. 99.
43. Randolph to Leicester 3 June 1565 CSP Scottish, Vol.1, p. 171; cited in Bingham, p. 100.
44. CSP Scottish; cited in Weir, p. 69.
45. Randolph to Cecil, 23 May 1565 CSP Scottish, Vol.2, p. 154; cited in Bingham, p. 100.
46. CSP Scottish; cited in Weir, p. 69.
47. Cited in Weir, p. 72.
48. CSP Scottish; cited in Guy, pp. 211-2 and in Weir, p. 69.
49. Cited in Antonia Fraser, p. 263 and Weir, p. 72.
50. CSP Scottish; cited in Guy, p. 214.
51. Cited in Weir, p. 72.
52. CSP Venetian; cited in Weir, p. 280.
53. Randolph to Cecil 16 July 1565, cit. Fleming, p. 346-7; cited in Bingham, p. 104.
54. CSP Spanish; Klarwill, p. 251; cited in Weir, pp. 73-4.
55. Randolph to Leicester in CSP Scottish, cited in Weir, p. 73.
56. Robertson; cited in Guy, p. 215.
57. Randolph to Leicester in CSP Scottish; cited in Guy, p. 217 and Weir, p. 75.
58. Robertson, Preface, pp. lxxxiv-lxxxv; cited in Bingham, p. 109.
59. From *Epithalamia Tria Mariana, trans. Revd. Francis Wrangham* (1837); cited in Bingham, p. 109.
60. Knox, II, p. 158, cited in Weir, p. 76.
61. Mauvissière to Charles IX, cited in Strickland, Vol. 4, p. 207; cited in Bingham, p. 118.
62. CSP Scottish; cited in Weir, p. 76.
63. Randolph to Leicester 31 July 1565, cited in Mumby, p. 387; cited in Bingham, p. 110; CSP Scottish; cited in Weir, p. 76.
64. Melville; cited in Weir, pp. 76-7.
65. Cited in Wormald *Mary, Queen of Scots*, p. 157.
66. Teulet; cited in Guy, p. 217 and in Weir, p. 78.
67. Cited in Guy, p. 220.

Chapter 15: Moray's rebellion

1. Keith; cited in Weir, p. 78.
2. Laing, Knox, p. 256; cited in Bingham, p. 113.
3. Laing, Knox, p. 272; cited in Bingham, p. 113.
4. Knox, II, p. 162; cited in Guy, p. 230 and in Antonia Fraser, p. 269; Knox V, p. 334; cited in Bingham, p. 114.

5. Knox, V, p. 333; cited in Bingham, p. 114.
6. Cited in Guy, p. 230.
7. Cited in Weir, p. 83.
8. Cited in Bingham, p. 117-8.
9. Cited in Guy, p. 231.
10. Cited in Guy, p. 254.
11. Patrick Hepburn, 1st Earl of Bothwell had married Margaret Gordon, daughter of George, 2nd Earl of Huntly.
12. Gordon; cited in Antonia Fraser, p. 285.
13. Sanderson, p. 38, cited in Weir, p. 102 and in Marshall, p. 131.

Chapter 16: Mary's efforts to govern with her husband without Moray and Maitland

1. Randolph to Leicester 3 July 1565, cit. Fraser, *The Lennox,* Vol. 1, pp. 480-1; cited in Bingham, p. 108.
2. Herries, pp. 74-5; cited in Bingham, pp. 120-1.
3. Cecil Papers; cited in Weir, p. 91 and in Marshall, p. 117.
4. Cited in Weir, p. p. 82.
5. Cited in Guy, p. 237.
6. Cited in Wormald *Mary, Queen of Scots,* p. 161 and in Weir, p. 86.
7. Cited in Weir, p. 88.
8. Guy, p. 238.
9. Bethune was the nephew of the Cardinal, born in 1517. In 1531, he went to France for his education and was later sent on a mission by Francis I to the queen dowager. After the Cardinal's death in 1546, he succeeded his uncle as an adviser to the queen regent and in 1552 was appointed Archbishop of Glasgow. He supported her loyally and was in Leith with her during the siege. On her death, he returned to Paris, taking with him the Catholic muniments from Glasgow Cathedral for preservation, passing them to the Scots College in Paris for safekeeping. Mary met him before her return to Scotland. As a man of unimpeachable integrity, he became her ambassador to the French court, remaining her mentor and closest *confidant.*
10. Cited in Guy, p. 240 and in Weir, p. 94.
11. Cited in Guy, p. 243.
12. Cited in Wormald *Mary, Queen of Scots,* p. 160, in Antonia Fraser, p. 280 and in Weir, p. 93. It is known that the Pope had been led to overstate the position as a result of Yaxley's diplomacy while in Brussels. He had promoted King Henry as the man who would achieve a Counter-Reformation in Scotland. As a result of the Pope's letter, Mary believed that the papacy would now support her claim to be the rightful Queen of England.
13. Cited in Guy, p. 243.
14. Cited in Guy, p. 243.
15. National Archives, State Papers, 52/11, f. 217.

16. Cited in Guy, p. 244.
17. Cited in Weir, pp. 90, 94.
18. CSP Scottish, II, p. 255; cited in Guy, pp. 245-6, in Antonia Fraser, p. 283 and in Weir, pp. 99-100.
19. Tytler, V, p. 334; cited in Guy, pp. 244, 247, and in Antonia Fraser, pp. 283-4.

Chapter 17: Riccio's murder

1. Cited in Weir, p. 96.
2. Cited in Weir, p. 96.
3. John Guy does not agree. He argues that the king had no motive to seek the queen's death unless he had the Crown Matrimonial, as Châtelherault would be her heir. Yet the bond for Riccio's murder promised him this and it also mentions the possible presence of the queen at the murder. If the king's motive were to gain the throne for himself, he needed both the queen and their unborn child to die, as the child would stand ahead of his own claim, even with the Crown Matrimonial.
4. Cited in Weir, p. 102.
5. CSP Scottish, Ruthven; cited in Keith, Buchanan, Knox and in Weir, p. 102.
6. Keith, III, p. 265; cited in Antonia Fraser, p. 284.
7. De Silva to Philip II 23 March 1566, CSP (Spanish) Vol. 1, p. 534; cited in Bingham p. 147.
8. Melville, p. 113; cited in Antonia Fraser, pp. 161, 286.
9. Melville; cited in Weir, p. 101.
10. Ruthven; Nau; cited in Guy, p. 249.
11. Ruthven; cited in Guy, p. 249.
12. Nau; cited in Weir, pp. 106, 107.
13. Birrell, p. 5 fn; cited in Antonia Fraser, p. 290 and in Weir, p. 107.
14. Randolph and Bedford; cited in Weir, p. 107.
15. Mary to Archbishop Bethune; cited in Weir, p. 107.
16. Melville; *Les Affaires du Conte de Boduel;* Teulet; cited in Weir, p. 109.
17. Melville; cited in Weir, p. 109.
18. Nau; cited in Guy, p. 251 and in Weir, p. 109.
19. Nau; cited in Guy, pp. 251, 252.
20. Weir, p. 108.
21. Guy, p. 251.
22. Ruthven; cited in Guy, p. 252 and in Weir, p. 89.
23. Nau; cited in Guy, p. 252 and in Weir, p. 89.
24. Nau, p. 4; cited in Antonia Fraser, p. 292.
25. Mary to Archbishop Bethune; Nau; cited in Antonia Fraser, p. 292.
26. Nau; cited in Weir, p. 110.
27. Nau; cited in Weir, p. 110.
28. Nau; cited in Weir, p. 110.
29. Nau; cited in Weir, p. 110.

30. Nau; cited in Weir; p. 111.
31. Nau; cited in Weir; p. 111.
32. Weir, p. 113.
33. Guy, p. 256.
34. Guy, p. 256.
35. Ruthven; cited in Weir, p. 114.
36. Nau, p. 16; cited in Antonia Fraser, p. 294 and in Weir, pp. 114-5.
37. Nau; cited in Weir, p. 114.
38. Cited in Guy, p. 258.
39. Cited in Weir, p. 115.
40. Ruthven; Melville; cited in Weir, p. 115.
41. Ruthven; cited in Weir, p. 116.
42. Nau; cited in Antonia Fraser, p. 295 and in Weir, p. 116.
43. *Les Affaires du Conte de Boduel;* cited in Weir, 116.
44. Nau; cited in Weir, p. 116.
45. Nau, p. 17; cited in Antonia Fraser, p. 295 and in Weir, p. 117.

Chapter 18: A time for compromise

1. Labanoff, I, p. 351; cited in Antonia Fraser, p. 296 and in Weir, p. 119.
2. CSP Venetian; cited in Weir, p. 119.
3. Melville; cited in Weir, p. 120.
4. Cited in Guy, pp. 260, 261.
5. Prebble; cited in Weir, p. 123.
6. Mary to Archbishop Bethune; cited in Guy, p. 260; *Diurnal of Occurrents;* Teulet; Buchanan; cited in Weir, p. 123.
7. Bingham, p. 147.
8. CSP Spanish; Teulet; CSP Foreign; Keith; cited in Weir, p. 122.
9. Teulet; CSP Scottish; cited in Weir, p. 127.
10. Melville; cited in Weir, p. 122.
11. Gore-Browne; cited in Weir, p. 122.
12. CSP Spanish; cited in Weir, p. 128.
13. Nau, p. 41; cited in Antonia Fraser, p. 303.
14. Gore Browne, p. 351; Herries, p. 80; cited in Antonia Fraser, p. 302.

Chapter 19: James's birth and its aftermath

1. Cited in Bingham, p. 156. Hume claims that the Countess of Moray was proposed as a mistress. There is no other reference to the countess being wayward; she was Mary's close associate and her husband, who seems to have been devoted to her, was now back at court. She also suffered a miscarriage in the following year causing Moray to travel to St Andrews to be with her.
2. Hume, p. 318; cited in Bingham, p. 156.
3. Nau, p. 28; cited in Antonia Fraser, p. 300.
4. Cited in Bingham, p. 156.

5. Nau, p. 7; cited in Antonia Fraser, p. 299.
6. De Silva to Philip II, 18 May 1566, CSP Spanish, Vol. 1, p. 549; cited in Weir, p. 130 and in Bingham, p. 149.
7. King Henry to Charles IX, 6 May 1566, BL MMS, Egerton 1805 fol. 7; CSP Scottish, Vol. 2, p. 277; cited in Weir, p. 131 and in Bingham, p. 148.
8. CSP Spanish; cited in Weir, p. 141.
9. William Rogers to Cecil, 5 July 1566, CSP Scottish, Vol.2, pp. 293-4; cited in Bingham, p. 164.
10. Cited in Guy, p. 266.
11. Cited in Guy, p. 266-7.
12. Cited in Guy, p. 269 and in Antonia Fraser, p. 305.
13. Melville; cited in Antonia Fraser, p. 307.
14. Melville, p. 56; cited in Wormald *Mary Queen of Scots*, p. 163 and in Antonia Fraser, p. 308.
15. 'Stainley' is the name used by Herries although it has often been supposed to be an error for Stanley. Yet the only known Sir William Stanley at this time had inherited as 3rd Lord Monteagle in 1560, and there is no evidence that he was involved in a diplomatic mission to Scotland. Caroline Bingham has conjectured that it was an error for Sir Anthony Standen.
16. Herries, p. 79; cited in Wormald *Mary Queen of Scots,* p. 163 and in Antonia Fraser, pp. 309-10.
17. Herries, p. 79.
18. Bannatyne Memorials, p. 238; CSP Scottish, II, p. 289; cited in Guy, p. 267.
19. Cited in Antonia Fraser, p. 311.
20. Both Buchanan in his Detectio and Lennox later claimed that Mary was already involved in an affair with Bothwell at Alloa and encouraged the king's departure, so that the liaison could continue. This was a complete fabrication as Bothwell was not there and it contradicts Buchanan's later assertion that their affair began in September 1566 (which was equally untrue). With Moray present, he would have done all he could to avert it, and Mar was extremely straight laced, having trained for the Church, and would not have condoned it. When Bedford reported the king's jealousy at the queen's intimate friendship with the Countesses of Argyll, Moray and Mar, he did not mention any concerns over her liaison with Bothwell. Yet Buchanan insinuated, 'What her usage was in Alloa need not be rehearsed but it may be well so said that it exceeded measure and all womanly behaviour ... but even as she returned to Edinburgh ... what her behaviour was, it needs not be kept secret being in the mouths of so many; the Earl of Bothwell abused her body at his pleasure, having passage in at the back door ... This she has more than once confessed herself ... using only the threadbare excuse that the Lady Reres gave him access ...' (Buchanan's *Detectio*; cited in Guy, p. 389) The pun was deliberate, to confirm Bothwell's taste for anal sex. There were unfounded reports that Lady Reres was acting as Bothwell's go-between with Mary on

later occasions but she did not travel to Alloa, as she was in charge of James's nursery arrangements. She was one of Bothwell's cast offs, and, according to Drury, she was so jealous when Bothwell later married Mary that she was replaced at court by his widowed sister Jean. This makes her promotion of an affair between Mary and Bothwell extremely unlikely.

21. Cited in Weir, p. 145.
22. CSP Forcign, VIII, p. 114; Keith III, p. 349; Fleming, p. 136; cited in Guy, p. 270 and in Weir, p. 312.
23. Bingham, p. 154.
24. Cotton MMS; Caligula Selections from Unpublished Manuscripts; CSP Foreign; Keith; cited in Weir, p. p. 146 and in Guy, p. 271.
25. CSP Foreign, VIII, p. 118, Fleming, p. 411; cited in Guy, p. 270 and in Weir, p. 146.
26. CSP Foreign; cited in Weir, p. 146.
27. Cited in Weir, p. 143.
28. Cited in Weir, p. 147.
29. Pollen, pp. 282 et seq.; cited in Antonia Fraser, p. 316.
30. Cited in Weir, p. 149.
31. Anthony Standen had arrived in Scotland as a diplomatic adviser to the king, but following the king's murder, he remained on the Continent and was recruited by Walsingham as a double agent, providing the English with valuable intelligence on the timing of the Armada in 1588.
32. Weir, p. 148.
33. Nau, p. 30; cited in Antonia Fraser, p. 312 and in Weir, pp. 148-9.
34. Mary to Archbishop Bethune, 20 January 1567, Mumby, p. 154; cited in Bingham, p. 164.
35. Buchanan records that Bothwell continued his illicit affair with Mary at the Exchequer House, whose secluded gardens backed onto the home of David Chalmers, shortly to be appointed by Bothwell as Common Clerk of Edinburgh. According to Buchanan, the 'dissolute' and portly Lady Reres assisted Bothwell in visiting Mary from Chalmers' house. The queen and Margaret Carwood apparently let her

> down by a sash over the wall into the next garden. But behold! The sash suddenly broke! Down with a great noise tumbled Lady Reres. But the old warrior, nothing dismayed by the darkness, the height of the wall or her unexpected flight to earth, reached Bothwell's chamber, opened the door, plucked him out of bed – out of his wife's embrace – and led him, half-asleep, half-naked, to the arms of the Queen. (Buchanan's *Detectio*; cited in Weir, p. 152).

There is no other evidence to corroborate this, and at the time Lady Reres was supervising the royal nursery at Stirling. Buchanan claimed that the king threatened to leave Scotland on hearing of it, but, if so, he never mentioned it during the next few weeks, despite ample opportunity. He had not, of course, been reticent in accusing Riccio, when similarly implicated with the queen. The story is yet again unthinkable..

36. Keith, II, p. 447, p. 450; cited in Antonia Fraser, p. 312.
37. Privy Council to Catherine de Medici; du Croc to Archbishop Bethune; cited in Keith; Teulet; cited in Guy, p. 272.
38. Du Croc to Catherine de Medici, 15 October 1566; Keith II, p. 451; cited in Guy, p. 272 and in Weir, p. 155.
39. Cited in Antonia Fraser, p. 312.
40. Cited in Weir, pp. 158-9.
41. Cited in Weir, p. 159.

Chapter 20: Mary's illness at Jedburgh and convalescence at Craigmillar

1. Archibald Douglas to Mary; cited in Keith; cited in Weir, p. 157.
2. Buchanan asserted that Mary went to Hermitage out of lust to see Bothwell, attributing her subsequent illness to 'having gratified her unlawful passions' with him and to 'her exertions both day and night'. (Buchanan's *Detectio*; cited in Weir, p. 161) Nothing could have been further from the truth.
3. There has been much speculation as to the true cause of Mary's illness, but there can be little doubt that it was the result of internal bleeding from a gastric ulcer, which also caused the recurrent pain in her side. Although there are also suggestions that she was suffering from porphyria, the hereditary disease that later afflicted George III, she never suffered the bouts of delusion that are its general symptom. One reason for assuming that Mary suffered from porphyria is that it could also explain her father's fatal collapse after Solway Moss. Yet no further symptoms of it recurred during her captivity in England, when her illnesses were well documented. Whatever the cause, there can be little doubt that her illness was exacerbated by acute depression at her predicament of being married to the king.
4. Nau; cited in Weir, p. 161.
5. Nau; cited in Weir, p. 161.
6. Cited in Guy, p. 276.
7. Cited in Tytler; Nau; Leslie; cited in Guy, p. 274 and in Weir, pp. 162, 163.
8. Nau; CSP Scottish; see Archives of Edinburgh University; cited in Weir, p. 163.
9. Cited in Guy, p. 276.
10. Cited in Guy, p. 277.
11. Tytler, II, p. 400; cited in Guy, pp. 275, 282, in Antonia Fraser p. 318 and in Weir, p. 162.
12. Cited in Guy, p. 278.
13. Neale; cited in Guy, p. 278.
14. Cited in Weir, p. 170.

15. CSP Spanish, I, p. 597; cited in Antonia Fraser, p. 328 and in Weir, p. 165.

16. Du Croc to Catherine de Medici, 2 December 1566, Keith, II, p. 474; cited in Antonia Fraser, p. 320 and in Weir, p. 170.

17. Nau, p. 32; cited in Weir, p. 170.

18. Du Croc to Archbishop Bethune, 6 December 1566, Mumby, p. 144; cited in Bingham, p. 163.

19. In 1567, when Mary was in Lochleven, Jean retired from Edinburgh to Argyllshire, but, finding her husband intolerable, soon left. Yet, when he tried to persuade her to divorce him, she refused.

20. Cotton MMS, Protestation, Keith; Goodall; Mumby; cited in Weir, p. 172.

21. Cited in Weir, p. 172.

22. Cited in Guy, p. 283 and in Weir, p. 173.

23. Buchanan claimed that Mary initiated the plan to be rid of her husband by saying,

    About the fifth day of November, removing from Jedburgh to Kelso ... she said that unless she were quit of the king by any means or other, she could never have one good day in her life, and rather that she should fail therein, she would rather be the instrument of her own death. Returning to Craigmillar ... she renewed the same purpose ... in an audience with my Lord of Moray, the Earl of Huntly, the Earl of Argyll and Maitland, propounding that the way to be rid of the king and make it look best was to begin an action of divorce against him ... whereunto it was answered how that could not goodly be done without hazard, since by the doing thereof the Prince her son 'should be declared bastard ... which answer, when she had thought over it, she left that conceit and opinion of the divorce and ever from that day forth imagined how to cut him away. (Buchanan, *Book of Articles*; cited in Guy, p. 391).

24. Cited in Guy, p. 283, in Wormald *Mary, Queen of Scots*, p. 164 and in Antonia Fraser, p. 321.

25. Written by Moray and Cecil in London and pasted to back of Protestation; cited in Weir, p. 175.

26. The 'Protestation of Huntly and Argyll' dated 5 January 1569 was probably drafted by the Bishop of Ross on Mary's behalf while in captivity in England and sent to them for signature. It was intercepted by Cecil en route, and he ensured that they never saw it.

27. Protestation, Keith, II, p. 475, cited in Guy, pp. 283, 391, and in Weir, p. 174.

28. Keith III, p. 290; cited in Wormald, Mary Queen of Scots, p. 164 and in Antonia Fraser, p. 321.

29. Goodall; cited in Weir, p. 175.

30. John Guy does not believe that a bond was signed at Craigmillar. He argues that the decision to murder the king was not taken until the meeting between Morton, Maitland and Bothwell at Whittinghame on about 14 January. Certainly

the detailed plan could not have been made until it became clear that the king would move to Kirk o' Field at the end of January. Although it was reported that Bothwell gave a document to the queen at Carberry Hill only to have it removed by her captors, John Guy argues that there was no contemporary evidence for it or that it was a bond. He claims that Mary would not have needed to ask for a copy to enable her to provide evidence at the Conferences at York and London, if she had already seen it. This does not seem convincing. It is more likely that she wanted the written evidence of a document she had already seen. He contends that Balfour concocted a story of a bond after the event to incriminate those who were then his enemies. Yet there are several pieces of evidence for the bond's existence and it seems unthinkable in a conspiracy for the king's murder between doubtful colleagues that they should not have felt the need for mutual protection.

31. Hosack, I, p. 532, cited in Antonia Fraser, p. 322 and in Weir, p. 177.

Chapter 21: The baptism of Prince James

1. Cited in Guy, p. 285.
2. Cited in Guy, p. 286 and in Weir, p. 261.
3. Labanoff, I, p. 395; cited in Antonia Fraser, p. 328.
4. Melville; cited in Weir, pp. 125, 180, 181.
5. Robertson, pp. 61, 63, 69; cited in Antonia Fraser, p. 324.
6. Du Croc to Archbishop Bethune; cited in Keith and in Antonia Fraser, p. 325.
7. CSP Venetian, Vol. 7, p. 387; cited in Bingham, p. 164.
8. CSP Venetian, Vol. 7, p. 387; cited in Bingham, p. 164.
9. Du Croc to Archbishop Bethune, 23 December 1566; Mumby, p. 145; cited in Bingham, p. 166.
10. Du Croc to Archbishop Bethune; cited in Keith, in Guy, p. 285 and in Weir, p. 184.
11. Caligula, B IV, p. 149; cited in Bingham, p. 166.
12. Cited in Weir, p. 188.
13. According to Buchanan, it was at this time, while in bed as lovers, that Mary and Bothwell arranged the plot to kill the king choosing as the murder location the house at Kirk o' Field. Yet as will be seen all the credible evidence shows that it was the king, while returning from Glasgow, who chose to recuperate at Kirk o' Field.
14. Knox; Buchanan; cited in Weir, p. 190.
15. Cited in Guy, p. 288.

Chapter 22: Mary's visit to Glasgow to persuade the king to return to Edinburgh

1. Nau, p. 31; corroborated by Drury to Cecil, 13 August 1575; cited in Antonia Fraser, p. 331 and in Weir, p. 202.
2. The fact that Moretta stayed with Balfour has been taken to suggest that Balfour was another party in the king's plot against Mary. Yet this implies a

level of deviousness that, even by Balfour's standards, seems implausible, as he was indisputably part of the plot to rid Mary of the king. During Moretta's visit, Balfour was purchasing gunpowder and arranging its transfer to Kirk o' Field. As he moved out of his home in the latter part of Moretta's visit, it is more likely that Moretta was simply there as a lodger.

3. Keith, I, p. ciii; cited in Antonia Fraser, p. 329.

4. Knox, V, pp. 349-50; cited in Bingham, p. 168.

5. Cited in Weir, p. 214.

6. According to Alison Weir, 'Beaton' is either Archibald Bethune, a long-standing member of her household, or John Bethune, Master of her household.

7. CSP Scottish, II, Appendix II, p. 722; Mahon, p. 111; Robertson; Caligula; CSP Foreign; cited in Guy, p. 401 and in Antonia Fraser, p. 454.

8. Paris, also known as 'French' Paris or Joachim, was a French servant whose real name was Nicholas Hubert. He had been in the queen's service for about a year having previously been employed by Bothwell, who continued to pay him. Before that he had worked for Seton. He later claimed under torture that Bothwell had bullied, kicked and beaten him. Yet they were on close terms while he worked for Mary, and he is known to have carried messages between them.

9. According to Scrope, Bothwell went as far as Jedburgh on the first evening from Edinburgh and from there moved into Liddesdale with about eighty men. They captured a dozen brigands including their leader, Martin Elwood, an associate of the Elliots. Elwood managed to warn his followers, who arranged a rescue, during which one of Bothwell's men was killed and five more captured. Bothwell went in pursuit, but despite a furious chase failed to catch up with them, and returned to Jedburgh empty-handed.

10. CSP Scottish, II, cited in Weir, p. 196 and in Guy, p. 401.

11. CSP Scottish, II, Appendix II, p. 722.

12. There is no doubt that the discussions at Craigmillar had leaked. On 18 January, de Silva reported from London, 'The displeasure of the Queen of Scotland with her husband is carried so far that she was approached by some who wanted to induce her to allow a plot to be formed against him, but she refused. But she nevertheless shows him no affection.' (Keith, I p. ciii; cited in Antonia Fraser, p. 329.) Mary had surmised that there must be a spy at court and it has been conjectured that she thought this was Balfour. The more likely candidates are Lutini and Joseph Riccio.

13. Crawford's Deposition, Cambridge University Library, ed. in CSP Scottish; cited in Weir, p. 208.

14. Crawford's Deposition, Cambridge University Library, ed. In CSP Scottish; cited in Weir, p. 209.

15. Antonia Fraser, p. 459.

16. Guy, p. 404, and Antonia Fraser, p. 455.

17. Cited in Guy, p. 406 and in Antonia Fraser, p. p. 456.

18. Cited in Guy, p. 406.

19. Cited in Antonia Fraser, p. 458.
20. Cited in Guy, p. 407.
21. Cited in Guy, p. 407.
22. Cited in Guy, p. 407, and in Antonia Fraser, p. 458.
23. Cited in Guy, p. 408.

PART 4: KING HENRY'S MURDER

Chapter 23: The planning of the murder of the king

1. Nau, p. 36; cited in Bingham, p. 188.
2. Pitcairn, I, pt. 1, p. 496; cited in Antonia Fraser, p. 340 and in Weir, p. 265.
3. Cited in Weir, p. 199.
4. Pitcairn I, pt. 1, p. 498; cited in Antonia Fraser, p. 340.
5. Weir, p. 201.
6. Gore-Browne, p. 293; Holinshed; cited in Antonia Fraser, p. 330 and in Weir, p. 201.

Chapter 24: The demise of the king

1. Buchanan recorded,

> In the meantime, the Earl of Bothwell, according to the device [plan with the queen] appointed between them, prepared for the king the lodging where he ended his life. In what place it stood enough know and enough thought even that it was a ruin unsuitable to have lodged a Prince into, standing in a solitary place at the uttermost part of the town, separate from all company. (Buchanan Book of Articles; cited in Guy, p. 392).

As will be seen, this is all patently untrue.
2. Cited in Guy, p. 392 and in Weir, p. 228.
3. Mahon, pp. 126-7; cited in Bingham, p. 178.
4. Cited in Weir, p. 228.
5. In fact, there was no known cure for syphilis. The treatment being administered cleared up the skin rash that affected the whole body, including the inside of the mouth, during which the patient was highly infectious. There were then periods of remission during which the patient was less infectious, until the rash broke out again. Irrational behaviour, particularly delusions of grandeur, was a recognised symptom of the disease. Eventually tertiary syphilis would develop causing insanity, paralysis and congenital deformity for unborn children. There is no evidence that the king had become permanently disfigured or had reached the stage of tertiary syphilis, and Mary still seems to have been attracted to him at Kirk o' Field, despite knowing of his affliction.
6. Cited in Weir, p. 233.

7. Darnley to Lennox, 7 February, 1566; Nau, p. 34; Mahon, p. 115; cited in Guy, p. 296, in Antonia Fraser, p. 339, in Wormald, Mary, Queen of Scots, p. 164 and in Weir, p. 234.
8. CSP Scottish, II, p. 728; cited in Guy, pp. 418-9 and in Antonia Fraser, p. 460.
9. Nau; cited in Weir, p. 235.
10. Cited in Weir, p. 235.
11. Melville; cited in Weir, p. 236.
12. Hatfield House, I, p. 376; cited in Antonia Fraser, p. 461.
13. Casket Letter IV begins, 'I find the fairest commodity to excuse your business that might be offered. I have promised him to bring him tomorrow. If you think it, give order thereunto.' Although this was deemed to refer to Lord Robert, it does not mention him by name and the suggestion that she is inciting Lord Robert to undertake Bothwell's dirty business by killing the king is conjectural. The remainder of the letter appears to be a rebuke by a loving writer to a way-ward recipient and makes no other reference to Lord Robert being involved in the murder. It continues, 'the thing of this world that I desire the most ... is your favour or goodwill ... Otherwise I would think that my ill luck, and the fair behaviour of those that have not the third part of the faithfulness and voluntary obedience that I bear unto you, shall have worn the advantage over me of the second lover of Jason. Not that I do compare you so wicked, or myself so unpitiful a person.' In Greek mythology the second wife of Jason was Glauce, who was murdered by his vengeful first wife, Medea. The letter has been taken to infer that Mary feels the same jealousy for Bothwell's first wife, Jean Gordon, as Medea did for Glauce. Yet, as Medea was the first wife of Jason and Mary would become the second wife of Bothwell, the analogy seems the wrong way round. The letter then moves into a different theme, suggesting that it comes from a different source. It refers to the Ronsard sonnet. The English translation presented at Westminster states, 'Watch well if the bird shall fly out of the cage, or without his father make as the turtle [dove] shall remain alone for absence, how short soever it be.' This suggests that Mary thought the king might try to escape from Kirk o' Field, not wanting to be absent from his father with so much plotting afoot; by implication Bothwell should take steps to prevent him leaving. Yet the word 'father' in the English translation is a mistranslation of the French 'per' as shown in the French transcript, and Cecil corrected his copy to 'mate' without saying anything. A more accurate English translation of the Ronsard original should read, 'Beware lest the bird flies out of its cage, or like the turtledove without its mate lives alone to lament its absence, however short that may be.' The corrected translation makes no sense as a letter from Mary to Bothwell, but could well have been one she wrote to the king, while she was contemplating divorce. As the king referred to the turtledove in his own poetry, he would have understood that she was threatening separation, if he stayed away, even for a short time, with some new mistress. The letter ends, 'That that I could not do [ie ask Bothwell to his face to murder the king], my letter should do it with a good will, if it were not

that I fear to wake you, for I durst not write before Joseph, Bastien and Joachim, who were but new gone from I began.' (Hatfield House; cited in Guy, pp. 421-3, and in Antonia Fraser, pp. 461-2.) Written immediately after the original French wording, this cannot be construed as an admission that she cannot bring herself to ask Bothwell to murder the king. It can only be a falsified addition to corroborate the English mistranslation, showing that she encouraged her bedfellow, Bothwell, to prevent the king's escape (and to explain why she needed to write to him, when they were in bed together). Her bedroom servants are named simply to imply that she is writing to Bothwell, her bed-companion at Holyrood, while the king is recuperating at Kirk o' Field.

14. Cited in Guy, p. 424.
15. CSP Scottish, II, Appendix II, p. 722.
16. Labanoff, II, p. 3; cited in Guy, p. 301; Antonia Fraser, p. 343 and in Weir, p. 244.
17. Cited in Guy, p. 298.
18. Nau, p. 34; cited in Guy, p. 298 and in Antonia Fraser, p. 344.
19. Buchanan made the most of this, recording: 'As soon as she saw [him] she knew that the powder was put in the lower house under the king's bed, for Paris had the keys both of the front and back doors of that house, and the king's servants had all the remaining keys of the lodging. And so with feigned laughter she said: "I have given offence to Bastian by not attending the masque in honour of his marriage tonight, for which purpose I will return to Holyrood."' (Buchanan's *Detectio;* cited in Guy, p. 393).
20. Buchanan's *Detectio;* cited in Weir, p. 247.
21. Mahon, p. 128; cited in Bingham, p. 182.
22. Pitcairn, I, pt. 1, p. 502; Herries, p. 84; cited in Antonia Fraser, p. 354.
23. Sloane MMS; cited in Weir, p. 250.
24. Cited in Weir, p. 250.
25. Sloane MMS; Keith; cited in Antonia Fraser, p. 353 and in Weir, p. 250.
26. Mondovi to Cosimo de Medici, Labanoff, VII, p. 108; cited in Guy, p. 307 and in Antonia Fraser, p. 352.
27. Deposition of William Powrie, in Pitcairn; cited in Antonia Fraser, p. 354, and Weir p. 251.
28. *Les Affaires du Conte de Boduel,* p. 13; cited in Weir, p. 252.
29. CSP Scottish; Clernault in *State Papers* in the PRO; cited in Weir, p. 252.
30. CSP Venetian; cited in Weir p. 252.
31. *Les Affaires du Conte de Boduel;* Knox; cited in Weir, p. 253.
32. Privy Council to Catherine de Medici, Sloane MMS; cited in Weir, p. 256.

Chapter 25: A review of what happened

1. Mahon; CSP Scottish, Cecil's description; cited in Weir, p. 271.
2. After Carberry Hill, there was a strong rumour that Archbishop Hamilton was implicated, but this is likely to have been malicious propaganda from the Confederates against one of the queen's supporters. As late as 6 February

1568, Archbishop Bethune in Paris reported that Moray was determined to prosecute Archbishop Hamilton in parliament, 'on the plea that he had had a hand in the murder'. (Cited in Weir, p. 427) If Moray considered doing so, it was not progressed, although Lennox and his supporters, no friends of the Hamiltons, continued to believe in his guilt. When the Archbishop was eventually arrested after the fall of Dumbarton, he was again accused on the flimsiest evidence of taking part. He was by then more justifiably implicated in Moray's murder, so that Lennox, who had become Regent, arranged his immediate execution without trial.

3. Paris's 1st Deposition, PRO; cited in Weir, p. 262.
4. *Les Affaires du Conte de Boduel;* cited in Weir, p. 289.
5. Cited in Antonia Fraser, p. 341 and in Weir, p. 264.
6. Buchanan's *Detectio;* cited in Weir, p. 271.
7. Cited in Weir, p. 271.
8. Cited in Weir, p. 273.
9. Reported by Drury in CSP Scottish; cited in Weir, p. 296.

Chapter 26: The immediate aftermath of the murder and Mary's reaction to it

1. Melville; cited in Weir, p. 254.
2. Cited in Guy, p. 318.
3. Cited in Weir, p. 302.
4. Keith; cited in Antonia Fraser, pp. 353-4 and in Weir, p. 257.
5. Labanoff, II, p. 3; cited in Guy, p. 300, in Antonia Fraser, p. 353 and in Weir, p. 257.
6. Sloane MMS; CSP Spanish; cited in Weir, p. 300.
7. Robert Melville to Cecil, 26 February 1567; CSP Scottish; cited in Weir, p. 307.
8. By breaking her mourning so quickly Mary was severely criticised by Buchanan in his Book of Articles. He claimed that her visit to Seton with Bothwell 'had so many conveniences that they had gone back there to the detriment of their reputations'. (Cited in Weir, p. 307.) Yet Bothwell did not arrive until the second visit on 21 January and it was the Council who had encouraged the trip for her health.
9. Cited in Weir, p. 276.
10. Cited in Weir, p. 311.
11. Cited in Guy, pp. 304, 313.
12. Keith; cited in Weir, p. 303.
13. CSP Venetian; cited in Guy, p. 302 and in Weir, p. 273.
14. Guy, p. 303.
15. CSP Spanish; cited in Weir, p. 301.
16. CSP Venetian, VII, p. 389; cited in Antonia Fraser, p. 356 and in Weir, pp. 280, 324.

17. CSP Venetian, VII, p. 388, cited Antonia Fraser, p. 353 and in Weir, p. 307.
18. Pollen; cited in Weir, pp. 280, 320.
19. Pollen; cited in Weir, p. 323.
20. Melville; cited in Weir, p. 312.
21. *State Papers* in the PRO; CSP Scottish; cited in Weir, p. 322.
22. Cited in Guy, p. 310.
23. CSP Foreign, Drury to Cecil, 30 March 1567; cited in Weir, p. 322.
24. Cited in Weir, p. 318.
25. Buchanan; cited in Weir, p. 306.
26. Labanoff; cited in Weir, p. 314.

PART 5: THE CONSPIRACY TO FORCE MARY TO ABDICATE

Chapter 27: Pawns in a game of chess

1. Teulet; cited in Guy, p. 313 and in Weir, pp. 284, 316.
2. Cited in Guy, p. 313.
3. Cited in Weir, p. 299.
4. Pearson, p. 11; cited in Bingham, p. 167.
5. Acts of Parliament; Henderson, Appendix D, p. 177; cited in Antonia Fraser, p. 407.
6. CSP Scottish, Moray to Cecil, 13 March 1567; cited in Weir, pp. 280, 321.
7. Cited in Guy, p. 321.
8. Robertson, p. 53; CSP Foreign, VIII, p. 198; Gore-Browne, p. 374; cited in Antonia Fraser, p. 360.
9. CSP Scottish; cited in Guy, p. 309 and in Weir, p. 312.
10. Register of the Privy Council of Scotland, I, p. 500; Anderson; cited in Antonia Fraser, p. 359 and in Weir, p. 322.
11. CSP Spanish; cited in Weir, p. 327.
12. Keith, II, p. 532; CSP, Foreign, VIII, p. 198; cited in Antonia Fraser, pp. 360-1 and in Weir, p. 328.
13. CSP Spanish; cited in Weir, p. 329.
14. CSP Spanish; De Silva to Philip II, 21 April, 1567; cited in Weir, p. 331.

Chapter 28: Bothwell's exoneration and marriage to Mary

1. Diurnal of Occurrents, p. 108; cited in Antonia Fraser, p. 361 and in Weir, p. 340.
2. Buchanan's *Detectio;* cited in Weir, p. 340.
3. Keith, II, p. 558; cited in Weir, p. 341.
4. Cited in Guy, p. 320 and in Weir, p. 302.
5. Nau, p. 37; cited in Antonia Fraser, p. 363 and in Weir, p. 347.
6. Nau; cited in Antonia Fraser, p. 363 and in Weir, pp. 346-7.
7. MacNalty; cited in Weir, p. 352.
8. Hatfield House, I, p. 379; cited in Antonia Fraser, p. 463.

9. Cited in Guy, pp. 425-7 and in Antonia Fraser, p. 463.
10. Cited in Guy, pp. 427-8.
11. Henderson, pp. 171, 172; Armstrong-Davison, p. 195; cited in Antonia Fraser, p. 464.
12. Henderson, pp. 171, 172; Armstrong-Davison, p. 195; cited in Antonia Fraser, p. 464.
13. Henderson, pp. 171, 172; Armstrong-Davison, p. 195; cited in Antonia Fraser, p. 465.
14. Hosack, Appendix F, p. 562.
15. Buchanan's *Detectio;* cited in Weir, p.361.
16. De Silva to Philip II, May 1567; CSP Spanish; cited in Weir, p. 354.
17. *State Papers in the PRO;* CSP Scottish; cited in Guy, p. 329.
18. Nau; cited in Weir, p. 354.
19. Labanoff; cited in Weir, p. 355.
20. Labanoff; cited in Guy, p. 361.
21. Melville; cited in Weir, p. 362.
22. Drury to Cecil, 6 May 1567, CSP Foreign.
23. Keith; cited in Weir, p. 365.
24. Cited in Guy, p. 331.
25. Cited in Weir, p. 364.
26. CSP Spanish; cited in Weir, p. 365.
27. Weir, p. 367.
28. Melville; cited in Weir, p. 368.
29. Ovid, *5th Book of Fasti;* cited in Antonia Fraser, p. 372 and in Weir, p. 375.
30. Plowden; cited in Guy, p. 335 and in Weir p. 352.

Chapter 29: The confederate alliance challenges Mary and Orkney

1. Cited in Weir, p. 375.
2. Cited in Weir, p. 378.
3. CSP Foreign; cited in Weir, p. 384.
4. Cited in Guy, p. 338.
5. Melville; cited in Weir, p. 380.
6. Melville; cited in Weir, p. 385.
7. Weir, pp. 361, 385-6.
8. Nau; Drury to Cecil, CSP Foreign, VIII, p. 246; cited in Guy, p. 341, in Antonia Fraser, p. 379 and in Weir, p. 387.
9. Cited in Guy, pp. 341-2.
10. Drury to Cecil, 18 June 1567, CSPO Foreign; Teulet, cited in Weir, p. 388.
11. CSP Scottish; cited in Guy, p. 343, Antonia Fraser, p. 381 and Weir, p. 389.
12. Cited by Sitwell and by Weir, p. 390.
13. Cited in Guy, p. 344.
14. Cited in Guy, p. 345 and in Weir, p. 390.

15. *Les Affaires du Conte de Boduel;* cited in Weir, p. 390.
16. Cited in Antonia Fraser, p. 382 and in Weir, pp. 390-1.
17. *Les Affaires du Conte de Boduel;* cited in Weir, p. 391.
18. Nau; cited in Weir, p. 391.
19. Nau; cited in Weir, p. 391.
20. *Les Affaires du Conte de Boduel;* cited in Weir, p. 392.
21. *Les Affaires du Conte de Boduel;* cited in Weir, p. 392.
22. Melville; cited in Weir, p. 392.
23. Melville; cited in Weir, p. 393.
24. Du Croc to Catherine de Medici, 17 June, 1567; Teulet; cited in Guy, p. 349 and in Weir, p. 393.
25. Nau, p. 48; cited in Antonia Fraser, pp. 383-4.
26. Nau; cited in Antonia Fraser, p. 38.
27. Cited in Neale, in Wormald *Mary, Queen of Scots*, p. 171 and in Weir, p. 393.
28. Melville, p. 156; Teulet, John Beaton in Sloane MMS; Fleming, p. 165; cited in Weir, p. 394.

Afterword

1. Diurnal of Occurrents, p. 129; cited in Weir, p. 432 and in Antonia Fraser, p. 419.
2. By all accounts, Charles had superficial charm, but was physically weak from consumption. Like his brother, he was self-centredly arrogant and given to outbursts of petulant temper. He infuriated his mother by slouching about. She lamented his lack of a father's control. By the age of 15, he seems to have been delinquent and she asked Cecil to take him into his household to exercise discipline onto him. She wrote to Cecil: 'He is somewhat unfurnished of qualities needful and I being a lone woman am less likely to have him well reformed at home ...' Cecil shied away from taking him in, but recommended a Swiss tutor, Peter Malliet, who, despite being a good teacher, failed to furnish him with the 'qualities needful'.

Index

Printed in Great Britain
by Amazon